*A*dventure Guide to

Texas

Kimberly Young

HUNTER

HUNTER PUBLISHING, INC.

130 Campus Drive, Edison NJ 08818

(732) 225 1900, (800) 255 0343, fax (732) 417 0482

1220 Nicholson Rd., Newmarket, Ontario,

Canada L3Y 7V1, (800) 399 6858

The Boundary, Wheatley Road, Garsington

Oxford, OX44 9EJ England

01865-361122; fax 01865-361133

ISBN 1-55650-812-3

©1999 Kimberly Young

Maps by Lissa K. Dailey, © 1999 Hunter Publishing, Inc.

Cover: Horses galloping in a meadow (W. Hille, *Leo de Wys Inc.*)

Back cover: Greater roadrunner (Bob Johnson)

Drawings by Donna M. Blackburn

For complete information about the hundreds of other travel guides offered by Hunter Publishing, visit our Web site at:

www.hunterpublishing.com

4 3 2

Contents

Maps

Dedication

To Joseph K. Young, whose silver Impala was my chariot across Texas.

About the Author

A native and life-long resident of Texas, Kimberly thinks that her home state is heaven and spends much of her time in its varied nooks and crannies. She is currently managing editor of a trade magazine. Kimberly is an avid sailor, but when she's not on the water you'll find her hiking and camping somewhere in Texas.

"Texas, Our Texas"

Capital: Austin

State Motto: Friendship

State Flower: Bluebonnet

State Bird: Mockingbird

State Tree: Pecan

State Song: Texas, Our Texas

Name: Texas, or Tejas, got its name from the Spanish pronunciation of the Caddo Indian word which meant "friend" or "ally."

Area: 266,807 square miles

Land Area: 262,017 square miles

Water Area: 4,790 square miles

Forested Area: 22.032 million acres

State Forests: Five

OKLAHOMA

100 MILES
149 KM

Texas

NEW MEXICO

OKLAHOMA

Amarillo

40

27

Lubbock

Wichita
Falls

44

NORTH TEXAS &
THE PANHANDLE

35

Texarkana

30

ARKANSAS

NEW MEXICO

20

Abilene

Dallas

20

El
Paso

GUADELUPE MTNS
NAT'L PARK

Odessa

Fort
Worth

EAST
TEXAS

Toledo Bend Reservoir

LOUISIANA

MEXICO

10

CENTRAL
TEXAS

35

45

WEST TEXAS

10

Austin

Houston

Beaumont

BIG BEND
NAT'L PARK

San Antonio

10

THE TEXAS COAST

Galveston

Rio Grande River

35

37

N

MEXICO

SOUTH
TEXAS

Corpus Christi

Gulf of Mexico

South
Padre
Island

Introduction

It's difficult growing up in Texas. Having to ride your horse to school each day, the noisy oil derrick squeaking behind your house. And then all that dust and those tumbleweeds. It's enough to make you kind of twangy.

The myths surrounding Texas have infiltrated even the most remote of outbacks and the most educated of minds. It's dusty and wild, filled with women and men not satisfied with one name. There's Sue Ellen, Mary Lou and Jim Bob. Hell, Texas must be the only state that lets parents use middle names.

All kidding aside, Texas really is like no other place. Its residents are proud and strong and united with the land they cover. Non-Texans might find the lack of humility disconcerting – Texans will tell them that they just don't understand. Being Texan, to many, is like being from a very large family. A really big family.

The areas that Texas covers are extreme. From the dank, Piney Woods of East Texas, to the sparse desert in the west, so many are surprised by the hidden treasures of the state. When unaware visitors first descend into Austin or San Antonio, peering around and above the undulating, verdant Hill Country, they are delighted, to say the least.

Legends are here. All around. There are big, bold voices, raised to speak their minds. There are big, strong men and women who take the world by the horns. There are big, beautiful vistas that inspire poets and artists. And with a land as broad and deep and varied as Texas, how could there not be legendary material.

The history of a state as big as Texas varies from region to region. You'll find highlights of the past throughout this book, but by no means will you find an intense study. There are much larger books for that, such as Leon Metz' *Roadside History of Texas.*

 Texans fancy themselves a bit unusual. Perhaps that's why Texas roads are something of a puzzle to outsiders. The acronyms you'll find preceding highway numbers look different from those in the rest of the world. Most have origins in rural Texas and actually used to mean something. Here's a guide so you won't feel lost.

Texas Highway Signs	
FM	Farm to Market
RM	Ranch to Market
RR	Ranch Road
CR or CO	County Road
PR	Park Road

Throughout the book, you will find sections listing places to stay in particular areas. Each entry will be followed by $ signs indicating a general price range.

Accommodations Price Scale

$ . . . . under $50 per night

$$ . . . . $50-$100 per night

$$$ . . . . $100-$150 per night

$$$$ . . . . $150+ per night

We've focused on bed and breakfasts and local establishments throughout the book. But here's a list of national chains that have a presence in Texas.

Chain Motels & Hotels

Best Western . . . . ☎ 800-528-1234

Comfort Inn . . . . ☎ 800-221-2222

Days Inn . . . . ☎ 800-325-2525

Doubletree . . . . ☎ 800-222-TREE

Econo Lodge . . . . ☎ 800-424-4777

Hilton Hotels . . . . ☎ 800-HILTONS

Holiday Inn . . . . ☎ 800-HOLIDAY

Howard Johnson Suites . . . . ☎ 446-4656

Hyatt Hotels and Resorts . . . . ☎ 800-233-1234

Sheraton . . . . ☎ 800-325-3535

La Quinta . . . . ☎ 800-531-5900

Marriott Hotels . . . . ☎ 800-228-9290

Motel 6 . . . . ☎ 800-466-8356

Radisson . . . . ☎ 800-333-3333

Ramada Inn . . . . ☎ 800-2RAMADA

Renaissance . . . . ☎ 800-HOTELS1

Westin Hotels and Resorts . . . . ☎ 800-228-3000

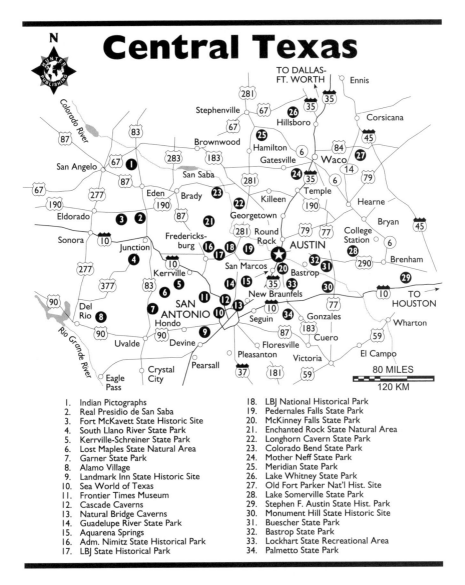

Central Texas

1. Indian Pictographs
2. Real Presidio de San Saba
3. Fort McKavett State Historic Site
4. South Llano River State Park
5. Kerrville-Schreiner State Park
6. Lost Maples State Natural Area
7. Garner State Park
8. Alamo Village
9. Landmark Inn State Historic Site
10. Sea World of Texas
11. Frontier Times Museum
12. Cascade Caverns
13. Natural Bridge Caverns
14. Guadelupe River State Park
15. Aquarena Springs
16. Adm. Nimitz State Historical Park
17. LBJ State Historical Park
18. LBJ National Historical Park
19. Pedernales Falls State Park
20. McKinney Falls State Park
21. Enchanted Rock State Natural Area
22. Longhorn Cavern State Park
23. Colorado Bend State Park
24. Mother Neff State Park
25. Meridian State Park
26. Lake Whitney State Park
27. Old Fort Parker Nat'l Hist. Site
28. Lake Somerville State Park
29. Stephen F. Austin State Hist. Park
30. Monument Hill State Historic Site
31. Buescher State Park
32. Bastrop State Park
33. Lockhart State Recreational Area
34. Palmetto State Park

Central Texas

■ The Land

Though many subscribe to the misguided notion that Texas is a land of desert with tumbleweeds serving as the state tree, Central Texas is a celebration of people and rich, dank earth. Interstate 35, the main road and artery that connects San Antonio, Austin and Waco, the three area hubs, also separates the mid-section of Texas into east and west.

The west is rocky terrain buffeted by rolling hills populated with cedar and oak. To the east is black prairie, flat with rich soil suitable for cotton and crops.

Culturally diverse, much of the region was settled by Europeans, particularly Germans and Czechs. In many of the smaller towns German is still spoken.

Central Texas has become a center for artistic pursuits and education, perhaps because of its liberal spirit, or because of its location. In Austin alone, there are over 75,000 students attending college at any one time. The district that encompasses Austin is usually the lone Democratic voting county in Texas, a blue dot in a sea of red. Ironic, because elected Republican leaders must come to this democratic city to serve out their terms.

■ Logistics

Let's get one thing straight. Texas is big. Unlike the East Coast, which was settled before mass transportation, Texans took advantage of their room and spread out. A car is your best bet and can be rented at any major airport.

There are major airports in San Antonio and Austin. However, the hubs in Texas run through Dallas and Houston, so you'll probably be stopping in one of them first. Waco also has a small airport; commuter planes and puddle-jumpers are the norm. Both American and Continental sends its smaller versions into the Waco airport.

Buses are cheap when going city to city, but, again, a car can give you the most access. If a car is not an option, try flying. Southwest, American and Continental all offer affordable fares for these small legs and a flight can be much quicker.

In the cities there are no real efficient and economical ways to get around. San Antonio, Waco and Austin each have mass transit bus systems – but they don't cater to the visitor who's looking for adventure. Adventure is usually found on the fringes of town in places buses don't frequent.

■ Weather & Seasons

The weather is predictable in the summer – hot. Perhaps it will be just warm, if you're lucky. Cold fronts usually only drop temperatures 5° or so. The winter is a different creature. It can be a beautiful 80° one day, and a frigid 10° the next (though most of the time it leans toward 70°). Be prepared for everything. Also, the warm coastal influence produces humidity that at times feels choking. The coast gets the worst of the humidity, but Austin and San Antonio can occasionally have bad days.

Spring and fall are both beautiful for Central Texas. Spring sometimes sneaks in during the late portions of February and is in full swing by March. While much of the nation is still digging itself out of snow and ice, Central Texas is alive with one of the most colorful wildflower displays in the world.

Oceans of deep blue (bluebonnets) spread sporadically across the state and are punctuated by the vivid reds, oranges, yellows and pinks that Indian blankets, buttercups and 5,000 other wildflower species provide. You'll know it's in full swing when you see the locals stopped on the edges of highways, hunting the embankments and adjacent fields for the perfect picture-taking opportunity. Dressed in their Sunday best, every Central Texan has had to pose (at one point or another) in a field of wildflowers.

Real fall comes late to Central Texas. There will be signs of it in September – brief periods of cool that follow Canadian air masses. But for the most part, October is when fall arrives. For the natives, October is heaven. As much as they love their festival-filled summer, by October they're ready for a break in the heat. They celebrate by doing everything outdoors – dining, watching movies, attending concerts and plays or just sitting.

Austin

Austin is an anomaly even in a state as broad and big as Texas. An oasis of lush rolling hills smack dab in the middle of the state, it is the most educated large city in America, a center for technology and a recreational mecca.

In addition to being the capital of Texas politics, it is considered the "live music capital of the world," offering dozens (and up to a hundred on a

Central Texas

busy weekend) of music venues every night of the week, with everything from blues to bluegrass, rock to folk and country to calypso.

It has earned a myriad of honors throughout the last few decades, from "Most Fit City in the US" to "Best City to Live In" to "Running Capital of the Nation."

✳ Take Care !

Unfortunately, most of the year Austin is also the allergy capital of the world (according to its residents), so be prepared if you know you have a weakness for molds, cedar and pollen. The things that make Austin one of the most beautiful cities in the nation – mild weather, dank earth, rich vegetation and flowering flora – also make it the perfect garden spot for things that make you sneeze.

■ History

Spanish friars were the first to fall victim to the charms of the Austin area. On their way to San Antonio in 1730, they discovered magical springs, which are now called Barton Springs, and built a temporary mission. It was more than a century later when pioneer Texans settled along a crook in the Colorado River and called their new home Waterloo, certainly a tribute to the springs, rivers and gushing water of the Edwards Aquifer that make this verdant area unique. In 1839 Waterloo was chosen as the new capital of Texas and renamed in honor of Stephen F. Austin, "Father of Texas."

Austin remained a quiet town into the 60s, while its counterparts, Dallas and Houston, skyrocketed to big city status. The high-tech and real estate booms in the 60s and early 70s turned Austin into one of the fastest-growing communities in the nation.

Austin quickly became a computer and scientific hub, partly because companies could feed off of the University of Texas' graduates, and partly because they could offer a quality of living that was no longer affordable in Silicon Valley. Austin became home to Dell, IBM, Motorola, Texas Instruments, Tracor, Apple, Advanced Micro Devices, 3M, Radian, and the list continues to grow.

Most recently the film industry has come calling on Austin. Some of Hollywood's youngest directors and actors have found Austin more economical and pleasant than California. Two young local directors, Richard Linklater *(Slacker, Dazed and Confused, Before Sunrise, The Newton Boys)* and Robert Rodriguez *(El Mariachi, Desperado, From Dusk 'Til*

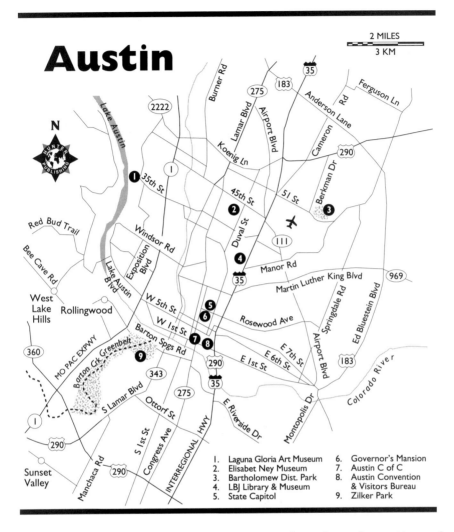

Austin

2 MILES
3 KM

N
HUNTER PUBLISHING

1. Laguna Gloria Art Museum	6. Governor's Mansion
2. Elisabet Ney Museum	7. Austin C of C
3. Bartholomew Dist. Park	8. Austin Convention
4. LBJ Library & Museum	& Visitors Bureau
5. State Capitol	9. Zilker Park

Central Texas

Dawn) and their friend Quentin Tarantino, have brought portions of Hollywood to town. Production industries are beginning to fill in the gaps, making Austin a full-service stop for both musical and movie ventures.

A large portion of the population consists of University of Texas graduates who couldn't bear to leave their favorite city. Their youth, spirit and free time only add to the festive dynamic the city enjoys. Now, closing in on a population of one million, Austin's massive growth shows no signs of abating.

■ Touring

THE CAPITOL COMPLEX: (11th and Congress, ☎ 512-463-0063) is the best place to start in Austin. Living up to the claim that things are bigger in Texas, the pink granite Capitol is just inches taller than the US Capitol in Washington DC, making it the tallest in the nation. Set on 26 acres of manicured lawns, the grounds are graced by dozens of monuments and sculptures. A recent two-year renovation not only restored the complex to its original splendor, but created an extensive new underground wing.

> **✻ Author's Tip**
>
> Frequent tours reveal all of the hidden treasures in the incredibly large building. Make sure you don't miss the grand mural-size paintings in both the Senate and House chambers. Each one, depicting special historical moments in Texas' action-packed colonization, is beyond life-size.

The Governor's Mansion (1010 Colorado St, ☎ 512-463-5516), just across the street from the Capitol, has been the official residence for every Texas governor since 1856. Built of local bricks and Bastrop (small

The Capitol.

town east of Austin) pine with a budget of $17,000, the house has a number of antique historical furnishings and pieces of art, including the writing desk of Stephen F. Austin. The Greek Revival house has been home to such colorful figures as Sam Rayburn, "Ma" Ferguson and, more recently, Ann Richards and George Bush III.

HISTORIC 6th STREET: You'll find this south of the Capitol complex, the heart of entertainment in Austin, stretching from Congress Avenue to Interstate 35. The abundance of restaurants, bars, dance halls and live music venues, all housed in structures from the late 1800s, make this concentrated area of festivities the Bourbon St of Texas.

6th Street at night.

Though the names of the establishments sometimes change with the season, many are perennial favorites. The corner of Trinity and 6th seems to be a lucky charm as three of its occupants have been around for more than a decade. **Wylie's Bar & Grill** is more bar than grill, and lays claim that its "big-a-rita" is the best margarita in town. **Maggie Mae's** attracts a more energetic crowd with its ability to facilitate three live bands at once. It has slowly engulfed its neighbors and has spread westward, making it the largest of the group.

The third neighbor, **Paradise Café**, accommodates the hungry crowd and was once the subject of a song by the now-defunct group Arc Angels. The **Iron Cactus**, the newest member to the fold, is showing its staying power with fine dining and one of the best rooftop decks in town.

On the corner of 6th St and Brazos you'll find the **Driskill Hotel** (604 Brazos, ☎ 512-474-5911). Offering elegant service for over a century, the 19th-century frontier palace has played host to many dignitaries, socialites and politicians, including President Lyndon Johnson, who awaited election results in the Driskill's splendorous halls during the elections of 1960 (Vice President) and 1964 (President).

THE WAREHOUSE DISTRICT: A second entertainment district has formed within the last decade a few blocks west of Congress around 3rd St. It includes a heavy concentration of some the finest Austin restaurants, including Mezzaluna (Italian), the Bitter End (bistro and brew pub), Sullivan's Steak House (steak and live jazz) and Gilligan's (gourmet seafood). The two districts – 6th St and the Warehouse District – have marked out distinctly different territories. 6th St is about clubs and dancing. The Warehouse District sees itself as the more refined, sit-down venue, with menus that offer martinis, cigars and Irish coffee.

Antone's (213 W 5th St, ☎ 512-320-8424), one of the finest blues clubs in the nation, lies between the two districts. It has been an Austin icon for as long as anyone can remember and its regulars have devoutly followed the smoky bar through several location changes. It boasts an international clientele – its legend has reached the far crevices of Europe and Australia. Clifford Antone, the blues-lover behind Antone's, has even created his own record label to promote the blues. You can pick up a catalog at the bar or visit the Web site (www.antones.com) to find some of the finest blues from both Austin and the world.

Named the Majestic Theatre when it opened in 1915, the lavish **Paramount Theatre** (713 Congress, ☎ 512-472-5411, www.pswtech.com/arts/paramount) welcomes Broadway shows, concerts and local productions.

Just south of the entertainment district is the **O. Henry Home and Museum** (409 E 5th St, ☎ 512-472-1903). O. Henry, one of the many pseudonyms for William Sydney Porter, became a proclaimed master of the short story in the early 1900s. His most enduring story, "The Gift of the Magi," still finds its way into every good Christmas celebration. In addition to being a renowned author, O. Henry was a published cartoonist and notable punster. The first weekend of each May, Austinites celebrate O. Henry with a "pun-off" in the shadow of his old house.

Party Town

The O. Henry Pun-Off is indicative of Austin's idea of a party. The town also annually celebrates spam, whose festival is aptly named "Spamarama," and Eeyore's Birthday Party, for the droopy donkey from *Winnie the Pooh*. Chili, hot sauce and jalapeños are also celebrated several times each year.

The **Congress Avenue Bridge** (Congress and Town Lake) is home to the largest urban bat colony in North America. At sunset each evening up to 1.5 million Mexican free-tails leave their roost for their nightly insect hunt. You can view the massive exodus from atop the bridge or from shore. It is truly one of the most memorable sites you will ever see.

The Hike and Bike Trail.

The **Town Lake Hike and Bike Trail** (best access and parking at Austin High School and Auditorium Shores) includes more than 10 miles of trail for walking, running and biking enthusiasts. Stretching along both sides of Town Lake, the downtown hotspot is packed with locals after work, and is a large reason Austin residents were at one time considered "most fit in America."

✳ Author's Tip

Springtime along the trail is mesmerizing, with wildflowers and fresh blooms paving the route. Take your camera.

Barton Springs Pool (2201 Barton Springs Rd in Zilker Park, ☎ 512-476-9044), a spring-fed local favorite for over a century, cools swimmers in its constant 68° spring waters. While at the pool, you can enjoy time in **Zilker Park**, a 485-acre affair that includes a grandiose children's playscape, a train that tours the grounds, soccer, rugby and lacrosse areas, picnic tables, a hillside amphitheater and canoe rentals. From June to August, you can also enjoy free musicals at the **Zilker Hillside Theater**, an unpretentious stage set at the bottom of a lush hillside where blankets and picnic baskets are the norm. Barton Springs and Zilker Park are not just any pool and park – they are the reason settlement commenced here in the 1700s and one of the reasons that residents consider Austin such a special city.

Austin by night.

Across the street, **Zilker Botanical Gardens** (2220 Barton Springs Rd, ☎ 512-477-8672) has preserved a 120-year-old schoolhouse and a Swedish cabin. The gardens offer a worldly collection of flowers and greenery, making it a local favorite for weddings and picture snapping. There are also a set of dinosaur tracks to be seen.

Umlauf Sculpture Garden and Museum (605 Robert E. Lee, just east of Zilker Park, ☎ 512-445-5582) might strike you as the perfect place for a wedding (many residents feel the same). Charles Umlauf's sculptures are spread throughout the lush gardens and the museum.

The University of Texas at Austin (bounded by Guadalupe, Red River, Martin Luther King Jr. Blvd and 26th St) encompasses over 350 acres and offers an array of historic sights and sounds. Centered around the UT Tower, unfortunately best remembered as where Charles Whitman splayed gunfire and despair decades ago, the University is one of the largest in the nation, with over 50,000 undergraduates.

On campus is the **Harry Ransom Center** (21st and Guadalupe, ☎ 512-471-8944), which counts a Gutenberg Bible as one of its prizes (one of only five in the US), and the **Lyndon B. Johnson Library** (2313 Red River, ☎ 512-916-5136), one of (I think the George Bush library just passed it up) the largest of the nation's presidential libraries. The presidential tribute includes an Oval Office replica and more than 39 million pages of historical documents.

Just a stone's throw away (quite literally) from the LBJ Library is the **Center for American History** (Sid Richardson Hall, ☎ 512-495-4515), which houses the Barker Texas History Center, the nation's largest collection of Texas history.

Some of the finest in college sports are played at the university. Texas football is legendary, boasting a past that includes coaches like Daryl Royal and players like Earl Campbell. It perennially has one of the top baseball teams in the nation, and the same can be said for the swimming, diving, volleyball and golfing teams. For information on attending any of the sporting events ☎ 512-471-4602.

The Drag, a stretch of Guadalupe that bounds the university on its western edge, has been an Austin icon for a century and is one of the code words you'll hear locals use a lot. No one actually says Guadalupe – you'll be branded an outsider if you do. The Drag used to be littered with eclectic shopping, dining and entertainment. Today it has turned more towards mainstream enterprises, with the Varsity Theater replaced by Tower Records and independent bookstores replaced by a massive Barnes & Noble. However, the street's energy is not all gone (though longtime Austinites will complain that it's just not the same). Captain Quackenbush's still caffeinates throngs.

The Renaissance Market at the heart of the Drag is also in for the long haul. Vendors used to amble up and down the street selling handcrafted wares, from jewelry to incense to art. Today, they gather at the market and offer original items you'll find nowhere else.

A favorite attraction since the 1850s, **Mount Bonnell** (3800 Mount Bonnell Rd, a mile past W 35th) boasts one of the most scenic spots in town, with a panoramic view of the Austin skyline, Lake Austin and the Hill Country. It will seem like you're going up the stone steps forever, but you'll find the climb worth it in the end.

✷ Author's Tip

There's a 10 pm curfew for the park, so enjoy it before dark.

The National Wildflower Research Center (4801 La Crosse Avenue, ☎ 512-292-4100, www.wildflower.org) invites you to stroll through its 23 display gardens and educate yourself on environmental issues and techniques. The brainchild of Lady Bird Johnson, who has endeared herself to Texas as a spokeswoman for various beautification projects since her husband's death, the Institute also includes a café, a research library and a stone pool.

Information Sources

You can always contact the **Austin Convention and Visitors Bureau** (201 E 2nd St #78701#, ☎ 800-926-2282, www.Austin360.com/acvb) for more information. The home page at www.Austin360.com has complete information for the entire Central Texas region. The **Greater Austin Chamber of Commerce** is at PO Box 1967, 78767, ☎ 512-478-9383. For information and maps on area parks, contact the **Austin Parks and Recreation Department** at ☎ 512-499-6700, www.ci.austin.tx.us/parks/default.htm.

■ Adventures on the Water

 With Austin's heritage deeply embedded in the limestone springs and creeks that populate the area, there is no shortage of water activities. The city lies at the foot of the **Highland Lakes** system, a series of six lakes that winds north through the Colorado River bed for some 600 miles. Each lake touts something unique.

Lake Travis plays host to sailors with its wide basin and winds that billow down its canyon walls. Water-skiers prefer **Lake Austin**, with its straight narrow stretches and protected water that barely reflects gale force winds. They are the jewels of Central Texas. For more information on them see the *Special Attraction* feature at the end of this chapter.

If you're out at Lake Travis, stop by the **Oasis Cantina Del Lago** (6550 Comanche Trail, off RR 620, ☎ 512-266-2441) for a drink (not for the food). It's a myriad of decks that sit high above the lake. Sunsets from here are some of the best in the country (yes, country) and are noted nightly with bells and thunderous applause.

Spoiled Austinites, though, are not limited to just the Highland Lakes. The next lake in the Colorado River chain is **Town Lake**, a narrow jig that separates north from south in a city whose directions are given with the lake's geography in mind.

Though not suitable for swimming and fishing, it is a good place to rent canoes and kayaks. Try **Zilker Park Boat Rentals** (downstream from Barton Springs in Zilker Park, ☎ 512-478-3852) and **Austin Canoe and Kayak** (9705 Burnet Rd, ☎ 512-719-4386).

Canoeing in Austin.

For the less physically ambitious, there are a variety of boat tours of the lake. The ***Lone Star*** paddle wheeler (208 Barton Springs, ☎ 512-327-1388) departs from the Hyatt Regency Hotel and South First St Bridge – its monolithic red, white and blue hull is hard to miss. **Capital Cruises** (☎ 512-480-9264) also offers excursions for bat-watching, private getaways and general lake-looking. It docks at the Hyatt, as well.

On the fringes of Austin, you can find **Hamilton Pool Preserve**, a long-treasured swimming hole created by a collapsed grotto that even the oldest of Austinites talk about with a smile in their eyes. Its centerpiece is a 60-foot waterfall that spills into a limestone-lined, jade-green pool. There are hiking and picnic areas in the **Travis County Park**. But go early, conservation officials limit park occupancy to the first 100 vehicles. Call ☎ 512-264-2740 for specific directions.

McKinney Falls State Park (US 183 south to Scenic Loop Rd, ☎ 512-243-1643), a stretch of Onion Creek just southeast of town, no longer allows swimming, but it remains a wonderful place to stroll beneath cypress and cedar trees. There are spots to fish, in addition to trails, group shelters and camping sites.

■ Adventures on Foot

A delicate portion of the Texas Hill Country has been guarded in the **Wild Basin Preserve** (805 N Capital of Texas Hwy, ☎ 512-327-7622). With more than 220 acres of protected wilderness, the preserve is home to two endangered species: the golden-cheeked warbler and the black-capped vireo. There are almost three miles of hiking trails and an education center.

The **Barton Creek Greenbelt** is certainly an extraordinary feat, if only for the fact that it entails over 16 miles of secluded trail right in the heart of downtown and west Austin. With multiple trailheads (the main one located in Zilker Park), the trail not only is a challenging hike, but a mountain biking mecca. You can pick up a map from the Austin Parks and Wildlife Department (200 S Lamar, ☎ 512-499-6700).

Barton Creek, which the park follows, can be navigated by tubers and canoeists during wet seasons. As you get away from Zilker Park the terrain gets more and more isolated.

✱ Author's Tip

Plan ahead on some kind of carpool system since the trail does not loop back. Also, watch out for bicyclists – the trail accommodates both hikers and bikers. If you're going by bike, bring spare tubes. The rocky and sharp terrain can get to even the best of mountain bikers.

The Greenbelt (even though Austin has several greenbelts, the Barton Creek Greenbelt has earned the official shortened moniker) is also a central starting point for rock climbing. Gus Fruh, New Wall, Great Wall and Seismic Wall have all been bolted. There are also several spots to boulder along the creek. To get there, take the Barton Skyway exit off of Mopac and head east. The road will dead end at Spyglass, which is an entrance to the Greenbelt. At the trail, turn right. New Wall and Great Wall are about a half-mile down, and Gus Fruh is a quarter of a mile further. However, unless you're already an expert climber, it would be much smarter to talk to an area expert.

One of the best places to check in would be **Pseudo Rock**, Austin's only indoor climbing gym (200 Trinity, 78701, ☎ 512474-4376). In addition to instruction and guidance, local climbers congregate there and you can probably find someone to tag along with.

The gym also carries *Texas Limestone II*, a guidebook to Central Texas climbing. It includes ratings and maps and was written by three local experts, Jeff Jackson, Kevin Gallagher and Rebecca Gonzalez. You can also find copies of the book at two local sports/outdoors stores: **REI** (9901 N. Capital of Texas Hwy, ☎ 512-343-5550) and **Whole Earth Provision Co.** (1014 N. Lamar, ☎ 512-476-1414). Even if you don't need or want the book, a stop one of the stores could be worth your while. Most of the employees are fans of the outdoors and are happy to share their local knowledge with visiting explorers.

■ Adventures on Wheels

Probably the best place to start an adventure on wheels is at Austin's **Veloway** (☎ 512-288-6086), located in the Circle C subdivision in South Austin. Joggers and hikers are not allowed on the 3.1-mile paved loop – only bicyclists and in-line skaters. Because it is paved, it is perfect for both novices and hard core riders. The International In-Line Skating Association has named the course one of the 10 best places in the country to skate. Beginning in-liners, however, might find a couple of the steep hills a little too challenging.

The loop meanders through the Texas Hill Country, curving with every break in the terrain. Most first-timers wonder if they're really going to end up where they began. There's a crossover point about half-way through the course for those who want to shorten the ride. Pay close attention to your lane – the left lane is for the speedsters. Many of the bicyclists that train here are professionals, and go faster than you can imagine.

There are two access points (there's no real visitor center) to park. One is behind the Bowie High School Campus (4103 Slaughter Lane), the other is on La Crosse Ave just east of Mopac. If you haven't been there before, call ahead for directions. Hours of operation are easy – from sun up to sun down. There are no lights for night time use. (There are also no water fountains, so bring plenty of your own water.)

While the Veloway offers a great paved surface for road bikes, mountain bikers looking for more challenging terrain have several options. The most popular mountain biking trail winds through the **Barton Creek Greenbelt** (see page 18 for information). If you begin at the trailhead in Zilker Park, there are some seven miles of criss-crossing paths before you end up at the golf course that anchors the Greenbelt's western end. A portion of the trail is very rugged and rocky, with boulders spread sporadically throughout. In places you'll find a mish-mash of smaller trails and it's not hard to get lost. But don't worry, the locals that you'll find here know these trails by heart. Just ask and they'll send you on your way. Because the scenery is so incredible and the trail so extensive and convenient, you'll find a crowd on the weekends.

❋ Author's Tip

Because of the rocky terrain, make sure you bring along (and use) a helmet. The ground is unforgiving. Also, plan to take a swim here after a sweaty ride. There are some great swimming holes along the creek bed and Barton Springs is just past the Zilker Park trailhead.

City Park (☎ 512-837-4500, Austin Parks & Recreation, or ☎ 512-346-1831), more formally known as Emma Long Metropolitan Park, provides what is considered some of the most difficult riding in town. While most visitors go for the park's Lake Austin access and sandy beach, bikers share the trails with motor cross vehicles. Mountain bikers have the advantage – you can hear dirt bikes before they see you. It's best to just get out of the way if you know they're right behind you. To get there, take RR 2222 west. Turn left on City Park Road, which will be the first light past Loop 360. The road will dead end at the park.

The **Bull Creek Greenbelt**, just north of City Park, has been evolving over the last two decades as new neighborhoods continually encroach on what once was country. But there is still a large portion of the greenbelt remaining. Loop 360 bisects the creek bed, with access points on either side of the road. Take Spicewood Springs Road east of 360 and then take your first right (before the big hill) – the trailhead, and some parking, will be just down the road. If you start here, you'll be going under 360 to get to a larger portion of the trail. There is also a parking lot on a small side road on the west side of Loop 360, .5 mile south of Spicewood Springs Rd. The lot is just to the right before the road goes through the creek.

Bull Creek is also a dog and dog owner's haven, so try not to run over anyone's pooch. Because of the creek's isolation owners don't feel hampered by leash laws. They're usually concentrated closer to the parking lots and along Bull Creek. Also, if the creek's running, bring your swimsuit for an after-ride dip.

■ Adventures in the Air

Nothing can afford you a better view of flourishing Austin than a **hot-air balloon** ride. While weather permits a year-round trade, the maze of lakes, creeks and rivers that spread across Central Texas provide a breathtaking panoramic performance. Most of the balloon companies will cater to your wishes, from romantic champagne breakfasts to touch downs on Town Lake.

One of the most scenic rides begins on the fields of Zilker Park at sunrise and follows the Colorado River toward Mount Bonnell. While the balloon owners and drivers are reticent to pick a favorite, this one certainly fits lots of bills. You can traverse the calm waters of Town Lake to the foot of the Hill Country, where bluffs surround lush Lake Austin. A trip out to the Wimberley/Dripping Springs area, just southwest of Austin, is another ballooning favorite.

Area Balloon Companies

Airwolf Adventures. . . . . (☎ 512-251-4024)

American Balloon Corp. . . . . (☎ 512-280-2558)

Austin Aeronauts . . . . (☎ 512-440-1492 or 800-444-3257)

Hill Country Balloons. . . . . (☎ 512-345-1575)

Skyride Balloons . . . . (☎ 512-310-7944)

Sunrise Celebrations . . . . (☎ 512-396-0759)

The **Austin Skydiving Center** (☎ 409-773-9100, http://austinskydiving.com), 40 minutes east of Austin, compresses your flight over the Hill Country into mere minutes. But for the thrill seeker, that's the point. Located in Lexington, the center is affiliated with Skydive University and certified by the US Parachute Association.

One of Austinites' favorite perennial pastimes has been **disc (frisbee) golf**. The town, long on people looking to play out of doors, was one of the first to truly embrace the sport. Back in the 80s, when the sport was still gaining momentum, Austin was rumored to be the disc golf capital of the world, a title no one can substantiate. Yet, there is no evidence to the contrary. There are five 18-hole courses around town, and one nine-hole course. One local disc golfer has set up a Web site (**www.ccsi.com/~khermes**) that can provide visitors with detailed information on course offerings, including hole length, pin placements and potential hazards.

The **Pease Park** course, which runs along a portion of Shoal Creek between 24th St and 15th St, is no doubt the most popular disc course in Austin. Its central location and nice variety, which includes several water and tree hazards, attracts the crowds. There are several places to park along the greenbelt. For access to the park try either the southwest corner of North Lamar and 24th St or go north on Lamar from 24th. There will be a small lot about four blocks up on the left.

Two other recommended courses are **Mary Moore Searight Metro Park** to the south and **Bartholomew Park** just east of I-35. Searight has no water hazards, but lots of trees. To get there, take I-35 south to Slaughter Lane. Go west on Slaughter. You'll see the park a few miles down on your left.

Bartholomew has good variety, but the water hazards are tough for beginners. Go three miles east of I-35 on 51st St and it will be on the left side of the street.

■ Where to Stay

For a listing of hotel and motel chains that have establishments all across the state, see above, page 3. For some local color try one of the following.

Driskill Hotel, 604 Brazos, 78701, ☎ 512-474-5911. $$-$$$. A historical attraction on its own, its decadence has been wowing visitors for over a century. In the heart of downtown, it is within walking distance of most everything.

Four Seasons Austin, 98 San Jacinto, 78701, ☎ 800-332-3442, 512-478-4500. $$$-$$$$. Just feet away from the convention center and on the Town Lake Hike and Bike Trail, it's a perfect way to mix business with pleasure. Its restaurant is one of the finest in town.

Hyatt Regency, 208 Barton Springs Rd, 78704, ☎ 800-233-1234, 512-477-1234. $$-$$$$. On the southern edge of Town Lake, the Hyatt has convenient access to the hike and bike trail (with complimentary bicycles) and two popular restaurants. Matthew McConaughey got his acting debut break here, meeting a casting director in the Hyatt's top-floor restaurant.

Omni Hotel, 700 San Jacinto, 78701, ☎ 800-843-6664, 512-476-3700. $$$-$$$$. With lots of glass and breathing room, the Omni embraces the modern rather than the antique. Includes a rooftop pool and is a block away from 6th St, the heart of Austin's entertainment district.

Renaissance Austin Hotel, 9721 Arboretum Blvd, 78759, ☎ 800-468-3571, 512-343-2626. $$-$$$$. On the northwest corner of town, the Renaissance is closer to most of the high-tech industry businesses. The Arboretum, an outdoor shopping center that the hotel anchors, is Austin's ritziest mall.

Sheraton Austin, 500 North IH-35, 78702, ☎ 800-325-3535, 512-480-8181. $$$-$$$$. Lush with imported art and antiques, the Sheraton is on the eastern edge of downtown, one block from 6th St.

Red Lion Hotel Airport, 6121 North IH-35, 78751, ☎ 800-547-8010, 512-323-5466. $$$-$$$$. At the corner of IH-35 and US 290, the hotel is convenient to north Austin and is close to Highland Mall.

Bed & Breakfasts

Austin's Wildflower Inn, 1200 W 22½ St, 78705, ☎ 512-477-9639. $$-$$$. Charm in the heart of Austin. Blocks away from the UT campus.

Carrington's Bluff, 1900 David St, 78705, ☎ 800-871-8908, 512-479-0638. $$-$$$. Old English Country. Very quiet with a large yard and gazebo. Writer's cottage.

Governor's Inn, 611 W 22nd St, 78705, ☎ 800-871-8908, 512-477-0711. $$-$$$. Neo-Classical Victorian with wraparound porches. Private baths, many with clawfoot tubs. Two blocks from UT campus.

Woodburn House, 4401 Avenue D, 78751, ☎ 512-458-4335. $$-$$$. Located in historic Hyde Park. Owners are resident innkeepers. The owners' dog is also a full-time resident.

Ziller House, 800 Edgecliff Terrace, 78704, ☎ 800-949-5446, 512-462-0100. $$$-$$$$. Genuinely eclectic with a Mediterranean exterior and German hunting lodge interior. Newly remodeled and includes natural stone hot tub and pool.

Austin International AYA Hostel, 2200 S Lakeshore Dr, 78741, ☎ 512-444-2294. $.

■ Where to Eat

Threadgill's, 6416 N Lamar, ☎ 512-451-5440. Also 301 West Riverside, ☎ 512-472-9304, www.threadgills.com. This Austin mainstay made its mark as the hangout of 60s legend Janis Joplin and more recently as the subject of a national VISA commercial (they don't take American Express). Traditional chicken fried steak and a black board brimming with vegetables of the day.

> **✷ Author's Tip**
>
> They've got their own cookbook if you want to take any of their recipes home.

County Line, 6500 Bee Caves Rd, ☎ 512-327-1742. Also 5204 FM 2222, ☎ 512-346-3664. The first location boasts a panoramic 20-mile view of the Texas Hill Country; the second is lakeside. Both provide heapings of

Texas-style barbecue and hot lemon napkins to clean off with afterwards.

Castle Hill Café, 1101 W 5th St, ☎ 512-476-7218. Don't pick a favorite dish here. There's a new menu every two weeks, though everything is distinctly Southwestern. Incredible atmosphere with a surprisingly affordable and expansive wine selection. You'll recognize the wait staff year after year.

Dirty's, 2808 Guadalupe, ☎ 512-478-0413. Since 1926 they've been serving it down and dirty. It's a humble joint just north of campus. Try the onion rings, fries and shakes.

Hyde Park Bar and Grill, 4206 Duval Rd, ☎ 512-458-3168. A 15-foot fork out front marks this cozy old home in one of the oldest neighborhoods in town. Battered French fries are a meal in themselves.

The Salt Lick, FM 1826, 30 minutes west of Austin in Driftwood, ☎ 512-894-3117, http://austin.data.net/saltlick. This barbecue mecca is definitely a destination hotspot for locals and is usually included on the Texas Best Barbecue lists. Casual setting is also BYOB. Be prepared to get dirty.

Fonda San Miguel, 2330 W North Loop Blvd, ☎ 512-459-4121. Austin's most celebrated Mexican cuisine set within a magnificent building. It has a more authentic feel to its food than the Tex-Mex genre that is more common in Texas, but it is still quite flavorful. The Sunday buffet is legendary.

Jeffrey's, 1204 W Lynn, ☎ 512-477-5584. One of Austin's most elegant dining establishment and one of the few that garners stars from national critics, though the price reflects it. Reservations are recommended.

Chuy's, 1728 Barton Springs Rd, ☎ 512-474-4452. Also 10520 N Lamar, ☎ 512-836-4852. Eating at Chuy's is entertainment in itself. Its decor changes from room to room – from hubcaps to fish to Elvis to piñatas. Celebrating Elvis' birthday with a bash each year, the restaurant and owners are noticeably involved in the Austin scene. They serve Tex-Mex. Next door, the owners have created **Shady Grove** (1624 Barton Springs Rd, ☎ 512-474-9991), which has a massive outdoor patio where they show vintage films and live music. So much atmosphere, you'll never want to leave. The food is a cross of Southern and chili peppers.

Hut's Hamburgers, 807 W 6th St, ☎ 512-472-0693. Great burgers for as long as anyone can remember. The memorabilia on the walls prove it. Weeknights there are two-for-one specials.

Las Manitas Avenue Café, 211 Congress, ☎ 512-472-9357. It just feels right. Small menu, fresh specials, prepared by people who know how to cook. Breakfast and lunch only.

Chez Nous, 510 Neches, ☎ 512-473-2413. Serves dinner only, Tuesday-Sunday. The French café-style food changes daily, depending on the freshest products the hosts find that morning. Your choices will be limited, but everything is good. You'll also probably meet the French owners.

The Hoffbrau, 613 W 6thth, ☎ 512-472-0822. Most Austinites won't tell you about this place – they try to keep it to themselves. Huge steaks and modest side dishes served at unpretentious prices.

Sullivans Steak House, 300 Colorado, ☎ 512-495-6504. The place to be seen with fine wine, incredible food, live music and valet parking. It's also a hotspot for the famous.

Mezzaluna, 310 Colorado, ☎ 512-472-6770. Fine Italian food with a lively ambiance. The party starts when the young guns get off work and continues all night long.

Z Tejas, 1110 W 6th St, ☎ 512-478-5355 and 9400 Arboretum Blvd, ☎ 512-346-3506. An eclectic collection of Southwestern and Tex-Mex goodies, all bundled into a colorful atmosphere. The first location recently closed for a period because of extensive fire damage, but it has opened again to the city's applause.

Waco

■ History

The large, cold springs of the Brazos River have enticed humans to Waco for centuries. The Hueco Indians – for which the town is named – were the first area residents. In 1837 Texas Rangers established an outpost on the banks of the Brazos, but it took another 12 years for settlers to make Waco home.

Its rich soil and location in the heartland of Texas brought quick money and fortune. It became a king when cattle, cotton and corn were blossoming on a national scale. The Civil War wreaked havoc on Waco, ending its brief period of prosperity. However, because of its location on the Chisholm Trail, Waco became a stopping point for cowboys and cattle on their way north. "Six Shooter Junction," as the town was called, again became a hub for commerce.

A suspension bridge, built in 1870, was the only bridge in existence to cross the Brazos, cementing the city's place in the Texas cattle economy. When the railroad hit town in 1872, it only furthered Waco's position.

The Great Train Wreck

A bizarre piece of the Waco area's history was the Great Train Wreck of 1896, which took place in the fictitious town of Crush, just north of Waco. The town – aptly named – was created as a piece of propaganda, and in September of 1896, 30 trains brought 30,000 visitors to Crush. They were to witness a head-on collision between two steam locomotives, each pulling six freight cars. And they did. However, two spectators were killed by flying debris.

Barbed wire and civilization meant the end of a lot of things in Texas, including cattle drives. In 1953 life changed irreversibly in Waco as a ferocious tornado ripped through town, killing 114 residents and taking out most of downtown. The town began a decades-long downward spiral. In 1966 the local airforce base closed, adding to the economic downturn. Over 3,000 military and civilian jobs disappeared.

The slide continued until the late 1980s, when locals took on a grand revival project that began with polishing up the beleaguered downtown district. New companies flooded to town. The warehouse district near the river is the new, hip social hub, boasting restaurants, clubs and bars. When Waco's population hit 200,000 – apparently the magic number – franchises began a mass ascent. The city is still in a tremendous period of revival.

Waco has transitioned into a town dependent on culture, recreation and education. The city attracted international attention in the spring of 1993 when the Branch Davidians and their leader, David Koresh, were killed in an eruption of flames after a 51-day stand-off with federal authorities.

■ Touring

 The Suspension Bridge that was so vital to Waco's place in the cattle industry still stands. It served as the model for its more famous sister, the Brooklyn Bridge, and was the longest single-span suspension bridge in the nation and the second longest in the world when it was built in 1870. The 475-foot structure, originally created by a group of private investors as a toll bridge, is now open only to foot traffic and appears on the National Register of Historic Places.

Dr. Pepper

Dr. Pepper, whose slogans have proclaimed it the "King of Beverages" and encouraged people to "Be a Pepper," had its humble beginning in a Waco drug store. The **Dr. Pepper Museum** (300 S 5th St, ☎ 254-757-2433, www.drpeppermuseum.com) traces the drink's rise from Morrison's Old Corner Drug Store in the 1880s to its place as a major player in the cola industry. It first received national exposure at the 1904 World Fair in St. Louis, where it was introduced to almost 20 million people. The same fair included the introduction of hamburgers and hotdogs on buns and the ice cream cone.

The **Texas Ranger Hall of Fame** (along I-35 at University Parks Drive, ☎ 254-750-8631, www.texasranger.com) documents all of the lore that surrounds this famed group of enforcers. Along with Indian artifacts and Western art, the museum contains a renowned collection of guns and weapons including James Bowie's flintrock (which was reportedly taken from his body after the fall of the Alamo.)

Along the same lines is the **Texas Sports Hall of Fame** (1108 S University Parks Dr, ☎ 254-756-1633), which highlights the achievements of sporting Texans including George Foreman, Nolan Ryan, Tom Landry and Babe Didrikson Zaharias.

Perhaps the best way to tour the town is to pick up a ride with the notorious **James S. Woods**. He offers a 45-minute mule-drawn wagon tour of Waco, complete with "more lies and stories about Waco than you ever heard." This self-proclaimed alligator wrestler serves as Waco's ambassador to hundreds of tourists who travel along the wagon route. Call the **convention and visitors bureau** at ☎ 254-750-8696 or 800-922-6386.

Waco's 416-acre **Cameron Park** (University Parks Dr adjacent to the Brazos River, reservations ☎ 254-750-5980) one of the largest municipal parks in Texas, was donated to the city by William Cameron, a successful Waco businessman and philanthropist. The park includes hiking and biking trails through lush vegetation, with two rivers – the Brazos and the Bosque – running through the park. Both of the rivers have receded considerably over the last several centuries, leaving behind massive cliffs and beautiful "pecan bottoms." The best known cliff in the park is **Lovers Leap**, where two Indian lovers from warring tribes took their lives (according to legend). Park maps, available at the gate, will point out the legendary overlook. Sports enthusiasts will enjoy the disc golf course and the open areas for volleyball, croquet and badminton. You can rent jet skis for fun on the water.

Within the park, on a 50-acre parcel, sits the **Cameron Park Zoo** (1701 N 4th St, ☎ 254-750-8400). Though not on the level of San Antonio's zoo, it is still a favorite with kids and adults.

The **Red Men Museum & Library** (4521 Speight Ave, ☎ 254-756-1221) exhibits an eclectic array of historic artifacts such as a bugle recovered from the battleground at Gettysburg, a watercolor by Adolf Hitler, circa 1912, and a Colt 45 and Colt 38 that once belonged to the notorious outlaws Bonnie and Clyde. The library is an American historical reference library and includes important papers of presidents, including a complete set of the Warren Commission report and the Nuremburg War Criminal Trials report.

The **Fort Fisher Park Campground** (IH-35 at University Parks Dr, ☎ 800-922-6386 or 254-750-8630) lies on the site of the original Fort Fisher, an encampment for the Texas Rangers. Broad oaks and pecan trees that are centuries old shade over 100 riverfront campsites and RV hook-ups.

Waco, well known for its religious fervor, is home to **Baylor University** (☎ 254-755-1921, www.baylor.edu) the largest Baptist university in the world. Chartered in 1845 by the Republic of Texas, the university is host to two world-class museums. The **Armstrong Browning Library** (700 Speight, ☎ 254-755-3566) contains the world's largest collection of materials relating to Robert and Elizabeth Barrett Browning. The **Strecker Museum** (Sid Richardson Hall, ☎ 254-755-1110) lays claim to being the oldest continuously operated natural history museum in the state.

Information Sources

Some helpful numbers for your stay: **Tourist Information Center**, ☎ 254-750-8696 or 800-WACO-FUN, the **Waco Convention & Visitors Bureau**, ☎ 254-750-5810 or 800-321-9226, and the **Waco Special Events Recording**, ☎254-752-9226.

■ Adventures on the Water

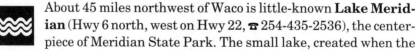

About 45 miles northwest of Waco is little-known **Lake Meridian** (Hwy 6 north, west on Hwy 22, ☎ 254-435-2536), the centerpiece of Meridian State Park. The small lake, created when the CCC dammed Bee Creek, is equipped for fishing, swimming and boating. Two trails, about four miles worth, circle the lake, which is densely surrounded by oak, pecan, cedar, elm and cottonwood.

Lake Waco (☎ 254-756-5359), with much of its 7,270 acres inside Waco's city limits, provides a little more room for boating activities. There are several shoreside marinas, camps and parks for visitors. It also has sandy beaches, a unique feature for an inland lake. Call before you go to get information on the eight boat ramps and five parks that line the 60-plus miles of shoreline. Among them, Airport Park, adjacent to the municipal airport, is a longtime favorite for its calm swimming waters and overnight camping facilities.

Speegleville II Park, on the west shore of Lake Waco, has recently re-opened. To get there, take Hwy 6 north from I-35, exit at Speegleville road to the right. The entrance to the park will be about a mile down the road at a stop sign. In addition to a boat ramp for access, the **Lacy Point Hike and Bike Trail** has been created for mountain bikers and those on foot (road bikers will find it too tough a ride).

The **Brazos River** cuts through the Waco area. The River makes its way to Cameron Park before turning sharply toward the coast. Between **Lake Whitney** and **Cameron Park** there are three good day canoe trips. There are no real obstacles and the runs can be enjoyed by the entire family. Local outfitters include **Dick's Canoes & Riverplace Realty** (☎ 254-622-8364). There is also a short trip (about four miles) between Lake Waco and the Brazos on the Bosque River – it's another enjoyable stretch of shaded canoeing.

■ Adventures on Wheels

Cameron Park (see page 27 for information) does a good job at being all things to all people. One of its greatest assets is its mountain biking trails, considered some of the best in the state and often included on "Top 10" Texas biking lists. The mammoth 416-acre park, which follows two rivers – the Brazos and the Bosque – offers both river valleys and limestone bluffs. The juxtaposition of the two make for some very challenging rides, with strenuous climbs and scary downhill rides. However, beginners and leisure riders are not left out.

The **River Trail**, three miles that follow the Bosque riverbed, is well-maintained and fairly simple. To add spice to the ride, take one of the splinter paths that branch off from the River Trail. There's an eight-mile singletrack course that winds through much of the park's interior, but it's sometimes difficult to navigate with so many criss-crossing paths. The park is small enough that you can't get lost for too long. Before you begin, check with the visitor's center to see if they have a trail map that was slated to be completed in 1998.

> ✳ **Author's Tip**
>
> You'll be sharing the trails with hikers and park rangers on horseback, so keep your eyes on traffic.

■ Where to Stay

 Waco Hilton, 113 S University Parks Dr, 76701, ☎ 254-754-8484, reservations 800-234-5244. $$. Just across the street from the Brazos River, it's convenient to most of Waco's attractions.

Courtyard by Marriott, 101 Washington Ave, 76701, ☎ 254-752-8686, reservations 800-321-2211. $$. With a whirlpool, spa and exercise room, it's about as fancy as Waco gets on the hotel scale.

Manor House Inn, 4201 Franklin Ave, 76710, ☎ 254-772-9440. $-$$. Some rooms recently remodeled. Located close to Waco's corporate center.

Old Main Lodge (Best Western), 4th St at IH-35, 76706, ☎ 254-753-0316, reservations 800-299-9226. $$. Across the street from Baylor University and close to several restaurants.

The Judge Baylor House, 908 Speight, 76706, ☎ 254-756-0273, 888-JBAYLOR. $$. Less than two blocks from the Baylor campus and the Armstrong Browning Library. The English country house also serves afternoon tea.

Colcord House Bed and Breakfast, 2211 Colcord Ave, 76707, ☎ 254-753-6856. $$. Room in both the main house and the detached carriage house in Waco's historic "Silk Stocking" district. Corporate rates available for extended stays.

■ Where to Eat

 Waco Elite Café, ☎ 254-754-4941, and **the Health Camp Restaurant**, ☎ 254-752-2081 (both S Valley Mills at I-35, on the circle). These two institutions have been drawing crowds for decades. The Elite's chicken-fried steak has been its mainstay since 1941. Don't let the Health Club's name fool you, as their specialty is great burgers and shakes. Its diner atmosphere replete with swiveling stools is straight from the 50s.

George's Restaurant,1525 Speight Ave, ☎ 254-753-1421, www.georgesrestaurant.com, has been a local gathering place for Wacoans and Baylor alumni since the 1960s. Famous for its chicken fried steak, it also boasts the Big'O, an 18 oz. goblet of ice cold beer for only $1.50.

Cadillac Jack's, 217 S 4th St, ☎ 254-714-2323. American cuisine from chicken fried steak to tasty burgers to fresh salads.

Dock's Riverfront Café, 100 N. Jack Kultgen Expressway, ☎ 254-714-2933. This has been a landmark on the Brazos River for decades. It's a tough call on which is better – their seafood or steaks.

Heitmiller Family Steakhouse, I-35 Exit 343, ☎ 254-829-2651. Waco's not shy about its affinity for steaks.

The Original Miller Family Lake Brazos Steakhouse, 1620 Martin Luther King, Jr. Blvd. (formerly Lake Brazos Parkway), ☎ 254-755-7797. Steaks, steaks, steaks. And all the fixins'.

The Northwood Inn, 1609 College Drive, ☎ 254-755-8666, www.the-northwood-inn.com. They call themselves the only fine dining experience in Waco, using a lovely home as their centerpiece. They also boast the largest wine selection in town.

Trujillo's, 2612 La Salle At The Circle, ☎ 254-756-1331. Another veteran on the circle, it's also one of the finer Tex-Mex choices in town.

Buzzard Billy's Armadillo Bar & Grill-o, 208 S University Parks Dr. ☎ 254-753-2778. Proving that there is a place for humor in our food and on our menu, Buzzard Billy's offers a wide range of Cajun selections, including the eclectic Chicken Alfredeaux.

San Antonio

San Antonio joins the ranks of cities like New Orleans and San Francisco – cities that have retained their ethnic flavor, even thrived on it, rather than bulldozing through history. While its sisters Houston and Dallas sent their buildings straight up to accommodate burgeoning business, San Antonio embraced its culture and set itself up as a tourism capital.

Not hard to do, especially when you have the Alamo. Remember it? It seems fitting that this small mission established in 1718 is still the city's main draw. Though its cracking adobe walls are engulfed by the downtown infrastructure, its magnificence is not lost on visitors.

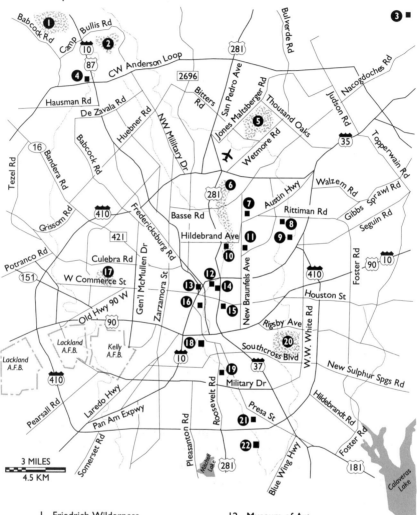

San Antonio

1. Friedrich Wilderness
2. Eisenhower Park
3. Natural Bridge Caverns
4. Six Flags Fiesta Texas
5. McAllister Park
6. Olmas Basin Park
7. McNay Art Museum
8. Fort Sam Houston National Cemetery
9. Fort Sam Houston
10. San Antonio Zoo
11. Botanical Gardens
12. Museum of Art
13. Convention & Visitors Bureau
14. The Alamo
15. Alamodome
16. J. A. Navarro State Hist. Park
17. Monterrey Park
18. Mission Concepcion
19. San José Mission
20. Southside Lions Park
21. Mission San Juan Capistrano
22. Mission La Espada

The Alamo.

Central Texas

■ History

When the governor of Spanish colonial Texas met with a tribe of Coahuiltecan Indians here in 1681, he paid tribute to the day – Saint Anthony's Day – by naming the area San Antonio. Mission leaders, having heard that the Coahuiltecan's were easily ruled, built a series of missions, among them Mission San Antonio, or the now fabled Alamo.

The Mexican Revolution in 1821 left San Antonio in Mexico's hands. However, that same year marked the entry of Anglo colonists to the city under the charge of Stephen F. Austin.

By 1836 there were 3,500 Anglos living in the city, and they, along with a number of native Hispanic Texans, led the rebellion against General Santa Anna at the Battle of the Alamo. It was later that year that Texas won its independence at San Jacinto.

■ Touring

It's hard not to remember the **Alamo** (300 Alamo Plaza, ☎ 210-225-1391) when thinking of San Antonio. Rescued and maintained by the Daughters of the Republic of Texas, the stone mission turned fort is dwarfed by the San Antonio skyline. Yet its appeal and integrity remain intact.

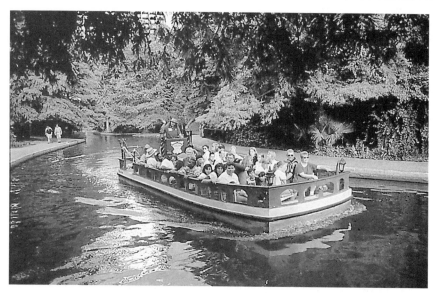

River Walk.

Its 189 defenders, including William Travis, Davy Crockett and Jim Bowie (of Bowie knife fame), all died during the 1836 battle but exacted a tremendous toll from Santa Anna's troops, whose depleted army went on to be defeated by Sam Houston's troops at the Battle of San Jacinto.

Just across the street from the Alamo is San Antonio's most photographed attraction, the **River Walk** (or the "Paseo del Rio"), accessible at Commerce and Losoya. Extending for miles one level below the downtown streets, the River Walk is accessible at several bridges. While the river was the center of settlement for early San Antonio, providing sustenance for thousands to thrive, its flow has been controlled and its banks are now lined with shops, restaurants, hotels and vendors.

After hosting the 1968 World's Fair, San Antonio was left with a bonus: **HemisFair Park** (bounded by Alamo St, I-37, Durango and Market St, ☎ 210-207-8522). This was the fair's site and it has become a focal point for entertainment and recreation in the city. Its centerpiece, the 750-foot **Tower of Americas** building, offers a panoramic view that few can surpass.

✳ Author's Tip

If you need to use the restroom while eating in the tower's slowly spinning restaurant take note of your seat. It will have moved by the time you get back.

The **Alamodome** (off I-37, Alamodome exit, ☎ 210-207-3600), a one-of-kind structure, is home to the San Antonio Spurs and the annual Alamo Bowl. Under its domed top are two permanent ice rinks.

The Institute of Texan Cultures (www.texancultures.utsa.edu) also in HemisFair Park, is one of Texans' favorite museums about Texans. Instead of focusing on specific events, the museum highlights 28 different ethnic and cultural groups that have made Texas what it is today.

If you haven't got your fill of Texas culture, try the **Pioneer, Trail Drivers and Texas Rangers Memorial Museum** (3805 Broadway, ☎ 210-822-9011), which traces the exciting path of the Texas Rangers with guns, photographs, sketches and individual accounts of a world that is far removed from the one we enjoy today. The museum is in Brackenridge Park, adjacent to the Witte Museum.

The **San Antonio Museum of Art** (200 W Jones Ave, ☎ 210-978-8100, www.samuseum.org) set up camp in the former Lone Star Brewery's castle-like building. Collections range from ancient art to contemporary, including magnificent Greek and Roman sculpture, and Latin American folk art.

The **Witte Museum** (3801 Broadway, ☎ 210-357-1900, www.wittemuseum.org) has been a city landmark for 70 years, featuring science, the humanities, hands-on exhibits of Texas history, natural science and anthropology. A life-size walk-through diorama, recreating the south Texas thornbrush, comes stocked with javelina, armadillo and jaguar. The EcoLab exhibits live Texas animals.

Fiesta Texas (☎ 800-IS-FIESTA, www.sixflags.com/sananton) is a 200-acre theme park that attempts to capture the spirit of Texas by combining amusement park fun with cultural entertainment. The "Lone Star Spectacular," a high-tech show that narrates the varied history of Texas on a cliff wall the size of a football field, serves as the crowning event for the theme park that aims to please both adults and children.

Texas Adventure (307 Alamo Plaza, ☎ 210-227-0388) is a theme park of the multi-media genre. Using a variety of state-of-the-art special effects, the Adventure allows you touch, feel and taste the story of Texas independence, in which the Alamo plays the lead role.

Watching the fall of the Alamo at the **IMAX Theater** (849 East Commerce, Rivercenter Mall, ☎ 800-354-IMAX, 210-225-4629) should complete your knowledge of the small mission's place in history.

Confounding those who know of San Antonio's distance to a large body of water, the city is home to **Sea World of Texas** (10500 Sea World Drive, ☎ 210-523-3611, www.4adventure.com/seaworld/sw_texas) and more

Central Texas

notably to its star, the world-renowned Shamu. This 250-acre affair is touted as the world's largest marine life display. In addition to Shamu, the lovable killer whale that piqued interest in treatment of whales on an international scale, there are exhibits that include dolphins, sharks, sea lions, walruses, otters and penguins. It's a full day, so start early.

A more extensive – and more land-oriented – collection of animals can be found at the **San Antonio Zoo** (3903 North St Mary's in Brackenridge Park, ☎ 210-734-7183, www.sazoo-aq.org), which is one of the best in the nation. Over 3,000 animals reside in the 25-acre park situated at the headwaters of the San Antonio River. The children's zoo features boat rides for $1. The zoo's captive breeding success is recognized interna-tionally – it was the first to hatch and rear Caribbean flamingos and pro-duced the first white rhinoceros born in North America. It is also the only zoo to exhibit the endangered whooping crane. You owe it to your-self to spend a day at the zoo.

While the zoo is the cornerstone of **Brackenridge Park** (2800 block of North Broadway, ☎ 210-736-9534), a day in the rest of the park can be quite extraordinary. The **carousel** features 60 antique Bradley-Kay horses and is the children's favorite. The **railroad** runs over three miles through the park, while the **skyride** affords a panoramic view of both the grounds and the San Antonio skyline. There are also horses for lei-surely strolls along the trails and paddle boats for a trip on the water.

The **Brackenridge Park Japanese Tea Gardens** (3800 North St Mary's St, ☎ 210-821-3120) wind along walkways, stone bridges and tranquil pools with colorful floral displays and a variety of plants. A 60-foot waterfall tops it off.

The city, very much a military town in modern-day terms (including Brooks, Kelly, Lackland and Randolph air force bases), boasts a favorite military post in **Fort Sam Houston** (N New Braunfels at Grayson, ☎ 210-221-1211). Established in 1876, this fort, which once detained Geronimo, is now a perfect place to take a picnic lunch. Deer and peacock roam the shaded grounds that include Victorian officers quarters. Don't let the serenity of the camp or the museum fool you – Fort Sam Houston is still a working military operation.

Information Sources

For more information on San Antonio, call the **San Antonio Convention and Visitors Center** (PO Box 2277, San Antonio, 78298, ☎ 800-447-3372, www.sanantoniocvb.com).

■ Adventures on Foot

Both the black-capped vireo and the golden-cheeked warbler can be found wandering the grounds of the **Friedrich Wilderness Park** (21480 Milsa Rd, ☎ 210-698-1057). Operated by the city as a nature reserve, this unspoiled wilderness boasts seven winding trails that take advantage of the Texas Hill Country bordering San Antonio to the northwest.

The flavor of a Spanish bazaar, usually only found south of the United States border, is alive at **El Mercado** market square (bounded by I-35, Santa Rosa, West Commerce and Dolorasa, ☎ 210-207-8600). Replete with crafts crammed into small vending spots, the market is festive and fun.

A tangible example of San Antonio's restoration into a premiere tourism hotspot is **La Villita National Historic District** (bounded by the San Antonio River, Nuevo, South Alamo and South Presa, ☎ 210-299-8610, hotx.com/sa/lavillita/). What began as a slum is now San Antonio history incarnated. You can amble among shops, cafés and galleries, taking in the eclectic artistic feel that the restored area exudes.

Another historic district worth strolling through is the **King William Historic District** (along King William St). Veiled by a canopy of trees, the street, named for King William I of Prussia, has been home to San Antonio's elite since its birth in the 1870s. The Victorian houses, many restored, are reminiscent of San Antonio's glory years.

The National Geographic Society once called the **Spanish Governor's Palace** (105 Plaza De Armas, ☎ 210-224-0601) the most beautiful building in San Antonio. At one time, with its spacious cobblestone patio and flowing fountain, it housed the officials of the Spanish Province of Texas.

The Alamo is but one of the missions established during the Spanish colonial period. Four others, one still in use, are still standing and make up the San Antonio Missions National Historical Park (www.nps.gov/saan). However, each mission stands alone at a different spot on the San Antonio River. The first, **Mission Concepcion** (807 Mission Rd, ☎ 210-534-1540) is believed to be the oldest unrestored Catholic church still being used in the nation. A few original frescoes adorn its tower walls.

Mission San Jose.

Mission San Francisco de la Espada (10040 Espada, ☎ 210-627-2021) is the most rural of the missions, lending it an authentic air. Little is left of the original mission walls, built between 1731 and 1756, but the interior, restored in the 1800s, remains preserved.

Considered the most picturesque and the site of endless weddings and postcard shots, is **Mission San Jose** (6539 San Jose, ☎ 210-229-4770). Each Sunday at noon a Mariachi Mass draws crowds. Ornate carvings make it one of the tourists' favorites. The last mission, **Mission San Juan Capistrano** (9101 Graf, ☎ 210-229-5734) is another pastoral masterpiece, complete with a small museum on mission life in the 1700s.

Eisenhower Park (19399 NW Military Hwy, ☎ 210-821-3000, 821-3120 camping permits), on the northwest edge of town next to Camp Bullis, covers 318 acres, with five miles of hiking trails. A wooden observation tower affords visitors a glimpse of surrounding nature, including the Friedrich Wildnerness Park and a view of the San Antonio skyline on a clear day. Unfortunately, it also offers a view of an adjacent rock quarry. There are several spots along the trail for primitive camping.

■ Adventures on the Water

One of the best ways to experience the **River Walk** is on the actual river. **Paseo Del Rio Boats** (Market St Bridge, across from the Hilton, ☎ 210-222-1701) floats gingerly among the shops and restaurants that line the heart of San Antonio.

Within the boundaries of San Antonio, there are not many activities on water. However, the city's position in the heart of the Texas Hill Country makes it an easy drive to a beautiful lake or river backdrop. See entries for New Braunfels, San Marcos and Gruene, which arise to the northeast, and for Boerne, Bandera and Concan, to the north and west. All are less than an hour's drive away.

Canyon Lake, which San Antonio considers its own, though it is north of New Braunfels, is a perfect opportunity to get away. Steep cliffs surround much of the 8,240-acre lake and park area. In addition to record-setting fresh water fishing, there are two yacht clubs, two marinas, several public parks and a host of recreational outlets.

■ Adventures on Wheels

McAllister Park, in north central San Antonio (San Antonio Parks and Recreation, ☎ 210-207-8480), began its career as a biking hotbed nearly three decades ago, long before biking ascended the recreational ranks. However, what began as a road biking mecca has been taken over by the mountain bikers, who have been carving out trails in the expanding city park. Road bikers are still welcome, but that's not the main attraction.

Trails offer a variety of terrains and cater to the beginner and intermediate. The areas near the pavilions lean more toward the beginner. The trails get more advanced, relatively, on the northern edges of the park and along some of the airport's property.

To get to the 20 miles of trails, head north on US 281. Take the Bitters exit, turn right and stay on Starcrest when the road splits. Take a left on Jones-Maltsberger and the entrance will be on your right.

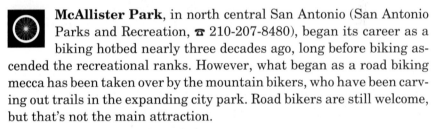

✳ Author's Tip

McAllister Park is also a favorite hiking and jogging spot for San Antonio residents. Watch the trails carefully for people on foot, especially during peak hours.

You'll find a little less traffic at **O.P. Schnable Park** (☎ 210-207-8480), which offers a variety of trails and some magnificent scenery. Just after the beginning of your ride, you'll find yourself atop a 40-foot cliff that overlooks a dry streambed. You can either follow the dry bed or climb up the cliffs for a spectacular view.

Central Texas

The ridgetop trails are forested, with fairly flat winding sections. The descent into the dry bed will send even a seasoned biker's heart racing with some fairly rough sections and large mounds.

To get there, take Hwy 16 (Bandera Road) north of IH 410 about 4½ miles. The park will be on your right. When the park road Ts, turn left and park near the pavilion. The trailhead is just to the right of the pavilion.

Road bikers can still enjoy the **Mission Hike and Bike Trail**, which connects Mission Concepción to Mission San Juan along the San Antonio River. The seven-mile route (14 miles round-trip), winds along a flat paved path that remains inaccessible to motorized vehicles. Trail maps can be found at any of the missions or at the San Antonio Convention and Visitors Bureau (☎ 210-270-8700).

B&J Bicycle Shop (8800 Broadway, Suite 106, 78217, ☎ 210-826-0177, www.bjbicycle.com) rents both mountain and road bikes on an hourly, daily and weekly basis. They are also chock full of local information.

■ Where to Stay

Days Inn Alamo Riverwalk, 902 E Houston St, 78205, ☎ 210-227-6233, 800-DAYS INN. $$. An affordable alternative to staying in the heart of downtown San Antonio. Amenities include cable, airport service, pool.

La Mansión Del Rio, 112 College, 78205, ☎ 800-292-7300, 210-225-2581. $$$$. www.lamansion.com. Built in 1852 as a private boys' school and looking over the historic River Walk, La Mansión has 337 luxury guest rooms, many with balconies and enchanting views. Conference quarters also available.

Menger Hotel, 204 Alamo Plaza, 78205, ☎ 800-345-9285, 210-223-4361. $$$. A tourist attraction in itself, the Menger was frequented by O. Henry, General Robert E. Lee (who rode his horse, Traveller, into the lobby), General Ulysses S. Grant, President Dwight Eisenhower, and Mae West. The opulent decor adds to all the rooms' ambiance, some of which face the Alamo.

Plaza San Antonio Hotel, 555 South Alamo, 78205, ☎ 210-229-1000, 800-228-9290. $$$-$$$$. www.plazasa.com. Nestled on six acres of sun-bathed courtyards and lush gardens in downtown San Antonio, this is a perfect escape for both leisure and business travelers.

Riverwalk Plaza Hotel, 100 Villita Steet, 78205, ☎ 800-446-4656, 210-226-2271. $$$. Overlooking the River Walk, it has all the amenities a grand hotel might offer, including proximity to San Antonio's downtown attractions.

Seven Oaks Resort & Conference Center, 1400 Austin Hwy, 78209, ☎ 800-346-5866, 210-824-5371. $$. Features a nine-hole golf course, an Olympic-sized pool and just about everything else. All the gadgets for big conferences.

A Victorian Lady Inn, 421 Howard, 78212, ☎ 800-879-7116, 210-224-2524. $$-$$$. Innkeepers Joe and Kate Bowski provide bicycles on request, as well as a book exchange on the premises. Rates include full breakfast, and private parking.

Academy House of Monte Vista, 2317 N Main, 78212, ☎ 888-731-8393, 210-731-8393. $$-$$$. Built by Attorney John H. Clark in 1897 on a hill named Monte Vista, the Academy overlooks nearby downtown San Antonio. A quiet evening walk in this neighborhood is a walk back in time.

Bed & Breakfasts

Adams House Bed & Breakfast, 231 Adams, 78210, ☎ 800-666-4810, 210-224-4791. $$$.

Beckman Inn and Carriage House, 222 E Guenther, 78204, ☎ 800-945-1449, 210-229-1449, http://cimarron.net/usa/tx/beck.html. $$-$$$. Located in the King William Historic District, the Beckman is across the street from the River Walk and minutes to the Alamo by trolley. It was built in 1886 by Albert Beckman for his bride, Marie Dorothea.

Bonner Garden Bed & Breakfast, 145 E Agarita, 78212, ☎ 800-396-4222, 210-733-4222. $$-$$$.

Brackenridge House B&B Inn, 230 Madison, 78204, ☎ 800-221-1412, 210-271-3442. www.brackenridgehouse.com. $$-$$$.

Brookhaven Manor, 128 W Mistletoe, 78212, ☎ 800-851-3666, 210-733-3939. $$-$$$.

Chabot-Reed House, 403 Madison, 78204, ☎ 800-776-2424, 210-223-8697. www.ivylane.com/chabot. $$$.

Joske House, 241 King William, 78205, ☎ 210-271-0706. $$.

Linden House, 315 Howard, 78212, ☎ 210-224-8902. $-$$.

Noble Inns Jackson House, 107 Madison, 78204, ☎ 800-221-4045, 210-225-4045. $$-$$$.

Noble Inns Pancoast Carriage House, 102 Turner, 78204, ☎ 800-221-4045, 210-225-4045. $$-$$$.

O'Casey's Bed & Breakfast, 225 W Craig Place, 78212, ☎ 210-738-1378. $$.

Ogé Inn River Walk, 209 Washington, 78204, ☎ 800-242-2770, 210-223-2353. $$$-$$$$. www.ogeinn.com.

River Haus, 107 Woodward, 78204, ☎ 210-226-2524. $$.

Riverwalk Inn, 329 Old Gilbeau, 78204, ☎ 800-254-4440, 210-212-8300. $$-$$$.

Terrell Castle, 950 E Grayson, 78208, ☎ 210-271-9145. $$.

■ Where to Eat

 La Fogata, 2427 Vance Jackson, ☎ 210-340-1337. While most of Texas concentrates on Tex-Mex, La Fogata's forte is strictly Northern Mexico cuisine. Patrons are tucked away in lush patios and among enchanting authentic Mexican settings.

Tomatillos, 3210 Broadway, ☎ 210-824-3005. Named for the little green tomato, Tomatillos offers both Tex-Mex and dishes with more of a Mexican influence in a festive, bright atmosphere.

Barrios, 4223 Blanco, ☎ 210-732-6071. "Casero" means home-style in Spanish, and that's exactly what Barrios serves up, courtesy of Mom Viola Barrios and her family recipe secrets. It's the real thing and legions of locals knock on the door every day.

County Line, Riverwalk-West Crockett St, ☎ 210-229-1941 and also at Loop 1604, one mile west of 281 North, ☎ 210-496-0011, www.countylinebbq.com. Though County Line has stores scattered around the Southwest, it hasn't sold out and retains it barbecue charm. With one location on the Riverwalk and one nestled among the Texas live oaks, you can't miss on the barbecue. Also, the hot lemon hand cleaners at the end of the meal make everything perfect.

El Jarro de Arturo, 13421 San Pedro, ☎ 210-494-5084, www.iads.com/eljarro.htm. For over 20 years El Jarro's has tried to make eating both a delicious and healthy experience. And because of its efforts, it's been recognized by both *Bon Appetite Magazine* and *Who's Who in America's Best Restaurants*. Minutes from the River Walk.

Boudro's on the River Walk, 421 E Commerce, ☎ 210-224-8484, www.boudros.com. Coupling East Texas/Louisiana Cajun with Texan mainstays, the offerings here are impeccable.

Paesano's, 555 E Basse, ☎ 210-828-5191. It moved, but the food remains the same. Superlative gourmet dishes topped with delectable sauces.

The I-35 Corridor

Temple, Belton, Killeen, Salado

■ History

Temple and Belton began as competitors. When the railroads began to lay their tracks across America in the 1880s, Belton paid big bucks to be chosen as the regional stop. But Temple, eight miles north and saturated with saloons and brothels, won that battle.

Urban spread and growth has blurred the lines between these dueling cities and, though residents will claim allegiance to one town or the other, a visitor would be hard pressed to tell the difference.

Famous Temple Residents

Famous Temple-ites include Dr. A.C. Scott, who was responsible for the care of all Santa Fe railroad employees. With partner Dr. R.R. White, he established Scott & White Medical Center, one of the largest and most respected in the state.

"Ma" (Miriam) and "Pa" (James) Ferguson also hailed from Temple. Both served as governor of Texas, Ma becoming the first female governor in 1924. After being elected to a second term in office, James was impeached in 1917. A feud with the Board of Regents of the University of Texas led to his dismissal. Ma Ferguson ran in his place in 1924. She lost her first reelection bid in 1928, but won a second in 1932 on the campaign promise of "two governors for the price of one," a not-so-subtle allusion to the fact that James was really running the show.

■ Touring

The Ferguson House (518 N 7th, not open to the public) was home for Ma and Pa Ferguson until they left for Austin and the Capitol.

The **Czech Heritage Museum** (520 N Main, ☎ 254-773-1575) traces not only the Czechs' contributions to the area, but to the state and nation. Preserved artifacts include a Bible from 1530 and quilts more than a century old.

Paying homage to the railroads that breathed life into the area, the **Railroad and Pioneer Museum** (710 Jack Baskin, ☎ 254-298-5172) features a restored depot and traces the significant role the steam trains played.

Downtown Belton boasts a unique history. The **McWhirter-Kimball House** (400 N Pearl) was the site of a revolution of sorts. Between 1870 and 1910, Belton's richest and best-educated women, under the leadership of Martha McWhirter, left their husbands and lived commune-style in this house under the auspices of the Sanctificationist religion.

The **Old Stone Jail** (210 N Pearl) became a hotel owned by the Sanctifictionists, who retired wealthy. In 1874 the jail, before being bought by the shrewd real estate mongers, was the site of mass murder – a mob stormed the structure and shot nine horse thieves.

Fifteen miles northwest of Temple lies **The Grove Country Life Museum** (TX 36, ☎ 254-986-3437 weekends, 512-282-1215 weekdays), a ghost town brought back to life by Moody Anderson, a definitive Texan. Anderson, among other things, collects Western antiques, many of which are used as props in Hollywood portrayals of the Old West. The Grove, open weekends only, includes a general store, post office, blacksmith shop and bank that recall the good old days with demonstrations and museum collections. Founded in the mid-1800s by Wendish colonists, Grove's growth followed the area's booming agriculture. Its demise was brought about by improved transportation through its larger neighbors like Temple.

Killeen, just west of Temple and Belton, started out as a railroad switching station. **Fort Hood** (US 190 west, ☎ 254-287-1110), which now provides most of the substance for the town, is home to more military personnel than any other place in the free world, being the only two-division post the US Army has ever created. Military aficionados would kick themselves if they skipped the **1**st Cavalry Division Museum and the **2**nd Armored Division Museum.

Just a short trip south of Temple is **Salado**, a small town that has retained its Scottish pride and charm. **The Stagecoach Inn** (1 Main, Salado, ☎ 254-947-5111) was originally the Shady Villa Hotel. From its balcony Sam Houston made an anti-secession speech. Other famous guests have included General George Custer, Charles Goodnight and Shanghai Pierce.

Antique collectors regularly check out Salado's Main Street, which is lined with antique shops. Another great place to gp out is the **Robertson's Home and Plantation** (I-35 south access road, ☎ 254-947-5613), with 22 rooms, old slave quarters, a family cemetery and stables. Built in the mid-1850s and often called "Sterling's Castle," the home is a premiere example of an antebellum plantation. Liz Carpenter, former staff director and press secretary to Ladybird Johnson while she was First Lady (and a very popular local figure), was born in the house. Her mother was a Robertson.

Information Sources

The **Temple Convention and Visitor Center** is located at 2 North Main, Temple, 76504, ☎ 800-479-0338. The **Temple Chamber of Commerce** can be reached at ☎ 254-773-2105 or you can visit www.temple-tx.org. The **Salado** chamber can be reached at ☎ 254-947-5040; **Belton's** is at ☎ 254-939-3551 (www.cityofbelton.org). The **Killeen Visitor and Convention Bureau** is at ☎ 254-526-9551 (www.gkcc.com).

■ Adventures on Foot

Mother Neff State Park (1680 TX 236, Moody, ☎ 254-853-2389, for reservations 512-389-8900), the first official state park in Texas, derives its name from Mrs. Isabella Eleanor (Mother) Neff, who donated six acres of land along the Leon River back in 1916. The riverbed is lined with huge pecan, cottonwood, sycamore and several species of oak trees. Many of the trees are over 250 years old.

Today the park contains 259 acres in Coryell County. Heavily wooded, the park is ideal for camping, hiking, picnicking and fishing. On weekends, the park hosts various special events – it is a favorite for reunions and family gatherings. The central hub of the park lies close to the Leon River and utilizes a charming building built in the 1930s by the CCC. The river bottom is richly canopied and remains cool in the summer's heat.

While swimming is not recommended in the Leon (its banks are very steep and slippery), fishing can produce healthy white bass and catfish. Bring your own fishing gear and bait – there's none available in the park.

Over two miles of trails begin at the river bottom and wind their way toward nearby prairie. The trails, lined with a mixture of hardwoods and cedar, are covered in areas by dense forest and by a limestone escarpment that hangs over the path.

Springtime is one of the best times to see a burbling spring and a neighbor pond. Just north of the springs is **Indian Cave**, where the escarpment is hollowed out and has been a haven for human activity for centuries. At least three Indian graves have been excavated at the park, whose grounds were home to several Indian tribes.

> ## ✳ Author's Tip
>
> Call ahead for reservationsith. With only 21 camp sites, it sells out fast.

The Chalk Ridge Falls Hiking Trail, made up of around five miles of paths just below the **Stillhouse Hollow Lake Dam**, is usually a serene spot for area hikers. It's also a favorite for local teachers to bring students on nature and ecology field trips. To get there, continue past the headquarters on FM 1670 and follow the signs.

■ Adventures on the Water

LAKE BELTON (3110 FM 2271, ☎ 254-939-1829), just west of Temple/Belton, meanders snake-like through the area. The upper portions are narrow and splintered. A broader, massive portion anchors the southern end of the lake. Fifteen different parks are scattered along its edges. Call the park for specific information on each access point.

Winkler Park, on the upper end, includes a two-lane ramp suitable to launch both medium and small boats. The upper region also affords access to the Leon River. To get there, follow Hwy 36 out of Temple. After you cross the Lake Belton bridge, the Winkler Park sign will be on your right.

Cedar Ridge Park, an access point toward the middle of the lake, includes a ramp suitable for all boats and is considered one of the best places by fishermen. Relatively calm waters surround the protected cove, making ramp launches smoother. The cove is also close to many creeks and inlets where bass, crappie and other fish are found in abundance. Cedar Ridge is also off of Hwy 36, but before the bridge. Look for signs on the left side of the highway.

Camping facilities, in general, are all at the southern end of Lake Belton. **Temple Lake Park** (west on FM 2305 to FM 317. Take a left and follow the signs) is just one of the southern access points that provides camping facilities. Park headquarters are also on the southern foot of the lake. To get there, take FM 439 west off of Hwy 317.

STILLHOUSE HOLLOW LAKE (US 190 west, Simmons Rd south, ☎ 254-939-2461), located 16 miles upstream of the confluence of the Lampasas and Leon Rivers, is a relative newcomer to the Central Texas water scene and is little visited. It boasts water that looks as if it came from your faucet and a rich mix of fishing and water sports. Its creators left several areas with stumps and undergrowth that allow different fish species to thrive. Other parts have been cleared for water skiers and boaters. And the most exciting part about Stillhouse Hollow – at least so far – is that very few people know about this lake. It is tucked into the limestone cliffs just four miles west of Interstate 35, the biggest north/south highway in Texas.

Check in at headquarters for current information. Of the several parks that line the lake's shores, **Union Grove Park** and **Dana Peak Park** seem to boast the most complete set of offerings, with all types of camping facilities, good water access and fishing piers. Union Grove includes a model airplance field, while Dana Peak is the site of a large hiking/equestrian trail (see below).

Outfitter

Mad Katter's Fishing Guide Service (☎ 254-721-8999), led by longtime area fisherman Mike Beck, specializes in crappie and catfish on Lake Belton. The service provides a pontoon boat, bait and all tackle. They are also available for lake cruises.

■ Adventures on Wheels

 Dana Peak Park, on the northern shore of Stillhouse Hollow Lake, has become a mecca for nearby mountain bicyclists, with miles of trails. Horseback riding has also come onto the scene of late, with a corral and water tanks provided by the park.

The park is in the process of building stables and establishing a system for hiring horses. To get there, take Hwy 190 west to Simmons Road (south). Take an immediate right on FM 2410 and another right on Comanche Gap.

■ Adventure in the Air

 Skydive Temple (☎ 254-947-3483) doesn't claim to be the biggest or the fanciest in Central Texas. Rather, it's a "small family drop zone" on a private airstrip. Jumps take place all day Saturday and Sunday and on holidays.

■ Where to Stay

 Brambley Hedge, A Fine Country Inn, ☎ 254-947-1914, www.touringtexas.com/brambley. $$-$$$. Located on 50 wooded acres just minutes from downtown Salado. The smell of warm chocolate chip cookies will greet you.

Stagecoach Inn, IH-35 North, Salado exit, ☎ 254-947-5111. www.touringtexas.com/stage. $$. Surprisingly affordable for staying in an area landmark. In addition to its renowned restaurant, the inn boasts tennis courts, walking trails and badminton areas.

Inn on the Creek, 600 Center Circle off Royal, Salado, ☎ 254-947-5554. www.inncreek.com. $$$. Furnished with antiques and including six different buildings (one from the 1850s), the inn is nestled up along the Salado Creek on 12 acres of prime real estate.

Rose Mansion, 1 Rose Way, Salado, 76571, ☎ 800-948-1004, 254-947-8200. www.touringtexas.com/rose. $$-$$$. Couples getting married flock to this beauty of a site that includes four cottages, many equipped with fireplaces.

The Inn at Salado, N Main at Pace Park, Salado, ☎ 254-947-0027. www.lnstar.com/innatsalado. $$. Best known for its homemade breakfasts (compliments of the on-site German chef), the Inn is convenient to all of Salado's downtown shopping district. Bicycles available to guests.

■ Where to Eat

 Bluebonnet Café, 705 S 25th, Temple, ☎ 254-773-6654. Cooking up southern fare for over four decades. Try the chicken-fried steak.

Old Stagecoach Inn, IH-35 north, Salado exit, ☎ 254-947-5111. A Central Texas landmark, serving good ol' steaks, prime rib and catfish. People drive in from across the state to enjoy its cuisine.

Salado Mansion, 128 S Main, north of Salado Creek, ☎ 254-947-5157. Mexican food can be enjoyed on the restaurant's patio, complete with a cabana.

Georgetown

■ History

The land that Georgetown occupies has a well-traversed history, first belonging to roving bands of Tonkawa Indians and then becoming a meeting place for Sam Houston and other area politicos. Established in 1848 as an agricultural trade center, the town was conveniently placed on the edge of the Chisholm Trail and enjoyed a booming cattle trade. But bust follows boom, and when barbed wire lessened the need for cattle drives, fewer people setted in the area. With a population just over 22,000 today, Georgetown has a small town feel but enjoys the culture of a major university and a major city (Austin) just 30 miles away.

■ Touring

 Chartered in 1840 and Texas' oldest university, **Southwestern University** (1001 E University Ave, ☎ 512-863-6511) has been ranked one of the nation's finest small liberal arts colleges.

A tad older than the city are **Inner Space Caverns** (4200 S IH-35, ☎ 512-863-5545). Formed over the last 100 million years, the caverns display the remains of a prehistoric mastodon, wolves, Ice Age animals and a breathtaking array of stalactites that hang from the caverns' domed ceiling.

Built during Georgetown's heyday in the late 1800s, the **Williamson County Courthouse Historic District** (Courthouse Square and surrounding) is a stunning example of a Victorian-era business community. The **Shaffer Saddlery Building** (711 Main) is the oldest building in the district, having been put up in 1870. Also of note is the **Williamson County Jail**, three blocks north of the square (312 Main), that still houses inmates, though it was built in 1888.

The **Mar-Jon Candle Factory** (4411 S IH-35, ☎ 512-863-6025, www.thecandlefactory.com) is a perennial favorite. Boasting hundreds of types of candles in every form imaginable, this warehouse for the candle enthusiast is designed around the formulas, colors and smells developed by a Southwestern chemistry professor, Dr. Sherman Lesesne.

Perhaps one of the most memorable things you can do while in the Georgetown area is visit **Walburg** (Exit 268, four miles east on CR 972, ☎ 512-863-8440), a small village just northeast of town. Its centerpiece is the Walburg Restaurant and Biergarten. With energetic polka bands playing at the outdoor biergarten, locals delve into their German roots and dance beneath the stars. The ambiance here – with the cicadas and accordions singing in unison – is nothing short of incredible.

Information Sources

Contact the **Georgetown Visitor and Convention Bureau** (PO Box 409, 78627, ☎ 800-436-8696, 512-930-3545, www.georgetown.org/tourism) or the **Chamber of Commerce** if you need more information (☎ 512-930-3535, www.gtwn-chamber.org).

■ Adventures on the Water

 LAKE GEORGETOWN (FM 2338, four miles west of Georgetown, ☎ 512-930-5253) offers over 1,300 acres of well-stocked fishing waters with designated fishing areas. Much quieter than its Colorado River counterparts (Lake Travis, Inks Lake and Lake LBJ are very close), here there is more solitude for camping, hiking, water-skiing and fishing.

Swimmers flock to **Russell Park** which has a washed pebble beach and 10 shelters for day-use. While the lake contains black bass, white bass, hybrid stripers, white crappie, channel catfish, flathead catfish, and blue catfish, among others, it is known for its smallmouth bass fishing.

A fishing dock is provided in the picnic area and campground at **Cedar Breaks Park** and near the boat ramp at **Jim Hogg Park**.

■ Adventures on Foot

 The **Good Water Hiking Trail**, 16½ miles long, comes close to encircling Lake Georgetown. However the trail does not make a complete loop so transportation arrangements should be made. Also, there's no potable water on the trail – bring your own.

Teeming with flowers, wildlife, vegetation and small springs, the trail is very rugged in places. Pick up a trail guide on your way into the park to direct you to one of the starting points and one of the four primitive campgrounds that lie along the route.

Call the Lake Georgetown headquarters (☎ 512-930-LAKE) for more information.

Adjacent to the lake are 1,200 acres of prime hunting ground managed by the US Army Corps of Engineers at Lake Georgetown. **Hunt Hollow Wildlife Management Area** is known for its high concentrations of white-tailed deer – the area's policy has designated bow hunting as the only legal means of hunting deer here. The deer hunting permits are available thorugh a lottery drawing. You can call ☎ 512-930-5253 for information.

■ Where to Stay

Claibourne House, 914 Forest St, 78626, ☎ 512-930-3934. $$. Charming historic home in Old Town with four rooms.

Page House B&B Inn, 1000 Leander Rd, 78628, ☎ 512-863-8979. $$. The Victorian ranch house is replete with special guest facilities, including a Polo Barn that is available for parties.

Patti Cakes Old Town Bakery, 812 Church St, 78626, ☎ 800-517-2253, 512-869-2253. With a bakery and bed and breakfast together, dining choices can't get any more convenient than this.

■ Where to Eat

Monument Café, 1953 South Austin Dr, ☎ 512-930-9586. While chicken-fried steak is their heart, home-style daily specials and vegetables bring in the crowds.

Walburg Restaurant & Biergarten, Exit 268, four miles east on CR 972, ☎ 512-863-8440. Who cares about the food (though their food is delicious); the ambiance will place you in another time. Authentic German fare.

Wimberley

 Everything that is Central Texas is in Wimberley, a picturesque village that may not be big enough to warrant a dot on the
map but that has become the main artistic outlet for the Central
Texas community. With a population around 3,000, it is between the
Blanco River and Cypress Creek, beneath towering cypress trees.

■ Touring

The **Blue Hole** (on Cypress Creek, a quarter-mile east of the square, off
CR 173, ☎ 512-847-9127) is the locals' favorite spring-fed swimming
spot. They also have camping facilities.

> ### ✷ Author's Tip
>
> They've recently changed the rules – you can only enjoy
> Blue Hole if you plan on camping or if you have a season
> pass.

The town square, a little hitch on RM 12, is a collection of galleries and
crafts shops. From quilts to glasswork to homemade jams, the folks in
Wimberley make pleasing visitors their full-time job. **Market Days**
(the first Saturday of every month, April through December) allow artists to visit with the public, providing workshops and demonstrations.
Go early so you don't miss anything – the morning hours are often the
most active.

Pioneertown is at the **7-A Ranch and Resort** (333 Wayside, one mile
south. Pioneertown, ☎ 512-847-9906; 7A Ranch, 512-847-2517). This is a
recreation of a complete Old West town. Its gallery boasts an impressive
collection of Remington bronzes and Western paintings. There's also
horseback riding, a chuckwagon supper, gunfights and wagon rides.

Information Sources

Because of Wimberley's attachment to the artistic and its infectious small-town glow, bed and breakfasts have popped up in amazing numbers. Call the **Chamber of Commerce** (☎ 512-847-2201) for help in finding the right place to stay, or **Wimberley Lodging** (☎ 800-460-3909, www.texhillcntry.com/wimberley), which provides reservations for a number of bed and breakfasts. Two others are **Country Innkeepers** (☎ 800-230-0805, 512-847-1119) and **Hill Country Accommodations** (☎ 800-926-5028, 512-847-5388, www.texasvacation.com).

■ Where to Stay

Bandits Hideaway, 2324 Flite Acres Rd, 78676, ☎ 512-847-9088. $$. Cottage and loft on the river just three miles from the town square.

Barrister's Guest Quarters, ☎ 512-847-6211. $$. Sleeps two.

Blair House, 100 Spoke Hill Rd, 78676, ☎ 512-847-1111 or 847-8828, www.blairhouseinn.com. $$$. Set on 85 acres with seven rooms, a full gourmet breakfast, private baths and jacuzzi. One mile from town square.

Bluebonnet Inn, 8 DeLuna, 78676, ☎ 512-847-2324. $$. Cozy cottage for two with a full kitchen, porch and use of a pool.

Dancing Water Inn, 1405 Mount Sharp Rd, 78676, four miles from square on Jacob's Well, ☎ 512-847-9391. $$-$$$$. Hot tub, fireplace and feather beds. There's also an art and furniture gallery.

Guest House at Gulley Creek, 300 Rogers Rd, 78676, ☎ 512-847-2953. $$-$$$. Two stories with loft, screened porch and open upper deck.

Hilcris Cabins, 300 Mill Race Lane, 78676, ☎ 512-847-2231. $$-$$$. Cabins on Cypress Creek with facilities for swimming and tubing.

The Homestead, RR12 at Scudder Lane (CR 316), ☎ 800-918-8788 or 512-847-8788, www.homestead-tx.com. $$-$$$. Eight cottages on the creek that come fully equipped.

The Inn above Onion Creek, 4444 Hwy 150 W., Kyle, 78640, ☎ 512-268-1617. $$$$. Six luxury rooms on 500 acres.

La Casita, 2337 Sandy Point Rd, 78676, ☎ 512-847-5417 or 847-2016. $$$. Two artistic country cottages that can sleep up to five.

Short Mama's House, 101 College St, Dripping Springs, ☎ 512-894-0023. $$-$$$. A Texas farm house with four bedrooms for rent.

Spencer Guest Cottages, 100 Blanco Bend West, 78676, ☎ 512-847-2134. $$$. Family accommodations on the Blanco River where you can swim, fish, tube and play tennis. Minimum two-night stay.

Bed & Breakfasts

Dabney House B&B, 701 Autumn Lane, Dripping Springs, ☎ 512-894-0161. $$. Private guest house set on 21 acres. Panoramic view of the Hill Country.

Heart House B&B, ☎ 512-847-1414. Log cabin that sleeps five.

Lonesome Dove B&B, ☎ 800-690-3683, 512-392-2921. An old west B&B village serving up gourmet breakfasts and offering big open porches.

New Tracks Ranch B&B, Kyle, ☎ 800-460-3909, 512-268-3211. Native Southwestern cottage on a working ranch. Offers swimming and tubing on the Blanco River.

Old Oaks Ranch B&B, ☎ 512-847-9374. Quaint cottages in the country.

Rancho Cama B&B, 2595 Flite Acres Rd, 78676, three miles from square, ☎ 800-594-4501, 512-847-2596. $$. Honeymoon cottage and bunkhouse with swings, pool, hot tub and miniature horses.

Rancho El Valle Chiquito B&B Resort, ☎ 512-847-3665. There's skeet shooting, a golf green, hiking, biking, horseshoe pits and horseback riding.

River Bluff B&B, ☎ 512-847-1230. Cedar cabin on the river.

Southwind B&B, 2701 FM 3237, 78676, ☎ 800-508-5277, 512-847-5277. $$-$$$. Only three miles to the square.

The Lodge at Creekside B&B, 11 Mill Race Lane, 78676, ☎ 800-267-3925, 512-847-8922, www.geocel.com/creekside. Three log homes on Cypress Creek.

Wide Horizon B&B, ☎ 512-847-3782. Deluxe accommodations with a long, sweeping view of the Hill Country.

■ Where to Eat

 Café on the Square and Brew Pub, ☎ 512-353-9289. They're open all day, every day, and serve everything from hamburgers to fish.

Casa Blanca Café, River Rd, ☎ 512-847-1320. Homemade Mexican food. Live music on summer weekends.

John Henry's Restaurant, ☎ 512-847-5467. Right on the square next to Cypress Creek.

San Marcos

■ History

One of the oldest continuously inhabited areas in North America, San Marcos thrives on the spring water of the Edwards Aquifer that makes it way through limestone cracks associated with the Balcones Fault. The pure water that erupts through here not only feeds the San Marcos River, it feeds the local economy. Locals and tourists flock to the brilliantly clear waters that are also instrumental in the watershed make-up of Central Texas.

When Spanish explorers discovered this verdant river in the 1700s, they named it for the day – St Mark's Day. The name stayed, but the explorers did not. The missions the Spanish attempted to build failed and the area remained unmolested until settlement in the 1840s.

San Marcos' other claim to fame, besides its bubbling springs, is President Lyndon Johnson, who earned his college degree in education at what is today Southwest Texas State University.

■ Touring

Though most of this gentle town's heart is centered around its waters, the earthquake-formed caves of **Wonder World** (1000 Prospect, at Bishop, ☎ 512-392-3760) are tangible and incredible manifestations of the Balcones Fault that lies beneath a large portion of Central Texas. In addition to the caves, there is a wildlife park, an anti-gravity house and a tower that offers a birds-eye view of the Hill Country.

If you happen to be around the area the third weekend in September, make it a point to visit the **Republic of Texas Chilympiad** (Hays County Civic Center, ☎ 512-396-5400). In the true spirit and taste of Texas, hundreds of teams concoct their unique versions of chili that include anything from armadillo to rattlesnake. A daily evening dance and an arts and crafts fair leave even true Texans feeling a little more Texanized.

Two outlet malls, **San Marcos Factory Shops** and **Tanger Outlet Center**, both located south on IH-35, provide super discounted merchandise for those who consider getting a good deal an adventure. Austinites, without their own outlet, regularly make the 30-minute run to this shopping hot spot.

Information Sources

Call the **Chamber Of Commerce/Convention and Visitors Bureau** (PO Box 2310, San Marcos, 78667-2310, ☎ 888-200-5620).

■ Adventures on the Water

 For those familiar with what used to be Aquarena Springs, you'll be glad to know the **Aquarena Center for Continuing Education** (Exit 206 on IH-35, ☎ 800-999-9767, 512-245-7575) is now fully operational. The center unites the idea of theme park with its indigenous fresh springs, coupling educational shows and rides with aerial tramways and a 220-foot Sky Spiral tower. Glass-bottomed boats hover over the aquatic wonderland. Operated by Southwest Texas University, the park is open seven days a week and is free to the public.

✳ Author's Tip

There have been changes since the park changed hands – Ralph the Swimming Pig, who provided decades of entertainment to visitors while the springs were a private enterprise, has been retired. You'll have to rely on pictures and your memory of Ralph if he was your favorite little guy.

The **San Marcos River**, one of the spring-fed jewels that goes through the heart of San Marcos, remains a constant 72° and boasts crystal-clear waters that are only clouded by occasional rapids. The lush assortment of elephant ears and hyacinths that line the river's banks seem almost tropical. Formed on the northern edges of San Marcos by several large springs, the river flows close to 75 miles southeast before uniting with the Guadalupe River.

The 16 miles of river directly downstream from City Park can be broken into three sections. The first, between City Park and Pecan Park Retreat, is relatively flat and subtle, great for tubers and beginning canoers and kayakers. The second section, between Pecan Park and Martindale Dam, is considered the most advanced section, with three series of rapids for canoes and kayaks. The last portion, between Martindale Dam and Staples Dam, is challenging but not overwhelming for the intermediate.

Both of the local canoe/kayak outfitters divide the river up similarly, with each section taking around four hours to navigate. Tubers, who put in at City Park usually take out at the Rio Vista Dam. Because tubers go about one-fourth the speed of a canoe, they can't make the entire river trip. For tubing, your best bet is the **Lions Club** in City Park (City Park Rec Building, ☎ 512-392-8255), which offers tube rentals and water taxis from May through Labor Day.

If you're going to attempt the mid-section, consult with one of the local outfitters first for guidance and instruction. While there are no Class V rapids, it can leave you wet and beat up if you don't approach of the hazards with some idea of what to expect.

This portion of the river has also become a haven for a few more extreme events. The second Saturday in June has become the starting point for the **Texas Water Safari** (PO Box 686, San Marcos, 78667-0686), a canoe race that begins in San Marcos and ends 260 miles later in the Gulf of Mexico. Hard-core paddlers have participated annually in the non-stop adventure since 1963. Contestants are expected to finish the trek – if they do finish – by the following Wednesday. As conditions vary, so do the finishes. One year saw only two teams of 60 make it to the finish line.

Also, Mike Spencer, owner of Spencer Canoes and Shady Grove Campgrounds, annually hosts the **Martindale Triathlon** (☎ 512-357-6113), a combination of canoeing (six miles), running (seven miles) and biking (16½ miles). The triathlon, held the last Saturday in October, can be split into teams (mens, womens and mixed) or be done solo.

Campers can soak up the tropical quietness of the San Marcos at both the **Pecan Park Retreat** (PO Box 219, Martindale, 78655, ☎ 512-392-6171), which caters to the RV crowd, or at **Shady Grove Campgrounds** (9515 FM 1979, Martindale, 78655, ☎ 512-357-6113), Spencer Canoe's sidekick. Both campgrounds cater to family crowds and insist on quietness. Pecan Park doesn't allow alcohol on the grounds. There's also one cabin available (with air conditioning) at Shady Grove.

San Marcos River Boat Rentals

T.G. Canoe Livery. Hwy 80, 2 miles SE of IH 35, PO Box 177, Martindale, 78655. ☎ 512-353-3946. Sales and rentals of canoes, kayaks and sit-on-tops. They also offer river and map information, along with shuttle service.

Spencer Canoes. On the San Marcos River, 9515 FM 1979, Martindale, 78655, ☎ 512-357-6113. Offers sales and rentals of canoes and kayaks, along with instruction, riverside camping (one cabin) and shuttle service.

Because the waters of the San Marcos River are incredibly clear (50-60 feet visibility at times), it attracts a number of **scuba divers and snorkelers**. At 15 feet deep, though, it's more for looking around than it is for serious underwater activity. Also, because the river is spring-fed, it's chilly. Bring your wetsuit if you're going to be swimming.

✸ Author's Tip

A good rain can unearth a variety of Indian artifacts around and in the river. The clear water makes it much easier to spot arrowheads and other finds.

One of Central Texans' favorite scuba diving spots, Aquarena Springs, is no longer open to the public. Since Southwest Texas State University (SWT) took over the park in the mid 1990s, it has been closed to recreational diving. However, the **Aqua Center** (its new name) *is* open to certified scientific divers. SWT periodically offers the scientific certification class that includes a large classroom section on the region's specifics and a skills section where divers must prove themselves agile enough not to harm the environment. You can then volunteer to dive and perform various chores for the university, while soaking in one of the most unusual diving spots in Texas. For information on the course and on volunteering call ☎ 512-245-7561.

For more information about area diving, contact **The Dive Shop** (1911 RR 12, ☎ 512-396-3483).

■ Adventures in the Air

 While the notion of jumping out of planes isn't particularly soothing to many people, **Skydive San Marcos** (PO Box 306, Fentress, 78622, ☎ 512-488-2214, www.skydivesanmarcos.com)

caters to the adventurous soul. Tandem skydiving – where you are physically attached to an instructor – can put you up in the air after only 30 minutes of training. A tandem jump, over beautiful Texas countryside, includes a 30-second freefall and a five-minute parachute ride. There are only two restrictions: Divers must be 18 years old and they must weigh less than 220 pounds. Experienced skydivers can also enjoy solo jumps from nearly 10,000 feet. The facilities are at **Fentress Airpark**, a 115-acre airport about 13 miles east of San Marcos off of Hwy 80.

■ Adventures on Wheels

One of the most spectacular ways to delve into Central Texas is to take a drive northwest of San Marcos on a stretch of road nicknamed the **Devil's Backbone** (RM 12 northwest to junction with RM 32). It's not a theme park; it won't entertain you. But it will amaze you. The windy stretch of road sharply meanders across a raised ridge that towers above the Texas Hill Country and gives you a look at the area's unspoiled grandeur. Springtime, with its greenness and wildflowers, is the best time for viewing. Bicycle riders love this area as well, but be prepared for lots of hills and a narrow road. It is not an easy bike ride.

■ Where to Stay

Aquarena Inn, 601 University Drive, 78666, ☎ 800-893-9466, 512-245-7500. $$. Right across the street from the Aquarena Center, the inn offers a continental breakfast.

Stratford Inn, 1601 IH-35 North, 78666, ☎ 512-396-3700. $-$$. Recently remodeled and right down from Southwest Texas University.

Crystal River Inn, 326 W Hopkins, 78666, ☎ 800-396-3739, 512-396-3739. $$. Small town goodness.

■ Where to Eat

Gordo's Grill, 120 E San Antonio St, ☎ 512-392-1874. Standard American and Southern fare with live music Thursday through Saturday.

Kismet Café & Espresso Bar, 220 North Edward Gary, ☎ 512-754-6760. Mediterranean, Italian, Tex-Mex and American dishes.

Palmer's Restaurant Bar and Courtyard, 16 West Moore, ☎ 512-353-3500, www.itouch.net/~palmers/map.html. In a historic 1920s building in west San Marcos, this is a showcase for dozens of plant species that include many rare Texas natives. Fare runs the gamut, from shrimp to fondue to quesadilla.

Gruene

On the northwestern edge of New Braunfels lies Gruene – pronounced like the color. A restored turn-of-the-century Texas town, Gruene might easily be overlooked on the Texas map. But its lack of size is made up for by its overwhelming and festive spirit.

■ History

Settled in the 1840s by German farmers on the banks of the fertile Guadalupe River, Gruene was hit hard by the Depression and it remained almost a ghost town until the 1970s. Today the town has it all: rafting, shopping, dancing and good food.

■ Touring

 Stroll the shops that line Gruene's square. Though all offer something unique, there are a few you don't want to miss. At **Buck Pottery** (1296 Gruene Rd, ☎ 830-629-7975), in a turn-of-the-century barn, you can watch craftsmen making wood-fired stoneware pottery. **Gruene General Store** (1610 Hunter Rd, ☎ 830-629-6021), selected as one of the 40 best places to visit in Texas, features a soda fountain, homemade fudge and a mixed bag of unique Texas foods and gifts.

Information Sources

The **Historic District** of Gruene (☎ 830-629-5077, www.gruene.net) has collected all the information you could possible need for a stay in the wonderful area.

■ Adventures on the Water

 There is no shortage of activity on the water in Central Texas – that much should be clear by now. Gruene and New Braunfels are no different. You'll have to pick a river to navigate before you even start here. Your choices include the Comal River and the Guadalupe River.

The **Comal**, which literally pours from one of the largest underground springs in the state, has earned the distinction of being the shortest river in the nation. It does a big turn, looking much like a horseshoe, before joining the Guadalupe in downtown New Braunfels.

The **Guadalupe River** stretches from the southern end of Canyon Lake through downtown and on to the coast. Outfitters provide guidance and rentals for the 22 miles between Canyon Lake and town.

The biggest hazard on this stretch of river is **Horseshoe Falls**, just over a mile from Canyon Lake. It has taken several lives and you'll want to put in below it. Most outfitters won't take you there anyway. The lower stretch is considered the most popular river running in the state, with exhilarating rapids for canoes, kayaks and rafts.

On the upper portion of the river, where Hwy 306 first crosses the Guadalupe, is a one-mile stretch called "Tube Loop." It is perhaps the most tubed mile of river in the country. You put in where Hwy 306 first crosses the river and take out on the second crossing. You can then walk the short distance back up the highway (there's a path for you) to start over again, if you so desire.

On the whole (other than Tube Loop), the Guadalupe is a much more serious affair – it requires both life jackets and alertness (and soberness). The Comal is a better choice for leisure and drinking.

Area Outfitters

Gruene River Raft Co. 1404 Gruene Rd, ☎ 830-625-2800, www.gruene.net/RiverRaftCo.

Rockin' R River Rides – Guadalupe. 1405 Gruene Rd, ☎ 800-55-FLOAT, 830-629-9999, www.rockinr.com.

Rockin' R River Rides – Comal. 193 S. Liberty, ☎ 800-55-FLOAT, 830-620-6262, www.rockinr.com.

Whitewater Sports. FM 306 on the Guadalupe, ☎ 830-964-3800. Canoes, rafts, kayaks, tubes, shuttles, RV hookups, showers and rainbow trout fishing.

Guadalupe Canoe Livery. Two locations on the Guadalupe. ☎ 830-885-4671, 830-964-3189. Complete outfitting for canoes, rafts and tubes.

Rio Raft Co. PO Box 2036, Canyon Lake, 78130, River Road. ☎ 830-964-3613. Rafts, canoes, tubes, shuttles, camping, showers, rainbow trout fishing, RV hookups and cottages for rent.

Bezdek's Rentals. 7308 River Road, between the second and third crossing. ☎ 830-964-2244 or 830-907-2141. Tubes, canoes, rafts, shuttle service, riverside camping and homemade barbecue.

Cedar Bluff Campground & River Rentals. ☎ 830-964-3639. Customized river trips, shuttle, riverfront campground.

Rainbow Camp & River Trips. 8690 River Road. ☎ 800-874-3745 or 830-964-2227. All rentals and riverfront campgrounds.

✳ Author's Tip

To be fully prepared for rafting make sure to bring sunscreen and shoes that you can get wet. Also, when the river is low, make sure you rent a tube with a bottom. Many people also choose to rent an additional tube for a cooler that you can drag behind (for the Comal). If you do this, be sure to tie it securely as there are a few minor waterfalls along the way, although a runaway beer cooler is always popular with the other tubers.

■ Where to Stay

 Gruene Mansion Inn, 1275 Gruene Rd, 78130, ☎ 830-629-2641. www.gruene.net/gruenemansion. $$-$$$. Offers a Victorian flair. Situated on a bluff overlooking the Guadalupe River.

Gruene Country Homestead Inn, 832 Gruene Rd, 78130, ☎ 830-606-0216. $$$. With 10 rooms, five suites and 15 private baths (along with a full continental breakfast), you'll be well taken care of.

■ Where to Eat

There are two different paths to take for dinner. For a more sophisticated (and air conditioned) adventure visit **Gruene Mansion** (1275 Gruene Rd, ☎ 830-620-0760). Overlooking the Guadalupe River, it offers an extensive wine list, pasta, steaks and seafood and is celebrated throughout Central Texas. **The Gristmill Res-**

taurant and Bar (1287 Gruene Rd, ☎ 830-625-0684) is also renowned as an area hotspot. Located in the ruins of a 100-year old cotton gin along the banks of the Guadalupe, the Gristmill is perfect for families. Its laid back atmosphere can be partly attributed to its large lawn and ample outdoor seating that accommodates visitors waiting for their tables. Also, its proximity to Gruene Hall, a live music dancehall, makes it a great way to hear quality music for free.

Gruene Hall (1281 Gruene Rd, ☎ 830-606-1281) is the perfect way to end the evening. Music enthusiasts come from all over the state to visit this place, Texas' oldest dance hall. Lyle Lovett, George Strait and Hal Ketchum all got their starts at this infamous honky-tonk and still frequent it today. Its dance floor is made for dancing and its beer is always cold.

New Braunfels

■ History

After Texas earned its independence from Mexico, it was portrayed as the utopia of the New World to Germans, who were eager to find prosperity while their own country faltered through a depression. Several princes and nobles formed a "Mainzer Adelsverein," or League of Nobles, to sponsor Germans who wanted to emigrate to Texas.

Prince Carl von Solms-Braunfels and 200 others striking out for a better life, arrived in present-day New Braunfels on Good Friday, 1845. Its name is the same as the village in Germany where Prince Carl's castle stood. Before the prince could build a new castle in Texas – as he had planned – he learned that his fiancée, Sophie, Princess of Salm-Salm, had decided not to venture to the New World. Prince Carl returned to Germany to wed Sophie, leaving the town that bore his name, and never returned.

Although New Braunfels enjoyed modest success, it's estimated that thousands of Germans perished while trying to reach the fabled land. By 1850 it was the fourth largest city in Texas, surpassed only by Galveston, Houston and San Antonio.

■ Touring

While New Braunfels' heyday might have been during the 1800s (its population still hovers somewhere below 30,000), many argue that its fun-per-capita ratio surpasses that of the busy cities. It enjoys what makes Central Texas unique – vast quantities of water and the recreation that accompanies it. The town also fancies itself a tourist mecca, with a convenient location smack dab between Austin and San Antonio, its bigger tourist counterparts.

The Hummel Museum (199 Main Plaza, ☎ 830-625-5636) is host to more than 300 paintings and drawings by Sister M.I. Hummel, a German nun whose entire collection of work numbers around 500 pieces.

Wurstfest (178 Landa Park Dr, ☎ 830-625-9167), the biggest celebration of the New Braunfels year, is held during the first two weekends of November. With average attendance of over 100,000 people – which more than triples the town's normal population – Wurstfest draws from a well of distinctly German activities for Central Texan's sake, from polka to oompah to dark ales and sauerkraut

The **New Braunfels Smokehouse** (140 Hwy 46 East, ☎ 830-625-2416, www.nbsmokehouse.com), which began as a smokehouse for local ranchers and farmers to bring in their own wares, has blossomed into a mega-enterprise. Not mega on the scale of McDonalds, but mega for a town of 27,000 inhabitants. Not only does it boast some of the best meats around (including kielbasa and bratwurst), it runs a national mail order business showcasing its meats and other local cheeses, jellies and gift packages.

Information Sources

Contact the **New Braunfels Chamber of Commerce** for more information (390 South Seguin, 78131, ☎ 830-625-2385, 800-572-2626, www.nbcham.org).

The Schlitterbahn.

■ Adventures on the Water

The Schlitterbahn or "slippery road" (400 N Liberty, ☎ 830-625-2351, www.schlitterbahn.com) probably buys more air time than any other New Braunfels attraction, and rightly so. Though it does have a little of that any-amusement-park, USA, feel to it, its German influence and original rides make it a unique water park.

As one of the nation's largest water parks, the Schlitterbahn includes 65 acres of water slides, tube chutes, a wave pool, children's play areas and hot tubs. Back in the '80s the Schlittercoaster was the ride of choice. Today the park boasts of the Surfenburg, the world's first body board surfing ride.

If being shot out of something with the prefix "schlitter" is not your style, the river is also lined with parks, including **Landa Park** (110 Golf Course Rd, ☎ 830-608-2180). Its 310 acres encompass glass-bottom boat rides, boat rentals, both traditional and spring-fed pools, miniature golf and a pint-sized train ride.

With over 8,200 acres of lake and seven parks, **Canyon Lake** (River Rd north off Hwy 46, ☎ 830-964-3341), just west of New Braunfels, provides facilities for boating, fishing, swimming, water-skiing, scuba diving and camping. Created out of a portion of the Guadalupe River, Canyon Lake boasts clear water and steep banks like many of its counterparts to the north in the Highland Lakes system.

■ Adventures on Foot

Not even discovered until 1960, **Natural Bridge Caverns** (26495 Natural Bridge Caverns Rd, ☎ 210-651-6101) was named for the 60-foot natural limestone bridge that spans its entrance. A subterranean labyrinth that takes a little over an hour to tour, the cave is a US Natural Landmark and considered a living cave, with many formations still developing a cubic inch every century.

Developers made the most of the natural caverns' tourist draw and

Natural Bridge Caverns.

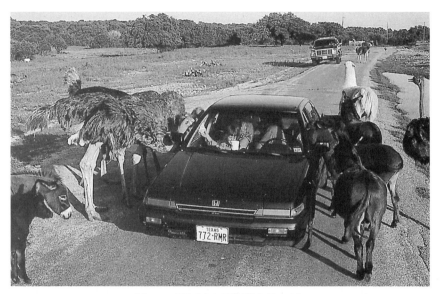

Natural Bridge Wildlife Ranch.

created the **Natural Bridge Wildlife Ranch** (26515 Natural Bridge Caverns Rd, ☎ 830-438-7400) as a visitor bonus. Home to over 600 exotic and indigenous animals, the 200-acre preserve includes Cape buffalo, llamas, ostriches, giraffes, bobcats and longhorns. There are also petting areas and a full range of primates, as well as exotic birds near the entrance in cages.

Misplaced as it may sound, **John Newcombe's Tennis Ranch** (Hwy 46 West at Mission Valley Rd, ☎ 830-625-9105, www.lnstar.com/newks) seems to be a cross between a dude ranch and a tennis camp. The three-time Wimbledon champion's spread includes 28 courts and usually a large number of Australian tennis instructors.

Though the collection of birds at the **Clear Springs Aviaries and Zoological Gardens** (5686 IH 35 South, ☎ 830-606-6029) in New Braunfels has been developing for some two decades, it wasn't open to the public until May, 1997. Piece by piece, the owners are opening up portions of their 35-acre parcel to show off over 200 exotic bird and animal species and a cast of over 1,000 tropical plant species.

Walking the paths that meander through the park, you encounter toucans, parrots and cranes, as well as more exotic and rare species from all over the world. Clear Springs boasts the only grouping of Australian bell magpies in the nation, a bird known more for its sweet song than its good looks. If you're stealthy and patient enough, you can get within two or three feet of many of the birds.

The walking trail that connects the aviaries is expected to grow each spring until the entire park is finished.

> ✳ *Author's Tip*
>
> Visitors enjoy spring, summer and early fall the most at Clear Springs. Though the park is open year-round – and the birds are always there – the tropical plants are seasonal.

■ Where to Stay

Camp Warnecke Resorts, Inc, 371 W Lincoln, 78130, ☎ 800-990-4386. $$-$$$. Luxury condominiums.

Log Cabins at Jacob's Creek, Canyon Lake, ☎ 830-964-2638. $$. Just what the name says they are.

New Braunfels Resorts, 1110 W San Antonio St, 78130, ☎ 830-629-5924 or 800-292-1617. $$-$$$$. They represent 95 individually owned houses and condos at different price levels.

John Newcombe's Tennis Ranch, Hwy 46 W at Mission Valley Rd, ☎ 830-625-9105 or 800-444-6204. www.lnstar.com/newks. Coupling tennis and resort, the ranch includes all the amenities.

Schlitterbahn Resort "At the Bahn," 305 W Austin, ☎ 830-625-2351. $$-$$$. Next to the original waterpark, the Resort boasts two pools and a pizza parlor.

Schlitterbahn Resort "At the Rapids," 500 S Union, ☎ 830-625-2351. $$-$$$. Motel rooms right on the river; you can go tubing out the back door.

Maricopa Ranch Resort, Hwy 306 at Canyon Lake, ☎ 830-964-3731. $$. Facilities for camping, RVs and normal motel areas. Includes just about everything and is packed in the wintertime as a home for a group of travelers often referred to as Winter Texans. These "Texans" annually leave the chilly winter confines of Canada and other northern reaches and make new homes and towns in the South. They even have their own magazine and Web site.

Maricopa Riverside Lodge. On the Guadalupe River, ☎ 830-964-3600 or 800-460-8891. $$-$$$. Right on the river, the lodge also acts as river outfitter. There are also volleyball courts and horseshoe pits.

Gruene Sunday Haus. 1950 Hunter Rd, 78130, ☎ 830-625-5818 or 888-760-0747. $$$. Guest houses that can accommodate groups of people. Just five blocks from the river and four blocks to Gruene.

Bed & Breakfasts

Aunt Nora's Bed & Breakfast, 120 Naked Indian Trail, Canyon Lake, ☎ 830-905-3989 or 800-687-2887. $$-$$$. Four private Country Victorian cottages. Twelve miles outside of town, four miles to the Guadalupe River and Canyon Lake.

Castle Avalon, 10900 Hwy 46 W, ☎ 830-885-4780. $$$-$$$$. An actual castle that offers royal opportunities, including a ballroom for special occasions. Ask about their special packages which can include a room, five-course meals, champagne and Sunday brunch.

Gruene Mansion Inn, 1275 Gruene Rd, 78130, ☎ 830-629-2641. $$-$$$. Victorian rustic elegance set high on a bluff overlooking the river. Most of the rooms come complete with a deck for better views.

Historic Kuebler-Waldrip Haus, 1620 Hueco Springs Loop, 78132, www.cruising-america.com/kuebler-waldrip. ☎ 830-625-8372 or 800-299-8372. $$-$$$. Its two buildings contain 10 different rooms, the price of each depending on its size.

Prince Solms Inn, 295 E San Antonio, 78130, ☎ 830-625-9169 or 800-625-9169. $$-$$$. Furnished as close to the 1800s style as possible, which means no television sets. One of the town's finest restaurants, Wolfgang Keller's, is right downstairs.

Stage Stop Ranch (Guest Ranch), 1100 Old Mail Route Rd, Fischer, 78623, ☎ 830-935-4455 or 800-782-4378. $$-$$$. Located at the base of the Devil's Backbone, the view couldn't be more spectacular. Contains private cabins and a main ranch house. Well stocked with fireplaces, spas, gardens and Victorian bathtubs.

■ Where to Eat

 Castle Avalon, 10900 Hwy 46 W, ☎ 830-885-2002. An authentic English castle. A little pricey, but the continental cuisine is worth it.

Grist Mill Restaurant, 1287 Gruene Rd, ☎ 830-625-0684. Large outdoor setting is perfect for families. The food is terrific for any palate.

Gruene Mansion Restaurant, 1275 Gruene Rd, ☎ 830-620-0760. An eclectic menu ranging from filet mignon to catfish to pasta at medium-ranged prices.

Guadalupe Smoked Meat Company, 1299 Gruene Rd, ☎ 830-629-6121. Texas barbecue by the plate or the pound. Right up the hill from the river.

Krause's Café, 148 S Castell, ☎ 830-625-7581. Wholesome German food coupled with daily specials like chicken and dumplings. A local favorite.

New Braunfels Smokehouse, 140 Hwy 46 E, ☎ 830-625-2416, www.nbsmokehouse.com. Though it runs a national mail order business for its wares, its food fresh can't be beat.

Wolfgang Kellers, 295 E San Antonio, ☎ 830-625-9169. In the basement of the Prince Solms Inn, it serves unique German dishes along with steaks.

East of the I-35 Corridor

Bastrop

■ History

For such a small town (population under 5,000), Bastrop has an extensive history as one of the oldest cities in the state. Nestled between a crook in the Colorado River just east of Austin and a curious patch of over 3,500 acres of pine trees, the town's name honors Felipe Enrique Neri, Baron de Bastrop, a Dutch nobleman.

Or so he told colonists. In reality he was Philip Hendrik Nering Bogel, an ordinary citizen who fled his home in Dutch Guiana with a 1,000 gold ducat price on his head for embezzlement.

Arriving as a "baron" in 1805, he received a colony grant and was later appointed second alcalde of San Antonio. The imposter baron was key in Stephen F. Austin's negotiations with Mexico allowing Anglo-American settlement and was instrumental in the establishment of the port of Galveston.

It wasn't long before tension between the area residents and the Mexican government grew, and in 1835 many local volunteers rushed to assist in the armed uprising against Mexico.

✳ Did You Know?

It was a Bastrop resident who was the first killed in the War of Texas Independence, at the Battle of Concepcion in October 1835.

When the Alamo fell to General Santa Anna, Bastrop settlers fled and what was left of their town was looted by Indians and the Mexican Army. Showing their resilience, the residents returned following Santa Anna's ultimate defeat and rebuilt their town. As one of the original 10 counties established by the Republic of Texas, they were considered a top contender for the site of the new Capitol. However, their western counterpart, Waterloo – now Austin – won that distinction.

■ Touring

 With over 125 structures on the National Register of Historic Places, Bastrop is a gentle step back in time. The first step could be **Lock's Drug** (1003 Main St), which has retained the furnishings and ambiance of a 19th-century doctor's office and drug store. Best of all on a hot Texas afternoon is its old-fashioned ice cream parlor.

For auto buffs, the **Central Texas Museum of Automotive History** (south on TX 304, ☎ 512-237-2635 call for hours and seasons) is a quiet treat of around 85 vintage cars. Its exhibits range from a Model T to a Napier to a Duesenberg.

Information Sources

Contact the **Bastrop Chamber of Commerce** (927 Main St, 78602, ☎ 512-321-2419) for more information on the town.

■ Adventures on Foot

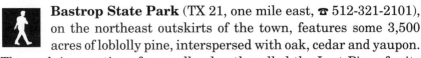 **Bastrop State Park** (TX 21, one mile east, ☎ 512-321-2101), on the northeast outskirts of the town, features some 3,500 acres of loblolly pine, interspersed with oak, cedar and yaupon. The park is a section of a woodland aptly called the Lost Pines for its

strange but lovely existence in the middle of Texas, isolated from the pines of East Texas. It is one of the most beautiful parks in the state.

Bastrop Park includes campgrounds for both tents and RVs, picnic areas, hiking trails, primitive cabins (reserve early), a 100-foot swimming pool and a golf course. The Lost Pines primitive trail contains over eight miles of loop hiking trails with some primitive camping areas. A 10-acre lake is stocked with bass, perch, trout and catfish.

The hiking trail is suitable for day-use or for backpackers who would like to make a weekend of it. Camping is permitted only east of the primitive road (pick up a map) and you'll need to bring your own water.

■ Adventures on the Water

Just 12 miles from Bastrop State Park is **Buescher State Park** (FM 153 north, ☎ 512-237-2241). Buescher, with over 1,000 wooded acres, offers camping, picnicking and hiking. The 25-acre lake allows fishing (crappie, bass, perch and rainbow trout) and non-motorized boating. Several intertwined trails wind through the forest, providing both short and longer day hikes (no overnight camping).

Lake Bastrop (FM 1441 or LCRA dam access road, call for details, north shore ☎ 512-321-3307, south shore 512-321-5048) is 906 acres of water recreation: water-skiing, boating, fishing swimming, picnicking and general lounging.

■ Adventures on Wheels

Mountain bikers can spend an entire weekend at **Rocky Hill Ranch** (FM 153, ☎ 512-237-3112), outside of Bastrop near Buescher State Park. Call for directions, but you'll know you're there when you see the old bike on the gate opening. As a privately owned ranch/venture, you'll need to pay for use of the trails and pick up guides at the saloon/restaurant. There are 38 miles of trails ranging from easy to expert winding through a small forest of pines, with water stations scattered along the paths. Afterwards, hang out in the bar/restaurant or even camp overnight.

■ Where to Stay

Tahitian Village Inn and Racquet Club, 2½ miles east at Loop 150, ☎ 512-321-1145. $-$$. Close to Bastrop State Park, each of the motel's units is equipped with a microwave, toaster and ice box.

Gonzales

■ History

"Come and Take It" was written on the flag Gonzales residents displayed to Mexican troops before the first shots of the Texas Revolution grazed the tiny but spirited town. The flag referred to the request by the Mexican government (which was feeling the vibes of a revolution) to return a small brass cannon it had lent to the Texans for defense against Indian attacks.

The town felt no need to return the cannon, the war began and Gonzales became the "Lexington of Texas." When Colonel Travis pleaded for support of his beleaguered Alamo, Gonzales was the only town to respond, sending 32 men, who perished in the celebrated battle.

■ Touring

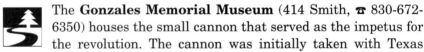 The **Gonzales Memorial Museum** (414 Smith, ☎ 830-672-6350) houses the small cannon that served as the impetus for the revolution. The cannon was initially taken with Texas troops when they left town, but its weight slowed them, so it was buried in Sandies Creek and forgotten. It was unearthed over a century later, in 1936, to become the centerpiece of this museum that pays tribute to the men who died in the revolution. Every year, on the weekend closest to October 2, the city commemorates the first shots of the revolution with a festival.

You can visit the **Site of the Battle of Gonzales** (US 183 south, TX 97 west) where monuments chronicle the battle's story. **The Old County Jail Museum** (414 St Lawrence, ☎ 830-672-6532) was still in use up to 1975. Though the gallows upstairs are replicas, the cells with initials and dates carved into its brick walls are the originals.

Noah's Land Wildlife Park (Hwy 304 north, ☎ 830-540-4664) allows for a hands-on experience, with 400 acres of rare species, including kangaroos, ostrichs, llamas, wildebeests, buffaloes and rhinos. Most animals you can feed from your car, with a petting zoo for some of the smaller species.

Just a tad further north, you'll find the **Lockhart State Recreation Area** (FM 20 southwest of Lockhart off US 183, ☎ 512-398-3479), which includes a swimming pool, hiking trail, camping area and nine-hole golf course.

Information Sources

Contact the **Gonzales Chamber of Commerce** at
☎ 830-672-6532, PO Box 134, 78629.

■ Adventures on Foot

Palmetto State Park (US 183 north, PR 11 west, ☎ 830-672-3266) delights both botanists and visitors. Located in what was once the Ottine Swamp, the unusual vegetation attracts naturalists from all over the world. The small, isolated vestige of swampland that flourished here more than 12,000 years ago would most likely have dried up if not for the intervention of the Civilian Conservation Corp. in 1934. The CCC added several mechanisms to keep the bogs damp and preserve the dwarf palmetto, a small palm-like plant with spiked fronds.

The unique physical make-up of the Palmetto Park attracts a variety of animals and critters, including flying squirrels. There are over three miles of hiking trails to enjoy – none are rugged, just scenic. Birders have counted over 240 species of birds in the park.

■ Adventures on the Water

Fun at the Palmetto State Park extends to the river and lake that are the park's vital components. The San Marcos River weaves a path through the swampland, inviting swimmers, tubers and paddlers. You can also fish for catfish, bass and crappie. But bring your own supplies (boats, bait, etc.) as the park supplies only paddleboat rentals.

✳ Author's Tip

Remember to bring insect repellent. Mosquitoes thrive here and will leave you feeling weak if you're not prepared.

Another park option is **Lake McQueeney** (FM 725, ☎ 830-557-9900), five miles northwest of Seguin, considered to be the "water-skiing capital of Texas." Skiing exhibitions are regularly presented here and facilities for boating, fishing and swimming are available.

Central Texas

■ Where to Stay

 Crooked Back Ranch, 14 miles west on FM 466 near Monthalia, ☎ 800-398-4052. $$-$$$. A collection of cabins along the tree-lined Guadalupe River that come fully equipped with modern conveniences, yet embrace the great outdoors.

The Houston House, 621 East St George, 78629, ☎ 830-672-6940. $$-$$$. Queen Anne Victorian mansion built in 1895 by a cattle baron with hand-painted murals in the parlor and dining room. Tours of Gonzales available in their antique car.

■ Where to Eat

 Kreuz Market, 208 S Commerce. Lockhart, ☎ 512-398-2361. If you're anywhere close to Lockhart you can't miss this barbecue heaven. Served on butcher paper since the turn of the century.

The Texas Hill Country

Burnet

Bluebonnets play an important role in every Texan's life. As the state flower, they are not to be picked. They are to treasured and admired. You'll see dozens of children propped up along roadsides and lying on hills – wherever there is a convenient patch of bluebonnets in the springtime – to get the ultimate picture. (It is a slow torture that every Texas child must learn to endure and ultimately like.)

■ Touring

 Burnet, designated the Bluebonnet Capital of Texas, takes its role seriously and annually hosts the **Bluebonnet Festival** (second weekend in April, Town Square, ☎ 512-756-4297), a splashing array of Texas' finest wildflowers.

Longhorn Caverns State Park (US 281 south to PR 4 west, ☎ 512-756-6976) has been home to prehistoric cave dwellers, Indians and outlaws. Confederate gunpowder was made in this two-mile underground dreamland. In the 1920s it served as a bar, its constant 64° luring overheated customers. The history of this grand dame of caverns is fascinating. The actual caves descend over a half-mile below the earth's surface. And while visitors are not privy to the entire (protected) network of caves, the one-hour walking tour takes you past a variety of geological wonders with names like Crystal City, the Hall of Gems, the Viking's Prow and Lumbago Alley. Above ground there are trails, picnic tables, a restaurant, a museum and observation tower.

Just West of Burnet is **Buchanan Dam**, one of the largest multi-arch dams in the country. It is the first dam in the Highland Lake system and creates the largest and highest of the lakes, Lake Buchanan. Views from atop the dam stretch hundreds of miles along the Colorado River. Eight miles across at its widest point, every water sport imaginable can be found here.

Information Sources

Contact the **Chamber of Commerce** (PO Drawer M, 78611, ☎ 512-756-4297). Visit their Web site as well (www.burnetchamber.org) for lots of good visitor information.

■ Adventures on the Water

 One of the most popular attractions the area offers is the **Vanishing Texas River Cruise** (reservations required, ☎ 800-728-8735 or 512-756-6986, www.highlandlakes.com/cruise/), which boasts a variety of tours on Lake Buchanan, a 23,000-acre parcel of the Highland Lake system. During winter months the tour boat takes you to the nesting ground of an American bald eagle. Another tour goes to the Colorado Bend State Park, where you can hike and swim. A recent tour addition makes a stop at Fall Creek Vineyards for a tour of the winery and a wine tasting.

Inks Lake State Park (TX 29 east to PR 4 south, ☎ 512-793-2223), to the south, provides tranquility. Many lake connoisseurs believe it is the gem – the most beautiful lake in the system. The **Inks Lake National Fish Hatchery** (☎ 512-793-2474), which adjoins the park three miles down the road, produces over a million fish annually to stock lakes across the Southwest. See the information at the end of this chapter on the Highland Lakes for more about both Inks Lake and Lake Buchanan.

■ Adventures on Wheels

 A perfect way to see the Texas Hill Country without having to drive is a ride on the **Hill Country Flyer** (reservations at 116 E 6th St, ☎ 512-477-8468, www.main.org/flyer), a train excursion between Cedar Park and Burnete. It begins and ends in Cedar Park, with a layover in Burnet for shopping, dining and sightseeing. After leaving the Cedar Park station, the train separates itself from the area's urban grandness and delves into the wooded valley of the South San Gabriel River, crossing an incredible trestle on its spectacular journey.

SP (Standard Pacific) locomotive #786 was originally put into service in 1916. It is one of only five of its kind left in the world. The 786 made her second debut to the world in 1991 after a complete restoration.

Information Sources

Call the **Burnet Chamber of Commerce** for more information (703 Buchanan Dr, 78611, ☎ 512-756-4297, www.burnetchamber.org).

■ Where to Stay

 The Edgewater, Southwest Lake Buchanan, Hwy 29 to 261 Lakeshore Dr, ☎ 512-793-2818. $$-$$$. Cabins along Lake Buchanan that include small fishing boats for rent. Designed for family vacations, with camping, fishing guides and souvenirs.

Hi-Line Resort & Marina, Northwest Lake Buchanan, ☎ 888-379-1065 or 915-379-1065, www.highlandlakes.com/hiline/. $-$$. Water activities for the entire family. Its 1,800 feet of waterfront includes a 24-hour crappy house, a beach area, jet ski rentals and fully equipped cottages.

Lake Point Resort, South Lake Buchanan, Hwy 29 near the dam, ☎ 888-793-2918 or 512-793-2918, www.hunt-fish.com/lpoint2. $-$$. The resort retains the charm of the 1940s with quaint cottages, fishing, canoes, paddle boats and skiing.

✻ Did You Know?

The 1997 movie remake of *Lolita*, a controversial film starring Melanie Griffith and Jeremy Irons, was filmed at Lake Point.

Lakeside Lodge, Lake Buchanan, ☎ 512-756-4935. $-$$. With only six rooms, the Lakeside Lodge is a quiet place to enjoy the lake, including a beach, fishing areas, free breakfast and massage therapy.

Main Street B & B, 808 N Main, Burnet, 78611, ☎ 512-756-2861. $$-$$$. Right in town, this quaint 1930s B&B offers weekly rates.

■ Where to Eat

Catfish Barge Restaurant, Southwest side of Inks Lake, FM 301, ☎ 512-793-6860. This floating barge can be accessed either by boat or car. Freshwater catfish any way you'd like it.

Marble Falls

Marble Falls is one of those places that inspire the best in song writers. Oscar J. Fox, Franklin D. Roosevelt's favorite composer for tunes like *Home on the Range* and *Get Along Little Doggie*, wrote the *Hills of Home* in tribute to his hillside view of Marble Falls. A Burnet County native, Fox took these memories with him as he toured the world.

■ History

The city is also the vision of another. Adam R. Johnson first envisioned the city he would build on these "Great Falls" (now covered by Lake Marble Falls) but was delayed by a number of things, including the Civil War. At that time the "Great Falls" poured over a series of marble ledges measuring up to 22 feet high.

When Johnson returned from the war, blinded by an injury, he built his town from memory with the help of his son.

With the coming of the railroad, business picked up, and in 1888 George and Elizabeth Roper built the **Roper Hotel** (located on the corner of US 281 and Third St). As one of the earliest hotels in the area, the Roper became a regular stop for travelers. The Roper was completely renovated in 1981, and the exterior looks much as it did in 1888.

■ Touring

 On the western edge of the town lies **Granite Mountain**, an 866-foot dome of solid pink granite. This mountain was used to build the state Capitol in Austin. Though quarrying has continued since then, the mountain's largesse has hardly been tapped – most of it remains and can be seen from RR 1431.

Several retirement communities have grown up in the area, including **Granite Shoals**, west of Marble Falls on RR 1431, and **Horseshoe Bay** (www.horseshoebay.com), south of town.

Both are snuggled against the shoreline of the area lakes. However, Horseshoe Bay also boasts several of the finest golf courses in Central Texas. The mode of transportation varies day-by-day, from golf cart to deck boat to wave runner. Horseshoe Bay, a relative newcomer to the scene, is still actively recruiting interested residents to buy lots and homes.

Information Sources

The **Marble Falls Chamber of Commerce** can help you with any specific questions you may have on the town and the area lakes (☎ 800-759-8178, 830-693-4449, www.Instar.com/marblefalls).

■ Adventures on the Water

 Lake LBJ and **Lake Marble Falls**, the third and fourth components of the Highlands Lake System, respectively, literally surround Marble Falls. Lake LBJ, with 6,300 acres, provides much more room than 780-acre Lake Marble Falls. Marble Falls, though, plays host to several drag boat racing events. Both lakes are perfect for boating, fishing, swimming and skiing. See the special entry on the Highland Lakes, page 113, for more information.

■ Where to Stay

 Krause Springs, Spicewood, ☎ 830-693-4181. (Two thumbs up from the author.) Provides facilities for primitive camping only. Its beauty is in the spring-fed pool, waterfalls and numerous trails under dense foliage.

Liberty Hall, 119 Ave G, Marble Falls, 78654, ☎ 830-693-4518, www.Instar.com/libertyhall. A three-story mansion built in 1887 by the founder of Marble Falls. It's 7,000 square feet of antique decadence.

Horseshoe Bay Resort, Horseshoe Bay Blvd, Lake LBJ, ☎ 830-598-2511 or 800-252-9363. $$$-$$$$. The lap of luxury. Staying at this lakeside resort gives you access to the spectacular pool and hot tub (which are surrounded by exotic birds), fine dining, golf range (golf packages available), the equestrian center and spa.

Sandyland Resort, 212 Skyline Drive, Sunrise Beach, 78643, west end of Lake LBJ, ☎ 915-388-4521, www.highlandlakes.com/sandyland. $$-$$$. Waterfront resort that functions as a bed and breakfast. Much quieter than its Horseshoe Bay counterpart, but still offers fishing, motor boating, swimming and captained sailing trips.

Tropical Hideaway, 604 High Crest Dr, Granite Shoals, 78654, ☎ 830-598-9896, 800-394-8181. $$-$$$. Tennis courts, beach, marina and on-site restaurant.

■ Where to Eat

 Blue Bonnet Café, 211 Hwy 281, ☎ 830-693-2344. Over seven decades of home-style cooking with Texas-type daily specials. Waylon, Willie and all the boys have frequented the restaurant, which relies on good food for its repeat business.

Jamin House Café, 710 Hwy 281, Marble Falls, ☎ 830-693-3979. Its owners brought their Caribbean heritage to the heart of Texas. Upscale food for the discriminating eater.

Texas Traditions, 19105 Hwy 2147 W, Horseshoe Bay, ☎ 830-598-6522. From catfish to cheeseburgers, the fare runs the gamut. Could satisfy any appetite after a day on the lake.

Rocky Top Restaurant, 1011 Hwy 1431 W, Granite Shoals, ☎ 830-598-1282. Another combination of American, Mexican and anything else you might want.

Sandyland Resort Restaurant, Sandyland Resort, 212 Skyline Drive, Sunrise Beach, www.highlandlakes.com/sandyland, west end of Lake LBJ, ☎ 915-388-4521. They serve groups only with prior reservations and prefer groups of eight or more. Your group will enjoy steak, quail, grilled butterfly trout or a range of other dishes. Exquisite continental buffet for lodge guests.

Johnson City

■ History

It's difficult to believe that Johnson City was not named for its most famous son, Lyndon Baines Johnson. But, in fact, it was named for his ancestors, Tom and Sam Ealy Johnson, LBJ's great-uncle and grandfather.

Lyndon Johnson was actually born near Stonewall, a small rural community a short distance from Johnson City that is now part of the LBJ Ranch District of the National Historical Park. But his family moved to town early in his life. The son of a school teacher and politician, he followed in both parents' footsteps, first becoming a school teacher and then the ultimate politician.

■ Touring

Johnson City serves as headquarters for the **LBJ National Historical Park** (100 Lady Bird Lane, ☎ 830-868-7128), which consists of two parts: the ranch unit and the Johnson City unit. In Johnson City you will find Johnson's boyhood home and the family settlement, which includes the log home of Sam Ealy Johnson. The ranch unit can be accessed only by a National Park Service tour bus, which picks up visitors at the LBJ State Historical Park west of town. The tour includes his ranch, the cemetery where he is buried and the schoolhouse that he attended and revisited to sign the National Education Act. Since Lady Bird Johnson still lives on the premises, and it is a working ranch, tours are subject to change.

The LBJ State Historical Park (US 290 west, ☎ 830-644-2252), across from the Johnson spread, was purchased by a group of LBJ's friends and donated to the state. Though the park includes much LBJ and Hill Country memorabilia, it also provides nature trails, picnic areas, swimming and tennis courts.

A fairly recent addition to the Johnson City historic district has been the **Feed Mill Complex** (103 W Main, ☎ 830-868-7299), a revamped version of a feed mill that encompasses a city block. It is home to two of Johnson City's more notable restaurants, the Feed Mill Café and Maya's Cajun Kitchen, and boasts a live theater, a high-end antique store, an old-time carousel and the Texas Music Hall of Fame.

Information Sources

The **Johnson City Chamber of Commerce** (☎ 830-868-7684, 868-7803, www.lnstar.com/johnsoncity) can help you with more of the specifics. **Bed & Breakfast of Johnson City** (☎ 830-868-4548) can help you find the most appropriate place to stay.

■ Adventures

Pedernales Falls State Park (FM 2766 east, ☎ 830-868-7304) offers more than six miles of river frontage on the beautiful Perdernales River. The river gained national fame during President Lyndon B. Johnson's administration – he was often found on its banks and it was one of his favorite spots in the world. There's swimming, tubing, fishing, camping, hiking and anything else you can find to do. The hiking can be spectacular, with both short, lazy walks and strenuous hikes.

Wolf Mountain Trail, a 7½-mile loop east of the river, includes four miles of very primitive trails for stronger hikers only. Just to get to this primitive terrain, you'll have to ford the Perdernales River at Trammel Crossing or at another appropriate spot. If your timing's right, stop at Arrowhead Pool for lunch or a mid-afternoon break. You'll enjoy a small waterfall feeding an unsullied oasis.

The actual falls are at the north end of the park and can be viewed from a designated scenic overlook. The river drops about 50 feet over a distance of 3,000 feet. Swimming, boating and other water activities are not allowed near the falls for safety reasons. But if you go further down the river, there's ample room to spread out and play (bring your own tubes and rafts). Usually, toward the end of the summer and during other dry seasons, the river's flow in inhibited and not suitable for kayaks, canoes and other rafts that need more water depth. Call ahead for information.

The park began as a working ranch and has left corrals as part of its legacy. **Horseback riding** is restricted to a 10-mile designated equestrian trail in the upper reaches of the park. While they do supply a place to keep your horse, they don't supply the horse. You'll have to bring your own.

There are several areas suitable for **rappelling** – for those experienced in the sport. Also, **mountain biking** has become increasingly popular in the park. The same trails that are challenging to hikers are challenging to bikers. Wear a helmet and take some extra tubes with you – otherwise you could be carrying your bike home with you.

■ Where to Stay

 Boot Hill Guest House, 107 Ranchview Drive, Johnson City, 78636, ☎ 830-868-4548. $-$$. The beds are made from welded horseshoes, cedar posts and wagon wheels; the dining room table is made from whiskey barrels. However, it's a lot more comfortable than the Old West that the house pays tribute to. A B&B service takes reservations for this location and several others.

Hillhouse Guest House, 105 Ranchview Drive, 78636, ☎ 830-868-4548, 868-7475, www.lnstar.com/hillhouse. $$. It's a quaint version of life way back when in one of the town's oldest homes.

■ Where to Eat

The Feed Mill Café. In the Feed Mill Complex, 103 W Main, ☎ 830-868-7771. Country cooking in a festive atmosphere.

Fredericksburg

■ History

A 19th-century German organization, the Adelsverein, or the Association of Noblemen, felt the sure-fire way to ease overpopulation in their homeland was to bring settlers to Texas, a utopia in their minds. Between 1845 and 1847 (when it went bankrupt), the Adelsverein brought more than 7,000 Germans to the Texas coast for delivery inland.

Fredericksburg, named after Prince Frederick of Prussia, was settled by many in this group and their leader, Baron Otfried Hans von Meusebach. Meusebach did what few others could, successfully negotiating peace with the Comanches, whose land they bordered.

The German influence of these settlers is tangible – many families are direct descendants and still speak German. Events throughout the year, like Schuetzenfests (markmanship contests) and Saengerfests (singing festivals), are uniquely German.

■ Touring

Admiral Chester Nimitz, Commander-in-Chief of the Pacific fleet during World War II, is Fredericksburg's favorite son. The **Admiral Nimitz State Historical Park** (340 E Main, ☎ 830-997-4379, www.Instar.com/nimitz) traces Nimitz's life from this small town to the far reaches of the Pacific.

The historic downtown district includes more than 100 of the town's original buildings. Included in these are **Sunday Houses**, one-room abodes built by ranchers and farmers who needed a place to stay when they were in town on weekends for church and other social activities.

Admiral Nimitz Museum and Historical Center.

The **Bauer Toy Museum** (233 E Main, no phone) displays toy soldiers, fire trucks, model airplanes and smaller toys from bygone eras. Also included is a hand-crafted village with toy cars and trains and a 35-foot diorama depicting Dickens' *A Christmas Carol*.

Fort Martin Scott (1606 E Main, ☎ 830-997-9895) was the first federal fort constructed in Texas to protect the frontier from Indian raids. However, since Meusebach had already established a treaty with the Comanches, the fort served more as a trading post for soldiers, Indians and settlers. It is still in the process of being fully restored.

Information Sources

Call the local **Visitors and Convention Bureau** (☎ 830-997-6523, www.fredericksburg-texas.com/cvb) or the **Fredericksburg Chamber of Commerce** (☎ 830-997-6523, www.fredericksburg-texas.com/coc) for more information.

■ Adventures on Foot

The huge pink granite domes that make up **Enchanted Rock**, formed over a billion years ago, have been mesmerizing area residents for thousands of years. Indians that lived here over 10,000 years ago were certainly "enchanted" by this rock, which is no

Enchanted Rock.

less than a mountain in size. The Tonkawa recorded strange noises and groaning from the mound – they believed magic was performed from its peaks. Modern-day geologists believe the noises were created when the rock rapidly heated during the day and cooled at night.

E-Rock, as frequent rockers call it, is one of the oldest exposed geological sites in America. It was designated a National Natural Landmark in 1970 and was included in the National Register of Historic Places beginning in 1984. And it is certainly awe-inspiring. Even if you can't afford to spend a weekend there, you should at least take a quick look. You will see nothing like it anywhere else – a round mountain of pink granite that stands as broad as a small city.

Adventure on E-Rock takes many forms. From hiking to biking to rock climbing and rappelling. Camping is walk-in only. Most visitors begin with a hike in the 1,643-acre park. A four-mile loop encircles the major rock formations, following creek beds that remain dry the majority of the year. The view from the trail can be fantastic.

Of course, the best view is from the top, with the majority of Central Texas stretched out beneath you. Just attack the rock from any side.

For backpackers there are three remote camping areas.

Rock climbers consider the Rock second only to Hueco Tanks in West Texas for climbing with a diverse set of both face and crack climbs. Climbers and rappellers are required to check in with the park headquarters for safety and to pick up a current map of available climbs.

Enchanted Rock State Natural Area (Route 4, Box 170, Fredericksburg, 78624, ☎ 915-247-3903) is west of Hwy 16 on RR 965, just north of Fredericksburg. For all camping, reservations are required (☎ 512-389-8900). This really is a local favorite – so call in advance to secure a camping spot. E-Rock is, at minimum, two full days of fun. Plan on taking your time. If the park begins to get overcrowded or the natural area is threatened by overuse, the park can indiscriminately shut the doors. Call ahead to make sure everything's OK before heading off.

■ Where to Stay

A Little Waltz Bed & Breakfast, 509 N Cherry, 78624, ☎ 830-997-5612. $$$. Traditional bed and breakfast with the owner on-site. Offers a bathtub for two.

Antonette Marie's Wedding Chapel and Social Manor, 208 E San Antonio, 78624 ☎ 830-997-1753. $$-$$$. Includes both a bed and breakfast for small groups and a social manor for up to 60 people. They'll even

*Fredericksburg Restaurant
and Biergarten.*

arrange the catering, flowers, carriage rides and music for your occasion.

Be My Guest, 110 North Milam, 78624, ☎ 830-997-7227. $$-$$$. Lodging service for several bed and breakfasts and ranches in the area, including a 1,000-acre ranch and a retreat one mile from Enchanted Rock.

Magnolia House Inn, 101 E Hackberry, 78624, ☎ 800-880-4374 or 830-997-0306, www.bbonline.com/tx/magnolia. $$-$$$. A Texas Historic Landmark, this 1923 stately home offers a full Southern breakfast and personal touches like fresh flowers and terry cloth robes.

Way of the Wolf Ranch. Midway between Fredericksburg and Kerrville, ☎ 888-929-9653, www.wayofthewolf.com. $$-$$$. This 61-acre Hill Country retreat offers room for groups in the ranch house or individuals in the Civil War cabin. There are hot German apple pancakes for breakfast, a fresh spring you can hike to, and a small herd of Texas longhorns that wander the estate. The owners are also trained to lead spiritual lessons if you would like a more formal retreat.

■ Where to Eat

 Altdorf Restaurant & Biergarten, 301 W Main, ☎ 830-997-7774. German dinners and specialty sandwiches. They offer a full-strength German beer that is sold under the label of malt liquor because of its potency. Locals call it the best biergarten in town.

Der Lindenbaum, 312 E Main, ☎ 830-997-9126. Another German establishment and more formal than the biergartens. There are steaks for the American palette. Located near the Nimitz Museum.

Friedhelms Bavarian Restaurant and Bar. 905 W Main, ☎ 830-997-6300. On the western edge of town, they serve traditional German fare.

George's Old German Bakery and Restaurant, 225 W Main, ☎ 830-997-9084. George still bakes all pastries, breads and goodies every morning. You're likely to have the pleasure of listening to a deep German accent.

Porky's Hamburger and Onion Rings, 904 W Main, ☎ 830-997-6882. A locals' hangout – they say it's got the best burgers in town. Its owner used to be in law enforcement. Thus the name "Porky's," reminiscent of the 80s movie with the same name.

Kerrville

■ History

Cypress trees that lined the Guadalupe River first attracted Joshua Brown to Kerrville in the early 1840s. Brown, a shinglemaker, was driven away by Indians, but returned in 1848 to resettle the town, then called Brownsborough. The town's name changed to Kerrsville and eventually the "s" was dropped.

Charles Schreiner, a Frenchman from Alsace-Lorraine who served as a Texas Ranger and Confederate soldier, became the area's prominent businessman. At one point he owned more than 600,000 acres of land. His legacy is two-fold: Schreiner College and Kerrville's status as mohair capital of the world, a "crop" that he introduced to the area.

The Guadalupe River, Kerrville.

Kerrville.

In the 1920s, Kerrville was called the healthiest spot in the nation – planting the seed for its growth as a destination for tourists and retirees.

Today, about 10,000 children flock to summer camps in the area, along with adults looking to enjoy the outdoors.

■ Touring

 The **Kerrville Folk Festival** (three weeks in May/June, Quiet Valley Ranch, ☎ 830-257-3600, www.kerrville-music.com) is the town's most visible face to the outside world. Over 100 musicians play this outdoor festival that has taken on an almost cultish following. Music lovers go for weeks at a time, and Austin, the "Live Music Capital of the World," sends most of its finest for this annual event.

> ✳ *Author's Tip*
>
> Kerrville has recently become a mecca for artists. Several art galleries in the area showcase their work.

If you're around in the summer, stop by the **Hill Country Arts Foundation and Point Theatre** (TX 39 west out of Ingram, ☎ 830-367-5121) for an evening production. Plays and musicals are staged Wednesday through Sunday evenings in the 700-seat outdoor theater.

Silver jewelry enthusiasts should visit **James Avery Craftsman** (FM 783, one mile north of I-10, ☎ 830-895-1122), the shop of the renowned jewelry artist who started a national business out of his Kerrville garage.

The **Kerrville State Recreation Area** (southeast on TX 173, ☎ 830-257-5392) provides 500 scenic acres of camping, hiking, swimming and fishing on the cypress-lined Guadalupe River.

Another notable attraction is **Camp Verde** (southeast on TX 173, ☎ 830-634-7722), on Verde Creek. It was an army base for the then Secretary of War Jefferson Davis' experiment using camels for transportation in the desert southwest. Active from 1855 to 1869, the experiment met with limited success and was interrupted by the Civil War.

Bandera Pass, 12 miles south of Kerrville, is a noted gap in the chain of mountains that camel caravans, wagons, Spanish conquistadors, immigrant trains and US troops passed through.

Information Sources

The **Kerrville Convention and Visitors Bureau** (1700 Sidney Baker, Suite 200, 78028, ☎ 800-221-7958, www.ktc.net/kerrcvb) can provide you with up-to-the-minute information.

■ Where to Stay

B&B on Cypress Creek, 816 N Creek Rd, PO Box 836, Comfort, 78013, ☎ 800-945-2479 and 830-995-2479. $$. The western boundary is Cypress Creek, which provides cool swimming, fishing and playing. The estate is full of wildlife, including a herd of longhorns, deer, raccoons and fox. Rocking chairs highlight the quietness of the escape.

Dietert Haus, Rt. 1, Box 74, Mountain Home, ☎ 830-792-9178 or 895-2235. $$-$$$. It's 50 miles from Kerrville and 10 from the Devil's Sinkhole. Very private and perfect for cycling.

Kerrville Bed & Breakfast, 2873 Bandera Hwy, 78028, ☎ 830-257-8750. $$. Traditional bed and breakfast with upstairs deck overlooking the Guadalupe River. The state park is just one mile down the road.

Nopalitos Ranch, 7117 Medina Hwy, 78028, ☎ 830-257-7815. $$$. Solitude is this 2,000-square-foot native stone house's calling card, offering

Horseback riding in Kerrville.

peaceful living on a small ranch. You get the entire house, along with access to the hot tub and a stocked refrigerator.

Guest Ranches

Las Campanas Guest Ranch, Hwy 187, half a mile north of Vanderpool, ☎ 830-966-3431. $-$$$$. A hunting ranch that caters to exotics. Most of their programs charge by the animal, depending on the type (ranging from fallow deer to blackbuck antelope). They breed a wide variety of the animals on the 2,200-acre ranch. Basic accommodations are affordable, the full package a little pricier.

Lazy Hills Guest Ranch, Henderson Ranch Rd, Ingram, ☎ 830-367-5600 or 800-880-0632, www.lazyhills.com. $$$$. They've got it all, from cookouts to hayrides to campfires to birding, hiking and horseback riding.

Wittlinger's Turtle Creek Lodge, 1520 Upper Turtle Creek Rd, south of Kerrville, ☎ 210-828-0377, www.stic.net/users/wittlodge. Single house with four bedrooms. Package plans for groups. Tons of things to do, including swimming, tubing, croquet, horseshoes, and birdwatching. Pets are welcome.

Y.O. Ranch, Hwy 41, 14 miles west of Mountain Home, ☎ 830-640-3222. Native and exotic game ranch encompassing 50 square miles. Established in 1880 by Charles Schreiner, the working ranch boasts zebras, giraffes and antelopes among the 56 species of game.

Mo Ranch, on FM 1340, 11 miles north of Hunt, HC1, Box 158, Hunt, TX 78724. ☎ 830-238-4455 or 800-460-4401. $$-$$$. Horseback riding, volleyball, tennis, swimming and fishing on the river. They also have canoes that you can use for a great river ride.

■ Where to Eat

Mamacita's Restaurant and Cantina, 215 Junction Hwy, ☎ 830-895-2441. Traditional Tex-Mex dishes with American choices, as well.

Patrick's Lodge, 2190 Junction Hwy, ☎ 830-895-4111, http://207.71.36.4/patrickslodge. The owner's French background is evident in the menu. Country location overlooking Goat Creek.

Sam Houston's, 2033 Sidney Baker St, ☎ 830-257-4440. Inside the local Holiday Inn, American fare is their forte.

Luckenbach

■ History & Touring

Certainly there are towns that have inspired songs. But there are few songs that have inspired towns. Such is the case for Luckenbach, Texas, where one visits with "Waylon and Willie and the boys." The town's humble roots, born of German immigrants in 1850, amount to a permanent population that never even reaches three digits and whose buildings can be counted on one hand.

There's the unpainted general store, which doubles as a beer tavern, a traditional dance hall and a blacksmith shop that only sees occasional action.

Luckenbach's fame actually started a bit before Waylon Jennings and Willie Nelson crooned about it, as a product of jokester cowboy J.R. "Hondo" Crouch who bought the town with a partner in the late '60s.

Crouch and his fellow funnymen turned the town into a destination for thousands with clever press releases and eccentric events. With their motto "everybody is somebody in Luckenbach," they scored their biggest coup in 1972 with the First Annual Luckenbach World's Fair, headlined by Willie Nelson. The event drew 20,000 – a stirring feat for a town who's official population rests between 20 and 30.

In 1977 Luckenbach's song hit the charts with record force, touting a Texas spirit where people can be themselves, no pretenses. Three decades later, tourists still flock to the tiny hamlet to drink and dance and do what they please.

To get to Luckenbach, which is more ambiance and history than place, head five miles south on FM 1376 from US 290 just east of Fredericksburg. Look carefully; souvenir hounds steal signs for the town regularly. Sundays are good days for spontaneity, with impromptu gatherings of singers, fiddlers, horseshoe throwers and whoever else happens by.

Information Sources

You can get more information on Luckenbach by calling ☎ 830-997-3224 or by visiting their Web site at www.luckenbachtexas.com.

■ Where to Stay

 The **Luckenbach Inn** (half a mile from the dance hall on Old Luckenbach Rd, ☎ 830-997-2205, www.luckenbachtx.com, $$-$$$) is about the only lodging you'll find close to the area. The traditional bed and breakfast has several rooms in the log cabin that Jacob Kunz, the area's first settler, built in 1867, along with rooms in the limestone farmhouse and a Sunday Haus.

West of San Antonio

Boerne

■ History

Boerne (pronounced "Burney") was settled by a group of German intellectuals around 1851 and named for Ludwig Boerne, a German journalist and satirist. The railroad arrived in 1887, conveniently connecting the city with its sister to the southeast, San Antonio. Beginning then and continuing today, Boerne acts as an escape valve for city folks trying to get away for a weekend or a week. It has retained all of its German flavor and thrives on the Hill Country's abundant energy.

> **❋ *Did You Know?***
>
> Boerne made national headlines in June 1997 when a local land battle between church and state worked its way to the US Supreme Court. The justices ultimately decided in *Boerne v. Flores* to overrule the 1993 Religious Freedom Restoration Act.

■ Touring

 Just about every village or city in the Texas Hill Country is a scenic tour, and Boerne is no different. Try any direction, particularly the small roads, and you can't go wrong.

A 90-foot underground waterfall furnished **Cascade Caverns** with its name (I-10 south, Exit 543, ☎ 830-755-8080). The views of this active cave are spectacular and include immense rooms and crystal pools. The guided walk is very relaxed and is not strenuous. Above the cave is a 100-acre park with camping facilities.

Another area cave, the **Cave Without a Name** (FM 474 east to Kruetzberg Rd, ☎ 830-537-4212), is more remote than its Cascade partner, but well worth the trip. It received its name from a contest won by a boy who remarked that the cave was too pretty to be named.

Sister Creek Vineyards (☎ 830-324-6704, 1142 FM 1376), is a relative newcomer to Central Texas. It began developing its wares in 1988 and opened to the public in 1994. Free tastings are available every day between noon and 5 pm and include two different Chardonnays. Their tasting room includes a dusty, two-story cotton gin built in the 1880s.

> ## Information Sources
>
> You can reach the **Boerne Chamber of Commerce** at ☎ 830-249-8000, One Main Plaza, 78006. Their Web site is at www.boerne.org.

■ Adventures on the Water

 A popular portion of the **Guadalupe River** meanders north of Boerne before connecting with Canyon Lake and continuing its path past Gruene and New Braunfels on its way to the Gulf of Mexico. It remains less commercialized and more remote than other area rivers. While other navigable rivers and streams have roads that run parallel to their course, the upper Guadalupe remains isolated. Access is restricted to roads that actually cross the river.

It is also very typical of the Texas Hill Country, featuring clear springs, commanding limestone bluffs and river banks lined with cypress and sycamores.

Between Bergheim and Rebecca Creek Road, 23 miles east, there are around 55 rapids to navigate. It can be a very technical trip, and even dangerous if the river is up and running faster than normal. Mueller Falls and Rust Falls, both at the tail end of this section, are considered the most powerful of the rapids.

The **Guadalupe River State Park** (13 miles east off Hwy 46 on PR 31, ☎ 830-438-2656 or 512-389-8900 for reservations), is bisected by the clear-flowing Guadalupe River and noted for its rugged but beautiful natural environment. The park wraps itself around the river, boasting four miles of river frontage right in the middle of a nine-mile stretch. The river courses over four natural rapids; two limestone bluffs serve as proof of the river's power. Camping facilities include both tent camping and RV hook-ups. There is also walk-in tent camping for backpackers, with water at the site. The park frequently fills up from March to November.

A guided interpretive tour of the adjacent **Honey Creek State Natural Area** (call Guadalupe Park) is conducted every Saturday at 9 am and emphasizes the history, geology, plant life and animals of the area.

Upper Guadalupe Outfitters

Bergheim Campground. ☎ 830-336-2235. FM 3351 N, Bergheim, 78004. The most upstream of the area outfitters. Offers all rentals and shuttle service, with primitive camping and RV hook-ups.

Bigfoot Canoes. ☎ 830-885-7106. They rent canoes, rafts, tubes, kayaks, and provide shuttle service for the upper Guadalupe.

Guadalupe Canoe Livery. ☎ 830-885-4671 or 830-964-3189. PO Box 8, Spring Branch, 78070. Complete outfitting right on the river with primitive campsites, RV hook-ups and shuttle service.

■ Where to Stay

Borgman's Sunday House B&B Inn, 911 S Main, Beorne 78006, ☎ 830-249-9563. $-$$. Each room has a private entrance and bath. Close to downtown antique shopping.

Guadalupe River Ranch, 605 FM 474, PO Box 877, Beorne, 78006 ☎ 830-437-4837, www.guadalupe-river-ranch.com. $$-$$$$. Perched on a bluff overlooking the Guadalupe River and Valley, the 360-acre ranch offers packages to any taste, including gourmet meals. Most of the activities (swimming, horseshoes, petting zoo, hiking, fishing) are free, and several others (tubing, mountain bikes and zip line trips (where you clip on to a cable, usually with a belt device that slopes down) are available for a small fee. They also offer massages and other spa treatments.

Joshua Creek Ranch, 132 Cravey Rd, 78006, between Boerne and Comfort, ☎ 830-537-5090. Primarily a hunting ranch offering a 10-station course for sporting clays. Between Oct. 1 and April 1 they offer a variety of bird hunting packages. Basic hunts, including the guide dog and lunch, start at $295 a gun. They can go up to $1,700 a gun for three-day driven pheasant and flighted mallard hunts. Hunting licenses can be purchased there. By reservation only.

Tapatio Springs Resort & Country Club. Off Hwy 46 west (Johns Rd), ☎ 830-537-4611, www.tapatio.com. $$-$$$$. They couple a championship golf course with luxury accommodations. Their packages can include everything a golfer might need.

Ye Kendall Inn, 128 W Blanco, 78006, ☎ 800-364-2138, 830-249-2138. $$. In addition to the 13 B&B rooms there is a designer boutique and a gift shop. In the village surrounding the inn, there are several other stores, including an antique shop, a quilting store, an art gallery and Christmas shops.

■ Where to Eat

Country Spirit, 707 S Main, ☎ 830-249-3607. Serving a little bit of everything, entrées include Mexican food, lasagna and grilled fish.

Peach Tree Kountry Kitchen, 448 S Main, ☎ 830-249-8583. A lunch-only establishment with small town appeal. Its owners invite you to join them. They take reservations.

Scuzzi's, 128 W Blanco, ☎ 830-249-2138. Within the Kendall Inn complex, the restaurant offers classy Italian food during the week and a buffet on the weekend.

Bandera

■ History

Saddle up and strap on your chaps. Bandera is not only the "Cowboy Capital of the World," the town of less than 1,000 also calls itself the "Dude Ranch Capital of the World." No small thing for a city that was first settled in 1852 as a cypress shingle camp and hasn't gotten much bigger since. As one of the oldest Polish communities in the United States, Bandera is surrounded by both working and guest ranches. City slickers from around the world come here to experience the cowboy way.

■ Touring

The **Frontier Times Museum** (510 13th St, ☎ 830-796-3864) includes more than 40,000 Old West relics from Buffalo Bill Wild West Show posters to buggy whips and saddles. If you're looking for an entry point in discovering the look and feel of the Old West, this is a great place to begin.

Also, the **Cowboy Artists of America Museum** (1550 Bandera Hwy, ☎ 830-896-2553) displays rotating exhibits by cowboy artists, including pieces by Joe Beeler and Melvin Warren.

Ranches, cattle and horses can be found from North Dakota to Mexico. What makes this area unique is the beautiful Hill Country that makes for a picturesque backdrop to campfires, round-ups and hayrides. Head out of Bandera in any direction and there is a scenic drive waiting for you with hairpin turns, canyons, sweet streams, long vistas and gentle hills.

Information Sources

Call the **Bandera County Convention and Visitors Bureau** (☎ 800-364-3833, 210-796-3045, PO Box 171, 78003, www.tourtexas.com/bandera.

■ Adventures on Foot

The **Hill Country State Natural Area** (FM 1077, approx. 12 miles southwest of Hwy 173, ☎ 830-796-4413) caters to hikers, mountain bikers and horseback riders with over 5,000 acres of open terrain. It has remained largely undeveloped – a stipulation agreed to by the state of Texas when it accepted much of the park's lands from the Merrick Bar-O-Ranch. The ranch insisted that its donated land "be kept far removed and untouched by modern civilization, where everything is preserved intact, yet put to a useful purpose."

The caliche road leading to the park's entrance is proof that the state is doing its best to keep its word. There are 36 miles of multi-use trails; four of those miles are restricted to hikers and horseback riders only. The Twin Peaks Saddleback Trail and the Cougar Canyon Overlook Trail will keep hikers breathless, taking them to the top of Cougar Canyon.

There are all types of primitive overnight sites, from developed equestrian camps, to walk-in sites, to creek-side locations. There's also a group lodge that can accommodate up to 12 visitors.

Many mountain bikers consider the nature area some of the best riding around because of the state's commitment to maintain the wild, natural setting. Expert riders have been forced to get off their bikes in places and walk because many paths are so narrow and irregular.

■ Adventures on the Water

If you have noticed, just about every entry in the Central Texas portion of this book is replete with river activities – there really are that many wonderful opportunities in the area. And while the rivers are not grand (rapid-wise) by Colorado standards, they have bewitched settlers for centuries.

The Medina River is no different, enticing locals and visitors with its limestone bluffs, clear free-flowing springs, towering bald cypress trees and oak-covered hills. The stretch of river between Medina ("Apple Capital of Texas") and Bandera is several different days of fun. Talk to outfitters to see which portion is most appropriate.

Outfitters include: **Fred Collins Workshop**, PO Box 1869, Bandera, 78003, ☎ 830-796-3553, with shuttle service and tube and canoe rentals; and **Yogi Bear's Jellystone Park**, PO Box 1687, Bandera, 78003, with rentals shuttles, riverfront camping and an RV park.

■ Where to Stay

(Including Dude Ranches)

Bald Eagle Ranch. Less than a mile off FM 1077, PO Box 1177, Bandera, 78003, ☎ 830-460-3012, www.baldeagleranch.com. $$$$. This is your city slicker-type dude ranch that puts the emphasis on horseback riding. All of the mounts are registered quarter horses and there are over 40 miles of trails to enjoy. There's also archery, skeet shooting, mountain biking and other activities. The ranch takes only 16 visitors at a time.

Dixie Dude Ranch, nine miles from Bandera on FM 1077, PO Box 548, Bandera, 78003, ☎ 830-796-4481 or 800-375-YALL, www.tourtexas.com/dixieduderanch. It's a working ranch with all the amenities you might expect from a dude ranch.

Flying L Guest Ranch & Resort, 1½ miles from Bandera off Hwy 173 south at Wharton's Dock Rd, PO Box 1959, Bandera, 78003, ☎ 830-460-3001 or 800-292-5134. A vacation spot for families and a conference resort. Caters to families with horseback riding, tennis, basketball, volleyball, swiming pool, an 18-hole golf course and trail rides that go through the State Natural Area. More of a retreat than a dude ranch, with modern structures (not rustic) and gourmet food (no cowboy campfire cuisine).

Las Campanas Guest Ranch, three miles from Lost Maples off Hwy 187, ☎ 830-966-3431. See entry on page 96.

Lost Valley Resort Ranch, Hwy 16 north, south of Bandera, PO Box 2170, Bandera, 78003, ☎ 830-460-8008. $-$$. Though it's no longer a dude ranch, it does offer horseback riding on its 580-acre spread. Also includes a swimming pool, banquet hall, 18-hole golf course, a scenic creek area and hayrides.

Mayan Dude Ranch, 6th and Pecan, two miles northwest from Bandera, ☎ 830-796-3312. $$-$$$. Packages include all meals, two daily horse rides (which are geared for novices and beginners – single file with a guide), wagon breakfasts with a country singer and complimentary beer and wine most of the day. The Medina River provides swimming and fishing. There is entertainment with each dinner, which varies by night and can include ropers, country dancing or Western bingo. Weekly rates are available.

Running R Ranch, nine miles west on FM 1077, Rt. 1, PO Box 590, Bandera, 78003, ☎ 830-796-3984. $$. The emphasis here is on the two-hour horseback ride through the State Natural Area next door. They also provide all meals.

Diamond H Ranch Bed & Breakfast, four miles west on Hwy 16, HCO2, Box 39-C, Bandera, 78003, ☎ 830-796-4820. $$. Offers a private spot on the Medina River along with a full breakfast.

Lightning Ranch, 818 FM 1283, Pipe Creek, 78063, ☎ 830-535-4096. $$. Their strong point is horseback rides that can last half a day. Three guest houses include facilities for horseshoes, swimming and volleyball. Day care for children is available.

Concan

There's not much town to Concan, a community that reportedly got its name from a Mexican gambling game called "coon can." What Concan is, though, is the hub for an area rich in dude ranches, resort camps, scenic countryside, gentle rivers and park sites.

■ Touring

Named for John Garner, former US Vice President (see above), **Garner State Park** (FM 1050 to PR 29, eight miles north of Concan, ☎ 830-232-6132, 800-792-1112) encompasses 1,420 acres, including 10 water acres of the Frio River.

The park is a Texas favorite, offering camping, hiking, nature study, picnicking, boating (non-motorized), fishing, swimming in the Frio River, paddle boat rentals (mid-March through November), bike riding, and a jukebox dance every night during summer. If you talk to enough Texans, you'll hear stories about a Garner State Park dance – they are well attended by both locals and tourists.

The park is no small affair. There is a dining hall, 5½ miles of unpaved trails for hiking, a seasonal concession with a gift store, a snack bar, a miniature golf course, paddle boats, inner tubes and laundry facilities. The park's 17 cabins are very popular, so call ahead for reservations.

Central Texas

Information Sources

Contact the **Frio Canyon Chamber of Commerce** (☎ 210-232-5222, PO Box 743, Leakey, 78873) for information about Concan and the Frio River recreational area.

■ Adventures on Foot

Lost Maples State Natural Area (two miles north of Vanderpool in extreme western Bandera County, ☎ 830-966-3413) includes almost 2,200 acres of park land and provides just about the only feel of fall (the season) in the entire state. Hungry for the sight of turning foliage, Texans and those who have moved to Texas flock to Lost Maples in October to catch a glimpse of autumn's beauty.

The park is a combination of steep, rugged limestone canyons, springs, plateau grasslands, wooded slopes and clear streams, featuring a large, isolated stand of unique Uvalde bigtooth maples, whose fall foliage can be sensational.

The maples were stranded in the area's moist canyons thousands of years ago when the last period of global warming began. While most of the surrounding area dried out and flora adapted to the arid conditions moved in, these maples survived.

Ten miles of trails connect eight different camping sites. The shortest of these trails – the Maple Trail at half a mile – passes through several stands of maple and sycamore trees. The longer trails, which are more strenuous, criss-cross the Sabinal River and Can Creek. A rich canopy covers Can Creek.

✹ Author's Tip

Generally, the leaves turn between mid-October and mid-November. Beginning in October, park rangers leave an updated telephone message as to the status of the changing foliage. Stay on designated trails as maples have a shallow root system and soil compaction from walking can damage the trees.

Visitors can enjoy picnicking, camping, backpacking, hiking, photography, birdwatching, fishing, swimming and nature study.

■ Adventures on the Water

 Concan anchors the southern end of a 31-mile stretch of the **Frio River** that is suitable for recreational purposes. With its roots in the northeastern portion of Real County, the entire Frio runs about 250 miles until in joins the Nueces and Atascosa Rivers, southeast of Concan. This easy-flowing, navigable section, which begins north of Leakey and ends around Hwy 127, is also known for its beauty, with cypress trees shading the outer fringes of the river and animals and plants native to the area. You're apt to see mountain goats scaling some of the rocky embankments or deer munching on local foliage. **Garner State Park** bisects this stretch of river.

You might want to avoid the hottest months of the year unless its been an especially wet summer. Otherwise, you'll end up walking your tube or canoe in the shallows. As a spring-fed river, it's also a bit cold. So the coldest times of the year aren't especially pleasant unless you come prepared.

There are several places to put in and take out, depending on what you're looking for and the time you want to be on the water. On the upper stretches, just south of Leakey, FM 1120 makes a half-loop off of Hwy 83, crossing the Frio on both ends. It's six miles between the two crossings. Two miles further down, FM 1050 crosses the river for another entry point.

The Frio follows the eastern edge of Garner for another three miles until CO 350 goes through the river at Magers Crossing. The longest stretch, at four miles, is next. Be on the lookout for a waterfall about one mile past the crossing. If the river is flowing swiftly, it could be hazardous. The next crossing, Third Crossing, occurs on the northern end of CO 348, which loops back across the river two miles further down. This crossing, creatively named Second Crossing, is three miles from Hwy 127, the last take out point for this section of the river. All of the last three crossings require going through the river to get to the other side. If the river is running high (or your car is abnormally low to the ground) don't attempt to cross. You can always loop around on the highways.

In general, tubers are found more frequently on the lower ends of this stretch, where the crossings are closer together. Canoes and kayaks are used more frequently on the upper stretches. The Frio is not a navigable river, so there's always a question of river depth for canoes and kayaks. (Tubers are a bit more mobile and not concerned with damaging the bottoms of their boat.) If you plan to bring your canoe or kayak, call ahead to make sure conditions are workable.

Central Texas

In 1998 there were no canoe rental facilities in the area. However, there were some in the works. Organized tube shuttle service is easily found, though it changes with the season. Rely on your lodging hosts for direction in that regard.

■ Adventures on Horseback

Both the Frio and the Sabinal River, which runs parallel to the Frio a few miles east, make this area of the world a hidden treasure. And they have historically been the main draw for outdoor enthusiasts. However, local tour operators have begun a new campaign emphasizing the area's other attributes. Horseback riding is but one of the adventures. A lot of the local bed and breakfasts will have their own horses to use, but if they don't you can call **Elm Creek Stables** (☎ 830-232-5365), two miles north of Garner State Park on Hwy 83. Also, **Neal's Lodges** (☎ 830-232-6118) has horses available.

There is an active movement to attract more **mountain bikers**. The lush terrain and river beds are perfect for a day on wheels. Between October and December, the fall foliage is absolutely breathtaking (see section on Lost Maples, Bandera, above). You can enjoy this view off-road or on-road, with either bike or car.

An interesting afternoon could be spent at the **Apple Valley Ranch** (☎ 830-232-5577), south of Leakey, west of Hwy 83. Apple harvesting begins the first week of July and you can pick your own or have them picked. They also offer orchard tours and apple tastings.

Birding has become popular as well and several rare and exotic species frequent the area. Several of the bed and breakfasts keep a careful eye out for these special birds and devote much time to taking care of them.

■ Where to Stay

These businesses offer camping and/or lodging on the Frio River outside of the Garner State Park. For the nearest hotel accommodations see the Uvalde entry.

Between 1880 and 1890, the town of Rio Frio was laid out using this big live oak tree (now the National Champion Oak) and Schoolhouse Mountain to the east as bearing points.

Yeargan's River Bend Resort, 2½ miles north of Garner State Park on Hwy 83, Concan, ☎ 830-232-6616. $$. Offers campsites, shelters, RV sites, cottages, kitchenettes and motel suites, with a café in the summer.

Neal's Lodges, Concan, ☎ 830-232-6118. $-$$$$. About 63 different cabins that vary from big and roomy to smaller and more affordable. Hayrides, horses for hire, a restaurant and volleyball courts round out the park. Neal's also offers tubes for the river and instructions on where to go. It's a seasonal enterprise running primarily between Memorial Day and Labor Day.

Rio Frio B&B and Lodging (☎ 830-966-2320), headquartered five miles east of Garner Park, offers 20 different houses, ranging from a bed and breakfast to a ranch with 16 miles of mountain biking and hiking trails. They can arrange for tubes, mountain bikes and horses. One of their newer accommodations boasts the National Champion Oak Tree for North America.

Utopia on the River, PO Box 809, Utopia, 78884, ☎ 830-966-2444, www.riverlodge.com, $$-$$$. A riverside lodge (Sabinal River), they offer tubing, fishing, hiking and jogging trails, a jacuzzi, and many more amenities.

Foxfire Cabins, HC01, Box 142, Vanderpool, 78885, ☎ 830-966-2200, $$. One mile south of Lost Maples Park.

Madrona Springs Cabins, PO Box 227, Vanderpool, 78885, ☎ 830-966-5198, $$. On the headwaters of the Sabinal River. Log cabins.

Seven Bluffs Cabins & RV Park, PO Box 184, Concan, 78838, ☎ 830-232-5260, $$-$$$. Country-style cabins (seven) in a pecan grove on the Frio.

River Oaks Resort, PO Box 303, Concan, 78838, ☎ 800-800-5773, 830-232-5117, $$$-$$$$. Hot tub and complete kitchen for each unit.

■ Where to Eat

House Pasture Cattle Country. River Road in Concan, ☎ 830-232-6580. The steaks bring in locals from 30 miles away. They also serve shrimp, quail and chicken on their property that looks out into the Hill Country.

Uvalde

■ History

A working city that depends on cattle, sheep, goats and honey production, Uvalde sits at the crossroads of two of the nation's longest highways: US 90 reaches from Florida to California and US 83 stretches from Canada to Mexico. The town has fathered and played host to several famous figures. Among them are John "Cactus Jack" Garner, who went from Uvalde to Washington DC to serve as a Senator and as Vice President under Franklin D. Roosevelt from 1933 to 1941, and Pat Garret, the lawman who killed Billy the Kid in 1881.

The most recent homespun hero is actor Matthew McConaughey, who is becoming one of the biggest box office draws in Hollywood.

■ Touring

The **Garner Museum** (333 N Park, ☎ 830-278-5018) pays tribute to "Captain Jack," who returned from Washington DC to live out the rest of his life here. He died in 1967, just before his 99th birthday.

✳ Did You Know?

Johm Garner was known for pure Texas demeanor, and for saying the vice president's office "isn't worth a bucket of warm spit."

Exhibits include a collection of over 100 gavels that were sent to Garner after he broke the gavel on his first day as Speaker of the House

The Grand Opera House (104 W North St, ☎ 830-278-4184) became a center for culture in the area after being constructed in 1891. It was one of the first two-story buildings in a mostly one-story town.

The **First State Bank/Briscoe Art Collection** (200 East Nopal St, ☎ 830-278-6231) houses an extensive array of art and antiques collected by former Texas Governor Dolph Briscoe and his wife Janey. Artists include Rembrandt, Gainsborough, and American Western artists such as Warren and Salinas.

Just south of the city on the Leona River at the base of an extinct volcano is **Fort Inge County Park** (FM 140, 1½ miles south), the site of an old US Cavalry post. The park includes hiking trails, camping, picnic tables and is a noted birdwatching locale.

Information Sources

The **Uvalde Convention and Visitors Bureau** (☎ 210-278-4115, 300 E Main Ave., 78801) can answer questions about the area. Much of the Hill Country, including Uvalde, is included on a comprehensive area Web page, www.texashillcountry.com.

■ Where to Stay

Amber Sky Motel, 2005 East Main Avenue, 78801, ☎ 830-278-5602. $. Affordable, with microwaves and refrigerators in some of the units.

Holiday Inn, 920 East Main Avenue, 78801, ☎ 830-278-4511. $$. Shuttles available, conference room, swimming pool, restaurant and guest laundry.

Casa de Leona Bed & Breakfast, 1149 Pearsall Hwy 140 (three miles from Uvalde), 78801, ☎ 830-278-8550. $$-$$$. Spanish hacienda on the

Leona River with fishing available off their pier. Located on the Fort Inge State Historical site.

■ Where to Eat

Los Alamos Mexican Restaurant, 1105 W Main St, ☎ 830-591-0083. Relatively new to Uvalde but popular with the locals. Traditional Tex-Mex fare.

Town House Restaurant, 2105 E Main St, ☎ 830-278-2428. A wide variety of standard American food.

Brackettville

■ History

Brackettville was built as a supply village for **Fort Clark** (☎ 830-563-2493, US 90, east edge of town), which was not deactivated until 1944 and included service by both General George C. Patton and General George C. Marshall. Though the fort's site is now a resort retirement community, it is open to the public and includes a number of historic buildings and museums. Of historical significance is the **Seminole Indian Scout Cemetery** (FM 3348, three miles south). Seminoles, descendants of slaves, found sanctuary among the Indians in Florida, where they began to intermarry and take up Indian identities. After the Seminole War, the black Seminoles were banished to Oklahoma.

Many Seminoles migrated south to Texas and Mexico. The US Army hired 150 of them to serve as scouts and they were assigned to Fort Clark. They served with distinction, with four receiving the Congressional Medal of Honor, the highest military award.

If you remember *The Alamo*, a movie starring John Wayne from 1959, you'll know what makes this town of 1,700 unique. **Alamo Village** (RM 674, seven miles north of town, ☎ 830-563-2580) the movie set built to film Wayne's movie, is still standing here and includes Western shows that are regularly interrupted by shootouts.

The movie industry still uses the village, complete with an Alamo, a blacksmith's shop, a bank and more than a dozen other buildings that make up an old Western set. It has been used for more than 30 feature films and movies and over 100 TV shows and commercials.

■ Touring

Kickapoo Cavern State Park (RR 674, 22 miles north – you must make arrangements before coming – ☎ 830-563-2342), formerly the Seargeant Ranch, straddles the Kinney/Edwards County line and includes more than 6,300 acres of the southern Edwards Plateau. Acquired by the state in December 1986, the park was opened to the public on a limited basis in 1991.

There are 15 known caves, two of which are large enough to be significant. Kickapoo Cavern is approximately a quarter-mile in length and boasts some impressive formations. Regularly scheduled tours are run by the Texas Parks and Wildlife division or by special arrangement. **Green Cave**, slightly shorter than Kickapoo, serves as a migratory stopover for large numbers of Brazilian freetail bats between mid-March and the end of October.

In addition to the caving, the park facilities include a primitive camping area, 14 miles of mountain biking trails and 18 miles of hiking trails.

■ Where to Stay

The **Fort Clark Springs Motel** (Hwy 90, east edge of town, ☎ 830-563-2493) might be your best bet for a place to stay. Besides Spofford, a small town 10 miles away, there are no other towns in Kinney County.

> **✳ Did You Know?**
>
> To put Kinney County on the Texas bigness scale, it is 22 square miles larger than Rhode Island.

Special Attraction

The Highland Lakes

■ History

With a course that stretches more than 900 miles, the Colorado River has nurtured human life for more than 12,000 years. It is only natural

Central Texas

that early man hovered near this water source. In many places the water literally pours from the limestone rock that encases it.

The Karankawa, a carnivorous coastal tribe, found the mouth of the Colorado a bountiful home. The Tonkawa, whose complex social system earned them their name (it means "the most human of men") lived just above the Balcones Escarpment near present day Central Texas and the Highland Lake system.

The most feared tribe in the area, the Apache most likely did not settle on the Colorado. Their semi-nomadic lifestyle followed the path of the buffalo. But the Colorado River ran smack dab through the middle of Apache territory and signs of their domination can be found up and down its bed.

The Spanish were some of the first European explorers to try settling the wild lands of Texas. Perhaps their most lasting influence is in the name they gave the river, Colorado, which means "red," and which more appropriately belonged to another river close by whose clay-silted banks are in fact deep red. That river, the Brazos, was earlier known as either "Los Brazos del Mar" (the arms of the sea) or "Los Brazos del Dios" (the arms of God.)

Apparently the name switch was a simple error. And though the early 17th-century mapmaker who transposed the names is long gone, his legacy remains.

■ Touring

Recreation on the Highland Lakes manifests itself in several forms and its economic effect on the area is tremendous. In 1993 alone, visitors made a $266 million impact.

Few lakes in the world can claim to be perfect, with moderate temperatures and clear, blue water untainted by dirt, silt or salt.

The Highland Lakes system, created by a series of dams put in place to harness the incredible and unpredictable lower Colorado River, is the jewel in Central Texas' crown. It is a testament to a new generation's ability to savor beauty in its truest form while using its power to produce electricity. It has become a vital part of both the local economy and local recreation.

Each of its six components – Buchanan, Marble Falls, Inks, LBJ, Travis and Austin – is known for something different. For water skiers, Lake Austin is a mecca. Sailors flock to Lake Travis with its wide, windy basin

Lake Austin.

and limestone-washed waters. Fishermen travel further west to harvest richer waters at Inks and Marble Falls.

Lake Austin

Long and narrow, Lake Austin is the muscle in the Highland Lake system – the souped up car that runs on pure alcohol. It is the place of choice for power boaters who revel in its unending course and flat, wonderfully ski-able water.

Austinites have built all the way up to its edges with grand estates and country cabins because its level is so constant.

Fed from the bottom of Lake Travis, it is cooler than the other lakes, which is perhaps part of its charm.

Don't let talk of numerous power boats deceive you – lined with lush trees, Lake Austin is breathtaking. As you head away from town, the grand Austin skyline at your back, there is one point where you pass beneath the beautiful rustic Loop 360 bridge. To the left is a sloping golf course. To the right, huge cliffs jut hundreds of feet straight out of the water.

Some of the best access to Lake Austin is from **Emma Long Metropolitan Park** (RR 2222, left on City Park Rd, ☎ 512-346-1831), or "City Park" as it's known to locals. With public boat ramps, designated swimming areas, camping facilities, volleyball and lots of room to spread a blanket, it's always a good place to start.

If you just need to dump your boat in the water, you can actually do that in town. Follow Lake Austin Blvd west until it dead ends at Boat Town and you'll find yourself at the southern tip of Lake Austin, with two free boat ramps at your disposal.

One of the most spectacular vantage points of Lake Austin (if you're not actually on the water) is found where Loop 360 crosses the river. On the northwestern corner of the intersection, there's a dirt turn-out for people to park and a steep path that goes up a pretty severe cliff. It doesn't take long, but it is a little difficult.

The view from the top – once you've gotten there – is breathtaking. The rustic, arched bridge lies at your feet and Lake Austin snakes through the Hill Country. To the east is the Austin skyline and you're close enough to the adjacent golf course to hear the crisp sound of golfers teeing off.

Boat Rentals

If you didn't bring your own boat, there are lots of places to rent one. For the most current selection look in the *Yellow Pages* or call the Austin Convention and Visitors Center.

Wet & Wild Rentals, ☎ 512-266-3644. Rent powerboats, ski boats, pontoon boats and party boats.

Hurst Harbor Marina. 2215 Westlake Dr, ☎ 512-347-7800. Rental and charter service.

Austin Party Cruises, ☎ 512-328-9887. Sunset cruises, company parties and catering.

Riverboats. 6917 Greenshores, ☎ 512-345-5220. Two large boats for charter.

Gilligan's Boat Rental, ☎ 512-708-8884. Late-model ski and pontoon boats.

Good Time Water Sports, ☎ 512-328-8457 or 913-4144. Boat rides, water-skiing and rentals.

Lake Travis

It's close to sunset and the crowd at the Oasis Cantina del Lago, perched on the rim of Lake Travis, knowingly turns toward the horizon. As if rehearsed, they stand as the sun dips below the verdant hillsides behind the lake and clap as the sun takes its final bow.

Seven days a week, every day of the year, the ritual continues in a symbolic gesture that signifies the place Lake Travis plays in the local mindset.

You'll hear a lot about sunsets in Texas. They seem to be a matter of local pride and Texans believe they are privy to some of the best. The deep burnt orange that crosses the sky can be attributed to the rich soils that reflect upwards and also to the people who make it a point to watch. University of Texas alumni would claim that the sunsets are a tribute to their alma mater.

The most heralded of the Highland Lakes, perhaps because of its vastness and its proximity to Austin, Lake Travis caters to all walks.

Your interests will determine where you start on this colossal recreational hotspot. Perhaps the most central place to begin is Windy Point, which offers all types of boat rentals and is a great place to spend a day or even a weekend. Located on a peninsula that juts into the main basin of Lake Travis (called simply the Basin), Windy Point is also a favorite spot for scuba divers, windsurfers and any general sunshine activity there is.

Two parks share the peninsula: **Bob Wentz Park** (☎ 512-266-3857), operated by the county, and **Windy Point Park** (☎ 512-266-3337, Comanche Trail at Ridge Top Terrace), which is privately operated. Bob Wentz is the more frequented park, offering a big empty space for sun seekers, swimmers and boaters. Windy Point Park, which charges a slightly higher entry fee, caters to scuba divers and overnight campers. They also maintain a nice, lush grassy area.

By far, the most talked about park on the lake is **Hippie Hollow** (☎ 512-473-9437), where it's acceptable to leave your clothes behind and seek the "all over" tan. Many debates have cropped up and have threatened to take away Hippie Hollow's status as a nude beach, but the park – and Austinites – have consistently held their ground. It's also OK to stay clothed if you prefer, but be prepared for an eyeful.

The **Austin Yacht Club** (5906 Beacon Dr, ☎ 512-266-1336) hosts most of the sailboat regattas on Lake Travis. All of the larger regattas are open to non-members, and each Wednesday night during the summer, the club hosts Laser and Sunfish races that are open to the public. (Boats are not provided.)

Central Texas

Boat Rentals

Lake Travis boasts a large number of charter and rental services. Call the visitor's center or use the phone book for the most current information.

Anchors Away, 16408 Stewart Rd, Yacht Harbor Marina, ☎ 512-266-2277. Boat rentals.

Commanders Point Yacht Basin, ☎ 266-2333. Rents 19- to 30-foot sailboats and can provide lessons.

Dutchman's Landing, ☎ 512-267-4289. Provides sailing instruction and rentals.

Flagship Texas, Lakeway Inn, ☎ 512-261-6484. Private charters and cruises.

Hurst Harbor Marina, 16405 Marina Point Dr, ☎ 512-266-1800. Rental and charter service.

Lakeway Marina, 103A Lakeway Dr, ☎ 512-261-7511. Rentals, charters and fishing guide service.

Resort Ranches of Lake Travis, ☎ 512-264-2533. Rental of personal watercraft up to 65-foot yachts.

Sail & Ski Center, ☎ 512-258-0733. Boat sales and lessons.

Texas Sailing Academy, ☎ 512-261-6193. Sailing instruction.

Utopian Cruises, VIP Marina at Volente Beach, ☎ 512-266-9803, Web site www.citysearch.com/aus/utopiancruises. Luxury yachts for short meetings or long vacations.

Lake Marble Falls

Lake Marble Falls is the baby of the bunch, although Inks Lake is technically smaller. Along with Lake LBJ, the two lakes virtually surround the quaint town of Marble Falls, one of the few cities in America with two lakes literally on its doorstep.

While there are traditional lake activities to enjoy on Lake Marble Falls – swimming, fishing, boating – the annual cigarette boat races are the biggest tourist attraction.

Lake LBJ

Named after native son Lyndon B. Johnson, Lake LBJ is much like Lake Travis. Big and wide on its southern edge, the lake narrows and winds north along the Colorado River. Besides being a recreational mecca, it has become a premiere retirement community. Its shores are dotted with weekend resorts and condominiums.

It's a lot like what Lake Travis used to be – calm and soft. Distance has kept the masses of Austin from overrunning the lake. It doesn't make sense for a day-trip, but it certainly does for the weekend. So it attracts a little different crowd, those that are content to soak in the sun from their porch and read a book.

> ✱ **Did You Know?**
>
> There are probably more watercraft here than cars and you're liable to see a resident hauling groceries home on a Wave Runner – it's faster by water.

Inks Lake

Inks Lake may be the shortest of the Highland Lakes, but it is one of the prettiest. Water-skiers that are serious about their sport will drive the extra distance to practice on its calm waters, undisturbed by the masses that flood Lake Austin.

Inks Lake State Park (TX 29 east to PR 4 south, ☎ 512-793-2223), to the south, provides tranquillity. Many lake connoisseurs believe it is the most beautiful lake in the system. The **Inks Lake National Fish Hatchery** (☎ 512-793-2474), which adjoins the park three miles down the road, produces over a million fish annually to stock lakes across the Southwest.

Lake Buchanan

When the Buchanan Dam was built it was considered the longest multiple-arch dam in the country, at just over two miles long. Views from atop the dam stretch hundreds of miles along the Colorado River. Eight miles across at its widest point, every water sport imaginable can be found here.

One of the most popular attractions here is the **Vanishing Texas River Cruise** (reservations required, ☎ 800-728-8735 or 512-756-6986, www.highlandlakes.com/cruise/), which offers a variety of tours on Lake Buchanan. During winter months their boat takes you to the nesting ground of an American bald eagle. Another trip takes you to the Colorado Bend State Park, where visitors can hike and swim. A recent tour addition makes a stop at Fall Creek Vineyards for a visit to the winery and a wine tasting.

■ Where to Stay

 The Edgewater, Southwest Lake Buchanan, Hwy 29 to 261 Lakeshore Dr, ☎ 512-793-2818. $$-$$$. Cabins along Lake Buchanan with small fishing boats for rent. Designed for family vacations, with camping, fishing guides and souvenirs.

Hi-Line Resort & Marina, Northwest Lake Buchanan, ☎ 888-379-1065 or 915-379-1065, www.highlandlakes.com/hiline/. $-$$. Water activities for the entire family. Its 1,800 feet of waterfront include a 24-hour crappy house (a building over water that has holes in the floor to fish through), a beach area, jet ski rentals and fully equipped cottages.

Lake Point Resort, South Lake Buchanan, Hwy 29 near the dam, ☎ 888-793-2918 or 512-793-2918, www.hunt-fish.com/lpoint2. $-$$. The resort retains the charm of the 1940s, with quaint cottages, fishing, canoeing, paddle-boating and skiing.

✳ Did You Know?

The 1997 movie remake of *Lolita*, starring Melanie Griffith and Jeremy Irons, was filmed at Lake Point Resort.

Lakeside Lodge, Lake Buchanan, ☎ 512-756-4935. $-$$. With only six rooms, the Lakeside Lodge is a quiet place to enjoy the lake. It offers a beach, fishing areas, free breakfast and massage therapy.

Main Street B&B, 808 N Main, Burnet, ☎ 512-756-2861. $$-$$$. Right in town, this quaint 1930s B&B offers weekly rates.

The Texas Coast

■ The Land

The Texas coast is like no other. Stretching about 367 miles as the crow flies along a gentle arc that makes up the northwestern edge of the Gulf of Mexico, there are actually over 3,300 miles of shoreline along its islands, bays and river mouths.

The Gulf of Mexico is gentle in its mix and mild in its temperature. Visitors from the Western and Eastern seaboards find the warm temperatures disarming. The beaches are wide and the sand is fine. Of course, it's no Riviera. Nor do Texans want it to be. There's a price to be paid for things like that.

No, Texas beaches are just what you'd expect if you mingled a Texan with the coast. Big, friendly, laid-back, hospitable and sometimes a little rowdy.

Barrier islands stretch all the way from Galveston to Brownsville. Padre, the longest of these islands, runs uninterrupted for 113 miles.

The anchor, both literally and figuratively, is South Padre Island. Many consider the seaside village of Galveston a natural treasure. Entertaining visitors is its sole purpose. With an opulent past that includes a myriad of mansions and a bundle of old Southern money, it anchors the northern end. But if you're looking for actual beaches, the farther south you go, the better.

The Texas coast continues to be a hub of activity for oil and gas industries. The coast produces a third of the entire state's wealth.

Houston sits at the crossroads of the coast and East Texas. It's not quite on the coast, yet its big industrial port is the largest in the state. Houston is an area of Texas unto itself, a sprawling mass of asphalt and people. But as the gateway to the south, it is inextricably coupled with Galveston and the rest of the coast.

The Texas Coast

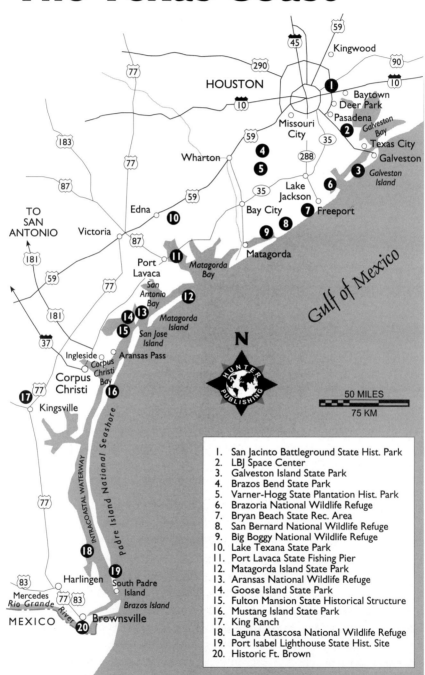

1. San Jacinto Battleground State Hist. Park
2. LBJ Space Center
3. Galveston Island State Park
4. Brazos Bend State Park
5. Varner-Hogg State Plantation Hist. Park
6. Brazoria National Wildlife Refuge
7. Bryan Beach State Rec. Area
8. San Bernard National Wildlife Refuge
9. Big Boggy National Wildlife Refuge
10. Lake Texana State Park
11. Port Lavaca State Fishing Pier
12. Matagorda Island State Park
13. Aransas National Wildlife Refuge
14. Goose Island State Park
15. Fulton Mansion State Historical Structure
16. Mustang Island State Park
17. King Ranch
18. Laguna Atascosa National Wildlife Refuge
19. Port Isabel Lighthouse State Hist. Site
20. Historic Ft. Brown

■ Logistics

There is no shortage of flights coming into town. With two airports – George Bush Intercontinental on the northern side and Hobby on the southeast (closer to the coast) – it is served well. Continental Airlines counts Houston as its hub.

Southwest Airlines has been the most visible, with service to South Padre Island (or Brownsville, next door), but other commuter flights frequent the region's southern tip.

A car is your best bet for enjoying the areas in between. It's a long drive to South Padre – consider a flight unless you especially enjoy driving.

■ Weather & Climate

The weather is usually gentle and predictable. Sunshine and a gentle breeze are the norm. Since Houston is a bit inland, it often receives a little more weather than the rest of the coast. In addition, it competes vigorously with New Orleans for the title of "Most Humid City in the World" during the summer months. There's not much advice for avoiding the humidity. You can just avoid the hot months or else go straight to the coast (or stay air-conditioned at all times, as the locals do).

Houston

■ History

Houston began like a lot of things in Texas – out of earnest braggadocio and temerity. John and Augustus Allen, two flamboyant brothers, purchased a spot of land where the San Jacinto River joins the Buffalo Bayou in 1836, cleverly named their new "settlement" for the contemporary and popular war hero Sam Houston, and then placed a newspaper ad enjoining settlers to come to their new oasis. The barely settled town, with a fancy map and a good game plan, was voted the capital of the Republic of Texas.

The town's success was briefly tested in 1839 when a yellow fever scare sent wagons carrying the Republic's archives into Austin. Houston never did recover the archives – or capital of Texas status – but by then its commercial pursuits and its wise placement 50 miles inland from the Gulf of Mexico made it the center of a booming economy, outdone only by its sister Galveston.

The Texas Coast

On Sept. 8, 1900, the day Galveston's opulence and grandeur were wiped out by the most devastating hurricane in American history, Houston became the star of Texas, a role it has never given up.

Today, the actual city of Houston covers 581 square miles, the metropolis covers 8,788 square miles – an area more than double the size of Rhode Island. The city sprawls across three counties – Harris, Fort Bend and Montgomery – and is the fourth largest city in the United States, with more than 1.7 million residents. The metropolitan area tops 4.1 million residents.

Houston serves as a major US gateway for international trade and commerce. Each year, more than 5,500 ships pass through its waters. The port runs along the Houston Ship Channel, a 50-mile inland waterway approximately six miles east of Houston's downtown business district, and is home to a $15 billion petrochemical complex, the largest in the nation and the second largest in the world.

Houston's airport system – fourth largest in the nation and sixth largest in the world – currently counts around 2,000 incoming flights a day. Its predictably warm weather has made it a hub for international travel – Continental Airlines uses the city as its southern hub. Getting to Houston by plane is no problem. Just about every airline provides service to the city's two airports: Intercontinental and Hobby.

Houstonions are still hot under the hat about the Oilers football franchise pulling up roots and landing in Tennessee, but there are several other professional sports teams that call Houston home, including the Astros (baseball), the two-time NBA world champion Rockets (basketball), the Hotshots (soccer), the Aeros (hockey), the Texas Terror (arena football) and a new professional women's basketball team, the Houston Comets.

Houston's claims to fame are many and varied. The world held its collective breath as Neil Armstrong and his fellow astronauts landed Apollo 11 on the moon. Armstrong's first words, "Houston, Tranquility base here. The Eagle has landed," sent shock waves around the world. Houston will forever be remembered for its ties with NASA and its role in space history.

Another Houston icon is the Texas Medical Center, which encompasses 42 nonprofit groups and is the largest medical center in the world. Estimated to have upwards of a $10 billion a year impact on the city, the Center is the largest employer in the city and more than 110,000 patients walk through its doors each day.

Located just south of Rice University, the "Harvard of the South," the Center's credits are immense. Heart surgery owes many of its innovations to the Center's doctors. In 1968 Dr. Denton Cooley performed the first successful heart transplant at St. Luke's Hospital in the complex. In 1969 he went further and implanted the first artificial heart.

Fellow doctor Michael DeBakey performed the first successful coronary bypass in 1964 here. M.D. Anderson Cancer Center has been instrumental in cancer research – chemotherapy was introduced here late in the 1940s, and the center continues to be one of the finest in the world in the fight against cancer.

The city's known for more obscure things. While Dallas represents old money, Houston is the new. Its high rollers cashed in on the oil boom and went bust in the glut. Its sequined women have big hair and bright lipstick. (Breast implants got their start here.)

Perhaps the saga surrounding Anna Nicole Smith, a large-breasted former dancer who married an elderly oil tycoon and made national headlines, says it best. Houston is loud and boisterous, not stoic and staid.

Lots of people call Houston home. Former President George W. Bush was sometimes snickered at by Texans when he ran on a Presidential ticket counting Houston as his home town. In his retirement, though, he is the revered son – both the Convention Center and International Airport honor his name.

Houston is cosmopolitan in its ethnic diversity, with more than 90 different languages spoken by its international ensemble. Caucasions represent 43% of Houstonions, 23% are Hispanic, 19% are African-American and 4% are Asian. Of more than 500 cultural organizations, close to 20% are devoted solely to minority art and multicultural enterprises.

Houston is the largest unzoned city in America – you'll notice there is no method to settlement, with odd pockets of commercial and residential properties cropping up where you wouldn't expect them. Houston leaders have historically believed capitalism is the best device for settlement.

Technically speaking, Houston hasn't earned the distinction of being the hottest Texas city – Dallas earns that honor – but you wouldn't be able to tell. Houston, like its fellow Gulf of Mexico sister New Orleans, has the potential to be downright miserable in the summer, with humidity that hovers near 100% at all times.

Houston

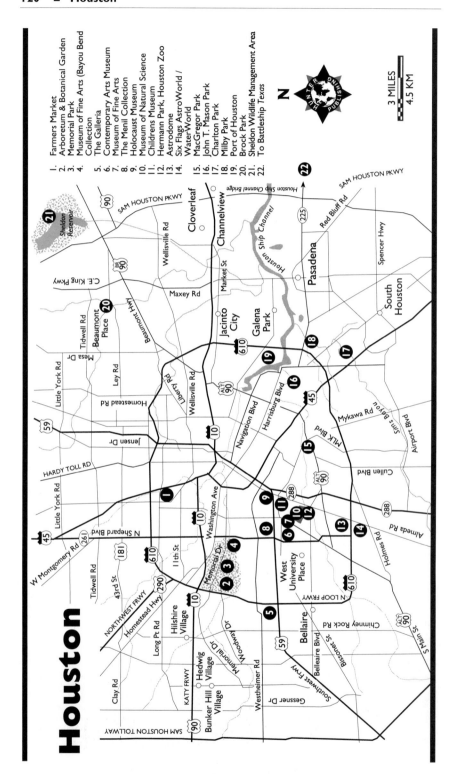

1. Farmers Market
2. Arboretum & Botanical Garden
3. Memorial Park
4. Museum of Fine Arts (Bayou Bend Collection
5. The Galleria
6. Contemporary Arts Museum
7. Museum of Fine Arts
8. The Menil Collection
9. Holocaust Museum
10. Museum of Natural Science
11. Childrens Museum
12. Hermann Park, Houston Zoo
13. Astrodome
14. Six Flags AstroWorld / WaterWorld
15. MacGregor Park
16. John T. Mason Park
17. Charlton Park
18. Milby Park
19. Port of Houston
20. Brock Park
21. Sheldon Wildlife Management Area
22. To Battleship Texas

3 MILES
4.5 KM

> **✳ Author's Tip**
>
> If you're coming to Houston just to see Houston, don't come during the late summer months. Spring, fall or the mild winters are a better time to visit.

■ Touring

Texans think large, but most Texans still think Houston is the biggest darn city they've ever seen. When someone asks you how long it takes to drive there, your answer is always "which part?" It's an easy hour – with no traffic – from end to end. You don't even want to know what it is with traffic. Congestion in the 90s has been lessening as the population surge crested and city planners were able to catch up. Though it's not as bad as Los Angeles (can any city be that bad?), you'll still want to take preventative measures when driving so that you don't hit rush hour.

Perhaps the easiest place to start is downtown. Like many cities, Houston's downtown deteriorated with the rise of the suburbs, but has enjoyed a recent revitalization that includes about $1 billion in different facelifts. It is again a thriving central hub for the area.

The most recent renovation is in the heart of the theater district in the Old Albert Thomas Convention Center. Pumping $23 million into the structure, investors have created **Bayou Place**, which they consider to

The Houston skyline.

be "the state's largest entertainment facility," with a concert performance hall, restaurants, cafés and several nightclubs.

Other developments along Buffalo Bayou include the **Houston Common**, a grand outdoor performance center and hub for the area, and **Sesquicentennial Park**, a 10-acre site developed to commemorate Texas' 150th birthday.

Tranquillity Park, bordered by Smith, Walker, Bagby and Rusk Streets, derived its name from the Moon's Sea of Tranquillity. Pleasant during the day – with huge copper fountains, lush grounds and futuristic pieces – it is not considered safe at night.

Beneath the buildings downtown you'll find a cool underworld, a maze of tunnels that wind beneath the city's streets. While Canadian and other cool-weather towns use similar systems to keep away from the cold, Houstonites find the tunnels an air-conditioned wonderland and make the most of them during the humid summer months. **TunnelWalks** (☎ 713-222-9255), hosted by Sandra Lord, will lead you through the labyrinth and provide an in-depth study of the why and how. Lord will also point out all of the shops, galleries, fountains and seasonal stops.

Still standing after several generations of renovations, **La Carafe** (813 Congress, ☎ 713-229-9399) holds the title of oldest commercial building in town, somehow having escaped the wrath of the wrecking ball and the asphalt zealots. The narrow bar, opened in 1845, is a popular hangout for locals to kick back and relax. In its lifetime it has operated as a trading post, apothecary, Confederate arsenal and bakery. It's perfect after a Thursday evening outing at **Party-on-the-Plaza** (Jones Plaza), a very well-attended free concert in the park series that runs from March through September. Every Thursday a large crowd gently descends on this downtown park to hear the sounds of Texas' favorite musicians.

Southwest of downtown, off Hwy 59 – referred to as the Southwest Freeway – is the museum district, with the highest concentration of art in town.

With no permanent collection, the **Contemporary Arts Museum** (5216 Montrose, ☎ 713-284-8250, www.camh.org) will never get stale. There are exhibit areas for both established and new artists. And the stainless steel exterior of the museum's building sets it apart from its surroundings, making it truly "contemporary."

Dominique de Menil and her husband, John, amassed more than 10,000 pieces of fine art – that's why the **Menil Museum** (1515 Sul Ross, ☎ 713-525-9400, www.menil.org/~menil) had to take up residence in a

100,000-square-foot building. The Menils' taste runs the gamut, from Byzantine to tribal to medieval.

Nearby is the **Rothko Chapel** (1409 Sul Ross, ☎ 713-524-9839), an all-denominational sanctuary featuring works by Mark Rothko, the American abstract painter.

The **Museum of Fine Arts** (1001 Bissonnet, ☎ 713-639-7300, http://mfah.org) is a sparkling jewel in Houston's cap, visited by hundreds of thousands of visitors each year. Its collections run the gamut – from Frederic Remington's work to Renaissance pieces from Italy and Spain to native arts from several different continents. As many as 20 different traveling exhibits a year stop by to complement the wide ranging collection.

Across the street is the **Lillie and Hugh Roy Cullen Sculpture Garden** (Bissonnet at Montrose, ☎ 713-639-7300), embracing abstract and modern sculpture.

For all you who dreamed of being fire fighters, **Houston's Fire Museum** (2403 Milam, ☎ 713-524-2526) can give a quick peek into the profession's past, which has progressed substantially since the days of the bucket brigade (which is documented). There's also an 1892 steam fire engine, a water tower truck and the coffee wagon that the Ladies Auxiliary used to operate. (They would bring coffee out to the working firemen.)

An actual Apollo capsule, along with artifacts from the Mercury, Gemini and Apollo missions, are in the basement of the **Houston Museum of Natural Science** (1 Hermann Circle Drive, ☎ 713-639-4629, www.hmns.mus.tx.us) in the Isaac Arnold Hall of the Space Science portion of the museum. But the beauty of this museum – more a complex – is that you can explore space travel, dinosaurs, medical science, petroleum or a planetarium. A confederation of exhibits and displays, the Museum of Natural Science has something for everyone. Perhaps the biggest draw is the **Wortham IMAX Theater** (☎ 713-639-4629 for shows and times), a six-story movie screen that can make you jump out of your seat.

Another six-story feature in the museum is the **Cockrell Butterfly Center** (☎ 713-639-4600), which invites visitors into a lush retreat complete with a 40-foot waterfall and hundreds of exotic butterflies.

The Children's Museum (1500 Binz, ☎ 713-522-1138), with its colorful face, is hands-on for infants to pre-teen. You can't miss its bright exterior.

The anchor of the museum district, **Hermann Park** (Hermann Drive at Fannin, ☎ 713-845-1000) contains a golf course, the zoo, Miller Outdoor

Theater and the Museum of Natural Sciences. Manicured flowers dot the large swathe of green. There's a duck pond, a tea garden, a miniature train and lots of room for strolling and picnicking.

Just west of downtown, on a 20-acre spread, **Sam Houston Park** (1100 Bagby St, ☎ 713-655-1912) maintains a number of the city's first buildings. The on-site Museum of Texas History changes its exhibits periodically.

One of the things Houston prides itself on is its arts – even for its size, it is a cultural mecca, with several organizations bringing in world-class shows. In addition to a sophisticated opera and symphony, the **Society for Performing Arts** (☎ 800-828-ARTS, 713-227-ARTS), **Theatre Under the Stars** (☎ 800-678-5440), **Main Street Theater**, the **Ensemble Theatre** (☎ 713-520-0055), the **Alley Theatre** (☎ 800-259-ALLE, 713-228-8421), **Da Camera** (☎ 713-524-5050) and the **Houston Broadway Series** (☎ 713-622-SHOW, 7469) make every night of the week a show night. It is possible to see a different play, musical, opera, etc. every day for weeks on end (though it might be a little costly).

Bayou Bend (1 Westcott St, ☎ 713-862-5890), a 28-room mansion, boasts a lifetime's collection of antiques and pieces of art. Given to the Museum of Fine Arts by Ima Hogg, a philanthropist who spread great wealth along the coast, the mansion has been open to the public since 1966 and includes 4,800 works that span several centuries. The 14-acre garden, bounded on three sides by the Buffalo Bayou, is comprised of both formal gardens and natural woodlands.

Another image of Houston etched into the world's brain is of the **Astrodome** (8400 Kirby Dr at Loop 610 South, ☎ 713-799-9500, home ground for the Houston Astros, the world's first indoor stadium, deemed the "Eighth Wonder of the World" when it originally opened in 1965. It made history with the introduction of a substance called "Astroturf" – now standard fare for sporting stadiums around the world. You can take a tour (unless an event is scheduled) through the behemoth that is home to the Houston Astros and used to be home to the NFL franchise, the Oilers.

Kids will more appreciate **Six Flags Houston AstroWorld** (9001 Kirby, ☎ 713-799-1234), with more than 100 rides designed to make you scream, and **Waterworld** (part of the same complex). The Texas Cyclone is considered one of the best roller coasters in the country; Runaway River boasts a number of what seem to be sheer drop-offs. AstroWorld's Batman the Escape coaster is one of the park's most recent additions; the Mayan Mindbender, an indoor roller coaster, is another

NASA/Johnson Space Center.

favorite. Waterworld (no relation to the Kevin Costner film) boasts a man-made beach, simulated ocean waves and a high dive.

The Houston Rockets, two-time world champions and the long-time home of perennial NBA favorite Hakeem Olajuwon, call the **Compaq Center** home (formerly the Summit, US 59 at Edloe, ☎ 713-961-9003). The center can accommodate almost 20,000 fans and is a part of the Greenway Plaza business complex.

People pay tribute to a lot of inanimate objects, sometimes in unique ways. Perhaps one of the most extraordinary examples of this is the **Orange Show** (2401 Munger, ☎ 713-926-6368), a tribute by the late Jeff McKissack to his fruit of choice. McKissack, described as a "trucker/postman/folk artist," built and decorated his own orange palace with murals and miscellaneous junk. Houston holds on dearly to this enterprise and since McKissack's passing in the 1980s, the Orange Show Foundation has kept the local pop icon's citrusy home open to visitors.

When the Eagle landed, Houston's place in the space spotlight was secured. A visit to the **NASA/Johnson Space Center** (I-45, 25 miles southeast of downtown, off NASA Rd 1, ☎ 281-244-2100), is a treat worth going out of your way for. This is where they train all of America's astronauts. Of course, they won't let you into the control booth or any other delicate area – NASA is very much a working operation, coordinating much of the design and development for the Shuttle and the US Space Station. But they have designed tours to give you both a working and historical perspective of the US space program. There are actual spacecraft to touch, flight simulators and tram tours.

Shopping is considered an adventure in Houston, with some of the finest malls the state has to offer. The **Post Oak-Galleria** area (I-610, Westheimer and Post Oak Rd) is perhaps the poshest, with a Neiman Marcus, Saks Fifth Ave, Macy's and more. The Galleria alone greets an average of 10,000 shoppers a day. For funkier and more eclectic musings, try the **Montrose** shopping district (bounded by Main, Sunset, Shepherd and West Gray) or the antique wonderland in the **Houston Heights** area (bounded by 11th, Heights Blvd, Studemont and Yale).

In February and early March, the social season hinges on the **Houston Livestock Show and Rodeo** (☎ 713-791-9000). While that may sound a little strange, Houston's relationship with the annual event is, well, unexplainable. More than 11,000 Houstonions volunteer to put on the world's largest rodeo. In 1996, 1.8 million people came to the two-week event. Auction sales topped $7 million. Held at the Astrodome (it's grown out of ordinary arenas), the rodeo features some of the best in country music. Even Elvis played here.

The **Houston Zoological Gardens** (1513 N MacGregor, ☎ 713-523-5888) may not be the best zoo in Texas, but recent additions and improvements have brought it close. Over 350 exhibits and 3,500 animals carouse here. There's a petting zoo for the kiddos.

The Rodeo.

If you're looking to dust your boots and can't make the rodeo, there are a number of ranches in and around Houston that cater to ranching adventure. The **Oil Ranch** (☎ 281-859-1616, Hockley) is the perfect family host, with hay rides, pony rides and a farm animal petting zoo. There's also a pool and paddleboats. You can watch ranchhands (it's a working ranch) perform their daily duties.

The largest equestrian center along the coast is just south in League City. **Stardust Trailrides** (☎ 281-332-9370) offers a variety of trail rides among its 1,000 acres. "The Taste of Texas," an evening trail ride, includes a barbecue dinner and a cowboy serenade.

If you prefer watching to participating, try the **4-N Ranch** (☎ 281-991-0671) on a Friday night for the weekly Bulls and Barrels rodeo. For another glimpse of the cowboy life go to the **George Ranch Historical Park** (☎ 281-545-9212, Richmond), which bills itself as a "living museum." The park is a portion of a 23,000 acre working cattle ranch. Costumed guides take you from the 1830s to present day with historic homes and a cowboy campsite.

Information Sources

There are several sources to contact for additional information on the Houston area. You can contact the **Houston Visitors and Convention Bureau** (☎ 800-365-7575, 801 Congress, 77002, www.houston-guide.com), the **Houston Chamber of Commerce** (☎ 713-522-9745, 2808 Wheeler Ave., 77004), and the **Clear-Lake/NASA Area Convention and Visitors Bureau** (☎ 713-488-7676, 1201 Nasa Rd. 1, Houston, 77058). Lycos maintains a Houston visitor spot, as well, at http://cityguide.lycos.com/southwest/HoustonTX.html.

■ Adventures on Foot

Nestled into the southeast corner of I-10 and Loop 610, two of the city's most important arteries, is **Memorial Park** (off Memorial Drive, ☎ 713-845-1000), a flash of green in a field of pavement. The park's two square miles of natural beauty, running up against the Buffalo Bayou, are perfect for jogging, canoeing and hiking. This "yuppie park" includes a three-mile jogging trail, tennis courts and cycling facilities.

Houston Arboretum and Nature Center (4501 Woodway, ☎ 713-681-8433) includes more than 450 native plants and covers almost 200 acres. Guided tours of the indigenous forest, as well as educational programs, are free throughout the day.

Rock climbers are pretty much out of luck in terms of natural geological formations in the flat Houston area. They've taken to what they term "buildering," an illegal and punishable art of scaling interesting buildings. Several area rock climbing gyms have jumped in to fill the weekday void, but if you're really looking for rock climbing, head west to the Austin area. Area gyms include: **Texas Rock Gym**, 9716 Old Katy Rd, Suite 102, ☎ 713-973-ROCK and 201 Hobbs Road, Suite A1, League City, ☎ 281-338-ROCK (www.texrockgym.com); **Exposure Indoor Rock Climbing**, 6970-C FM 1960 West, ☎ 281-397-9446.

■ Adventures on Wheels

 The **Alkek Velodrome** (19008 Samus Rd, ☎ 281-578-0858), created for the 1986 Olympic Festival, will let you pedal away to get your bicycle fix. Call ahead for the agenda of the day – track bikes only on certain days. You can rent a bike there if you prefer.

Using wheels of a different sort, you can get a good look at some of Houston's opulence by driving through **River Oaks**, a magnificent series of mansions.

■ Adventures on the Water

 Clear Lake and Galveston are extensions of the Greater Houston Metroplex, providing all the water activities you could possibly want. The Gulf of Mexico's warm tropical waters are a year-round resource for sailors, wind-surfers, etc. Some try their hand at surfing these beaches, but you'd be better off heading further south down to Padre Island and Corpus Christi where the waves are a little larger.

Two boat charters to try out are **At the Helm** (Kemah, ☎ 281-334-2840), a sailing school and team building enterprise, and **Galveston Party Boats** (Pier 19, Galveston, ☎ 281-222-7025 or ☎ 409-763-5423). They will do all the work for you.

The **Armand Bayou Nature Center** (8500 Bay Area Blvd, ☎ 281-474-2551, www.ghgcorp.com/abnc/), at 2,000 acres, is one of the area's largest preserves, boasting a variety of different terrains. It protects some of the last remnants of the area's original ecosystem, which included wetlands, bottomland forest and tall grass prairies.

Clear Lake.

There are over five miles of walking trails winding through the woodland and prairie regions. The trails are primitive and not suitable for bicycles or strollers.

Discovering the Armand Bayou – one of the last bayous in the Houston area that has not been channelized – can be done in various ways. Canoe trips (reservations required) take off on specified Saturday mornings for a three-mile adventure. Pontoon boat rides are also available at breakfast and sunset on Saturdays. When the moon is full or close to it, a moonlight cruise is offered. Bring your own boat for a more personal tour.

■ Where to Stay

 Angel Arbor Bed & Breakfast, 848 Heights Blvd, 77007 ☎ 713-868-4654, 800-722-8788, www.angelarbor.com. $$-$$$. Minutes from downtown, this 1923 landmark is known as the McTighe-Durham House. In addition to accommodations, there are Marguerite's renowned Murder Mystery Dinner Parties (Marguerite is the host).

Crown Plaza Galleria, 2222 W Loop South, 77027, ☎ 713-961-7272. $$-$$$. Central to all major freeways, the Crown Plaza is convenient for most business travelers.

Double R Ranch, Sealy, ☎ 409-732-5999. A working cattle ranch with a hunting preserve that's open from September through March. Has camping facilities, as well.

Patrician Bed & Breakfast, 1200 Southmore Ave, 77004, ☎ 800-553-5797, 713-523-1114. $$$. Right in the museum district, walking distance from Hermann Park. A 1919 three-story colonial revival house.

Hotel Sofitel, 425 N Sam Houston Parkway East, 77060, ☎ 800-231-4612, 281-445-9000. $$$. The outdoor tropical pool is just one of the hotel's elegant touches. Very close to Intercontinental with luxury dining and accommodations.

Houston Marriott Airport Hotel, 18700 John F. Kennedy Blvd, 77032, ☎ 281-443-2310. $$$. The revolving restaurant on top is a sure crowd pleaser. Easy access to Houston's Intercontinental Airport by underground courtesy tram. All amenities; health club is open 24 hours.

Four Seasons Hotel, 1300 Lamar, 77010, ☎ 713-650-1300. $$$-$$$$. For the more high-end traveler, there's no skimping. Underground access to the airport and some very fine dining.

Lancaster, 701 Texas, 77002, ☎ 713-228-9500. The 1920s-style building (recently renovated) lacks some of the high-end amenities, but has a better atmosphere than most.

Lovett Inn, 501 Lovett Blvd, 77009, ☎ 800-779-5224, 713-522-5224. $$-$$$. A bed and breakfast for anyone's taste.

Nassau Bay Hilton and Marina, 3000 NASA Rd 1, 77058, ☎ 800-634-4320, 281-333-9300. $$$. Just across the street from the Johnson Space Center on the shores of Clear Lake.

Omni Houston In the Galleria, Four Riverway, 77056, ☎ 713-871-8181. Elegant, with spectacular views. A bit off the beaten path (but not by far), the Omni offers a town car that will ferry you to close attractions.

Robin's Nest Bed & Breakfast, 4104 Greeley St, 77006, ☎ 800-622-8343, 713-528 5821, www.houstonbnb.com. In the heart of the arts and museum district. The owner has restored the two-story house to its original state (plus indoor plumbing as a bonus).

Sara's Bed & Breakfast Inn, 941 Heights Blvd, 77008, ☎ 800-593-1130, 713-868-1130. $$-$$$. The century-old dwelling offers 12 rooms, many of which have clawfoot tubs and other treats.

■ Where to Eat

 With over 7,000 restaurants in Houston – lots of them with stars attached to their stature – it's impossible to do justice to Houstonites' culinary skill in just a few pages. They range from the hole-in-the-wall to the ultra-formal.

Américas, 1800 Post Oak Blvd, ☎ 713-961-1492. The exotic interior is a tell-tale sign of the restaurant's experimental nature, using indigenous New World foods to create exotic menu items like potato-crusted calamari.

Andy's Home Café Breakfast, 1115 E 11th St, ☎ 713-861-9423. Close to several live music venues, Andy's is an all-nighter. The food is average, but it seems better than that at 4 am.

Anthony's, 4007 Westheimer, ☎ 713-961-0552. Anthony's has been a place to be seen for decades in one of the city's trendiest and poshest neighborhoods. The menu is American with lots of zing and the wine list is extensive.

Arcodoro, 5000 Westheimer, Ste. 120, ☎ 713-621-6888. Under the direction of a couple of native Sardinians, the Arcodoro ("Arch of Gold") is real Italian with risottos and fresh, simple dishes.

Benihana of Tokyo, 707 Westheimer, ☎ 713-789-4962, and 1318 Louisiana, ☎ 713-659-8231. Benihana's has been a Houston mainstay for decades. It's one of the most revered Japanese restaurants.

Berryhill Hot Tamales, 2639 Revere, ☎ 713-526-8080. Locals flock here for tasty fish tacos and tamales.

Brennan's Of Houston, 3300 Smith, ☎ 713-522-9711. You get to sign the walls, attesting to this Creole kitchen's culinary accomplishments. Jackets are required at dinner; brunch is a trendy time to hob-nob.

The Brownstone Restaurant, 2736 Virginia, ☎ 713-520-5666. One of the city's best places for a romantic interlude. The menu embraces European fare, with a touch of Creole.

Cavatore Italian Restaurant, 2120 Ella, ☎ 713-869-6622. Fine dining, including veal and seafood, in a restored 90-year-old barn.

Chez Georges, 11920-G Westheimer, ☎ 281-497-1122. Monique and Georges Guy have created one of the most authentic French restaurants in town. Leave room for dessert.

Dave and Buster's, 6010 Richmond Ave, ☎ 713-952-2233. For kids and kids-at-heart, it's food mixed in with billiards, shuffleboard, blackjack and a gaming paradise.

Goode Co. Barbecue, 5109 Kirby and other locations, ☎ 713-522-2530. Caféteria-style access means that you can get to the tender barbecue all the faster. The walls are littered with pieces of Texana. Popular with the locals.

The Texas Coast

Great Caruso, 10001 Westheimer, ☎ 713-780-4900. Your baked Alaska will be lots of fun with a singing waitstaff that carouses around in a re-created Victorian music hall. Reservations are required.

Joe's Crab Shack - An Embarrassment To Any Neighborhood, 6218 Richmond, ☎ 713-952-5400; 14901 North Frwy, ☎ 281-875-5400; 2621 South Loop West, ☎ 713-683-7383; and 12400 Gulf Freeway, ☎ 713-910-3232. Though they've branched out across the state, the same lively fishing camp atmosphere remains. Boiled crabs and other seafood.

Kim Son, 2001 Jefferson, 5731 Westheimer and 8200 Wilcrest, ☎ 713-222-2461, 713-783-0054 and 281-498-7841. A true rags-to-riches story. The La family, with its exquisite Vietnamese dishes, has made Kim Son a Houston icon. The downtown location is the centerpiece of their newly created dynasty.

La Colombe d'Or, 3410 Montrose, ☎ 713-524-7999. French food found its place in the former home of Walter Fondren, founder of Exxon.

La Griglia, 2002 W Gray, ☎ 713-526-4700. Things are hopping at this Italian hotspot where many Houstonians go to be seen.

La Mora, 912 Lovett Blvd, ☎ 713-522-7412. A welcome change from the frenzied pace of Houston dining, La Mora makes its home in a converted house. A loyal following enjoys its intimate nature and its Italian fare.

La Tour D'Argent, 2011 Ella Blvd, ☎ 713-864-9864. French cuisine served up in a log cabin. Reservations recommended.

Magnolia Bar & Grill, 6000 Richmond Ave, ☎ 713-781-6207. Further evidence of Houston's demand for neighboring Louisiana's Cajun cui-sine, Magnolia's has appeared on several lists (local and national) as a favorite dining spot.

Michelangelo's, 307 Westheimer, ☎ 713-524-7836. Don't mind the massive oak in the middle of the dining room – it's been in this down-town Italian eatery for three decades.

Ouisie's Table, 3939 San Felipe, ☎ 713-528-2264. The herb garden produces fresh ingredients daily for their American dishes. Set in a re-stored ranch house.

Billy Blues Bar & Grill, 6025 Richmond, ☎ 713-266-9294. The 63-foot saxophone tells you you've reached your destination; this sumptuous barbecue place is one of the city's landmarks.

Pappasito's Cantina, 6445 Richmond and other locations, ☎ 713-784-5253. The Pappas brothers have maintained and grown a restaurant chain and still the waiting lists are an hour long. Their huge warehouse-size restaurants are always packed because they serve some of the best Mexican food in town. Exquisite fajitas (with incredible pico de gallo and spicy butter cream) and fresh ceviche.

The Pappas Brothers

Though the Pappas brothers started with Mexican food, they didn't stop there. The city has what seem to be hundreds of restaurants with the name Pappas – all of them considered among the best in town. You will not be able to go down any major street without seeing them – their addresses are too numerous to list. If you see one, look around. They seem to come in clumps (that way you have a choice). Some of their other restaurants include: Pappas Brisket House, Pappadeaux Seafood Kitchen, Pappamia Cucina Italiano, Little Pappas Seafood Kitchen, Pappas Seafood House and Pappas Bros. Steak House.

Ruggles Grill, 903 Westheimer, ☎ 713-524-3839. A spirited stop for locals looking for good food at reasonable prices. American cuisine with pastas, seafoods and a huge selection of fresh vegetables.

Sammy's Lebanese Restaurant, 5825 Richmond, ☎ 713-780-0065. Another fine example of Houston's cultural diversity, Sammy's serves up some of the best Middle Eastern food in the state.

Taste Of Texas, 10505 Katy Freeway, ☎ 713-932-6901. Big steaks with all the trimmings, it's Texan any way you look at it.

Tony Mandola's Gulf Coast Kitchen, 1962 W Gray, ☎ 713-528-FISH. The Dixieland bands help inspire this New Orleans-style joint that boasts standards like shrimp étoufée and po'boys, along with more unusual selections.

Treebeard's, 315 Travis and other locations, ☎ 713-225-2160. More Louisiana-inspired food served buffet-style. It's fast, but don't underestimate its serious lunchtime crowd.

The Texas Coast

Galveston

■ History

Besides claiming the lives of over 6,000 people, the hurricane that devastated Galveston in 1900 chilled a booming economy and drove surviving merchants and businessmen up to the safer confines of protected Houston. The hurricane, which is still considered the greatest natural disaster in American history, scarred the heart of Texas inland.

Up until the hurricane, Galveston was the third largest port in the nation, the largest city in Texas and the second wealthiest city in the United States. Antebellum mansions were commonplace and plush hotels signaled the city's cultural wealth.

Galveston's roots, though, were planted well before 1900. In 1528, colorful Spanish explorer Cabeza de Vaca was shipwrecked on the shores of Galveston. For six years he and his crew were held captive by the native Karankawa Indians, a tribe known for both their occasional cannibalism and the black tar (alligator grease and fish oil) they smeared on their bodies to keep mosquitoes away.

In the mid-1700s a group of Spanish soldiers stayed in the area and named their settlement after Count Bernardo de Galvez, viceroy of Mexico. Jean Lafitte, famed for his heroism in aiding General Andrew Jackson in the Battle of New Orleans, set up camp in 1817 and used the area as home base for pilfering and pirating vessels traveling through the Gulf of Mexico.

After he made the unfortunate decision to pirate an American ship, the US government forced Lafitte to leave. Legend has it that on the eve of his exit, Lafitte threw a grand party, burning his own village to the ground and leaving buried treasure that has yet to be found. Settlers, no longer frightened by the presence of Lafitte and his unsavory crew, flooded the area.

Galveston grew quickly and splendidly. The Strand, a waterfront banking center, was dubbed "the Wall Street of the Southwest" and as cotton became king, the city's natural deep port made it a hub for all that was coming and going. The city became the port of entry for all Europeans, developing into what many consider to be the most culturally diverse Texas city. Galveston Island was second only to Ellis Island as an immigration station.

Galveston Trolley.

The Texas Coast

Galveston's past opulence lends itself to a booming tourist trade. Its beaches, threatened in the 80s by pollution, have been cleaned and its close relationship with the Gulf of Mexico adds balance for those seeking ocean adventure.

∎ Touring

 Situated on a 32-mile barrier reef island with an average width of two miles, Galveston has no choice but to embrace the balmy Gulf waters that surround it.

Getting around town can be done by traditional methods – walking, biking or renting a car – but there are some interesting alternatives. The **Galveston Island Trolley** (2100 Seawall or 2016 Strand, ☎ 409-762-2950) will transport you from the Seawall to the Strand in fixed-rail trolley cars built in turn-of-the-century style (similar to those used in Galveston from the late 1800s on). **Air Tours of Galveston Island** (2115 Terminal Drive, ☎ 409-740-IFLY) touches on most of the city's highlights during its 30- to 40-minute aerial tours. The **Treasure Isle Tour Train** (departs from the Moody Civic Center, ☎ 409-765-9564) offers a 90-minute tour of the island's highlights, leaving periodically and weather permitting.

Capturing the spirit of Galveston can be easy with a trip on the ***The Colonel*** (☎ 409-740-7797, Moody Gardens), a triple-deck paddle wheeler that departs from Moody Gardens regularly April through Labor Day. Named to honor Colonel W.L. Moody, who came to Texas in 1854 to practice law, the 152-foot replica of an 1860s stern wheeler can carry up to 800 passengers.

The **Texas Seaport Museum** and the *Elissa* (Pier 21, ☎ 409-763-1877) are two other labors of love that allow visitors to breathe in the fresh salt air.

The Elissa

The third oldest ship afloat in the world (only outdone by the *Cutty Sark* in England and the *Star of India* in San Diego), this is an iron-hulled, 150-foot square rigger that carried cargo to and from more than a hundred ports during its heyday. The Galveston Historical Foundation conducted a massive search for a boat to represent the city's role as an important 19th-century port. When they found the *Elissa* in Greece, they towed her home and restored her at a cost of more than $4.5 million.

Several of the older homes in town exemplify the incredible wealth that Galveston attracted in its golden era. Among them are the Ashton Villa and the Bishop's Palace. **The Moody Mansion and Museum** (2628

The 1877 tall ship Elissa.

The Strand.

Broadway, ☎ 409-762-7668) vies for the role of prima donna in this beautiful array of 19th-century grandeur.

Built of limestone and brick (and one of the first houses in the state to use a steel frame), the 42-room mansion was acquired by the Moody family after the 1900 hurricane. The Moody family, whose influence and name you can't escape in present-day Galveston, capitalized on a thriving cotton trade and banking industry. The Moody Foundation has attempted to restore the home to its 1911 splendor, the year of Mary Moody Northern's debut.

Galveston boasts a spectacular assortment of restored iron-front buildings in a six-block area called **The Strand**. Back when cotton reigned and Galveston was a hub for commerce, the Strand was fittingly called the "Wall Street of the Southwest." Today the Strand, fueled by tourism, has turned into the "Bourbon Street" of Texas (competing with Austin's 6th St), hosting an annual Mardi Gras celebration that is second only to New Orleans. More than 100 shops, restaurants and art galleries are enveloped by the 36 square blocks here. Shoppers can't seem to get enough of the eclectic mix of old country antiques, Victorian jewelry and assorted collectibles.

Moody Gardens (One Hope Blvd, ☎ 409-744-1745, www.moodygardens.com) is an enormous project expected to be completed by the year 2006. However, much of the eight-phase, $150 million project is already open to the public. The actual construction of the Gar-

Moody Gardens and the Rainforest Pyramid.

dens began in the mid-80s with only a horse barn and riding arena. The purpose was to establish a hippotherapy riding program for people with head injuries. While it still retains its original therapeutic goals, it has since become an entire complex of educational and recreational opportunities.

The **Rainforest Pyramid**, unmistakable in any current Galveston photograph, is an enormous greenhouse containing replicas of the major tropical rainforests of the world. With IMAX and 3-D capabilities, it is just one of the complex's educational tools.

The **Learning Place**, another completed phase, is an animal-assisted therapy facility. Palm Beach, a freshwater, white sand beach, is also completed.

A comprehensive look at Galveston's past is available at the **Galveston County Historical Museum** (2219 Market, ☎ 409-766-2340) housed in the 1919 City National Bank building. Notable exhibits include displays on Native American occupation during the 1500s and on the Great Storm of 1900, which includes actual footage from the storm taken by Thomas Edison's assistant.

The **Grand 1894 Opera House** (2020 Postoffice, ☎ 800-821-1894, 409-765-1894) ranks among the nation's finest historical restorations. Designated the "Official Opera House of the State of Texas" by the 73rd Legislature, no seat in the house is more than 70 feet from the stage.

The Texas coast's success is indelibly tied to the oil and gas industry. **The Ocean Star** (Pier 19, ☎ 409-766-STAR, 713-975-6442), a recent addition, invites visitors to go aboard an actual offshore rig and be a part of the oil and gas experience. The rig, while in operation, made over 200 successful oil well hits. It was retired in 1991 and moved to its present location just off Pier 19 for use as a museum.

The world's longest mural, the **SEE-Wall Mural**, stretches from 27th St to 61st St along Seawall Blvd. Depicting marine life, local birds and area attractions, it took 14,000 volunteers and 8,500 school children to finish the 14,760-foot mural.

Information Sources

Contact the **Galveston Convention and Visitors Bureau** for more information (☎ 888-GAL-ISLE, www.galvestontourism.com).

■ Adventures on the Water

The **Galveston Island Beach** stretches 32 miles south along the coast, and is edged with condominiums, restaurants and tourist stops. It's nice, but if the only reason you're visiting the Texas coast is for a trip to the seashore, you will do better heading south to Port Aransas or Padre Island.

✹ Did You Know?

Galveston joins cities like Miami Beach and Fort Lauderdale in its completion of a beach renourishment project that cost $6 million and dredged 700,000 cubic yards of sand from the ocean floor onto eroding beaches. The project added as much as 150 feet of sand to a four-mile stretch of beach that follows Seawall Drive.

Perhaps the most popular place to go along the beach is the 10-mile **Seawall**, built in the aftermath of the 1900 hurricane. Buffering the city from unpredictable and, at times, violent ocean weather, the 17-foot-high structure stretches along the coast offering a platform for joggers, bikers, in-line skaters and walkers.

Galveston Island State Park (FM 3005, six miles south, ☎ 409-737-1222) is rich in both bird life and outdoor fun, and also offers camping facilities. Elevated boardwalks make viewing the birds easier. During the summer months, plays are held nightly in the park's 1,700-seat outdoor theater.

Pelican Island, just across the channel from Galveston's port, is home to **Seawolf Park** (51st St Causeway to Pelican Island, ☎ 409-744-5738), which serves as both a picturesque vantage point to watch sea-going traffic entering the harbor and as a fishing hotspot off a commercially operated pier. Several World War II combat ships, including the *USS Cavalla* (submarine) and the *USS Stewart* (destroyer escort), are open to the public. A fairly new addition to the island are the **Galveston Harbour Tours** (Pier 22, ☎ 409-765-1700), which provide a narrated 45-minute tour of everything from the sugar, banana and cotton docks to the *Elissa* and the "Mosquito Fleet" shrimping boats. They also offer periodic dolphin watches.

Across the shipping channel from Galveston – via a free ferry ride – the **Bolivar Peninsula** (☎ 800-FUN-SUN3) closes the gap to Galveston Bay, encircling the harbor and providing a natural buffer. The peninsula boasts three things (among others): the Bolivar Lighthouse, white beaches unstressed by the nearby presence of a popular resort town, and fabulous fishing from the long jetties and empty shores.

Though the lighthouse officially retired in 1933 after guiding sailors for over six decades, visitors can still marvel at the 117-foot edifice. At this time it is not open to the public, but can be seen off of Hwy 87.

> ✷ *Did You Know?*
>
> Movie buffs will remember the lighthouse as the backdrop for the 1968 film *My Sweet Charlie* starring Patty Duke and Al Freeman Jr.

Crystal Beach (10 miles northeast on Highway 87) still enjoys small community status, though motels, hotels and condominiums are beginning to dot its shores. But if a brief respite from the busy whirl of the big city is what you're looking for, a trip to Crystal Beach could bring a lazy smile to your face.

■ Where to Stay

Hotel Galvez, 2024 Seawall Blvd, 77550, ☎ 800-392-4285, 409-765-7721. $$$-$$$$. Nicknamed the Grand Old Lady of Galveston, this 1911 luxury hotel has been restored to its original splendor.

The Tremont House, 2300 Ships Mechanic Row, 77550, ☎ 800-874-2300, 409-763-0300. $$-$$$$. Just a block off the Strand, every amenity you might want they have, including privileges for Galveston Country Club's golf course and a trolley stop at the hotel's front door.

Gilded Thistle (circa 1892), 1805 Broadway, 77550, ☎ 800-654-9380, 409-763-0194. $$$-$$$$. A privately owned bed and breakfast that has been recognized nationwide for its fine service and beautifully decorated interior.

The Victorian Condo-Hotel, 6300 Seawall Blvd, 77551, ☎ 800-231-6363, 409-740-3555. $$-$$$$. All the amenities of home, including a full kitchen and bunk beds for the kids. They'll even fix up picnic lunches for guests to take out.

Bed & Breakfasts

Many of these were built before the turn of the century:

Away at Sea Inn/Jacuzzi Suites (1877), 1127 Church, 77550, ☎ 800-762-1668, 409-762-1668. $$-$$$.

Carousel Inn (1886), 712 10th St, 77550, ☎ 409-762-2166. $$-$$$.

Coppersmith Inn (1887), 1914 Ave M, 77550, ☎ 800-515-7444, 409-763-7004, www.cimarron.net/usa/tx/copper.html. $$-$$$.

The Inn at 1816 Postoffice (1886), 1816 Postoffice, 77550, ☎ 409-765-9444. $$$.

Inn on the Strand (1856), 2021 Strand, 77550, ☎ 409-762-4444. $$$.

Madame Dyer's Bed and Breakfast (1889), 1720 Postoffice St, 77550, ☎ 409-765-5692. $$-$$$.

Michael's Bed & Breakfast Inn, 1715 35th St, 77550, ☎ 800-776-8302, 409-763-3760. $$-$$$.

The Queen Anne Bed and Breakfast (1905), 1915 Sealy, 77550, ☎ 800-472-0930, 409-763-7088. $$-$$$.

Victorian Bed & Breakfast Inn (1899), 511 17th St, 77550, ☎ 409-762-3235. $$$-$$$$.

■ Where to Eat

Gaido's Seafood Restaurant and Casey's Seafood Café, 3828 Seawall Blvd, ☎ 409-762-9625. The Gaido family still operates this casual but quality seafood restaurant. A recent patio addition provides a great view of the Gulf.

Joe's Crab Shack, 3502 Seawall Blvd, ☎ 409-766-1515. If you don't mind employees jumping on your table to croon their rendition of "YMCA" or other popular ditties, then this is the place for you. Outside seating provides a Gulf view.

Fish Tales, 2502 Seawall, ☎ 409-762-8545. With room for up to 150 patrons on its second-story deck, every seat has a good view.

Landry's Seafood House and Oyster Bar, 5310 Seawall (seafood), ☎ 409-744-1010; 1502 Seawall (oyster house), ☎ 409-762-4261. This one's so popular they had to have two. Their signature seafood toppings include the Pontchartrain, Etoufée and Landry. The establishment also has an oyster bar on Pier 21 that serves sandwiches and po' boys. During peak seasons, Landry's Seafood will serve up to 10,000 guests in one week.

Fisherman's Wharf, Pier 22, ☎ 409-765-5708. Located right next to where the *Elissa* is docked. It also includes the 1944 *Ursula M. Norton* from Martha's Vineyard, a restored shrimp/clam boat, now used for lunch and cocktails.

Queen's Bar-B-Que, 35th and Ave S, ☎ 409-762-3151. For something different in a fish town, try this barbecue joint that has guarded the recipe to its sauce for decades.

Brazosport

Southern Brazoria County, and more specifically an area called Brazosport, considers itself one unit, though it is made up of six different cities: Brazoria, Clute, Freeport, Lake Jackson, Quintana Beach and Surfside Beach. Three other towns – Jones Creek, Oyster Creek and Richwood – also fall under the area's broad blanket. Less than an hour from Houston, it even shares one chamber of commerce and school district, an obvious indicator that the area has one economic pursuit – fishing the rich waters of the Gulf.

Surfside Beach and Quintana Beach share the eastern edge of the area, occupying space on a narrow strip of land between the Gulf of Mexico and the Intracoastal Waterway. Freeport is just up the road at the mouth of the Brazos River. As the river winds its way inland, you'll find the towns of Clute, Lake Jackson and Brazoria, in that order.

■ History

In 1821 the first 18 of Stephen F. Austin's settlers arrived at the mouth of the Brazos River, making Brazoria County the first portal for Anglos in Texas. At the same river's mouth General Santa Anna, defeated by Sam Houston, boarded a ship and signed the Treaties of Velasco, giving Texas its hard-fought-for independence. The Brazos River Delta still celebrates its important role in the formation of Texas.

■ Touring

 Though the area is best enjoyed in a pair of waders, there is plenty to do in this loose confederacy of towns. The **Brazoria County Historical Museum** (100 East Cedar, Angleton, ☎ 409-849-5711, www.tgn.net/~bchm) is housed in the 1897 Brazoria County Courthouse, built using elements of the Italian Renaissance, popular at the time. Its exhibits are unique to the area. Quiet plantation life is preserved at the **Varner-Hogg State Historical Park** (northern edge of West Columbia via FM 2852, ☎ 409-345-4656). The main house was built in the 1830s by the Patton family and was bought by former Texas Governor James Hogg in 1920. His children, including the infamous Ima Hogg (a persistent rumor held that there was also a daughter named "Ura"), remodeled the plantation into its current colonial revival style and donated the house, complete with its furnishings, to the state as a historical park.

If fishing is your game, a trip to **Sea Center Texas** (Lake Jackson, ☎ 409-238-9222 for reservations) is right up your alley. The $13 million facility, built in partnership with Dow Chemical Company, is expected to produce 20 million fingerlings each year. In addition, the hatchery includes touch tanks for the kids and three aquariums. Then there is the annual **Great Texas Mosquito Festival** (Clute, last weekend in July, ☎ 800-371-2971). Organized perhaps on the theory of "if you can't beat 'em, join 'em," the festival only half-jokingly refers to the beloved mosquito as the Texas State Bird. "The Swat Team," the event's ambassadors, organizes three days of non-stop activities.

The Texas Coast

Information Sources

Brazosport Area Chamber of Commerce (☎ 409-265-2505, 420 W Hwy 332, Clute, 77531) or the **Southern Brazoria County Convention and Visitors Bureau** (☎ 409-265-2508, 420 W Hwy 332, Suite B, Clute, 77531). Or visit www.brazosport.com.

■ Adventures on the Water

 All kinds of fishing records are set and reset in Brazosport, a natural deep sea fishing port. Water depth changes from 20 feet just offshore to 80-100 feet 80 miles out, creating a habitat that is attractive to hundreds of fish types, including trout, sharks, mackerel, bonito, ling, flounder, red snapper, amber jack, tarpon and marlin.

Angler Hot Spots

A publication put out by the Brazoria County Visitor and Convention Bureau named the following locations as "Angler Hot Spots," though they point out that "the best fishing spot is where someone else just caught one."

Swan Lake off County Rd 257. Crabbing, redfish, speckled trout.

Old Brazos River off Hwy 288, Freeport. Saltwater fish of all kinds.

Buffalo Camp Bayou, Hwy 332 near Lake Jackson. Bass, catfish and crappie.

Christmas Bay off Bluewater Hwy, San Luis Pass. Wade fishing.

Chocolate Bayou on FM 2004 to Halls Lake. Bass and catfish.

Surfside and Quintana Jetties extend a mile into the ocean. All species of saltwater fish.

Fishing outfitters seem to represent about half of the area's businesses. Call the **Brazoria Visitor's Center** at ☎ 800-WET-GULF for a complete listing of current guides. **Captain Elliott's Party Boats** (1010 West 2nd, Freeport, ☎ 409-233-1811) and **Johnston's Sportsfishing** (Freeport, ☎ 800-460-1312 or 409-233-8513) are just two area outfitters.

Offering a primitive setting on undeveloped beaches, the **Bryan Beach State Recreation Area** (FM 1495 south of Freeport, take a right at Bryan Beach, ☎ 409-737-1222) is more accessible by boat than by car. With no roads or facilities, your privacy is interrupted only by splashing fish and cawing birds.

A more conventional beach experience can be had at **Surfside Beach** (TX 332 to its eastern edge), the major beaching community for the Brazosport area, with facilities for swimming, sailing, fishing, surfing, eating, drinking and sleeping.

> ✷ *Did You Know?*
>
> Shelling is sport for the area, with over 600 known shell species living along the Gulf Coast. The lightning welk, named the Texas state shell in 1987, can be found only on the west coast of the Gulf of Mexico (mainly Texas) and is one of the few shells that naturally opens to the left. It is also one of the first shells selected by the US Postal Service to appear on a stamp.

■ Eco-Tours

The Brazoria National Wildlife Refuge (FM 523 north of Freeport, ☎ 409-849-6062). Access is limited, so call ahead for directions and reservations. This has become one the finest waterfowl viewing spots on the Texas coast, with sightings of sandhill cranes and wintering white-tailed hawks. Its 46,000 acres provide a home for more than 400 wildlife species, including 270 bird species.

The San Bernard National Wildlife Refuge (County Rd 306 southwest of Freeport off FM 2918, ☎ 409-849-6062) is another renowned viewing area for birds. The blue and snow geese make winter homes at the 24,000-acre refuge.

■ Where to Stay

Ramada, 925 Hwy 332, Lake Jackson, 77566, ☎ 800-544-2119. $$. One of the few luxury hotels in the area. Bring back the day's catch and the restaurant will prepare it for you with all the fixins'.

Anchor B&B at San Luis Pass, 342 Anchor Drive, Freeport, 77541, ☎ 409-239-3543. $$-$$$. With fishing on a private pier and offshore access, this waterfront B&B is a great place for the fisherman to clean up and relax.

Brannan Swan Lake Division, ☎ 409-233-1812 or 888-233-1812. Offers daily, weekly and monthly rentals of over 75 furnished beach homes.

■ Where to Eat

Smithhart's Downtown Grill, 104 That Way, Lake Jackson, ☎ 409-297-0082. Lots of finger-licking food – chicken-fried steak, steak finger baskets, mega burgers and all the trimmings.

Windswept Seafood Restaurant, 105 Burch Circle, Oyster Creek, ☎ 409-233-1951. All-you-can-eat broiled and fried shrimp at reasonable prices round out the seafood menu. Call for times.

Port Aransas

Port Aransas, on the northern tip of Mustang Island, remains a fishing village. The smell of fresh fish permeates the air from all of the town's public and private docks, evidence of Port A's (the local lingo) close working relationship with the sea. However, the tourism industry has delivered condominiums and hotels to the beachfront, rounding out this town of about 2,500 residents. Connected to its mainland sidekick Aransas Pass by a free five-minute ferry trip, Port Aransas lets you enjoy what the Texas coast is all about without making you fight Texas-size crowds.

■ History

The Karankawa Indians, a man-eating bunch that reportedly swathed themselves in tar to keep pesky mosquitoes away, were the first residents of this island, which experts believe began as a submerged sandbar.

> **✱ Did You Know?**
>
> Mustang Island received its name when the Spaniards began bringing wild horses, "mestenos" (mustangs), there in the 1800s.

Always maintaining an active fishing industry (the natural pass to the north, Aransas Pass, helped this flourish), Port Aransas went through a variety of name changes and was beset by several hurricane disasters. Despite that, the town is still alive and kicking. It is estimated that over 600 species of saltwater fish inhabit the waters surrounding the island.

■ Touring

Port Aransas is all about being outside, about smelling the pungent but sweet scent of fresh fish and hearing the caws of thousands of gulls that fish the waters alongside the locals. You can feel the town just by walking around and seeing fishermen performing their daily duties. If the weather doesn't permit outdoor recreation, drive down Padre Island to Corpus Christi, which provides big-city accommodations. (See *Corpus Christi,* page 153, for activities.)

The Texas coastal eco-system is under constant scrutiny at the **University of Texas Marine Science Institute** (Cotter St across from Port Aransas Park, ☎ 512-749-6711). A self-guided tour of the visitor's center includes research on natural phenomena and the impact of man on the environment.

The Tarpon Inn (200 E Cotter, 78373, ☎ 512-749-5555), originally built in 1886 and since rebuilt following several hurricane wipe-outs of the structure, is not only a hotel, but a slice of history. The tarpon, once a prized sports fish native to the area but now rarely seen, has attracted sports fishermen for over a century. They've taken one scale from each fish – they're big – and recorded the date they were caught and the name of the fisherman for each on the back. The prize catch is a tarpon caught by President Franklin D. Roosevelt in 1937.

Information Sources

If you need more information on Port Aransas, contact the **Chamber of Commerce and Visitors Bureau** (421 Cotter, 78373, ☎ 512-749-5919, 800-45-COAST, www.portaransas.org).

■ Adventures on the Water

 The Gulf side of Mustang Island is one long beach, tempered only by high tide. It's worth pointing out that the beaches on the barrier island chain are very wide. When Texans migrate to the East and West Coasts of the US they can't help but feel the beaches are puny in comparison, though the waves are usually bigger and the water much, much cooler. People used to the colder waters will find the Gulf of Mexico in the summer a lot like a bath tub.

You can purchase a permit to park on the beach at just about any local store. The very northern point of the island houses **Port Aransas Park**, a 1,670-acre affair that includes a lighted fishing pier over 1,200 feet long.

San Jose Island (Jetty Boat at Woody's Boat Basin, ☎ 512-749-5252), the next island north across the natural water break, is private and accessible only by boat. You pick up a round-trip ticket for the 15-minute boat ride in Port A and can return periodically throughout the day.

> ### ✳ Author's Tip
>
> Part of San Jose Island's beauty is that there are NO facilities. So whatever you plan on eating or drinking, bring it along. The uncrowded shoreline boasts some of the best shelling on the coast.

Just south of Port Aransas, at a midway point between it and Corpus Christi, is the **Mustang Island State Park** (TX 361 south, ☎ 512-749-5246), containing more than five miles of beachfront. It is perfect for nature walks and camping.

There are several fishing outfitters in the area for trips that range from a couple of hours to a couple of days. Among them are **Dolphin Docks** (300 W Cotter, ☎ 800-EYE-FISH) and **Woody's Private Charters** (☎ 512-749-5252). In addition, Dolphin Docks takes certified divers out for eight-hour dives with a divemaster and Woody's offers sailboat rides, jet ski rentals and boat rides, including bird- and dolphin-watching tours.

Two city piers, one at **Roberts Point Park** and another at the north end of **Station Street**, offer free fishing to the public in the ship channel. The **Horace Caldwell Pier** in Port Aransas Park offers public fishing at the very low price of 50¢ per person.

■ Eco-Tours

In town you can birdwatch from the **Port Aransas Birding Center** (Ross Ave off Cut-Off Rd, ☎ 512-749-5307). A free guided tour begins at the center every Wednesday at 10:30 am. Just up the road, in Rockport, you will find the Aransas National Wildlife Refuge, the principal watering hole for the rare whooping crane.

■ Where to Stay

The Tarpon Inn, 200 E Cotter, 78373, ☎ 512-749-5555. $$. Basic accommodations set within a living museum.

Avian House, 1110 Sea Secret, PO Box 1408, 78373, ☎ 800-867-2248. Bed and breakfast accomodations.

Harbor View Bed & Breakfast, 340 W. Cotter, 78373, ☎ 512-749-4294. Four rooms on the harbor plus one house near beach. Includes a boat dock and fishing pier.

Aransas Princess Condominiums, 720 Access Rd 1A, PO Box 309, 78373, ☎ 512-749-5118. Over 100 units with condos on the beach, tennis courts, a boardwalk to the beach, fishing house and a heated swimming pool.

Cline's Landing, 1000 N. Station, PO Box 1628, 78373, ☎ 512-749-5275. All the upscale amenities you could need plus penthouses/condos with view of ship channel.

Executive Keys, 820 Access Rd 1A, PO Box 1087, 78373, ☎ 512-749-6272. Just a walk to the beach. Includes a game room, shuffleboard, tennis courts and volleyball court.

Sandcastle Condominiums, 800 Sandcastle Drive, 78373, ☎ 512-749-6201. Nearly 200 units with kitchenettes.

Sea Gull Condominiums, 6649 State Highway 361, 78373, ☎ 512-749-4191. Over 100 condos on the beach, with a swimming pool and tennis courts.

Port Royal, TX 361, seven miles south, ☎ 800-242-1034, 512-749-5011, www.port-royal.com. $$$. Just one of the condominium complexes that reserves a portion of its room for rentals. Everything you can imagine is included at this heavy-duty resort, including swim-up bars in the huge lagoon-style pool.

Call the **Port Aransas Chamber of Commerce** for a more complete listing of available condominium units at ☎ 800-45-COAST.

■ Where to Eat

 Crazy Cajun, corner of Station and Beach Sts, ☎ 512-749-5069. Cajun-style seafood, gumbo, red beans and rice, dirty rice, shrimp, stone crab claws, crawfish and baby-back ribs – served on butcher paper family-style. Live entertainment on weekends. Enjoy a drink outside in their beer garden before dinner.

Steamer's, 914 Tarpon, ☎ 512-749-4602. Serves up lobster, oysters, shrimp and clams for seafood lovers. Their specialty, the Boston Bucket, is filled with steamed shellfish.

Trout Street Bar & Grill, 104 W Cotter, ☎ 512-749-7800. You can enjoy dining on the boardwalk with dishes that embrace a tropical Cajun taste, including tequila shrimp and grilled red snapper with angelique sauce.

Yankee and Betty's Flounder Run, 129 N Alister, ☎ 512-749-4869. Home of the motto, "you catch 'em, we cook 'em." Not only is it BYOB, it's BYOF (bring your own fish). They do have fish there, however, if you didn't just get off the boat.

Venetian Hot Plate, 232 Beach St at Station, ☎ 512-749-7617. Authentic Italian cuisine in a nice, relaxing atmosphere with a variety of made-to-order appetizers, salads, pasta and unique entrées.

Corpus Christi

■ History

Corpus Christi natives are the first to chime in that their town is aptly named for the "Body of Christ." They believe they're in heaven. And most water enthusiasts would agree. Nestled behind Mustang and Padre barrier islands, Corpus Christi is the second most popular vacation destination in Texas.

With an average temperature just above 71°, the jewel of a city is a year-round outdoor recreation mecca. In addition to fishing (bay and offshore), sailing, golf and windsurfing are popular sports.

The city owes its name to Alonso Alvarez de Pineda, a Spanish explorer who discovered a beautiful bay in 1519 and decided to name it for the religious feast day, Corpus Christi. It was more than three centuries later, in 1839, that US troops, under the command of General Zachary Taylor, set up a small tent city in preparation for battle with Mexico. Among Taylor's troops were three future Presidents: himself, Franklin Pierce and Ulysses S. Grant. He and his troops moved on, but their legacy remains today in a city with over a quarter-million residents.

In the 1920s the US government made Corpus (most Texans shorten the name) a deep water port, dredging its bay and shipping channel, thereby attracting the oil industry to its gates. It remains the deepest port in Texas to this day and still thrives on shipping.

■ Touring

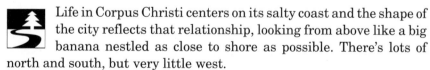

Life in Corpus Christi centers on its salty coast and the shape of the city reflects that relationship, looking from above like a big banana nestled as close to shore as possible. There's lots of north and south, but very little west.

However, Corpus does offer entertainment off the water. Living displays at the **Texas State Aquarium** (2710 N Shoreline Blvd, 78402, ☎ 800-477-GULF, 512-881-1200), which include sharks and endangered sea turtles, are designed to give the sensation of gradually im-

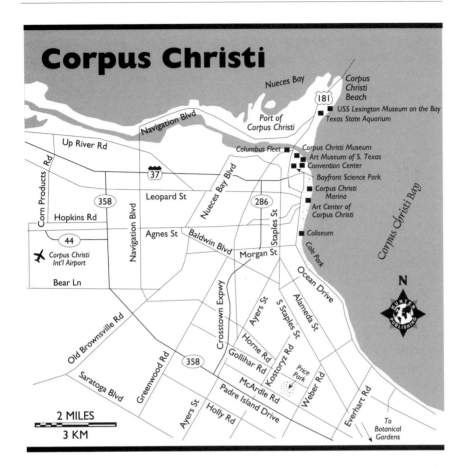

mersing yourself in the Gulf of Mexico waters. It is the first aquarium in the country to concentrate on the ecosystems of the Gulf and the Caribbean, and is being designed in phases as a world-class institution with a budget over $60 million.

Replicas of the **Ships of Columbus** (☎ 512-883-2862), the *Niña*, the *Pinta* and the *Santa Maria*, are moored at the C. Storm Pavilion under the Harbor Bridge. These reproductions provide a fascinating look at their legendary voyages in what are surprisingly small vessels. There are activities to join and watch.

Another famous vessel docked in Corpus (this is the real one) is the *USS Lexington*, an acclaimed aircraft carrier that served longer and set more records than any other US Navy carrier. It was decommissioned in 1991. The **USS Lexington Museum on the Bay** (2914 N Shoreline Blvd, ☎ 512-888-4873, 800-LADY-LEX) includes five tour routes, educational exhibits, a restored aircraft and a collection of historical artifacts.

Fishing off Corpus Christi.

Corpus Christi Botanical Gardens (8510 South Staples, ☎ 512-852-2100) includes 290 acres of natural area with over 1,000 native plants in display areas, greenhouses, wetlands and along the one-mile "Mesquite Trail." It's an excellent spot for birdwatching, with flocks of herons and cranes.

The **Corpus Christi Greyhound Racetrack** (5302 Leopard St, ☎ 512-289-9333, 512-580-1223) touts itself as a state-of-the-art facility with live pari-mutuel wagering and simulcasts from Galveston and Miami.

Cultural entertainment in the city is concentrated in the Bayfront Arts and Science Park on the north end of Shoreline Blvd. The area includes several museums and parks. **The Harbor Playhouse** (1 Bayfront Park, ☎ 512-888-7469) also resides in the district. The oldest continually performing community playhouse in Texas, it's has been in operation since 1925 and its members present about 15 plays each year.

The **International Kite Museum** (3200 Surfside, inside the Best Western, ☎ 512-883-7456) provides a fun escape from the sun. The museum traces the history of kites throughout the Orient, Europe and the United States, including their uses in science and warfare.

An easy and relaxing way to take in the area's ambiance is to catch a **trolley** that meanders along the bayfront and through the downtown area. You can also catch a trolley over the Harbor Bridge to Corpus

Christi Beach. Call the **Regional Transportation Authority** for schedules and fares at ☎ 512-289-2600.

You can also walk along the **seawall**, a two-mile stretch of walkway designed by famed Mt. Rushmore sculptor John Gutzon Borglum. It offers visitors a natural area to rest and enjoy the sights, with steps down to the water's edge.

Information Sources

Call the **Corpus Christi Convention and Visitors Bureau** (☎ 800-766-BEACH, www.cctexas.org/cc) for more information.

■ Adventures on the Water

 This is the joy of Corpus Christi. Fishermen love it. Sailors adore the winds, which are some of the breeziest in the nation. And swimmers relax on its clear, unpolluted beaches. Corpus Christi is the sixth largest port in the nation, with ships from around the world tying up at its docks. The town also provides access to Padre Island, which is known to the younger generation as a beaching hotspot, and to older generations as a spectacular wildlife and bird refuge.

Corpus Christi Beach is only three miles from downtown, just over the Harbor Bridge. It's a gem of a beach, but don't forget suncreen and water. Glass bottles are not recommended.

✳ Take Care!

As for the jellyfish, don't touch. A standard take-along is meat tenderizer or vinegar, both of which treat jellyfish stings.

You can get to the beach in a **water taxi** operated by the Regional Transportation Authority. It picks up at the barge dock on Shoreline Blvd. Call ☎ 512-289-2600 for schedules and fares.

The **Padre Island National Seashore** (at the end of Park Rd 22, ☎ 512-937-2621) is one of the longest stretches of primitive, undeveloped ocean beach in the United States, embracing 80 miles of white beaches, windswept dunes, grasslands and warm offshore waters. Visitors can enjoy swimming, fishing, hiking, beachcombing, camping, bird-

The Texas Coast

watching, surfing, water-skiing and off-roading. The surfing is not as adventurous as on the West and East Coasts, but the warm waters make it a more enjoyable experience.

At the **Corpus Christi Marina** (People's St T-head, i.e., at the end of the dock) you'll find a wide variety of sightseeing cruises, private pleasure craft, and commercial shrimp boats. Fresh seafood can be bought right off the boats. You can also rent jet skis, paddleboats, sailboats, or other water toys on the People's St T-Head. Every Wednesday evening sailboats race in an ongoing series. Any spot along the bay or at the pier will give you a birds-eye view of the racing.

Oleander Point (2000 block of Ocean Dr), on the south end of Cole Park, is internationally renowned for fantastic windsurfing, with consistently windy conditions between 15 and 25 miles per hour. It has repeatedly been the site of the US Open Windsurfing competition and has hosted the Mistral World Championships. The city built a breakwater at Oleander Point to cut down on chop and in the process created a windsurfing heaven.

If you would rather try your hand at sailing, you can begin at the **Corpus Christi International School of Sailing** (Cooper's Alley L-head, ☎ 512-881-8503, www.constant.com/sailing), which offers lessons for beginning, intermediate and advanced sailing.

Scuba diving is another activity for adventurers. While it's not Corpus Christi's most alluring activity – sailing and wind surfing take that

Corpus Christi windsurfing.

honor – it is worth a trip. Outfitters can take you to various reefs and often dive near offshore oil rigs, where plant and fish life thrive.

Area Scuba Diving Outfitters

Ascuba Venture, 6121 S. Padre Island Dr, ☎ 512-985-1111.

Copeland's Inc., 4041 S. Padre Island Dr, ☎ 512-854-1135.

See Sea Divers, 4012 Weber Rd, ☎ 512-853-DIVE.

Tours of Corpus Christi Bay are available on **Capt**. **Clark's Flagship** (People's St T-Head, ☎ 512-884-1693, 512-884-8306), a 400-passenger paddle-wheeler. The narrated cruise proceeds along the downtown bayfront, passing close to the *USS Lexington* and the Texas State Aquarium.

The Dolphin Connection (5151 East Causeway Blvd, ☎ 512-882-4126) tours Corpus Christi Bay and offers the chance to see dolphins.

Fishing opportunities abound in this city by the sea. Call the local Visitors and Convention Center for information.

Water Rentals

Wind & Wave Water Sports, 10721 S Padre Island Dr, ☎ 512-937-9283. Windsurfing lessons and rentals. Surfboard, boogie board and kayak rentals. Surf accessories.

WorldWinds, 14225 S Padre Island Dr (Bird Island Basin), ☎ 512-949-7472 or 800-793-7471. Boards, wetsuits and booties for rental.

M.D. Surf & Skate, 4016 Weber, ☎ 512-854-7873. In-line skates.

■ Eco-Tours

 Geography and climate have made Corpus Christi a birding paradise. Rare seabirds, shorebirds and marsh waders, as well as songbirds, game birds and raptors, call the area home.

Over 500 species of birds have been documented on the barrier islands of Texas, including brown pelicans, the rare masked duck and the endangered whooping crane. The list of good sites for birdwatching is extensive. Call the local bird hotline at ☎ 512-364-3634 for current and detailed information.

Two birding tours of note: **Bird Song Natural History Adventures** (3525 Bluebonnet, ☎ 512-882-7232), which are conducted by Gene W Blacklock, co-author of *Birds of Texas: A Field Guide* and *Birds of the Texas Coastal Bend; and* **Captain Ted's Whooping Crane Tours** (Sandollar Pavilion in Rockport, ☎ 512-729-9589, 800-338-4551), where you can enjoy close-up views of the endangered whooping cranes.

The **Hans A. Suter Wildlife Park** (Ennis Joslin at Nile) is one of the best birdwatching locations in Texas. The coastal marshland park has a viewing tower, hiking trails and a boardwalk.

■ Where to Stay

 Villa Del Sol, 3938 Surfside, 78402, ☎ 800-242-3291. $$$-$$$$. Furnished condos on Corpus Christi Beach with kitchens, pool and hot tubs.

Holiday Inn Emerald Beach, 1102 S Shoreline Blvd, 78401, ☎ 512-883-5731. $$$-$$$$. The only downtown hotel on the beach.

Wes-Tex Management, ☎ 800-221-1447. They handle condo rentals on Mustang and Padre Islands on a daily, weekly or monthly basis. Many of the condos come fully equipped.

Majestic Mayan Princess, Mustang Island, ☎ 800-662-8907, 512-749-5183. $$$-$$$$. An ocean-front resort that offers one of the finest ocean views.

■ Where to Eat

 Crystal's Restaurant, 4119 S Staples (Parkdale Plaza), ☎ 512-857-8081. This tropical setting boasts frozen margaritas, baby back ribs and homemade desserts. One of the city's most popular spots.

The County Line of Corpus Christi, 6102 Ocean Dr, ☎ 512-991-7427. Be careful what you wear to the County Line. The barbecue here is as Texans intended it to be – all over you.

The Lighthouse/Landing Restaurant, 444 N Shoreline Blvd, ☎ 512-883-3982. The outdoor deck is the perfect place to watch sailboat races. Great seafood, steaks and more to go with the view.

Water Street Oyster Bar, 309 N Water St and the **Water Street Seafood Company**, ☎ 512-882-8683. Daily blackboard specials at these two restaurants add some of the spice that locals treasure.

South Padre Island

It's a narrow thread that connects South Padre Island with Texas – a 2½-mile stretch called the Queen Isabella Causeway. But the well-worn bridge to this natural barrier island that stretches endlessly up the coast is crossed by over one million beach enthusiasts each year. No small feat for an island with a year-round population of about 2,000.

There are almost two hotel/motel/condominium rooms for every resident – an unmistakable indicator that tourism is king, representing nearly 100% of the local economy.

The well-tended white sand beaches sit flush against the Gulf of Mexico on its outer edge and the Laguna Madre on its western rim. Hwy 100 winds its way north along miles of undeveloped beach front, ending abruptly at the man-made Mansfield Cut, a water passage that splits the barrier island in two. To the north lies Padre Island, accessible through the Corpus Christi area.

Spring Breakers, in their annual rite, descend on the island, numbering at times over 100,000. Winter Texans from Canada and the Midwest call the island home in the colder months, finding the mild temperatures much more amenable to their spirits. Mexican Nationals and Texans find summers on the island a perfect retreat.

■ Touring

As in most towns of the coastal bend, life revolves around the water here. Port Isabel lies just west of South Padre Island – the first link with mainland Texas.

The **Port Isabel Lighthouse State Historical Park** (421 East Queen Isabella Blvd, ☎ 800-527-6102, 956-943-2262) was constructed in 1852 and extinguished in 1905. It fell into neglect until being restored in 1947 and is now the only lighthouse of the 16 originally constructed along the Texas coast that is open to the public. With a perch 50 feet above the ground and a backdrop that includes South Padre Island and the Gulf of Mexico, the lighthouse is popular with photographers, visitors and couples getting married.

One of the things that makes South Padre such a Spring Break mecca is its proximity to **Brownsville** and **Matamoros**, Mexico, with its drinking age of 18. Mexico has historically been very willing to accept the American tourist dollar. Most people prefer to leave their cars on the US side of the bridge and walk across the border, which costs less than a dollar each way for passage. There are free buses to the Matamoros market, where bartering is the norm. If you decide to take a taxi, negotiate the price before hopping in; that way there'll be no misunderstanding.

✳ Take Care!

If you do take your own car, make sure to buy specific insurance for Mexico. You can be arrested if you are involved in an accident without the proper insurance. And a Mexican jail is not where you want to spend your time.

Customs

When returning to the US, remember that all articles acquired in Mexico must be declared. You are allowed $400 exemption for gifts and personal articles. You may bring back one liter of alcoholic beverage and one case of beer per person over 21. Fruits, meats and articles made from endangered species (sea turtle boots, etc.) are not allowed back into the States. US Customs has recently changed its policy regarding intoxicated partiers returning on foot from Mexico. They can and will arrest you for public intoxication if you are visibly drunk.

Information Sources

Contact the **South Padre Island Convention and Visitors Bureau** (☎ 800-343-2368, 600 Padre Blvd, PO Box 3500, 78597, www.sopadre.com).

■ Adventures on the Water

 Where does one start? There's surfing, wave running, parasailing, kayaking and banana boating. Consistent Gulf breezes make this a popular windsurfing and kiting destination, and fishing in the Gulf and Laguna Madre is fine too. The soft, silty beach sand provides excellent sand castle-building material.

Andy Bowie Park ($3 per vehicle, ☎ 956-761-ANDY), at the northern limits of South Padre Island proper, features two beachfront pavilions, boogie board and umbrella rentals, barbecue areas and a car-free environment.

On the southernmost tip of the island lies **Isla Blanca Park**, which includes boat ramps, a fishing jetty, daily charters, a marina and beachfront facilities.

The prime **windsurfing** seasons are mid-October through early December and April through mid-May, with winds averaging between 15 and 25 knots. South Padre is essentially a deserted island during the main windsurfing seasons (excepting March).

Beginners should try their luck in the Laguna Madre, on the west side of the island, where you can sail for several miles in water that is only waist-deep. More advanced sailboarders will find the Intracoastal Waterway and the jetties more challenging.

A more conventional outpost for kids can be found at **Jeremiah's Landing** (100 Padre Blvd, ☎ 956-761-2131), a small water park with seven water slides, a miniature golf course and an arcade.

Adults might enjoy a cruise on **Le Mistral** (1250 Port Rd, Port Isabel, ☎ 956-943-SHIP). With room for 450 passengers, this cruise ship travels south past the banks of Mexico and international waters, where Las Vegas-style gambling is legal. Call them for specific cruise offerings.

Just about anything you might want to rent is available somewhere on the island. It's a fairly safe bet that you will find whatever you're looking for just by walking or driving down the beach. Or you can call the **Convention and Visitors Bureau** for detailed information at ☎ 800-343-2368.

■ Adventures on Horseback

A gentle breeze. Soft sand. Water lapping at the shore. And you astride a horse, running along the beach. It's a picture South Padre Island sells often to its visitors. And for good reason – SPI has all the ingredients. The perpetually warm island is a natural fit for horseback riders. You can rent horses by calling the **Island Equestrian Center** (☎ 800-761-4677).

The Texas Coast

■ Where to Stay

 Bahia Mar Resort and Conference Center, 6300 Padre Blvd, 78597, ☎ 800-292-7502, 956-761-1343. $$-$$$$. Provides both hotel and condo accommodations. May cost a couple of extra pennies, but the amenities are worth it.

Padre Island Rentals, 3100 Padre Blvd, 78597, ☎ 800-926-6926, 956-761-5512. $$-$$$$. Provides rental information and reservations for more than 15 different condominium complexes and hotels. They've got options for any budget and any specific requests.

■ Where to Eat

 Amberjacks, 209 West Amberjack St, ☎ 956-761-6500. www.dockndine.com. The restaurant overlooks the Laguna Madre, making it a pleasant spot to munch on gulf shrimp, ceviche or a Texas sweet onion blossom.

Blackbeard's, 103 E Saturn, ☎ 956-761-2962. The beach crowd appreciates the juicy burgers and outdoor fare, but seafood remains the emphasis here.

Grill Room at the Pantry, 708 Padre Blvd, ☎ 956-761-9331. Entrées include a variety of well-prepared seafoods, steaks, and specialty items, like lamb chops. Open for dinner only and their schedule depends on the season.

Sea Ranch Restaurant, 1 Padre Blvd, entrance to Isla Blanca Park, ☎ 956-761-1314. Nestled up along the water and the Sea Ranch Marina, Sea Ranch offers fare for any palate, from Tex-Mex to steaks to fresh ceviche.

Special Attraction

■ Offshore Fishing

With so much of Texas snuggled up along the Gulf of Mexico, deep sea fishing is more than sport. It is a way of life and the economic heartbeat for many Texans. With so many miles of coast, fishermen ritually take to the Gulf waters.

Fishing in Texas is different from many places. It remains relatively shallow for a good 25 to 30 miles out (around 100 feet deep). The further south you go, the quicker the depth falls off, making for a great variety of fish. The warm, almost tropical waters are very different from what you would find on the Pacific and attract a much more active crowd. While the West Coast is much better for sightseeing – with its regal cliffs and crashing waves – the Gulf Coast invites you to swim. Its waves are mellow, its sand is soft (though hot) and its temperature is mild.

Texas coastal fishing is concentrated between Port Aransas and Port Isabel, with Port Aransas and Corpus Christi the dominant hubs for visitors. You'll find many of the small towns that land between these larger centers are all about fishing – but they are about fishing for a living, not charters. Galveston and Clear Lake Bay also offer some charter service, but fishing enthusiasts will tell you to move south for the better catches.

Texas Parks and Wildlife (☎ 512-389-4505, fishing information, www.tpwd.state.tx.us) regulates all fishing permits and current rules and regulations. Visit their Web site if you need timely information – they provide a weekly fishing update at various saltwater and freshwater locations across the state. Following are some of the coastal area guides.

Fishing Guides

Port Aransas Area

Elliott Guide Service. Ralph Elliot. Bay fishing, ☎ 512-643-7351.

Private Deep Sea Charters. Ron Pierson. Gulf fishing, ☎ 512-749-7311.

Bill Busters. Sportfishing, Bay and Gulf fishing, ☎ 512-749-5223.

Fishin' Fever. Mark Rochester. Bay fishing, ☎ 512-749-6957

Crystal Blue Charters. Clark Miles. Bay and Gulf fishing, ☎ 512-749-5904, 800-920-0931.

Beacon Charter Service. Charles (Chuck) Bujan. Bay fishing, ☎ 512-749-4273, 800-693-6220.

Neptune Charters. Charters, fishing, sightseeing, boat rides, nature tours, ☎ 512-749-6969.

Investigator Fishing Charters. Bob Coons. Gulf fishing, ☎ 512-776-5223.

Happy Bottoms Charters. Marty Millard. Gulf fishing, ☎ 512-758-5316.

Hook Guide Service. Gene H. Frost. Bay fishing, ☎ 512-749-4925.

Marshall's Guide Service. Monte Marshall. Bay fishing, ☎ 512-749-6633.

G&S Marine Inc. Scott Andrews. Scuba diving service and fishing, ☎ 512-270-7292.

Shallow Water Charters. Gary Einhauf. Bay and fly fishing, duck hunting and birdwatching, ☎ 512-749-6525.

Charlie's Guide Service. Charlie Hutchins. Bay fishing, ☎ 512-749-3231.

Freespool & Ladyfish Charters. Jeff & Mary Ann Heimann. Bay and Gulf fishing, ☎ 512-749-6278.

Ala Cat Fishing Charters. Alan & Cathy Neimann. Gulf fishing, ☎ 512-749-6393.

Waterworld Charters. Brad Barwise. Gulf fishing, ☎ 512-749-3556.

Ironhead Charter Service. Keith Schoolcraft. Gulf fishing, ☎ 512-949-0910.

Corpus Christi Area

Capt. Byron Hough. Corpus Christi, ☎ 512-937-4229.

Capt. Phyllis Ingram. 4518 Janssen. Corpus Christi, ☎ 512-857-0702, 800-368-6032.

Capt. Joe Mendez. 2901 Caprice, Corpus Christi, ☎ 512-937-5961.

Capt. Wallace E. Kelly Jr. 4102 Wyndale, Corpus Christi, ☎ 512-939-8045.

Don's Guide Service. Corpus Christi, ☎ 512-993-2024.

South Padre Island Area

A convenient way to check on conditions and to find out more about booking a trip is to contact **Jim's Pier** (☎ 956-761-2865), **Fisherman's Wharf** (☎ 956-761-7818), or the **Sea Ranch Marina** (☎ 956-761-5493).

Breakaway Cruises. Dolphin watches, ☎ 956-761-7646.

Murphy's Charters. Gulf fishing, ☎ 956-761-2764.

Nite Chart. Bay fishing, ☎ 956-399-3459.

R&R Charters. Bay fishing, ☎ 956-943-7507.

Skipper Ray. Bay fishing, ☎ 956-761-4565.

Hospitality Docks. Gulf and Bay fishing, ☎ 956-943-1621.

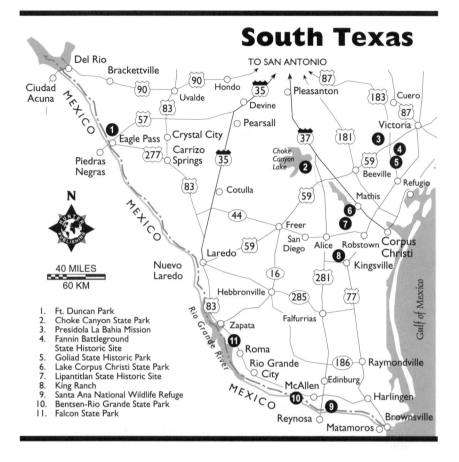

South Texas

■ The Land

The terrain making up South Texas is markedly different from the rest of the state. This "Brush Country" stretches south of San Antonio to the Rio Grande River, the United States' southern border, encompassing 20 million acres of dryland vegetation. You'll likely see no trees once you've traveled past San Antonio and the Edwards Plateau, only squatty mesquite, prickly pear and dwarf oak trees. The oceans of green that crop up along the extreme southwestern portions are a product of intense irrigation. Farmers take advantage of the 330-day growing season.

While much of the region raises stock (cattle), the "Valley" (the irrigated southeast region buttressed by the Rio Grande) is a haven for citrus, primarily oranges and grapefruit. The oranges are not as good as the California and Florida varieties, but they are heavily used for commercial orange juice. The grapefruit, with famous names like "Ruby Red," are some of the most sought-after in the country.

Other products grown in the Valley and dispersed around the world are carrots, onions, lettuce, broccoli, cucumbers and tomatoes. Most of the nation's aloe vera comes from this small strip of land.

To the north and west, and enveloping the rest of South Texas, the earth is mostly parched and dry (caliché). It is home to wildlife that can withstand the demands of an arid country. And it is a hunters' paradise.

■ History

Ownership of South Texas was hotly contested and a volatile subject well into the 1800s. The portion of land between the Nueces River and the Rio Grande was claimed by both Texas and Mexico during Texas' stint as an independent nation, though nothing substantial was done to resolve the border dispute.

But when Texas joined the Union on Dec. 29, 1845, they gained a formidable and powerful ally. The dispute became a real problem for the two bickering nations, reaching a feverish pitch.

In 1846 General Zachary Taylor built a fort just across the river from Matamoros, Mexico, casting the first stone in the Mexican War. The United States ultimately won the war and Mexico conceded the area of land known as the "Nueces Strip."

Ironically enough, historians believe that if Mexico had conceded the area without going to war, the country might not have lost most of its Western possessions, including California, Arizona and New Mexico. As it was, the riled Americans kept moving west at the expense of our southern neighbor.

The cultural make-up of South Texas is predominantly Hispanic by virtue of its proximity and close-knit relationship with Mexico. It is also the poorest region in the state, with its populace subsisting on sometimes marginal farming.

NAFTA is changing things, though it has not been fully implemented. Investment income has flooded into the area, easing some of poverty's pangs.

■ Logistics

Not to sound like a broken record, but you'll need a vehicle to get around in South Texas. If you're only going to South Padre Island for some beach time you can probably do without a car by flying into Brownsville and then shuttling to the island. Any other trips, though, require four wheels. San Antonio is the other closest city to fly into and, as the gateway to the south, it's a good place to start. Many travelers will actually start in Austin, one hour north of San Antonio, because it consistently seems to have a better variety of competitive flights.

■ Weather & Climate

In the winter, you'll believe you're in heaven. Weather is mild and frontal systems often fizzle before they reach the southern plains. This seasonal mildness is the reason "Winter Texans" make annual pilgrimages from their homes in Canada, the Northeast, and other cold places to spend a few months in South Texas. If you're there, you'll see them in their RVs and their influence is undeniable. The retired folks (and whoever else doesn't have to work during the winter) make socializing and enjoying the good outdoors their full-time profession.

The summer is two different beasts. The coastal influence keeps those portions near the shore pleasant and beachy. Inland, where the sun bakes and cracks the earth, you'll often feel baked and cracked yourself.

> ✳ *Author's Tip*
>
> Heat can be an issue here. So be prepared if you're going during the hot months.

Goliad

The soundbite that resonates through the nation's memory – "Remember the Alamo" – doesn't quite get it right. The actual battle cry that rose among Texas patriots as they fought for their independence at the Battle of San Jacinto was "Remember the Alamo! Remember Goliad!" Goliad, a small hamlet southeast of San Antonio and an integral part of Texas history, has been historically slighted ever since.

South Texas

■ History

One of the oldest municipalities in the state, Goliad's roots date back to 1749 when a Spanish mission (Nuestra Senora del Espiritu Santo de Zuniga) and presidio (Nuestra Senora de Loreto) were moved here. Operating under the name La Bahia, missionaries taught Indians the art of cattle raising and the area quickly became a boon for the developing beef industry. In 1829 the government decided that La Bahia was no longer functioning as a mission and needed to change its name. The community adopted the name Goliad.

The town, which remains small (around 2,000 residents), became one of the key sites in Texas' fight for independence from Mexico. On Oct. 9, 1835, just days after the first shots of the Texas Revolution were fired in Gonzales, Texans seized the fort in Goliad. In December the same group of colonists drafted a premature version of a Declaration of Texas Independence and raised a symbolic flag of independence.

The flag they raised – a severed arm and bloody sword to illustrate that they would rather lose life and limb than submit to Mexican rule – would serve as a tragically ironic piece of history. Three months later Colonel James Walker Fannin and his troops were captured following the Battle of Coleto, fought close to Goliad. The 350-plus soldiers and Fannin were brought back to the fort in Goliad.

On Palm Sunday, as the soldiers milled about, they were gunned down by the Mexican army. A few deft and lucky Texans escaped, but all of the others, including Fannin, died in what is termed the Goliad Massacre.

■ Touring

 The wealth of history that encompasses Goliad is what the town is about. The **Presidio La Bahia** (US 183, two miles south, ☎ 512-645-3752), a National Historic Landmark, is considered the world's finest example of a Spanish frontier fort. The oldest fort in the western United States, nine flags have flown over the Presidio. The fort's restoration was completed in 1967 and it is operated by the Catholic Diocese of Victoria. Chapel service still takes place every Sunday.

Military historians have never really figured out Colonel Fannin's tactical decision that delayed his troops' retreat to Victoria, as ordered by General Sam Houston after the fall of the Alamo. But the delay ended up costing them their lives. They were overtaken and surrounded near Coleto Creek before being taken back to Goliad to be executed. The **Fannin Battleground State Historic Site** (US 59 east to Park Rd 22 south, ☎ 512-645-2020) is where the battle and surrender took place. The 13-acre park includes picnic areas.

The actual **Fannin Monument and Grave** is behind the Presidio de Bahia. After the massacre, the Mexican forces partly burned the victims' bodies. It wasn't until June, several months later, that the bodies were buried properly with military honors here. Fannin and 342 of his men are believed to be buried in the mass grave site.

The downtown district includes a number of historic buildings. The **Goliad County Courthouse** (town square), built in Second Empire style, was completed in 1894 by noted Texas architect Alfred Giles. The limestone used to build it was hauled from Austin by oxcart.

The oak tree on the north courthouse lawn served as the county's **Hanging Tree** until 1870. Death sentences proclaimed inside the court's chambers were carried out immediately with a strong piece of rope on one of the tree's sturdy limbs. The tree is a Recorded Texas Historic Landmark.

The **Market House Museum** (205 Market, ☎ 512-645-3563) was built by the city in the early 1870s and contained stalls that were rented to farmers for the sale of meat and produce. Today the building houses a museum and serves as the office for the local chamber of commerce.

The centerpiece of the **Goliad State Historical Park** (one mile south on US 183 to Park Rd 6, ☎ 512-645-3405) is the mission **Nuestra Senora del Espiritu Santo de Zuniga**. Originally established in 1722 on Lavaca Bay to the east, it was moved to its present site in 1749. In its heyday, it controlled a large portion of land between the Guadalupe and San Antonio Rivers, along with a huge herd of cattle. It was restored in the 1930s, after having fallen into disrepair.

Included in the rest of the park, 178 acres of gently rolling hills, is **General Zaragoza's Birthplace**. One of the most famous Goliad prodigies. Ignacio Zaragoza was born in 1829. He was too young to take part in the Texas Revolution, but he was a leader for the Mexican Army. After working his way up to the rank of General, he defeated French forces at the Battle of Pueblo on May 5, 1862. That day – Cinco de Mayo – is a celebrated holiday every year in Mexico and Zaragoza is one of Mexico's most revered heroes.

The ruins of **Mission Nuestra Senora del Rosario** are found four miles west of the Goliad State Historical Park headquarters. The mission had been established in an attempt to settle the Karankawa Indians.

South Texas

Goliad State Park offers facilities for picnicking, hiking, tent and trailer camping, as well as history and nature study. Fishing and boating are permitted in the San Antonio River.

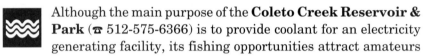

Information Sources

For more information, call the **Goliad County Chamber of Commerce** at ☎ 512-645-3563 or visit their Web site at www.goliad.org.

■ Adventures on the Water

Although the main purpose of the **Coleto Creek Reservoir & Park** (☎ 512-575-6366) is to provide coolant for an electricity generating facility, its fishing opportunities attract amateurs and tournament fishermen by the thousands. In addition to native species of large-mouth bass, crappie and catfish, Coleto Creek has been stocked with Florida and hybrid striped bass, and copper-nosed blue gill perch. Most of the lake is only 11 feet deep, extending to around 40 feet as you work into many of the original stream beds.

To get there, go east of Goliad on Highway 59.

■ Where to Stay

Dial House B&B Inn, 306 W Oak, 77963, ☎ 512-645-3366. $$. A 1905 Victorian original with five rooms. They serve you dessert in the evenings – on the large wraparound porch if you like.

Goliad Inn Motel, 124 S Jefferson, 77963, ☎ 512-645-3251. $. Basic amenities, with microwaves, cable and phone in each room.

The Quarters, Presidio La Bahia, 1½ miles south of town on Hwy 183, ☎ 512-645-3752. $$$. Lodging in an 18th-century Spanish Colonial fort. You get the two-bedroom abode to yourself.

■ Where to Eat

The Empresario Restaurant, 141 S Courthouse Square, ☎ 512-645-2347. Mexican food, steak and shrimp – they cover all the bases.

La Bahia Restaurant, US Hwy 183/77A S, ☎ 512-645-3651. They too are all things to all people, with a menu that ranges from Tex-Mex to catfish.

Kingsville

Kingsville marks its birthday on July 4, 1904, the day the first regular passenger train of the St. Louis, Brownsville and Mexico Railroad arrived. And while that might be fine for civic celebrations, the town actually owes its existence to Captain Richard King, who had come to the area more than half a century before that.

■ History

In 1853, Captain King purchased what was the beginning of a Texas ranching empire that is maintained by his heirs today. Building upon 75,000 acres that had been a part of the Santa Gertrudis Spanish land grant, King began his legacy. Before his death, King had stretched his boundaries to some 600,000 acres. However it was his wife, Henrietta, who after King's death, took the bull by the horns. She proved just as tenacious as her husband in building and maintaining an empire.

With the help of her son-in-law, she saw to it that the railroads came through her neck of the woods and grew the King Ranch to what is today around 825,000 acres, a spread larger than Rhode Island. At its peak the King Ranch included 1,125,000 acres, with holdings of over 10 million acres around the world. Recognized as the birthplace of the American ranching industry, the King Ranch developed the Gertrudis and King Ranch Santa Cruz cattle breeds, along with the first registered American quarter horse. As one of the largest ranches in the world, it is home to over 60,000 cattle and 300 quarter horses.

South Texas

■ Touring

Kingsville, with a population over 25,000 and its own university (Texas A&I University), is still very connected with the ranch that prompted its settlement. Perhaps the first stop to make is the **King Ranch Museum** (405 N 6th St, the Henrietta Memorial Building, ☎ 512-595-1881), which welcomes visitors with an award-winning photographic essay on life at the King Ranch in the 1940s. The museum also offers a collection of saddles from around the globe and several antique carriages and vintage cars, including a 1950 custom-built hunting car.

The **John E. Conner Museum** (821 Santa Gertrudis, Texas A&I campus, ☎ 512-593-2819) houses one of the largest displays of cattle brands and branding irons in the state. However, the museum's rotating exhibits touch on varying topics, from the bicultural heritage of South Texas to fossil findings at local dig sites.

If you want to take some of South Texas home with you, stop by the **King Ranch Saddle Shop** (201E Kleberg, ☎ 800-282-KING or 512-595-5761), where you can pick up custom goods with the Running W brand and exquisite Indian saddle blankets. The shop resembles a high-dollar boutique, with jewelry, cactus jelly and antler candlestick holders.

It would be difficult to avoid a visit to the **King Ranch** (TX 141, around three miles west of town, ☎ 512-592-8055) as it engulfs the area with its massive presence. The ranch has worked hard to maintain a variety of habitats that attract a rich collection of animals. Nature tours allow visitors to enjoy South Texas wildlife, from white-tailed deer to javelinas, coyotes to migratory and tropical birds.

Information Sources

For more information on the Kingsville area, visit the **Kingsville Visitor Center** (101 N 3rd, 78364, ☎ 800-333-5032) or visit the Chamber of Commerce's Web site at www.kingsville.org.

■ Adventures on the Water

 Fishermen flock to the Kingsville area to visit **Baffin Bay**, a few miles southeast of town. There is little development along the bay's shores because the King Ranch and the Padre Island National Seashore encompass them. It is considered one of the finest fishing spots in the state and is world famous for its spotted sea trout. It is also famous for its prop-eating rocks that make for great fishing.

✳ Take Care

Rocks lie submerged just below the water's surface. If you're going to navigate the bay on your own, make sure you bring a good map and a sensitive depth finder. Otherwise, you'll join the ranks of fishermen with their weekends cut short because of "technical difficulties."

Guide Services

Ingram's Guide Service, Corpus Christi, ☎ 512-857-0702 or 800-368-6032, www.davlin.net/ingram/baffinba.htm.

Capt. John E. Wooten Jr, Kingsville, ☎ 800-324-8227, www.hammer-time.com/wooten.htm.

Capt. Don Hand, Corpus Christi, ☎ 512-993-2024, www.seatrout.com/donhand.

Other useful numbers are: **Williamson's Boat Dock** (☎ 512-297-5221) and **Kaufer-Hubert Park,** for accommodations next to Baffin Bay (☎ 512-297-5738).

■ Where to Stay

 The B-Bar-B Ranch Inn, 325 East County Rd 2215, RR 1, Box 457, 78363, off US Hwy 77, ☎ 512-296-3331. $$$. www.seatrout.com/bbarb. Originally part of the historic King Ranch, this ranch house has been completely restored and offers a unique retreat experience for those on either business or pleasure.

Wild Horse Lodge, Baffin Bay, ☎ 512-584-3098. $$$. It's on the water, with a lighted pier and fishing charters available. There are three different houses that vary in price and number of beds (the biggest has 12). You get to hang out with your fishing buddies all day long.

■ Where to Eat

 The B-Bar-B Ranch Inn, 325 East County Rd 2215, off US Hwy 77, ☎ 512-296-3331, www.seatrout.com/bbarb. Home-cooked meals. Call for reservations before you go.

Harrel Drug Co, 204 E Kleberg Ave, ☎ 512-592-3355. Old-fashioned soda fountain goodness with floats, shakes and juicy burgers.

King's Inn, US 77 south 11 miles, FM 628 east nine miles, ☎ 512-297-5265. Texans plan their travel around the King's Inn lunchtime and dinnertime schedules. It's in the middle of nowhere, but reservations are recommended for this joint that has no menus and serves its fresh seafoods by the pound. Many consider it a Texas tradition.

Lydia's Homestyle Cooking, 819 W King Ave, ☎ 512-592-9405. Mexican food for the hungry. They're closed on Sundays.

Helena

Things went tragically wrong on a fateful night in 1884 for Helena, Texas. That was the night 20-year-old Emmett Butler was killed in a saloon gun fight. No one fessed up to the murder so Emmett's father, Col. William Butler, a wealthy area rancher, decided that he would make the town pay for his loss.

He enticed the railroad to bypass Helena by giving them free land far away from the town. Without the railroads, the town suffocated and its residents wandered away.

What remains of Helena makes for a great historical visit. Buildings include a turn-of-the-century farmhouse, the old post office, part of the original jail and a barn. The abandoned courthouse has been retooled into a museum that offers area history, artifacts and period settings.

The remnants of Helena are located on Texas 80 between Karnes City and Gillett.

Brownsville/Matamoros

■ History

When Texas became a part of the United States, Texas' problems also became national problems. One of those problems – whether the southern boundary of the state was the Nueces or Rio Grande River – became an intense battle with Mexico.

In 1846 General Zachary Taylor, with his nation's best wishes, instigated the Mexican War by building a fort just across the Rio Grande from Matamoros. Mexico considered the fort an invasion (they were of the opinion that the Nueces, to the north, served as the boundary) and attacked.

Major Jacob Brown was among the first killed – Brownsville was named in his honor. Things quieted, for a while at least, after the Mexican War.

While much of Texas remained untouched during the Civil War because of its inaccessibility, Brownsville played a pivotal role, with each side alternately taking and re-taking the town. Eight miles east of Brownsville, at Palmito Ranch, the last battle of the Civil War was fought.

Today, Brownsville's population has soared above 115,000 and is continuing to rocket. Matamoros, established well before Brownsville was even a tactical idea, has a population of around half a million. The two, like all border towns, consider themselves one. Residents of one town regularly cross the international border to do business, go to work and visit friends.

While much of South Texas and the Valley have been depressed through the 1970s and 80s relative to the rest of the state, this area has been on a meteoric rise. Much of the rise is speculative and related to the recent enactment of the North American Free Trade Agreement (NAFTA), which will have a substantial impact on all Texas border regions.

■ Touring

For a historical journey – Brownsville counts itself as one of the top historical sites in the state – you can begin at **Fort Brown** (600 International), whose mere presence spawned the Mexican War. Founded in 1846 and closed over a century later in 1948, the Fort's original name belied its intent. "Fort Texas Across from Matamoros" was built strictly to incite Mexico and provide tangible evidence of the United States' belief that north of the Rio Grande was its territory. The stout posturing worked, and Fort Brown became just the first step in the United States' ultimate win over Mexico. The fort was also occupied by both the Union and the Confederacy during the Civil War. The outpost defended against bandits well into the 1900s.

While the fort instigated the Mexican War, the actual **Mexican War Battlefields** lay 10 miles away from the fort. The first battle, at Palo Alto, was won by the Americans, who were outnumbered 3-to-1. Only nine Americans were killed, compared to 300 Mexicans.

The next day General Zachary Taylor pressed on and encountered a Mexican outpost that was literally lying in wait in the dry creekbed of Resaca de la Palma. Casualties were higher, but Taylor won again. Ulysses S. Grant, second lieutenant, was one of the commanders present at this battle.

South Texas

✴ Author's Tip

A marker commemorating the Battle of Palo Alto (www.nps.gov/paal) is at the intersection of FM 1847 and FM 511. The marker for the Battle of Resaca de la Palma is on FM 1847 between Coffeeport and Price.

The battle fought at the **Palmito Ranch Battlefield** (TX 4, 14 miles east) is one of those historical footnotes that is indelibly imprinted on every military historian's mind. Despite the fact that the Civil War had ended six weeks earlier, Confederate and Union troops clashed. Word of General Lee's surrender had not yet made its way to the far reaches of South Texas. Nonetheless, 300 Confederate soldiers drove off over 1,500 Union troops in order to recapture some cotton stored in a downtown warehouse.

The **Gladys Porter Zoo** (500 Ringgold, ☎ 956-546-7187, www.gpz.org) is consistently ranked as one of the best zoos in the state, despite being in one of the smaller cities. The zoo, which features 1,800 mammals, birds and reptiles, some of which are the world's rarest and most endangered species, has no cages. Large open areas that resemble native habitats allow the animals to roam freely and intermingle. Many species live together, as they would in the wild.

There are several interesting museums about town. The **Stillman House and Museum** (1305 E Washington, ☎ 956-542-3929) was built by Charles Stillman, the founder of Brownsville, back in 1850, and is listed on the National Register of Historic Places. Antiques date back to the mid-1800s, with the exception of a 1790 grandfather clock that adorns the main hallway.

The **Historic Brownsville Museum** (641 E Madison, ☎ 956-548-1313) might be a good place to start before heading out to area battlefields – it contains a comprehensive history of the area. The 1920s Southern Pacific Railroad depot serves as the museum's home. It's run by a private organization, so call ahead for visitor hours.

If you can't be in New Orleans for Mardi Gras, you might as well be in Brownsville and Matamoros for **Charro Days** (Thursday through Sunday on weekends, varies from mid- to late February). Celebrating the Charro – landowning Mexican horsemen who are identifiable by their black pants, bolero jacket exquisitely embroidered, and decorative sombrero – and life in general, the two cities' host parades, dances, fiestas, rodeos and anything else they can find during this long weekend.

Tours of Brownsville are available on the **Historic Brownsville Trolley Tours** (Convention and Visitors Bureau: ☎ 956-546-3721), aboard a charming replica of a turn-of-the-century trolley. The two-hour narrated trips vary between tours of Historic Brownsville, the Port of Brownsville or Brownsville's historic churches. Call for the day's itinerary. **Gray Line Tours** (☎ 956-761-4343) regularly hosts tours of Matamoros. For more information on Brownsville, contact the **Conven-**

tion and Visitors Bureau (US 77 at FM 802, ☎ 800-626-2639, 956-546-3721, http://brownsville.org).

Information Sources

Contact the **Brownsville Convention and Visitors Bureau** (☎ 800-626-2639, PO Box 4697, 78523, http://brownsville.org) or the **Chamber of Commerce** (☎ 210-542-4341, PO Box 752, 78522). The city also maintains a Web site at www.ci.brownsville.tx.us.

■ Eco-Tours

The Brownsville area is home to many tropical bird species found nowhere else in the nation. More than 370 species share the areas in and around Brownsville with endangered animals like ocelots and jaguarundis. Because of the abundance of birding habitats along the Rio Grande Valley, a Wildlife Corridor has been created by area conservation groups and the US Fish and Wildlife Service. This refuge system is designed to protect the native brush along the river, providing safe passage for animals.

The **Sabal Palm Audubon Center & Sanctuary** (call for directions, ☎ 956-541-8034, www.audubon-tx.org/sanctuary/sabal.html) harbors some of the most distinctive and critical ecosystems, including the sabal palm, in South Texas and Northern Mexico. Only a small portion of the sabal palms that used to line the Rio Grande 80 miles upstream remain, and they are being preserved here in this preserve of over 500 acres.

Birders find great pleasure in sighting some of America's most elusive birds, as well as the endangered jaguarundi. At sunset, watch for bobcats and other native species that prowl the park's grounds. There are also two short nature trails that begin at the visitor's center.

You can reach the sanctuary by following US 77/83 south until it ends. Turn left on International Blvd, right on Southmost. The entrance will be six miles after you turn.

■ Where to Stay

Best Western Rose Garden Inn & Suites, 845 N Expressway, 78520, ☎ 956-546-5501, 800-528-1234. $$-$$$. Standard amenities.

South Texas

Colonial Hotel, 1147 E Levee, 78520, ☎ 956-541-9176. $. The economical way to see South Texas.

Four Points by ITT Sheraton, 3777 N Expressway, 78520, ☎ 956-350-9191, 800-325-3535. $$-$$$. In addition to standard amenities, there is a restaurant, heated pool, jacuzzi, and a work-out facility.

Holiday Inn Fort Brown Resort, 1900 E Elizabeth, 78520, ☎ 956-546-2201, 800-465-4329. $$$. They've got everything, from tennis, golf and shuffleboard facilities to jacuzzis and live musical entertainment.

Rancho Viejo Resort, Hwy 77, N 83 Rancho Viejo, 78575, ☎ 800-531-7400, 956-350-4000. $$$-$$$$. A country club with two 18-hole par-71 golf courses.

■ Where to Eat

Antonio's, 2921 Boca Chica Blvd, ☎ 956-542-6504. Mexican food to its core.

Miguel's Restaurant, 2400 Boca Chica Blvd, ☎ 956-541-8641. Offers both Tex-Mex and American fare. Fajitas are their most popular dish.

Garcia's Restaurant, Obregon near the bridge. Matamoros, Mexico. It burned down awhile back, but seems to be back stronger than before. A long-time favorite.

Palm Court Restaurant, 2235 Boca Chica Blvd, ☎ 956-542-3575. The menu stretches from gazpacho to tortilla soup to elegant crêpes.

The Vermillion, 115 Paredes Line Rd, ☎ 956-542-9893. From seafood to steaks to Tex-Mex, they've got a well-rounded menu. Try the ceviche, fresh from the Gulf. It's a favorite of the locals.

Harlingen

■ History

Considering the age of many of the border towns that were settled well before American colonization, Harlingen is very young. Lon C. Hill, Sr. first came to the Lower Rio Grande Valley in 1900. Hill became so enthralled with the area that in 1903 he gave up his law practice and began settlement of what is today Harlingen.

He picked the townsite's name from a map of Holland, where Harlingen is a town. He believed the area's irrigation canals must have looked a lot like the Dutch counterpart.

By 1910, the town had incorporated, but was known as "Six Shooter Junction," a reference to the wildness of the town. They say there were more guns in town than citizens. It took the presence of both the National Guard and the Texas Rangers to calm the bandit-riddled town down.

Today, Harlingen thrives as a harvesting center for the Lower Rio Grande Valley ("the Valley" to Texans), which is rich with fruit orchards and vegetable farms.

■ Touring

 The **Rio Grande Valley Museum Complex** (Boxwood and Raintree off Loop 499, ☎ 956-430-8500) rolls four distinct buildings into one. The Historical Museum traces both the cultural and physical steps the Valley has taken in its short lifetime. Railroads truly opened the area up to commerce. Their role is celebrated with schedule cards, lanterns, spikes and photographs.

One of the buildings on display is the 1905 house of Lon C. Hill, the town's founder. Hill was responsible for creating 26 miles of irrigation canals, which opened all kinds of agricultural opportunities for the town. Memorabilia from Hill's life are on display, including photographs and clothing worn by his family.

The city's first hospital, built in 1923, now serves as a medical museum in the complex. The fourth building is the Paso Real Stagecoach Inn, which has been restored to its original 19th-century state.

> **✱ Did You Know?**
>
> The Paso Real Stagecoach Inn, at the turn of the century, would charge visitors 35¢ for food and a night's lodging.

If you are inspired by the precision of the military, then you should drop by the **Marine Military Academy** (320 Iwo Jima Blvd, ☎ 956-423-6006), where you might catch the private military school cadets doing drills or maneuvers. If your timing is off, visit the **Texas Iwo Jima War Memorial** (on campus). It is the original model used to cast the bronze memorial that stands in Arlington National Cemetery. The figures stand 32 feet high – the flagpole they are erecting stands 78 feet high.

South Texas

Across from the memorial is a small museum and gift shop that contains World War II artifacts and memorabilia.

To truly taste – in the literal sense – what the Valley is all about, go shopping at **Sugar Tree Farms** (Bass Blvd off US 83 west, ☎ 956-423-5530). You can buy their wares, which differ with the season, by the pound, the sack or the box.

Information Sources

Contact the **Harlingen Chamber of Commerce/Convention and Visitors Bureau** (☎ 800-531-7346, 311 E. Tyler, PO Box 189, 78550, www.harlingen.com).

■ Where to Stay

Hudson House Motel, 500 Ed Carey Drive, 78550, ☎ 800-784-8911, 956-428-8911. $. Modern accommodations at fair prices.

Marriott Courtyard, 1725 W Filmore, 78550, ☎ 800-321-2211, 956-412-7800. $$. Shuttle service and a heated swimming pool top off the amenities.

Ross Haus B&B, PO Box 2566, Harlingen, 78551, ☎ 800-580-1717, 956-425-1717. Corporate suites.

Vieh's Bed and Breakfast, Hwy 675, Rt. 4, Box 75A, San Benito, 78586, ☎ 956-425-4651. $$. It's out in the country, and the proprietors cater to the birding clientele. Their 15 acres of property are a prepared habitat, complete with walking trails and a lake right outside the house. The hosts will pick you up at the airport and help you with your plans. This B&B is relatively close to three or four bird refuges.

■ Where to Eat

Lone Star, 4201 W Bus. Hwy 83, ☎ 956-423-8002. Barbecue, barbecue and barbecue. That's what they do best. There are a few other items for those not in the mood.

Vannie Tilden Bakery, 203 E Harrison, ☎ 956-423-4062. Give in to their pastry delights for breakfast and lunch. They've been around almost as long as the town. Open Tuesday through Saturday.

McAllen

■ History

John McAllen, a Scotland native, arrived in South Texas in the 1850s. His persistence and temerity made him one of the largest landowners in the Valley. By 1904, he had acquired some 80,000 acres and established a town, West McAllen (though there was no East McAllen or even a McAllen). It wasn't long before there was an East McAllen, created in 1907 by James Brigg, another developer.

The two towns vied for dominance. Finally Brigg came up with the more creative answer – installing a horse trough. Cowboys and ranchers began to water their horses at the trough, provisioning at the same time. McAllen's western settlement faded away and East McAllen became McAllen.

The biggest economic impact came not with the railroads (though they certainly had an effect), but with irrigation canals trenched by the Rio Bravo Irrigation Company. Over 27,000 acres of land were opened up for cultivation and the Valley became an agricultural hub.

■ Touring

 The large influx of "Winter Texans," usually retired travelers who migrate to South Texas to escape the cold winters of Canada and northern states, has helped a great deal in making McAllen the "Square Dance Capital of the World." From December to March, fueled by the enlarged population, there's dancing and lessons to be enjoyed just about every hour of every day. To find out current information and times on **square dancing** events, call the **Convention and Visitors Bureau** at ☎ 956-682-2871.

Try picking your own fruit at **Eggers Acres** (Shary Rd west of town, ☎ 956-581-7783), a family-run citrus market owned by Mardi Eggers. Eggers has long been in the citrus business – her grandfather developed the Ruby Red grapefruit. The citrus season usually runs from October to April.

The **Shrine of La Virgen de San Juan del Valle** (400 N Nebraska, San Juan, ☎ 956-787-0033) is one of the most traditional Catholic churches around. The $5 million project, funded by small private donations, seats 1,800 worshippers and includes a magnificent array of stained glass, an impressive alter and an incredible shrine to the Virgin of San Juan.

A quick side trip to the **Old Clock Museum** (929 Preston Lane, Pharr, Texas, ☎ 956-787-1923) is a unique trip into a working history of clocks. There are only five museums with similar collections in the nation. James Colvin, who began collecting clocks in the 1960s, now has over 1,000 timepieces, ranging from antique cuckoos to weathered grandfathers. Colvin's collection grew so immense that he had to move it next door into its own building. If you have a moment, you should stop to talk with the owner – he's an interesting character and a real Texas gem.

Of course, if you're in a border town, you're always just a step away from Mexico. McAllen's sister city is **Reynosa**, 10 miles south across the border. With over half a million residents, Reynosa is much larger and more established than its Texas counterpart.

✳ Take Care!

As at most border towns, it's usually better to leave your car on the US side of the border if you're just going across for the day and aren't familiar with the territory. If you do drive in (there's nothing really difficult about it), just make sure you have the proper insurance. If you have an accident and aren't covered, there could be problems.

A large congregation of shops and restaurants are in the **Zona Rosa** district, just a short walk from the international bridge.

Information Sources

Call the **McAllen Convention and Visitors Bureau** (☎ 210-682-2871, PO Box 790, 78505, www.mcallen.org) for more information.

■ Eco-Tours

The **Bentsen-Rio Grande Valley State Park** (five miles south of Mission off FM 2062, ☎ 956-519-6448, www.tpwd.state.tx.us) hugs the Rio Grande. The 588 acres of subtropical resaca woodlands and brushland of thicket-forming thorny shrubs and small trees allow visitors to study plants, animals and birds unique to South Texas.

Park naturalists conduct daily birdwatching and wildlife tours from December through March and they are very thorough, lasting between six and eight hours. You can also rent bird observation blinds on your own. The park rents out bikes and offers two hiking trails, one that takes you through the wilderness and another that brings you to the banks of the Rio Grande.

Birders especially enjoy the spring months when migration patterns bring several different species to the area, like paraques, groove-billed anis, green kingfishers, blue buntings, black-bellied whistling ducks and tropical parulas. The park is also one of the last natural refuges in Texas for cats such as the ocelot and jaguarundi.

The area is rich in birding opportunities. Another favorite is the **Santa Ana/Lower Rio Grande Valley National Wildlife Refuge** (☎ 956-787-3079, 956-787-7861, www.hiline.net/santaana/index.shtml), where many of the species are considered threatened or endangered. It provides a preserved thorn forest habitat for various species – over 95% of the area's original thorn forests have been cleared to make way for industrial and farming needs, making the refuge vital to the survival of many animals.

Over 300 species of birds can be found in the park, as well as half of all butterfly species native to North America. The annual migrations – and some of the most dynamic times to visit – occur in September/October and March/April.

There are over 12 miles of trails to enjoy, but there is no camping or picnicking allowed. Bring insect repellent if you go – the weather is so mild in the winter that mosquitoes thrive year-round. There are guided nature tours and bird walks throughout the winter months. Check with the visitors' center for details.

■ Where to Stay

 Doubletree Club Hotel Casa De Palmas, 101 North Main, 78501, ☎ 956-631-1101, 800-222-TREE. $$-$$$. All of the modern amenities you could ask for in a restored 1918 Spanish-style hotel, a Texas Historical Landmark. There's a beautiful courtyard, a heated swimming pool, covered parking, complimentary breakfast and free shuttle service.

South Texas

Fairway Resort Hotel, 2105 S 10th, 78503, ☎ 956-682-2445. $$. There are about 40 rooms for rent, including several nice suites. They've recently downsized their establishment.

■ Where to Eat

 La Cucaracha, Reynosa, three blocks southwest of bridge. Although the famed song *La Cucaracha* is about cockroaches, there's none of that here. It's plush, with lobster and flaming desserts, plus nightly dancing.

Johnny's Mexican Food, 1012 Houston, ☎ 956-686-9061. It's basic Mexican and Tex-Mex fare with no pretenses. Menu includes migas, cabrito and chili rellenos.

Tom and Jerry's, 401 N 10th, ☎ 956-687-3001. You'll feel at home here, because you're literally enjoying your dinner in a home. Chicken fajitas and chicken-fried steak are their specialties.

Laredo/Nuevo Laredo

■ History

Laredo's roots run clear back to 1755, when Captain Tomás Sánchez, along with three families, was granted permission to settle an area just north of the Rio Grande near an Indian ford. By 1757 there were 11 families operating the ranch and by 1767 they had laid out the town. Originally a Spanish colony, it became a Mexican city in 1821 when Mexico won its independence from Spain.

However good the location, Laredo was still a target for the Comanche and Apache raiders and the town was frequently wiped out. Mexico's apparent complacency in protecting their city, along with local discontent over rule by a dictatorship, led Laredo residents to support the creation of the Republic of the Rio Grande in 1840. Their grand plans for a new nation – with Laredo as the capital – were destroyed after only 283 days. Laredo became, once again, a part of Mexico. But not for long. The town, which existed under a myriad of flags, became a part of Texas after the Treaty of Guadalupe Hidalgo established the Rio Grande as the southern boundary of the state.

Loyalists to Mexico simply moved across the river to form Nuevo Laredo. The two cities, although belonging to different nations, have considered themselves one unit ever since.

The railroads came to town in 1881, sealing the town's fate. It was to become a large city and international gateway. A coal mine 29 miles northwest of town fueled the railroad engines and ensured their path through the area well into the 20th century.

Known today as the city under seven flags, Laredo has emerged as the principal port of entry into Mexico. It has consistently been one of the fastest-growing cities in the nation for the past decade. Nuevo Laredo is the bigger of the two towns, often referred to as Los Dos Laredos (the two Laredos), topping a quarter-million residents.

■ Touring

 Though the Republic of the Rio Grande lasted only 283 days, its existence is immortalized at the **Museum of the Republic of the Rio Grande** (1003 Zaragoza, San Augustin Plaza, ☎ 956-727-3480). An 1834 stone building that served as the capitol for the short-lived republic is now home to the museum, which traces the makings of the revolution.

There are several things you can't miss when you visit **Nuevo Laredo**. **La Fiesta bullfight ring** (six miles from the International Bridge #1, ☎ 956-722-9895, Laredo Visitors Center) hosts bullfights, usually from the spring through September. If it's hot outside, shell out the extra admission for a seat on the shady side of the stadium. It will make a world of difference.

Near the bullring is the **Handcraft Museum** (Bravo St), with replicas of important art objects of the principal pre-Hispanic cultures, including Maya, Aztec, Olmeca, Huasteca, Totonaca and Teothihuacan.

Nuevo Laredo's main shopping strip is located on Guerrero, just across bridge #1 when you enter town. Bartering is par for the course, so whittle prices down as low as your bargaining prowess permits.

✳ Author's Tip

Do research if there's a particular item you want – you'll usually find it available from several vendors. You'll also probably find that there is a threshold that none of the vendors will go below on each item.

South Texas

Also, if you're in Mexico, don't miss some of the great foods. Nuevo Laredo is famous for its fresh Gulf seafood at cheap prices.

Information Sources

Contact either the **Laredo Convention and Visitors Bureau** (☎ 210-795-2200, 501 San Augustin, 78040, www.visitlaredo.com) or the **Chamber of Commerce** (☎ 800-292-2122, PO Box 790, 78042).

■ Adventures on the Water

Some of the state's finest black bass fishing can be found at **Lake Casa Blanca State Park** (US 59, eastern edge of town). The 1,656-acre park, offers camping facilities, along with a boat ramp and fishing pier. Only 10 minutes away from downtown Laredo, you can either breeze in and out in an hour or hunker down for an entire day of recreation. There's a complete bait-and-tackle shop and boat rental.

■ Where to Stay

Executive House Hotel, 7060 N San Bernardo, 78041, ☎ 956-724-8221. $$. Just about everything you might need plus free transportation to the airport and the bridge to Nuevo Laredo. Weekly rates available.

Family Gardens Inn, 5830 San Bernardo, 78041, ☎ 800-292-4053 or 956-723-5300. $$-$$$. All the amenities you could want including out-door pool, whirlpool, free breakfast, dry cleaning service and free airport transportation. Units in the Garden Square building are built around a garden, complete with waterfall.

Posada Hotel & Suites, 1000 Zaragoza St, 78040, ☎ 956-722-1701. www.laposadahotel-laredo.com/laposadahotel-laredo. $$$-$$$$. Once a 19th-century Spanish-Colonial convent, this historical edifice overlooks the Rio Grande, along with lush tropical courtyards and pools. Right next to International Bridge #1, so access to Nuevo Laredo is right out the door.

■ Where to Eat

Charlie's Corona, 3902 San Bernardo Ave, ☎ 956-725-8227. Live entertainment and international cuisine.

Cotulla-Style Pit Bar-B-Q, 4502 McPherson, ☎ 956-724-5747. Breakfast tacos here go by a different name – mariaches. And they're also not just for breakfast. Served all day to locals' delight.

Laredo Bar & Grill, 102 Del Court, ☎ 956-717-0090. Caters to the upscale crowd with eclectic offerings that are unique to South Texas.

The Tesoro Club, 1000 Zaragoza, 3rd Floor, ☎ 956-722-1701. Tableside cooking and exceptional choices. Part of the Posada Hotel.

El Dorado (Cadillac Bar), Beldon Y Ocampo, Nuevo Laredo, ☎ 12-00-15. The finest in international food and drink.

Del Rio

■ History

When 17th-century explorers stopped at present day Del Rio on the Day of San Felipe, they crowned their campgrounds San Felipe del Rio. That was the name it kept for around two centuries until it became a part of Texas. There was already a village bearing the same name, so the town graciously agreed to change its name to Del Rio. The moniker "San Felipe" survived as a community within the city.

The first real settlement of the area happened after the Civil War, when ranchers tapped the San Felipe Springs for irrigation. The verdant springs gushed forth with around 90 million gallons of water a day, making life in the semi-arid climate possible. Agriculture, established by the spring's grandeur, became the economic heart.

It remains important today, but it was quickly discovered that sheep and goats thrived in the climate and Del Rio now proclaims itself the "Wool and Mohair Capital of the World." The title is contested (Sonora, up the road, says it is Mohair Capital of the World, as well), but the annual bumper crops of wool and mohair are not in dispute.

In 1969, with President Nixon in office, the Amistad Dam on the Rio Grande River was dedicated. Just 12 miles north of Del Rio, the dam created the Amistad Reservoir, a recreational resort.

Around the same time, the city began to see an economic future in attracting *maquiladoras* to its border. American and European businesses flocked to the town to set up *maquilas* (assembly and industrial plants) across the Rio Grande, while administrating their affairs in Del Rio.

South Texas

■ Touring

The Perry Mercantile building that sits on South Main has been big in many ways. Back in the late 1800s it was the biggest store between San Antonio and El Paso, making it a vital stop on travelers' itineraries. Now it is part of the **Whitehead Memorial Museum** (1308 S Main, ☎ 830-774-7568), which was deeded to the city in the 1960s for a museum and now includes seven different buildings – big by any museum standards. The first building – the Hacienda – serves as the visitor's center, gift shop and chapel. The actual Perry Store provides the backdrop for exhibits on pioneer history. Some of the other buildings include displays on the Seminole Indian Scouts, prehistoric man and native Indians, and on Judge Roy Bean (the infamous "Law West of the Pecos" that ruled just up the road in Langtry – see entry on Langtry, page 371, for details).

The oldest winery in Texas, **Val Verde Winery** (100 Qualia, ☎ 830-775-9714) began selling its wares in 1883 and continues operating today under the same family. A tour of the Qualia family's winery includes everything from seeing the grapes ripening on their vines, to the aging process, to a final taste. They produce eight different varieties, one of which is the Lenoir, the wine they began their legacy with back in the 1880s. If you like what you taste, you can, of course, purchase some to take home. The Muscat Canelli, a sweet fruity white wine, is their biggest seller.

With Mexico literally in your backyard, a visit to **Ciudad Acuña** (Garfield Ave west to International Toll Bridge) is worth it. Although almost all Mexican border towns suffer poverty that seems worse than in the interior, it is not as defined here. Most everything on the border is transacted in English and with the American dollar.

✳ Take Care!

You can take your vehicle across, but if you don't need to, it's better just to leave it north of the border and either walk or taxi across. It's less than a mile from the bridge to the shopping district, but probably a bus or taxi ride to downtown. If you do take your car across, be sure to purchase auto insurance from an authorized Mexican insurance agent (you'll find them at the border). Most American insurance policies do not cover travel into Mexico. And if you're involved in any accident in Mexico without the proper insurance, you might wind up in a Mexican jail.

Contact the **Del Rio Chamber of Commerce** at ☎ 830-775-3551 or visit their Web site at www.chamber.delrio.com.

▪ Adventures on the Water

 With the **Amistad Reservoir** (US 90 northwest, ☎ 830-775-7491, park service, or 830-775-6722, ranger station) only minutes away from Del Rio, recreational choices are simple. The truly international lake offers 851 miles of shoreline, including several rivers: the Rio Grande, the Pecos and Devils River. The joint venture between the US and Mexico is spanned by a toll road atop the bridge that impounds its waters.

More than 1.2 million visitors come to the US side of the lake each year for swimming, fishing, water-skiing, camping, hiking, biking, and anything else you can think of. The reservoir's water is so clear that scuba diving is also popular. You can fish in Mexican waters as well if you've purchased a Mexican fishing permit.

The **Lake Amistad Resort and Marina** (US 90W at Diablo East Recreation Area, ☎ 830-774-4157) offers all normal resort and marina facilities, including houseboat rentals. Visitors can rent 50-foot or 36-foot houseboats for a day or longer. The **Rough Canyon Inn & Country Store** (Hwy 277N, RR2, ☎ 830-774-6266) also offers boat rentals.

Tours

Several touring companies put Amistad at your fingertips. **High Bridge Adventure** (Comstock, ☎ 915-292-4495) tours include trips to see Indian pictographs – some that are 8,000 years old – that dot many of the reservoir's canyon walls. Some of the pictographs are accessible only by boat.

Guides

Fishing guides could help on a lake as large as Amistad. Two servicers are: **Jim Holder Guide Service** (Box Canyon, ☎ 915-292-4581), catching catfish only, and **Lake Amistad Guide Service** (☎ 830-774-3484).

South Texas

Special Attraction

■ The Big Hunt

If a Texan tells someone they're going to South Texas, more often than not the response will be "What are you hunting?" While that is a little too simplistic – considering that Mexico borders the southern edge and the Texas Coast and Padre Island lie to the east – it is representative of what South Texas is about. Sparsely populated with wild game that multiplies rapidly in the mild climate, South Texas is a hunters' paradise.

Hunting in Texas is by no means isolated to South Texas. There are different opportunities across the state. More than one million hunters spend over a billion dollars per year in Texas – a telling statistic. But South Texas – the Brush Country – offers some of the finest.

The area stretches south of an imaginary line that connects Del Rio, San Antonio and Corpus Christi. Ranging from areas that appear pancake-flat to those with gently rolling hills, South Texas is covered with thick growths of brush and cacti, both well-equipped with thorns. Hunting is expensive, a reflection of the fact that most of the state's trophy bucks are nurtured here. Bucks average 125-145 pounds dressed weight in most seasons, depending on the year's rainfall. December is typically the best month for finding bucks in the Brush Country – they are preoccupied with mating rather than caution. October and November are good times for Central Texas, which has a thicker population of whitetail (but they are typically smaller than those you would find in the south).

While deer are one of the main attractions of Central and South Texas, quail hunting is considered unparalleled in the south. Also, turkey, dove and cottontail turn in good seasons. Texas has pretty much declared war on the feral hogs, which can be hunted any time of the year, with a few exceptions.

Perhaps the biggest challenge to hunting in Texas is finding a place to hunt. Ninety-seven percent of wildlife live on private land. Hunters depend on leasing alliances to access trophy specimens. The Texas Wildlife Association annually puts out a leasing registry (see the end of this chapter) that can help you obtain access to private land. The Parks and Wildlife people also put out an annual list of leasing opportunities, along with chambers of commerce in some of the key hunting areas (like Uvalde, Del Rio, Laredo, etc.). A good start to any hunting trip would be to talk to the **Parks and Wildlife Department** (☎ 512-389-4800, 4200 Smith School Road, Austin, 78744) or visit their Web site at www.tpwd.state.tx.us/.

Types of Hunting Leases

1. **Day lease** – a specified fee is paid to the owner for each day of hunting.

2. **Package lease** – a specified number of hunting days are arranged. This is often included with other services, such as guiding, lodging and meals.

3. **Season lease** – a specified pasture or area is leased for an entire season, or, more rarely, for the full year. Commonly, a group of individuals will share the cost, as in a "hunting club."

The Texas Hunting Guide, published each August by the Parks and Wildlife Department, provides season information, license description and requirements and bag limits. You can pick up a license in just about any sporting goods, hardware, gun or convenience store, especially those in hunting territory.

The **Texas Wildlife Association** annually puts out a lease registry that is available to hunters for $3. It is updated continually, so the information will change over time. Perhaps the best way to get current information is to visit their Web site at www.texas-wildlife.org. You can also contact them at Texas Wildlife Association, 1635 NE Loop 410, Suite 108, San Antonio, Texas 78209, ☎ 210-826-2904; fax 210-826-4933.

Useful Addresses for Hunters

Texas Wildlife Association
1635 NE Loop 410, Suite 108
San Antonio, Texas 78209
☎ 210-826-2904; fax 210-826-4933
(Lease registry $3; general information)

Texas Parks & Wildlife Department
4200 Smith School Rd
Austin, TX 78744
☎ 512-389-4800
(Hunting/fishing regulations/information; state parks information)

South Texas

Texas Dept of Highways & Public Transportation
Division of Travel and Information
Dewitt C Greer Building building
125 E. 11˚ St
Austin, TX 78701
☎ 512-463-8585
(Highway maps; county maps)

Exotic Wildlife Association
PO Box 705
Ingram, TX 78025
☎ 830-895-4997, 800-752-5431
(Information on non-native hoofed species)

■ Where to Stay

Inn on the Creek, Rose Ave, 78840, ☎ 830-774-6198. $$$.
Very private with shade trees and wrought iron fence. The
creek runs through the front yard and the owners live off-site.

Villa Del Rio, 123 Hudson Dr, 78840, ☎ 830-768-1100, 800-995-1887,
www.villadelrio.com. $$-$$$. A late-1800s Alamo-styled mansion nes-
tled between 22 centurion pecan trees and 15 century-old palms and
magnolias. A wonderful find, complete with ballroom, chandeliers, and
hacienda ambiance.

The 1890 House, 609 Griner St, 78840, ☎ 830-775-8061. $$-$$$.
Breakfast is served by candlelight at this five-room house.

Laguna Diablo Resort, 1 Sanders Point Rd, 78840, ☎ 830-774-2422,
www.delrio.com/~ldresort. $$-$$$. Enjoy this rustic resort built of na-
tive stone and rough-sawn wood only three miles from Rough Canyon
Marina, where you have access to Lake Amistad and can launch or rent
a boat.

■ Where to Eat

Cripple Creek Restaurant, Hwy 90 West, ☎ 830-775-0153.
www.drtx.com/cripplecreekrestaurant. With a logged exterior
and muraled interior, Cripple Creek does its best to bring back
the Old West. They specialize in prime rib, steaks and seafood.

Lando's Restaurant and Bar, 270 Hidalgo, Ciudad Acuña. Both Mex-
ican and American cuisine are served at this plush place that's topped

off with a chandelier. Reservations are recommended for the weekends. Thursday through Saturday are disco nights.

Memo's, 804 E Losoya, ☎ 830-775-8104. The family restaurant has been around since 1936, surely a testament to their Tex-Mex and American fare.

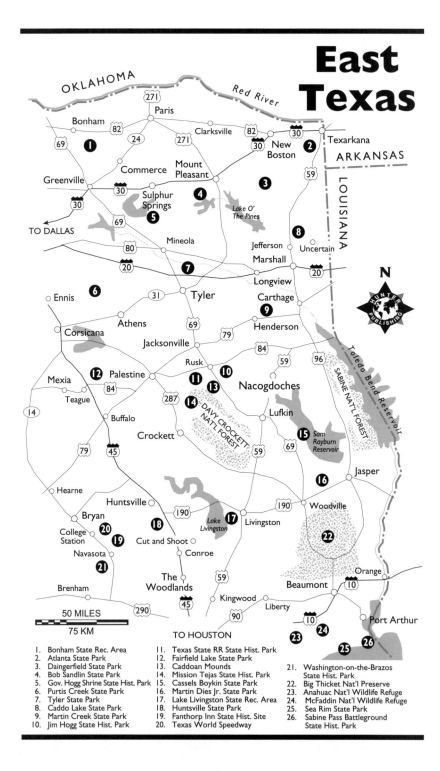

East Texas

1. Bonham State Rec. Area
2. Atlanta State Park
3. Daingerfield State Park
4. Bob Sandlin State Park
5. Gov. Hogg Shrine State Hist. Park
6. Purtis Creek State Park
7. Tyler State Park
8. Caddo Lake State Park
9. Martin Creek State Park
10. Jim Hogg State Hist. Park
11. Texas State RR State Hist. Park
12. Fairfield Lake State Park
13. Caddoan Mounds
14. Mission Tejas State Hist. Park
15. Cassels Boykin State Park
16. Martin Dies Jr. State Park
17. Lake Livingston State Rec. Area
18. Huntsville State Park
19. Fanthorp Inn State Hist. Site
20. Texas World Speedway
21. Washington-on-the-Brazos State Hist. Park
22. Big Thicket Nat'l Preserve
23. Anahuac Nat'l Wildlife Refuge
24. McFaddin Nat'l Wildlife Refuge
25. Sea Rim State Park
26. Sabine Pass Battleground State Hist. Park

East Texas

■ The Land

They say Texas is a Whole Other Country. East Texas certainly proves that. While West Texas provides the dusty backdrop that the world expects, and Central Texas has its cedar-topped rolling hills, East Texas is a piney wooded paradise.

The first time you drive along some of its narrower roads, you have to pinch yourself to remember which state you're in. You usually don't find the words "Texas" and "forests" in the same sentence, but there you are, driving by dense collections of pine and more green than you can imagine.

The greenness comes from the more than ample rainfall – an average of 30 inches a year, with the easternmost portions recording double that amount.

■ History

The first Indians arrived here 37,000 years ago. The French and Spanish arrived in the 16th century. But it was the tenacious, westward moving American colonists that planted the deepest roots in the Piney Woods of East Texas. The Spanish were never completely comfortable here.

Texas lore does not much mention the eastern stretches of the state – talk is reserved for tourist attractions like the Alamo, South Padre Island and the like. Which is ironic, because East Texas is where it all began, from colonization to cotton to cattle to oil. Nacogdoches, settled by Europeans in 1716, is the oldest town in the state.

The first Texas settlers were primarily farmers and planters looking for new land to cultivate. And they found it – in large, fertile masses. They brought their slaves, cleared the land and set up brisk cotton and sugar trades. They extended the Old South of Mississippi, Alabama and Georgia, but eventually bumped against what is now the I-35 corridor boundary, where the soil was unsuitable for plantation growth.

The coming of the railroads changed the social and economic fabric of the nation. For East Texas, it meant easy transportation for sawmills and lumbering enterprises.

✳ *Did You Know?*

With the coming of the railroads, the plundering of the great Piney Woods began. Between 1890 and 1940, 16 million acres of virgin pine were "harvested." Today, the virgin pine exists only in protected areas.

Corsicana was the site of the state's first big oil strike just before the turn of the century. Ultimately, over 350 wells were dug in and around the town, producing a half-million barrels of oil a year. Spindletop blew its top near Beaumont in 1901. During its first year the well produced more than three million barrels of oil. From these two massive discoveries – along with smaller ones that cropped up across the wooded landscape – some of the world's largest oil companies arose: Texaco, Mobil and Gulf Oil. To the south, utilizing the Gulf shore for its access to the world, refineries took root in Port Arthur, Beaumont and Orange.

Those three cities became known as the "Golden Triangle," a tribute to the wealth that the oil industry created. With all of the oil, industry and wealth being pumped and shipped to the Gulf Coast, it is no surprise that Houston quickly became one of the largest cities in America.

Today, East Texas enjoys a peace and solitude it never had in its wildcatting days. Working-class people still man its wells, refineries and farms and enjoy the myriad fishing holes that dot the countryside. Accents are strong here, as are family bonds. And the pace is nice and slow.

■ Logistics

There is really no good way to travel the windy backroads that snake around the Piney Woods other than by car. But you'll be flabbergasted by the forested beauty that makes up the area.

East Texas is flanked by Houston to the south and Dallas to the west, both major hubs for air transportation. Virtually every airline, large and small, services the two cities. Commuter and jet service is spotty and changes with the season. However, if you're trying to get straight into the interior, ask questions about Tyler. It often picks up jet routes from various airlines.

■ Weather & Climate

The price East Texas pays for its lush undergrowth is a longer rainy season than the rest of the state. But you'll barely know the difference. What you will notice will be the humidity and the mosquitoes during the warmer months. The dank surroundings are perfect breeding grounds for the pesky creatures. Make sure you bring a full can of repellent during the warm stretches.

The Northern Reaches

Greenville

■ History & Touring

 Greenville very well could have been named for the lush color that covers the area's fertile, dank earth. However, the town of 23,000 received its moniker from Gen. Thomas Jefferson Green, a military man who achieved only mediocre success and died in the Civil War while serving as a Confederate commander.

The residents who chose the Greenville settlement chose well, placing it squarely amid the Blackland Prairie. The dark earth proved especially well suited for a variety of crops, including cotton. When the railroads arrived in 1880 the town became an agricultural hub. Although the small community has diversified through the years, cotton and other crops remain central to its economy.

Audie Murphy

Greenville's most famous son, Audie Murphy, the most decorated soldier during World War II, later became a film star. He was actually born up the road a couple of miles, but it was in Greenville that he enlisted in the army on his 18th birthday. He is immortalized in the **Audie Murphy Room** at the Walworth Harrison Public Library (3716 Lee St) through a collection of medals, uniforms and photographs. For Murphy fans – or World War II history buffs – it's a treasure.

You probably wouldn't guess that a large portion of those mail order Christmas fruitcakes come from Greenville. **Mary of Puddin Hill** (4007 I-30, ☎ 903-455-2651, www.puddinhill.com/puddin) churns out a huge chunk of them. She sends out 1.6 million catalogs a year. Mary and Sam Lauderdale began the enterprise in 1948, using an old family rec-

East Texas

ipe for pecan fruitcake. That first year they sold 500 of the hand-crafted novelties and they've been growing ever since. The majority of the site is dedicated to the mail order business, but there is a store attached for visitors. In addition to serving their famous pies and candy, they offer fresh soups and sandwiches.

The **American Cotton Museum** (600 I-30 east, ☎ 903-454-1990) not only pays tribute to cotton, but to Murphy and other local celebrities like *Voyager* copilot Jeana Yeager and baseball pitcher Monty Stratton.

Shoppers passing through town might want to check out the town square, which boasts a fascinating array of antique shops and boutiques. Greenville has earned a solid reputation as a bargain hunter's dream.

Information Sources

Call the **Greenville Chamber of Commerce** (2713 Stonewall St, PO Box 1055, 75403, ☎ 903-455-1510, www.greenville-chamber.org).

■ Adventures on Foot

The **Heard Natural Science Museum and Wildlife Sanctuary** (One Nature Place, McKinney, 75069, ☎ 972-562-5566, www.heardmuseum.org) has sought to preserve a small portion of the once-vast Texas Blackland Prairie, setting aside 100 acres of what began as 12 million acres. The preserve, which has never been plowed, stands as it did a century ago with native grasses and wildflowers. Birdwatchers and wildflower lovers are particularly drawn to the site that serves as a living history of the earth before human involvement.

The actual museum is a result of one woman's passion. Miss Bessie Heard (1884-1988) was a devout collector of butterflies, nature prints and seashells, among other things. When her collection was too large to fit in her house (especially the butterflies), it was moved to this present-day museum.

There are over five miles of trails throughout the 287-acre wildlife sanctuary. There is also a canoe trail. More than 240 species of birds, mammals, reptiles and amphibians and nearly 150 species of wildflowers and other plants inhabit the park. Children appreciate the outdoor learning center, with an observation deck, a floating study laboratory and a boardwalk.

■ Adventures on the Water

 Some of the state's best fishing lakes are located near Greenville. **Lake Tawakoni** (take US 69 southeast 16 miles, ☎ 903-447-3020), with 200 miles of shoreline, weighs in as one of Texas' largest lakes, spreading itself over three counties. In addition to fishing, visitors enjoy boating, camping, swimming, beaches, picnic areas and water-skiing. At least 10 different fishing clubs run tournaments from the lake; it boasts an ample supply of striper, catfish and largemouth bass.

Lake Fork (State Hwy 515, 35 miles southeast) lies just a little farther away and is a perfect getaway for fishing and boating.

■ Where to Stay

Greenville

Iron Skillet Inn Bed & Breakfast, 664 Forester, 75401, ☎ 903-455-0074. $$. This recently restored bed and breakfast is a tourist attraction itself. With 5,000 square feet of house and "scads" of antiques, Bonnie, Clyde and World War II hero Audie Murphy all stayed here at one point.

The Friendly Ghost

According to its owners, the Iron Skillet is also home to a friendly ghost. The legend begins with a Mrs. Williams divorcing her husband because of his lack of the finer things, and marrying a Jewish man who could quench her worldly tastes. Mr. Williams then proceeded to build this 5,000-square-foot mansion. The Jewish man mysteriously "disappeared," leaving Mrs. Williams free to remarry Mr. Williams and take up residence in the massive abode. A walled-in fireplace within the house, legend has it, was the final resting spot for the jilted Jewish man. But his spirit, supposedly, still wanders the house.

Lake Tawakoni

429 Marina, a quarter-mile south of FM 751 on 429, ☎ 903-356-2125. RV sites and ramp access.

East Texas

Anchor Inn Marina & Resort, Hwy 276 at Tomahawk (half-mile south), ☎ 903-447-2256. Fishing guide service, on-site restaurant, hotel, cabins, tent sites, two boat ramps and rental facilities for paddleboats, canoes and bikes.

Cedar Cove Landing, off Hwy 35, ☎ 903-447-2169. Includes a store replete with needed supplies.

Finstad's Kitsee Ridge, off 741 at County Rd 3622, ☎ 903-356-3573. Campgrounds with facilities for both tents and RVs.

Holiday Marina, Hwy 47 N at spillway (near Wills Point), ☎ 903-560-0630. With a bait shop and lighted fishing pier.

Lone Star Marina, ☎ 903-447-4843.

Rabbit Cove Landing, ☎ 903-447-2278. Slips for your boats and facilities for RVs.

Tawakoni Marina, Inc. Rabbit Cove, End of County Line Rd, ☎ 903-447-2255.

Walnut Cove Marina & Resort, off FM 276 on Mays Lane, ☎ 903-447-2855. A bait and tackle shop, lighted fishing pier, campgrounds, RV hook-ups and wet and dry slips.

■ Where to Eat

 The Spare Rib, 7818 Wesley, ☎ 903-455-0219. You'll smell the food long before you get it – barbecue is baked right into the walls. There's fried ice cream for dessert.

Canton

■ History

The town's major claim to fame humbly began after the town was laid out in 1849 when the area folk gathered on the first Monday of the month (when the district judge was in town) to "hear court." Court day was also the day – Hoss Monday – when stray horses were auctioned, attracting farmers from all over who were interested in trading their own wares and livestock. Historians note that Hoss Monday developed much more quickly than Canton, drawing more and more bargain hunters to its town square.

It took on a more competitive nature, with vendors beginning to fetch customers the day before First Monday. Soon the mega-event was moved to encompass the entire weekend prior to First Monday. Today the 150-acre affair starts the deal-making late Thursday night and by Sunday afternoon most of the vendors are packed up and gone.

■ Touring

 Three weekends a month Canton is a sleepy bastion of small-town feel-good with just over 3,400 residents. But on the fourth weekend preceding the first Monday of every month, hundreds of thousands of professional and amateur shoppers flock to town, located one hour southeast of Dallas, for what is billed as the largest flea market in the state and perhaps even the nation.

First Monday Trade Days (☎ 903-567-6556) includes more than 3,000 independent trinket dealers and unofficially boasts that if you can't find it here, it probably doesn't exist.

> ### ✳ Author's Tip
>
> Roads are clogged with RVs and campers and day shoppers during First Monday. Hotels are booked to capacity and standing in line is the norm. Local residents grin and bear the delays, considering that income from the market accounts for almost two-thirds of the city's operating budget.

If you're going to be in town anyway, a good place to visit is the **Brewer's Bells Museum** (two miles west on Hwy 64), Belle Brewer's collection of 3,200 bells, many of which are rare. Tours are by reservation only, so call before you venture out.

> ### Information Sources
>
> Call the local **Chamber of Commerce** (☎ 903-567-2991, www.cantontx.com).

■ Where to Stay

 East Texas Reservation Service, ☎ 888-EAST-TEX. Represents dozens of local bed and breakfasts in Canton and the surrounding area.

■ Where to Eat

 Susie's Tea Room on the Square. West side of the square, ☎ 903-567-6221. Homemade selections of soups, salads and desserts.

Genya's Kitchen. N Hwy 19, ☎ 903-567-2606. Try the chicken-fried steak.

Jewel's Family Restaurant. Intersection of I-20 and Hwy 19, ☎ 903-567-4440. A local favorite known for its flame-broiled steaks.

Tyler

■ History

Named for the 10th president of the United States (John Tyler), Tyler became a destination for a number of nurserymen following the Civil War. By the 1900s, after they failed to make fruit work as an area industry, rose production was established.

Roses temporarily took a back seat to oil production, but regained their hold in the 1940s with the inauguration of the Texas Rose Foundation. Today, Tyler roses bloom around the world and are celebrated on several fronts. More than one-third of the field-grown rose bushes sold in the nation are harvested from the Tyler area.

The other Tyler claim to fame is Earl Campbell, the legendary football player whose name is inexorably linked to the town where he was raised. Campbell, who won the Heisman Trophy while playing for the University of Texas in Austin and went on to play for the Houston Oilers, is Tyler's "Yellow Rose."

Tyler residents split their allegiance between the roses that have become their economical mainstay and the man that put their city on the map.

In addition to lending color to the town of 75,000, roses and other flowers also adorn the county's agenda. The annual **Azalea and Spring Flower Trail** and the **Texas Rose Festival** (October) are considered some of the biggest events in East Texas.

■ Touring

The **Municipal Rose Garden** (1900 W Front, ☎ 903-531-1370) is the largest city rose garden in the nation, with more than 30,000 rosebushes. Mid-May is when blooming peaks and the colorful garden keeps its brilliance through October. At the same location, adjacent to the Rose Garden building, is the **Rose Museum**. Not only does it trace the historical and economical significance of the rose to the county, but it is the site for an extensive display of Texas Rose Festival memorabilia, including gowns and photos.

The **Caldwell Zoo** (2203 Martin Luther King Blvd, ☎ 903-593-0121) has earned a reputation as one of the finer small-city zoos in the state. More than 800 species live among the 35 acres. The zoo includes a petting area, a herpetarium, a nature trail and an aquarium.

Antique shoppers cluster around Vine and S Broadway for hidden treasures. There are a wide variety of antique shops on these downtown streets.

Information Sources

You can get a brochure from the **Chamber of Commerce** (407 N Broadway Ave, 75702, ☎ 903-592-1661, www.tylertexas.com) for detailed information.

■ Adventures on the Water

Tyler State Park (FM 14 north to PR 16, ☎ 903-597-5338) counts a 64-acre spring-fed lake, stocked with trout, as its centerpiece. Fishermen are the first to extol the virtues of the park, but they're not the only ones. There's also a small beach, hiking and mountain biking trails, summer boat rentals and camping facilities.

Though it's a little further down the road, **Lake Palestine** (TX 155 south 15 miles) is considered one of the prettiest lakes in Texas, sheltered by a thick patch of East Texas pine. It has developed considerably over the last several years and you can find marinas, motels, camping areas and boat ramps along its edges. Locals have also staked out a large portion of the lake for homes and many city dwellers have summer cottages on the lake's shores.

East Texas

Lake Tyler and Lake Tyler East (FM 346 east from Whitehouse) are two more alternatives for water lovers. The twin lakes offer 4,800 acres of boating, fishing, camping and swimming.

■ Where to Stay

Heathwood Manor, 600 W Rusk, 75239, ☎ 903-596-7764. $$. A lush garden tops off the amenities.

Shiloh Bed & Breakfast, 15714 CR 1130, 75762, ☎ 903-561-4604. $$. The log cabin is done up old-style, complete with a dog trot design for breezy afternoons.

Castle on the Lake, PO Box 667, 75710, ☎ 903-566-3682. $$. They only have two rooms, but that makes things better for peace and solitude seekers.

Mary's Attic, 417 S College, 75702, ☎ 903-592-5181. $$. A mom-hosted B&B, the owner has it stocked with sweet goodies at all times.

Woldert-Spence Manor, 611 W Woldert, 75702, ☎ 800-965-3378, 903-533-9057, www.tyler.net/woldert_spence. $$-$$$. This 1859 Historical Landmark bills itself as the "Closest B&B to Downtown." Each of the six rooms is unique, with some boasting enclosed, private balconies.

Charnwood Hill Inn, 223 E Charnwood, 75701, ☎ 903-597-3980, www.tyler.com/charnwood/. $$$-$$$$. The owners of this 1861 grande dame will provide everything from in-room dining to horsedrawn carriage rides. The two-acre parcel includes extensive gardens.

Rosevine Inn, 415 S Vine Ave, 75702, ☎ 903-592-2221. $$$-$$$$. There are six rooms and they cater to life outdoors, with several outdoor fireplaces and a hot tub.

Annie Potter' s Victorian Village Bed & Breakfast, Hwy 155 North, PO Box 928, Big Sandy, 75755, ☎ 903-636-4355. Country inn and guest house.

Chilton Grand, 433 S Chilton, 75702, ☎ 903-595-3270. $$-$$$. A restored 1910 home that sits along a brick street. Two rooms available.

The Seasons Bed & Breakfast, 313 E Charnwood, 75701, ☎ 903-533-0803. $$$. The hosts have decorated this 1911 Colonial home with the seasons – each room represents a different time of year. They serve a full breakfast.

■ Where to Eat

 Bernard Mediterranean, ☎ 903-534-0265. A very popular lunch spot with the ladies. Gifts are also sold here. Boasts fresh seafood, steaks and rack of lamb. Bernard caters in the evenings and is a local favorite.

Cace's Seafood, 7011 S Broadway, ☎ 903-581-0744. Grandfather Cace served as an oyster fisherman in New Orleans and imported his brand of Cajun to East Texas. His family carries on the tradition.

Coffee Landing, 8386 State Hwy 155 north, ☎ 903-876-4923. The huge seafood buffet is their calling card.

Current's French Restaurant, ☎ 903-597-3771. All kinds of wonderful things with beef tenderloin. The rest of the menu is delicious as well.

Potpourri House, 2301 S Broadway, ☎ 903-592-4171. The ambiance is almost church-like, with stained glass windows and a garden courtyard. Steaks and seafood dominate the menu.

Kilgore

■ History

Oil and hard work were two of the main ingredients that propelled Kilgore into the ranks of successful settlements. Oil came easily, the first well being tapped in 1930. The downtown block soon boasted the highest concentration of oil wells in the world.

"Lone Wolf" Gonzaullus

Hard work was difficult to quantify, but Texas Ranger Manuel T. "Lone Wolf" Gonzaullus found his own way of keeping the town's streets clean of the criminal element. He asked to see the palms of residents. If they were rough, he left them alone. If they were smooth, he considered them gamblers or thugs and held them in his jail, which was really a Baptist church.

East Texas

The oil boom has, of course, lost some of its luster. But oil remains a primary industry for this town of 11,000.

■ Touring

 The biggest contemporary draw in the town is its junior college drill team, the **Kilgore Rangerettes**, who introduced the world to half-time high kicks. The Rangerettes have performed across the world in shows and performances and are internationally known for their precision and perfection. Their history is preserved at the **Rangerette Showcase** (Kilgore College campus, ☎ 903-984-8531) with thousands of photographs, props and costumes. The shrine also includes a 10-minute video of one of their performances.

The **East Texas Oil Museum** (Kilgore College campus, ☎ 903-983-8295) has been touted as the "best of its kind." The museum's core is built around a boom town replica, making it easy for visitors to imagine what the 1930s in Kilgore must have felt like. Original footage of wildcatters taming their grisly wells is shown at the Boomtown Cinema.

Information Sources

You can contact the **Kilgore Chamber of Commerce** (PO Box 1582, Kilgore, 75662, ☎ 903-984-5022, www.ci.kilgore.tx.us) for more information.

■ Where to Stay

Days Inn, 3505 US Hwy 259 N, 75662, ☎ 903-983-2975. $-$$. Standard for a mid-range motel.

Ramada Inn, 3501 US Hwy 259 N, 75662, ☎ 903-983-3456 or 800-2-RAMADA. $$. Modern amenities, including an outdoor pool and restaurant.

Jefferson

■ History

Established in 1845 as a river port, Jefferson served as a stopping point for settlers migrating westward. After the Civil War, Jefferson's population hit 35,000. Southern mansions and plantations were commonplace. However, the bust that followed left Jefferson only the remnants of its opulent past. A log jam on the Red River was destroyed in 1873, making

Courtyard of The Excelsior House, Jefferson, which has been in continuous operation since the 1850s.

the river channel that ran across Caddo Lake and up to Jefferson too shallow for steamboat travel. Without that access, the community floundered and never fully recovered.

Only 2,000 people actually live in Jefferson, although another 8,000 who live in the country count it as their hub. Tourism, along with agriculture, livestock and forestry, dominate the area economy. Lake O' the Pines lies to the west and Caddo Lake, Texas' only natural lake, is just east of town.

A renaissance of sorts has taken place recently in Jefferson as a flourishing tourism industry has gained speed. Antique dealers, bed & breakfasts and 19th-century theme restaurants dot the town square.

■ Touring

"You have found a place, oh not far away, where history repeats itself every day of the year. Where porch swings are the best seats in the house.... Where the corner drugstore still has your favorite malt... and the crickets and owls sing a soft lullaby. This is something special...." So boasts a Jefferson Web site, and you'd be hard-pressed to prove any differently.

The **Jefferson Historical Museum** (223 W Austin, ☎ 903-665-2775) is packed with pieces of the town's past. With more than 3,000 items on display, it's difficult to absorb it all. Among the displays is a working 200-year-old loom and a gun collection.

Touring options include the **Bayou Queen** (Jefferson Landing, ☎ 903-665-2222), which provides one-hour tours of Big Cypress Bayou, and the **Jefferson and Cypress Bayou Railroad** (north end of Austin St, ☎ 903-665-8400). The live-steam train takes a five-mile, one-hour tour along the rim of the Big Cypress Bayou.

Mullins Narrated Tours (302 Dallas St, ☎ 903-665-2857) take advantage of a horsedrawn surrey to give visitors a gentle, slow-paced tour of the historic downtown district. Rides start at the home of J.N. Mullins, a "retired" gentleman who has been providing tours of his town for around two decades.

Many of the opulent buildings of Jefferson's past serve as incredible forays into history. The **Excelsior House** (211 W Austin, 75657, ☎ 903-665-2513), which still welcomes overnight guests, is the second oldest hotel in Texas. Ulysses S. Grant and Oscar Wilde are among its long list of notable visitors.

The **Freeman Plantation House** (TX 49 west, ☎ 903-665-2320) is an antebellum structure that has been carefully restored. Set on a 1,000-acre cotton and sugarcane plantation, the original house was built by slave labor in the 1850s.

Information Sources

There are several services that will give you an in-depth tour of the area. Call the **Marion County Chamber of Commerce** (118 N. Vale, Jefferson, 75657, ☎ 903-665-2672) for a current copy of vendors.

■ Adventures on the Water

With Caddo Lake and Lake O' the Pines flanking Jefferson on either side, there's no shortage of water fun. **Caddo Lake** (☎ 903-679-3351) is the only natural lake in Texas and consists of an extensive labyrinth of bayous and channels. The State Park anchors itself on the northern end of the 32,500-acre lake. Cypress groves line the shoreline and more than 40 miles of "boat roads" have been mapped by the state. They've got all the facilities you might need.

You can rent canoes or set up a lake tour at **Caddo Canoe Rentals & Boat Tours** (☎ 903-673-3743). Another option is a ride with the **Caddo Lake Steamboat Co.** (Bois D'Arc Lane on Taylor Island, ☎ 888-325-

Caddo Lake Steamboat Co.

5459 or 903-789-3978). **Mystique Tours** (Bayou Landing Dock at Uncertain, ☎ 903-679-3690) offers tours of Caddo Lake.

Lake O' the Pines (☎ 903-665-2336) is about half the size of Caddo, but still an excellent area for fishing, swimming, boating and many other water sports. These two lakes are among the most scenic in Texas.

■ Where to Stay

Ashley Mountain, Rt. 2, Box 424, Avinger, 75630, ☎ 888-922-5663. www.prysm.net/~ashleymt. $$-$$$. Overlooking Lake O' the Pines, Ashley has hiking trails, a heated pool, horseshoe pits and panoramic views. It can house up to eight guests and is available for weddings and special events.

Anne's Arbor, 205 S Alley, 75657, ☎ 903-665-3180 or 903-755-2240. $$. A recently restored five-bedroom cottage with breakfast at a local restaurant included in your room rate.

Azalea Inn, 203 E Dixon, 75657, ☎ 903-665-2051. $$. You'll want to rock away on the porch and enjoy the home-cooked breakfasts in this restored Victorian home, circa 1873.

Baker St Inn, 409 E Baker St, 75657, ☎ 903-665-3662. $$. Tea is served at 3 pm every afternoon in this 1856 home.

Bell's View of The Bayou on Caddo Lake, Mound Pond Rd, Rt. 2, Box 85-C, Karnack, 75661, ☎ 903-679-3234. $$. Two bedrooms for rent. Privacy comes with the view.

Blue Bayou Inn on Caddo Lake, Rt. 2, Box 95-AB, Karnack, 75661, ☎ 903-789-3371/3240. $$. On the banks of the Big Cypress Bayou, there's private fishing, a nearby boat launch and continental breakfast each morning.

Breckenridge Garden Cottages, 502 Houston St, 75657, ☎ 800-665-7758, 903-665-7738. $$. Each cottage offers its own small kitchen, sitting area and front porch for rocking.

Bullfrog Marina on Lake O' The Pines, Hwy 729 & Johnson's Creek, Lake O' the Pines, ☎ 903-755-2712. $$. A fisherman's resort with covered boat slips, fishing licenses, gas docks and full-service marina.

Busy B Ranch, Hwy 59 North, 1100 W Prospect Rd, 75657, ☎ 903-665-7448. $$-$$$. Each private log cabin cottage is nestled only a few steps from its own private trophy bass lake. They also offer complete outfitter service, guided fishing trips and seasonal hunting opportunities.

Caddo Cottage on Caddo Lake, Mossy Brake Drive on Taylor Island, ☎ 903-789-3988. $$$. A little out of the way, but way out of the ordinary. There's a boathouse, deck, patio, gas grill and much more.

Captain's Castle, 403 E Walker, 75657, ☎ 903-665-2330. $$$. Also known as the Rogers-McCasland home, it was so named by Captain Thomas J. Rogers, a Confederate officer and local pioneer banker.

Captain's Quarters, 604 E Elizabeth, 75657, ☎ 903-665-1246. $$. Sleep beneath a breezy canopy net in your queen-sized bed.

Chapelridge Bed & Breakfast, Hwy 59 West (one mile), ☎ 800-794-4009 or 903-665-6730. $$. You'll be surrounded by 12 acres of beautiful oak trees and nature trails.

Charles House Bed & Breakfast, 209 E Clarksville, 75657, ☎ 903-665-1773. $$$. Two-story Dutch Colonial Revival home with a wrap-around porch.

Claiborne House, 312 S Alley, 75657, ☎ 903-665-8800. $$. Down home goodness.

Clarksville Street Inn, 107 E Clarksville, 75657, ☎ 903-665-6659. $$$. An 1860 Classic Greek Revival home with spacious rooms and clawfoot tubs.

Cottonwood Inn Bed & Breakfast, 209 N Market St, 75657, ☎ 903-665-2080. $$-$$$. The innkeeper lives off-site, giving you total privacy.

Excelsior House Hotel, 211 W Austin, 75657, ☎ 903-665-2513. $$-$$$. The historic Excelsior House Hotel, circa 1858, was built by riverboat captain William Perry and has a total of 13 guest rooms, each furnished in exquisite period furniture. The ballroom and dining room each feature large French chandeliers and oriental rugs.

Faded Rose, 1101 S Line, 75657, ☎ 903-665-2716. $$. Charming 1920s home.

Falling Leaves Inn, 304 Jefferson St, 75657, ☎ 903-665-8803. www.jeffersontx.com/fallingleaves. $$. An antebellum Greek Revival home.

Gingerbread House & Honey Do Inn, 601 E Jefferson, 75657, ☎ 903-665-8994. $$-$$$. Two- and three-room suites with covered porches, a courtyard and a big breakfast.

Governor's House, 321 Walnut, 75657, ☎ 800-891-7933 or 903-665-7933. $$-$$$. Built in 1870 for Charles A. Culberson, 20th governor of Texas.

Hale House, 702 S Line, 75657, ☎ 903-665-8877. $$$. A Carpenter Gothic built in 1865 with a large side porch and gazebo.

Hodge Plantation, Hwy 49 W, 75657, ☎ 903-665-7442. $$-$$$.

Holcomb Lodge at Lake O' The Pines, Crestwood West, Hwy 729, 75657, ☎ 903-665-3236. $$$. A romantic getaway close to the lake.

House Of The Seasons, 409 S Alley, 75657, ☎ 903-665-1218. $$. The most fascinating interior feature is the dome containing beautiful frescoes.

Ice House Guest Cottage, 209 Jefferson St, 75657, ☎ 800-263-5319 or 903-665-1945. $$-$$$. Privacy is assured.

Kennedy Manor, 217 W Lafayette, 75657, ☎ 903-665-2528. $$$. Lakeshore Hideaway On Lake O' The Pines. Hwy 729 & Ferrell's Point, Avinger, ☎ 800-413-7351 or 903-755-3072. Perfect for families, fishermen or hunters.

Maison Bayou, 300 Bayou St, 75657, ☎ 903-665-7600, www.maisonbayou.com. $$$. Located on the ancient riverbed of the Big Cypress, amid 55 wooded acres. Nature trails, fishing and birdwatching.

McKay House, 306 E Delta, 75657, ☎ 800-468-2627 or 903-665-7322. $$$-$$$$. Recognized for more than a decade as one of the best B&Bs in Texas. Several notable guests have stayed here, including Lady Bird

East Texas

Johnson, Alex Haley, Martin Jurow and Fabio. Has been rated one of the "10 Most Romantic Inns in America."

Pace House, 402 N Polk St, 75657, ☎ 800-850-1433 or 903-665-1433. $$. It was the first brick house built in Jefferson. Serves a full East Texas breakfast, with biscuits and gravy.

Pine Needle Lodge on Caddo Lake, Hwy 49 East & FM Rd 805, 75657, ☎ 903-665-2911, www.prysm.net/~caddo_lk. $$. Sit, swing, rock, walk, fish or paddle – they've got all the goods at this log lodge.

Pride House, 409 E Broadway, 75657, ☎ 903-665-2675, www.jeffersontexas.com. $$-$$$. They claim to be the first B&B not only in Jefferson, but in the state.

Secrets of Lake Claborn, Hwy 59 North, No. 1 Lois Lane, 75657, ☎ 903-665-8518. $$. A cottage surrounded by green forests overlooking a five-acre pond.

The Daniel House, 502 Taylor St, 75657, ☎ 903-665-7840. $$$. A wide veranda wraps around three sides of this stately house.

The Jefferson Hotel, 124 W Austin St, 75657, ☎ 903-665-2631. $$-$$$. An 1861 masterpiece in the heart of the Riverport District. Twenty-four rooms available.

The Town House Bed & Breakfast, 504 Polk St, 75657, ☎ 903-665-6767/6327. $$$. You get the whole house.

Twin Oaks Country Inn, Hwy 134 South, 75657, ☎ 903-665-3535 or 800-905-7751, www.twinoaksinn.com. $$$. Located on a Pre-Civil War plantation site nestled among towering pines, graceful oaks and rolling meadows. There's swimming, croquet, badminton, horseshoes, a gazebo, sunning porches and tree swings.

White Oak Manor Bed & Breakfast, 502 Benners, 75657, ☎ 903-665-1048 or 903-665-1271. $$$. The largest white oak trees in Texas are on the front lawn (there's also a 50-foot pecan out back). Clawfoot tubs, fireplaces, a parlor and a wrap-around porch complete the amenities.

Winborn Haven & Guest Cottage, 408 Houston, 75657, ☎ 903-665-7745, www.jeffersontx.com/winbornhaven. $$-$$$.

■ Where to Eat

 Diamond Bessie's Saloon & Dance Hall, 124 E Austin, ☎ 903-665-7454. They not only have a restaurant, but a nightclub/dance hall.

Plantation Restaurant, 400 S Walcott (US Hwy 59 South), ☎ 903-665-2131/7456. Their buffet is their forte, but they also serve steaks and sandwiches.

The Bakery, 211 N Polk, ☎ 903-665-2253. Specializing in American and Italian dining.

Bayou Landing Restaurant, 300 Cypress Drive, Uncertain, ☎ 903-789-3394. Catfish might be the house specialty, but shrimp (of all sorts) and red snapper are also served.

Galley Restaurant, 121 W Austin, ☎ 903-665-3641. Steaks and seafood.

Sleepy Hollow Catfish & Steakhouse, Hwy 59 North (eight miles), ☎ 903-665-1148/8118. Specializing in catfish, they also offer great gumbo shrimp any way you like them.

Texarkana

■ History

Caddo Indians, less mobile than Comanches and Apaches, were the first to settle what has become Texarkana. They built their village at the crossroads of two great Indian trails. Seventy Caddo ceremonial mounds are found near the city today.

Modern-day Texarkana's history – it sits astride the border of Texas and Arkansas – is a little more vague. Popular mythology relates that a railroad surveyor picked his site and then the settlement's name by using three letters from each state: TEX for Texas, ARK for Arkansas and ANA for Louisiana, even though Louisiana was 30 miles away. A problem with this theory is the fact that Oklahoma is also 30 miles away and is not represented in the town's moniker.

The more acceptable version of events has two cities growing up side by side and eventually merging at the Texas/Arkansas border. If you live in Texarkana, you're more likely to live in Arkansas than Texas – about two-thirds of the combined population lives east of the state boundary.

The two state legislatures, faced with a unique opportunity, devised a **Bi-State Justice Center** (State Line and Broad, ☎ 903-798-3000), the only endeavor of its kind in the country. Legislation was passed to insure that the physical location of a trial did not hinder the justice pro-

East Texas

cess. An Arkansas judge can rule on a case while physically sitting in Texas and vice versa.

■ Touring

 Photographer's Rock (State Line and 5th) provides an opportunity to take those indulgent photos of family members (or family pets) with a foot in each state. Civic leaders have made it a snap to capture a winning pose.

Scott Joplin, the ragtime composer posthumously recognized with a Pulitzer Prize, is enshrined in the **Scott Joplin Mural** (3rd and Main), which marks his contributions to American music. Ross Perot is the city's other famous son, with the **Perot Theater** (219 Main, ☎ 903-792-4992) bearing his name. The opulent affair is a throwback to what theaters were like in the early 1900s.

There are two places to get a firmer feel for the history surrounding Texarkana and the Piney Woods it calls home. The **Texarkana Historical Museum** (219 State Line, ☎ 903-793-4831) is the first and a natural choice. Housed in one of the oldest buildings in town, the Offenhauser Insurance Co. building, the museum traces the town's path from the Caddo Indians through the railroad and timber industries.

Another stop is the **Draughn-Moore House** (420 Pine St, ☎ 903-793-7108), aptly called the "Ace of Clubs" for its floor plan. An octagonal rotunda is surrounded on three sides by more octagonal rotundas and the fourth side is a rectangular room. The 1884 Victorian masterpiece is listed on the National Register of Historic Places and has a gift shop that insures you'll remember it forever.

Information Sources

Contact the **Texarkana Chamber of Commerce** (819 State Line Avenue, ☎ 903-792-7191, www.texarkana.org) for current information.

■ Adventures on the Water

 The entire family can get wet at **Crystal Springs Beach** (US 67, 18 miles west, ☎ 903-585-5246), which offers a spring-fed lake and sand-covered beach with swimming, picnicking and camping. But there are also toys for the kids in the form of a 400-foot waterslide, paddleboats and a cable swing. They open in May and stay open throughout the summer months.

Perhaps a little more low-key and providing more solitude is **Lake Wright Patman** (US 59 12 miles southwest, ☎ 903-838-8781), which includes 165 miles of shoreline and more exploration possibilities than you can cover in a day. The best way to check out the hiking, camping, boating and fishing spots is to talk to park managers.

■ Where to Stay

Four Points Hotel, 5301 North State Line, 75503, ☎ 903-792-3222. $$. An affordable price with some luxury items, including a concierge floor.

Holiday Inn Express, 5401 North State Line, 75503, ☎ 800-342-4942, 903-792-3366. $$. Express service means free breakfast.

Mansion on Main, 802 Main St, 75501, ☎ 903-792-1835. $$-$$$. Each of the six rooms in the century-old home is different. The hosts are from New Orleans, so your culinary choices include authentic Cajun.

The Farm House, 4802 South Kings Hwy, 75501, ☎ 903-838-5454. $$. Two rooms are available in this 1905 gabled roof country farmhouse. Open Monday through Friday, catering to corporate travelers.

■ Where to Eat

Cattleman's Steak House, 4018 State Line, ☎ 870-774-4481. Everything a steak house should offer, along with a lively atmosphere.

Bryce's Cafeteria, 2021 Mall Dr, ☎ 903-792-1611. An institution in Texarkana for more than half a century. Expect great food, a casual atmosphere and friendly service.

Pier 27, Hwy 237, ☎ 870-691-3096. Fifteen miles south of Texarkana off Hwy 71 South. Overlooking the Sulphur River, Pier 27 serves up catfish, seafood, steak and chicken.

Brangus Feed Lot, 1301 Arkansas Blvd, ☎ 870-772-6988. Specializes in steaks, burgers, Western pie, and Cajun peanuts.

Dixie Diner, 3200 N. State Line Ave, ☎ 870-773-4943. Southern fare at its best, chicken-fried steak is a house specialty. Homemade desserts top off a full meal.

Moving South

Mexia

■ History

The Chamber of Commerce's slogan for their town, "A great place however you pronounce it," is a casual indication that this town isn't as simple as it seems. Mexia (Meh-hay-ah) derived its name from Mexican General Jose Antonio Mejia, who changed parties and took part in an unsuccessful uprising against General Santa Anna of Mexico. Mejia wound up in front of a firing squad for his actions.

His family, who changed their name to "Mexia," donated the land for the town. In its beginnings, the town was no more than a cotton and cattle community. But when oil seekers hit pay dirt in 1920, the population skyrocketed from 4,000 to 40,000 or more. The oil fizzled as fast as it came and Mexia remains a small town to this day (population 7,200).

Peaches are the town's current claim to fame. An early resident, Joseph W. Stubenrauch, was an educator as well as a horticulturist. He developed about 100 new varieties of peaches and created one of the largest peach-producing counties in the state.

Cynthia Ann Parker

Nine-year-old Cynthia Ann Parker was kidnapped by Comanche Indians. Parker became completely assimilated into the Comanche way of life, married and bore the last great Comanche chief, Quanah Parker. Both she and her daughter, Prairie Flower, were later "saved" by Texans, but they hated the unfamiliar life, tried to escape on several occasions and died four years later.

■ Touring

Old Fort Parker State Historic Site (TX 14 south to PR 35) offers a historical glimpse into the Texas frontier. The fort was established to protect a settlement of eight or nine families, including the family of Elder John Parker. But in 1836 it was destroyed by Comanche Indians, who killed many of the residents and took others into captivity. The historic site has frontier artifacts, original log block-houses and a stockade.

Information Sources

Contact the **Mexia Area Chamber of Commerce** (☎ 817-562-5569, PO Box 352, 76667).

■ Adventures on Foot

Fort Parker State Park (TX 14 south four miles, ☎ 254-562-5751) is 1,400 acres of park including 750 acres of lake. Thickly wooded areas surround Lake Fort Parker and make for great hiking and camping. Though the actual plotted hiking trail is only one mile long, there's great walking and hiking along the Navasota River basin, which feeds the lake. Park rangers are also continually adding trails to the map. Birds often find refuge in the park in their annual migrations, attracting photographers and birders.

The lake in recent years has been low, making it suitable only for fishing and boating in shallow boats. The park will rent both paddleboats and canoes to visitors. The park offers a canoe trip, approximately three hours long, in which park rangers drop you off up the Navasota River and let you paddle/fish your way into the main lake. There are all types of camping facilities, from primitive to RV hook-ups. Contact **Texas Parks and Wildlife** in Austin (☎ 512-389-8900) for reservations.

■ Adventures on the Water

The Navasota River also feeds **Lake Mexia** (US 84 west to FM 2681), which is about eight miles upstream of Fort Parker. Most of Lake Mexia which is lined with residential neighborhoods. However, there are public facilities to provide access to the 1,200-acre lake, as well as places for camping, fishing and hiking.

■ Where to Stay

Economy Inn, 807 E Milam St, 76667, ☎ 254-562-2811. $. Nothing fancy, but the price is right.

Triangle Motel, 508 Hwy 14 N, 76667, ☎ 254-562-2838. $. Another basic choice.

East Texas

Crockett

■ History

Steeped in rich history, Crockett is a not-so-subtle reminder of small town spirit. A.E. and Elijah Gossett, a father/son team who were both veterans of the Battle of San Jacinto, donated a large portion of land for the creation of the town. They, in turn, got to pick the name of both the town and the county.

The county was named for Sam Houston. The town was named for Elijah's friend Davy Crockett, who died in the Alamo. The entire town burned down in 1865, but bounced back. Today it counts agriculture as its chief economic base. Davy's name is immortalized at every turn in this part of the world. He has a memorial park, a national forest and a spring, among other things.

■ Touring

Two major homes are open for display in Crockett. **The Downs-Aldrich Home** (206 North 7th St, ☎ 409-544-4804) is an example of a combination of Eastlake, Victorian and Queen Anne architecture and is listed in the National Register of Historic Places.

The Monroe Crook House (709 East Houston, ☎ 409-544-5820) is recognized as one of the finest early Greek Revival houses in Texas. It was built in 1854 by the grand nephew of President James Monroe.

At every turn you take, you're apt to see a historic marker. Almost 200 of them are located in Houston County alone, attributable to the area's status as the first county in the Republic of Texas and its position at the crossroads of Texas history.

Lists of markers can be obtained from the Houston County Historical Commission or from the **Chamber of Commerce** (700 E Houston, 75835, ☎ 409-544-2359).

The 1909 Crockett Railroad Depot now serves as the **Visitor Center Museum** (629 N 4th St). The Great Northern Railroad Company built

the depot that includes two passenger waiting rooms, ticket offices, a freight room, freight and baggage storage areas and a concrete loading platform. It has provides exhibits and century-old memorabilia relating to the history of Houston County, its cities and its 53 communities.

The **Caddoan Indian Mounds State Park** (TX 21 north 28 miles, ☎ 409-858-3218) marks the southwesternmost ceremonial center of the great Indian Mound Builders, one of the most sophisticated prehistoric Indian cultures in Texas. A self-guided tour takes you through a reconstructed dwelling, mounds and a village area.

Set on 118 acres in the hills of the East Texas Piney Woods, **Mission Tejas State Park** (TX 21 northeast to PR 44, ☎ 409-687-2394) was named for the first Spanish mission in the province of Texas. The park has two historic buildings of interest. The **Rice Family Home** is an original stage coach house that was moved to this location from its site on the El Camino Real Hwy, and the **Mission Tejas Church** is located in an area where priests and Indians worked together. The mission ultimately failed and moved to San Antonio in 1730.

Camping and RV sites are available, along with hiking and nature trails, a playground and picnic tables.

Information Sources

Houston County Historical Commission or the **Chamber of Commerce** (700 E Houston, 75835, ☎ 409-544-2359).

■ Adventures on Foot

 When you begin your trek into the great outdoors, start with the **Davy Crockett National Forest** (TX 7 east, 1240 East Loop 304, Crockett, 75835, ☎ 409-544-2046), the largest national forest in Texas, covering 161,000 acres.

Only one mile of the 20-mile **Four C National Recreation Trail** is not on national forest park land. Beginning at the Ratliff Lake Recreation Area and ending on the northern end of the park at the Neches Bluff Overlook, this mammoth trail got its name from the Central Coal and Coke Company, which logged area virgin timber in the early 1900s. Some of the trail actually follows abandoned tramways built by the company. Today's forest is a combination of some of the original trees and newer additions that sprouted after the company finished its logging in the 1920s.

The trail passes by several ponds that can be fished. It also passes through a portion of the **Big Slough Wilderness Area**, which is free from modern development and very primitive. Though the trail can be hiked year-round, spring and fall are your best bets. Summer gets steamy and winter gets a little frightening – deer hunters also occupy the park during November and December. Only hikers are welcome on the Four C.

Ratliff Lake, at the Four C's trailhead, was originally a timber pond for the loggers, complete with a sawmill. Today the area is a developed recreation area, with 75 camping units, a swimming beach and bathhouse, a fishing pier and an amphitheater. The area offers interpretative talks and walks throughout the summer. Non-motorized boats are allowed on the lake.

The **Walnut Creek camp site**, located around mile 13 of the Four C Trail, is on a small ridgetop close to the creek.

■ Adventures on Horseback

The **Davy Crockett Horse & Rider Camp** (Hwy 21 east 12 miles, ☎ 409-546-0690) adjoins the forest and offers a beautiful scenic trail ride, plus horses. Or you can bring your own horse.

■ Adventures on the Water

Houston County Lake (FM 229 west, ☎ 409-544-8466) is known for its trophy bass and is considered a great spot for all water sports. In addition to traditional camping and tent facilities, there are also cabins for rent.

■ Where to Stay

Arledge House, 718 East Houston, 75836, ☎ 409-544-8120. $$-$$$. All of the rooms have sitting rooms and king-size beds. The rocking chairs on the big front porch make for pleasant breakfasts and sunsets.

Country Blessings, Rt 3 Box 80-H, 75835, ☎ 409-544-7329. $$$. Located on 42 acres, five miles north of town, the host provides a gourmet breakfast and robes for guests.

Warfield House Bed & Breakfast, 712 East Houston, 75835, ☎ 888-988-8800 or 409-544-4037, www.virtualcities.com/ons/tx/z/txz4601.htm.

Built in 1897, the huge wrap-around porch is a perfect place to enjoy
your gourmet breakfast.

■ Where to Eat

Wooden Nickel, 510 Loop 304 E, ☎ 409-544-8011. The
chicken-fried steak and fajitas have kept them in business for
more than a decade.

Brass Lantern, 1117 E Loop 304, ☎ 409-544-4091. An affordable choice
for sandwiches, burgers and fried fish baskets.

Nacogdoches

■ History

One can't even begin a history of Texas without Nacogdoches, dubbed
the oldest city in Texas and one of the best kept secrets in the state.
Things started very early for the area. Evidence shows that Paleolithic
settlement began around 10,000 BC, with the Caddoan tribe setting up
camp between 1250 and 1450 AD. The Caddoan site, near present-day
downtown, was surrounded by mounds, some of which have been preserved.

> **✷ Did You Know?**
>
> The Caddo word "tejas," meaning friend, was the basis
> for the name of "Texas."

The first contemporary descriptions of the area were from French explorer LaSalle in 1685. The town, and much of East Texas that served as
the gateway to the West, became a pawn in the struggle between Spanish and French for supremacy.

The Spanish established several missions in the early 1700s, including
Nuestra Señora de Guadalupe de los Nacogdoches and Mission Concep-
tion. In 1779, Don Antonio Gil Y'Barbo built the Old Stone House, laid
out the modern streets, and wrote the first law code. The Stone House
remained a hub of political activity throughout the various regimes that
passed through. At the turn of the 19th century, Nacogdoches was the
second largest city in Texas.

East Texas

Old Stone Fort Museum, Nacogdoches.

The city was part of three independent republics before the Lone Star Republic and has flown nine flags: Spanish, French, Mexican, The Magee-Gutierrez Republic, The Long Republic, The Fredonia Republic, The Lone Star, The Confederacy and The United States.

The very first oil well in Texas was found in Nacogdoches, but its effects were minimal. The well only produced about 10 barrels a day and was eventually abandoned. Cotton, tobacco and timber provided strength to the economy into the 20th century, but today the most important economic asset is Stephen F. Austin State University, with 12,000 students and a budget over $24 million.

■ Touring

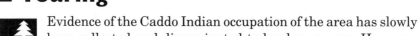 Evidence of the Caddo Indian occupation of the area has slowly been collected and disseminated to local museums. However, you can view one of their **Indian Mounds** (500 block of Mound St), the only one that has withstood the test of time and settlement. The mounds designated ceremonial sites and up until the 1930s mounds stood on either side of Mound Street.

The **Old Stone Fort Museum** (Griffith and Clark on SFA campus, ☎ 409-468-2408) served as headquarters for the Spanish, the Mexicans, three independent republics and Sam Houston's first law offices. The replica of the original Old Stone Fort houses a collection of area artifacts.

Another place to delve into the town's rich history is at the **Oak Grove Cemetery** (N Lanana and Hospital St), established in 1837 and the burial ground for countless historical figures. Among them are four signers of the Texas Declaration of Independence (Thomas J. Rusk, Charles S. Taylor, John S. Roberts, and William Clark), two veterans of the Battle of San Jacinto (E.E. Hamilton and Captain Hayden Arnold), Haden Edwards, leader of the Fredonia Rebellion, General Kelsey Harris Douglass, Commander-in-Chief of the forces that drove the Indians out of East Texas in 1839, and Frost Thorn, Texas' first millionaire.

The **Sterne-Hoya Home** (211 South Lanana at Pilar, ☎ 409-560-5426) is the most historic house in Nacogdoches. Nicholas Adolphus Sterne, an immigrant from Cologne, Germany, built the house for his bride after their wedding. The house was both the social and the political center of activity in the years prior to Texas independence. Sam Houston boarded with the Sternes when he first arrived in Texas and was baptized into the Catholic Church in the front parlor of the house, with Mrs. Sterne serving as his godmother. The diary that Sterne kept provides an interesting look into the day-to-day life of the Texas pioneers.

An entire cluster of houses and buildings has been preserved at **Millard's Crossing** (6020 North St, ☎ 409-564-6631). It resembles a small village.

Information Sources

Call the **Nacogdoches Chamber of Commerce** (513 North St, 75961, ☎ 409-564-7351) for information.

■ Adventures on the Water

You have many options in area lakes. Here are three of the best. **Lake Nacogdoches** (FM 225 west 12 miles, ☎ 409-564-4693) is managed by the city and offers boating, fishing, swimming, water-skiing and nature trails.

However, if you have the time, you would be better served to head south and spend a few days at **Lake Sam Rayburn**. It's one of the most popular outdoor spots in East Texas and is tucked away in the heart of the Angelina National Forest. The largest body of water wholly contained within the state, Sam Rayburn covers 114,500 acres and offers some of the finest freshwater fishing in the South.

East Texas

There are boat roads through flooded timber areas that are home to black bass, white bass, striped bass, Florida bass, walleye, crappie, catfish and bream. Call the Army Corps of Engineers for specific details on lake facilities (☎ 409-384-5716). The **Rayburn Country Resort and Country Club** (1000 Wingate Blvd, ☎ 800-882-1442), with golf course and clubhouse, is popular (and posh), frequented by East Texas residents.

A joint effort by Texas and Louisiana led to the formation of the **Toledo Bend Reservoir** in 1966. When it was created, the lake was the second largest man-made lake in the nation – today it is the fifth largest. Eighty miles long and covering 186,000 square acres, Toledo Bend was formed by damming the Sabine River. There are 1,200 miles of shoreline.

Toledo Bend has earned a reputation as a fishing mecca. By some estimates, there are over 55 million pounds of game fish swimming in its waters. You can contact the **Sabine River Authority** (Rt. 1. Box 270, Burkville, TX 75932, ☎ 409-565-2273) for more information. The **Sabine National Forest** (101 South Bolivar, San Augustine, 75972, ☎ 409-275-2632) lines much of the reservoir's western shore. It includes 157,951 acres and offers a variety of spots for camping, hiking, boating, birdwatching and fishing.

The **Trail Between the Lakes** extends 28 miles from Lakeview Recreation Area on Toledo Bend Reservoir to US 96 within sight of the easternmost point of Sam Rayburn Reservoir.

■ Adventures on Foot

Southeast of Nacogdoches, the **Angelina National Forest** (701 N. First St., Lufkin, 75901, ☎ 409-639-8620) wraps itself around the Sam Rayburn Reservoir, one of East Texas' fishing treasures. The smallest of the four national forests in Texas, Angelina preserves portions of what was a grand piney forest.

Connecting Bouton Lake and Boykin Springs Recreation Area, the **Sawmill Hiking Trail** on the southern shore of Sam Rayburn travels some 5.5 miles. A short spur off this trail will take hikers to the historic **Aldridge Sawmill**, first constructed in 1905. After the mill began production, a small village sprang up in its shadow, including more than 75 buildings. The sawmill closed its doors in 1923 and the township that surrounded it finally abandoned ship in 1927. All that remains of the foresting village are the shells of the four concrete mill buildings, the mill pond and portions of the old railroad tram.

Bouton Lake, on one end of the trail system, is called "one of the best kept secrets about the Angelina National Forest" in the literature prepared by the park system. Primitive camp sites (no water) complement the rich fishing and hiking among bottomland hardwoods and cypress. In addition to fishing on Bouton Lake, Little Bouton is just a few hundred feet away.

Anchoring the opposite end of the trail system, **Boykin Springs Recreation Area** offers a little of everything, from camping to fishing and hiking. Bubbling springs that feed Boykin Springs Lake cascade through a series of falls and meander through the campground.

The **Sandy Creek campground**, on the shores of Sam Rayburn, provides a panoramic view of the surrounding country. Three other campgrounds edge the lake: **Caney Creek Recreation Area, Harvey Creek** and **Townsend Park**. Caney Creek is the largest of the three, with 123 sites to choose from and a large picnic shelter and an amphitheater. Harvey Creek maintains a popular boat ramp that remains open even when the lake recedes.

The **Lanana Creek Trail** follows a six-mile trail once traveled by Indians along Lanana Creek and through Pecan Acres Park. Call the Nagodoches Chamber of Commerce (☎ 409-564-7351) for details on access to the trail.

■ Adventures on Horseback

While there are no marked trails for horseback riding in the **Angelina National Forest**, riders and their horses are welcome to use numerous unmarked dirt roads and trails. Horses are also permitted in the **Upland Island Wilderness Area**. Check in with a park ranger to purchase a trail map.

Letney, a former developed campground, permits camping with horses. Call ☎ 409-639-8620 to make reservations. Many of the more popular horse trails begin close to this camp site.

■ Where to Stay

Anna Raguet House, 816 West Main, 75961, ☎ 409-564-2735. $$. Two bedrooms available. The owner lives off-site, giving guests all the privacy they could want.

Anderson Point Bed & Breakfast, 29 East Lake Estates, 75961, ☎ 409-569-7445. $-$$. A two-story French home surrounded by 300 feet of lake and boasting a double verandah. You can fish off the pier.

Eagle's Aerie Bed & Breakfast, 12 East Lake Estates, 75961, ☎ 409-564-7995. $-$$.

The Fredonia Hotel & Convention Center, 200 North Fredonia St, 75961, ☎ 409-564-1234 or 800-594-5323. $$-$$$. Originally built by the citizens of Nacogdoches, it has been lovingly restored and serves as a local institution.

Haden-Edwards Inn Bed & Breakfast, 106 North Lanana St, 75961, ☎ 409-559-5595. $$. An 1890s restored masterpiece.

Hardeman Guest House Bed & Breakfast, 316 North Church, 75961, ☎ 409-569-1947. $$-$$$. Two blocks from the downtown square. Many of the antiques and crafts displayed may be purchased.

Holiday Inn, 3400 South St, 75961, ☎ 409-569-8100. $$-$$$. Just minutes from downtown, it includes everything from a jacuzzi to an exercise room.

The Little House Bed & Breakfast, 110 Sanders St, 75961, ☎ 409-564-2735. $$. Pure country style.

Llano Grande Plantation Bed & Breakfast, Press Rd, Nacogdoches, ☎ 409-569-1249. $$. Three separate houses. Rates includes a hearty breakfast.

Mound Street Bed & Breakfast, 408 N Mound, 75961, ☎ 800-247-1687, 409-569-2211. $$-$$$. The two-story Victorian home (circa 1899) is close to everything in Nacagdoches. The sun porch is perfect for dining.

Pine Creek Lodge Bed & Breakfast, Farm Rd 2782, Rt. 3, Box 1238, 75961, ☎ 888-714-1414, 409-560-6282. $$. Three rustic buildings situated on the bend of a flowing creek in the middle of a 140-acre farm. You can fish, walk, read, rock or laze to your heart's content.

Stag Leap Retreat Bed & Breakfast, Farm Rd 2782, 75961, ☎ 409-560-0766. $$-$$$. Includes fully equipped kitchen, living room, bathroom, washer & dryer and a golf cart for sightseeing on nature trails. When you cross the waterfall bridge, you'll know you're there.

Stratford House Inn, 3612 North St, 75961, ☎ 409-560-6038. $$. Over 40 rooms are available, with whirlpool bathtubs and a continental breakfast.

■ Where to Eat

Blank & Company, 207½ East Main, ☎ 409-560-0776. All the normal fare, from sandwiches to burgers and salads to steaks.

Café Fredonia, 200 N Fredonia St, ☎ 409-564-1234. Part of the historic Fredonia Hotel, their food is upscale seafood, pasta and steaks.

Cotton Patch Café, 3117 North St, ☎ 409-569-6926. It's country-style all the way around. Try the chicken-fried steak.

Clear Springs Restaurant, 211 Old Tyler Rd, ☎ 409-569-0489. Their catfish platter and the baby back ribs are the biggest winners.

La Hacienda, 1411 North, ☎ 409-564-6450. They discriminate between Mexican and Tex-Mex fare, but offer both. A local favorite.

Bryan/College Station

■ History

The boundaries that separate these two cities are beyond murky. A native will more than likely say they are from "Bryan/College Station" rather than pick one or the other. They share everything.

Bryan was first settled by colonists with Stephen F. Austin, the "Father of Texas." They put to good use the fertile Brazos bottomlands that are indigenous to the area. When William Joel Bryan, one of those first settlers, donated some land in 1855, the town took his name.

Perhaps the defining moment in the area's history happened in 1876 when the Agricultural and Mechanical College of Texas opened as the first school of higher learning in the state. The university, now called Texas A&M, planted itself in College Station, a stop on the Houston & Central Railroad line.

Students, faculty and staff for Texas A&M number close to 50,000. The combined population of both College Station and Bryan is over 110,000, revealing the predominant role the university plays in the community.

■ Touring

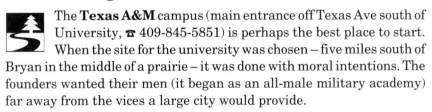

The **Texas A&M** campus (main entrance off Texas Ave south of University, ☎ 409-845-5851) is perhaps the best place to start. When the site for the university was chosen – five miles south of Bryan in the middle of a prairie – it was done with moral intentions. The founders wanted their men (it began as an all-male military academy) far away from the vices a large city would provide.

East Texas

✳ Author's Tip

One of the best views of the campus is from atop the Rud-
der Tower.

The **George Bush Presidential Library and Museum** (1000 George
Bush Drive West, College Station 77845, ☎ 409-260-9552,
www.csdl.tamu.edu/bushlib) is the most recent addition to the A&M
campus. With much fanfare, and a host of dignitaries and media stars,
George W. cut the ribbon in late 1997. It is being touted as one of the finest libraries in the country and is worth a side trip.

Other interesting side trips would include a stop at the **Messina Hof
Wine Cellars** (TX 6, south to Old Reliance Rd, ☎ 409-778-9463). The
owners hailed from Messina, Italy and Hof, Germany. They provide
wine tastings and tours on a regular basis. If you're in town in mid-April,
you should try to catch the grape stomp.

Entertainment of the more roguish kind can be found at the **Texas
World Speedway** (TX 6, south of TX 30, ☎ 409-690-2500), with a three-
mile grand prix course and a two-mile oval speedway. As one of the premiere tracks in the nation, they play host to stock cars, motorcycles,
Indy cars and 18-wheelers.

For some local flavor, try out the **Dixie Chicken** (307 University,
☎ 409-846-2332, www.dixiechicken.com) or **Dudley's Draw**, long-time
haunts of the college crowd. Neither will show up on the suggested dining lists – they cater to the greasy-finger crowd – but tradition runs ram-
pant at both digs. If you go by the Chicken (the locals' term for the joint)
be sure to check out the massive rattlesnake they keep in the glassed
aquarium behind the pool tables.

Information Sources

Bryan/College Station Chamber of Commerce
(☎ 409-260-5200, www.rtis.com/reg/bcs).

■ Where to Stay

Angelsgate Bed & Breakfast, 615 East 29th St, Bryan,
77803, ☎ 888-779-1231, 409-779-1231, www2.cy-net.net/~an-
gels. Greet the morning with a sumptuous breakfast served in a

setting varying from the formal dining room to a private sunroom breakfast nook. The cottage out back offers the ultimate in privacy.

Beaver Lodge Bed & Breakfast, 2202 E Placid Dr, College Station, 77845, ☎ 409-690-0204. $$$. This is a log cabin on a lake, and you'll wish you could stay forever. The wide porch complete with rockers is the perfect place to end your day. There's a separate cottage if you want more privacy.

Hilton Hotel and Conference Center, 801 University Dr East, College Station, 77840, ☎ 800-445-8667, 409-693-7500. In addition to normal amenities, they offer free airport transportation, an outdoor pool and an exercise room.

The Vintner's Loft at Messina Hof Wine Cellars, 4545 Old Reliance Rd, Bryan, 77808, ☎ 409-778-9463. Call ahead for this one-room loft. Having a winery and restaurant on the premises adds to the experience.

■ Where to Eat

 Black Forest Inn, TX 30, 21 miles east, ☎ 409-874-2407. It's a little off the beaten path, but you'll be glad you took it. Crossing fine European and American cuisine, dishes include veal cordon bleu and rainbow trout amandine.

Fajita Rita's, 4501 S Texas Ave, ☎ 409-846-3696. Affordable and tasty Tex-Mex.

The Kaffee Klatsch, 106 North Ave, Bryan, ☎ 409-846-4360. Their blackboard lunches include quiches, crêpes and other tasty fare. The garden surroundings add to the atmosphere.

La Barronena, 102 Live Oak St, ☎ 409-694-8232. Appetizers are all made fresh, from risotto to fried zucchini. Their trout has won rave reviews.

T-Bone Jones, 809 University Dr E, ☎ 409-846-6823. Steaks, seafood and all the trimmings in a family atmosphere.

The Texan, 3204 S College. Bryan, ☎ 409-822-3588. For more than 20 years this humble-looking restaurant has served up the finest dining in town, from Alaskan king crab to escargots to lobster. Reservations are recommended. Closed on Sundays.

Brenham

■ History

Named for Richard Fox Brenham, a Kentuckian who fought as a Texan on several occasions against Mexico, the town began to attract a large number of Germans during Reconstruction. It retains much of its German influence today and remains primarily a gentle, farming community.

> **✳ Author's Tip**
>
> Brenham is synonymous with Blue Bell Ice Cream, "the best ice cream in the country," if you believe its commercials. Many Texans are likely to agree. Vermont can keep Ben & Jerry's.

■ Touring

 Blue Bell Creameries (S Horton St, ☎ 800-327-8135, 409-836-7977) has been making ice cream since 1911. That first year they produced two gallons a day. Today, they produce 20 million gallons a year. The end of the tour is always the best, with a tasty treat to whet your ice cream appetite.

The town's other famous residents are the **Monastery Miniature Horses** (Monastery of St Clare, ☎ 409-836-9652), raised, shown and sold by the nuns of St Clare to support their monastery. They usually keep about 60 of the pettable miniatures on display for visitors. You may also support their cause by purchasing items at their gift shop and ceramics studio.

Flowers with mass appeal and in massive quantities can be found at **Ellison's Greenhouses** (2107 East Stone St, ☎ 409-836-6011), where mums, azaleas, begonias and poinsettias are grown for distribution. You can always arrange a guided tour by appointment, or stop by on Friday and Saturday when the greenhouses are open to the general public.

The **Brenham Heritage Museum** (105 S Market, ☎ 409-830-8445) seeks to preserve the area's rich agricultural history. The building that houses it – a 1915 Federal building – is a piece of history itself. Another glimpse into the area's farming past is at **Burton Farmers Gin** (US 290, 12 miles west, ☎ 409-289-3378), a 1914 creation that is now recognized as a National Historic Landmark. If you've never laid eyes on a real cotton gin, this is a rare chance to see a working model.

Blinn Junior College may not be big by college standards, but it is huge on the baseball scale. Blinn is a premiere academic destination for aspiring baseball players on their ladder to professional status. The **Texas Baseball Hall of Fame Museum** (Blinn campus, ☎ 409-830-4000) proves the college's allegiance to the sport. More than 450 items have been collected and include Mickey Mantle's 515th home run ball and a life-size wax figure of Nolan Ryan.

Information Sources

Contact the **Brenham/Washington County Convention and Visitors Bureau** (☎ 409-836-3695, 314 S. Austin St., 77833, www.brenhamtx.org) for more information.

■ Where to Stay

Ant Street Inn, 107 W Commerce, 77833, ☎ 800-481-1951 or 409-836-7393. $$-$$$. Rocking chairs on the back balcony are just one of the many gentle pleasures at this 14-room abode. Breakfast included.

The Brenham House, 705 Clinton St, 77833, ☎ 800-259-8367 or 409-830-0477.

Campbell's Country Home, Hwy 50, eight miles north of Brenham, ☎ 409-830-0278. $$. Serene country setting in a 100-year-old renovated country home, complete with a hearty breakfast.

Captain Tacitus T. Clay House, Fieldstone Farm, 9445 FM 390 East, 77833, ☎ 409-836-1916. $-$$. Stroll to the creek or enjoy the wide open vista. You can also relax in the hot tub, which is enclosed in the gazebo.

1865 Country Home, ☎ 281-367-2280. You get the entire 50 acres and house to yourself (unhosted). Comes complete with clawfoot tub, porch swings and antique furniture. Sleeps up to nine people and is priced at about $250 a weekend, or $525 weekly.

Creekside House B&B, 11299 Palestine Rd, 77833, ☎ 409-830-0888. $$. From the guest house, visitors can enjoy the view of hills, cattle, trees and rolling pastures.

East Texas

Dewberry Hill Bed & Breakfast, ☎ 409-836-6879. $$-$$$. You can choose between two rooms in the 100-year-old farmhouse or the secluded guest house that overlooks the lake. Pretty enough for country weddings.

Far View, 1804 South Park St, 77833, ☎ 888-FAR VIEW or 409-836-1672. $$-$$$. A Texas Historic Landmark. Period furnished guest rooms that can be rented either individually or together.

Heartland Country Inn, 9402 Palestine Rd, 77833, ☎ 800-871-1864 or 409-836-1864. Hilltop location and a gentle lifestyle.

The Inn at Nueces Canyon, 9501 Hwy 290 West, 77833, eight miles west of Brenham, ☎ 800-925-5058 or 409-289-5600. Choose from their bed and breakfast house or their inn, all set on a 135-acre working ranch. They also have an elegant restaurant that overlooks an equestrian arena, several lakes, hiking trails, a gift shop and flowing streams.

■ Where to Eat

 The Great Ant Street Restaurant, 205 S Baylor, ☎ 409-830-9060. It has charm, along with a century-old bar and an antique collection. Call for hours – they vary from day to day.

Country Inn II, 1000 E Horton, ☎ 409-836-2396. They specialize in beef, including sirloins, T-bones, ribeyes and chicken-fried steak.

Design II, 1200 S Austin, ☎ 409-830-0450. Housed in a Victorian cottage, Design II specializes in the unusual and exotic and is open to the public for lunch only. All other meals are for groups by appointment only.

Fluff Top Roll Restaurant, 210 E Alamo St, ☎ 409-836-9441. Plate lunches and daily specials, with homemade soups, stews, chili and salads.

The Grand at Nueces Canyon, 9501 US Hwy 290 West, ☎ 409-289-5600 or 800-925-5058. Open Friday and Saturday evenings only, but it's a treat to dine on prime rib, blackened red fish or steaks.

Santa Fe Café, 302 W 1st St, ☎ 409-836-0573. Good, old-fashioned café cooking with generous helpings and daily specials.

Huntsville

■ History

There have been more notorious people than you can shake a stick at come through Huntsville at one time or another – not to be expected in a town of 33,000 until you consider that it has been home to the Texas State Penitentiary ("The Walls") since 1847. Ruffians and criminals have been emprisoned in Huntsville for well over a century, some of them less lucky than others. "Old Sparky" electrocuted 361 inmates between 1924 and 1964. In early 1998 Karla Faye Tucker, a convicted pickax murderer, was executed here, causing a sensation around the world.

■ Touring

 But Huntsville, whose name is a tribute to Huntsville, Alabama, offers a lot more than a morbid step into prison life. Its terrain is as varied as the sites that surround this hidden recreational hotspot. To the north and east is **Lake Livingston**, one of the largest lakes in Texas. To the south is **Lake Conroe**, one of the most popular lakes in the state. It has become a retirement mecca. And then there's the **Sam Houston National Forest** that surrounds the city. If you can't find something to do outside in Huntsville than you're probably on the wrong side of the prison's walls.

Of course, you can go visit the **Texas Prison Museum** (1113 12th St, ☎ 409-295-2155) just to see what the Huntsville prison is all about. A unique relic and one-of-a-kind opportunity, the museum's roll call is dotted with memorable criminals. "Old Sparky," no longer in use, is on display.

Sam Houston, one of Texas' greatest leaders, made Huntsville his home and relics of his existence are found throughout the county. Of course, you can't miss the Sam Houston National Forest or the city of millions to the east that bears his name.

Sam Houston in Huntsville

In the 1840s Houston purchased a plantation, Raven Hill, 14 miles from town. He also kept up his Woodland Home that was closer to town. He was elected governor of Texas in 1859, but was removed from office when he refused to desert the Union. He returned to Huntsville humble and dejected, living out his life in the Steamboat House, which resembles a Mississippi steamboat. He died in 1863 and it is reported that his last word was "Texas."

Sam Houston's Grave and Monument (Oakwood Cemetery, 9th and Ave I) are simple tributes to one of the state's most popular heroes. A more audacious display of the area's affection for Houston is a statue of the man that can be seen from six miles away (I-45 south of town, adjacent to visitor's center). Standing 66 feet tall and incorporating 60,000 pounds of concrete, there is absolutely no way you can miss it. More of Houston's history and contribution to the Republic of Texas can be enjoyed at the **Sam Houston Memorial Museum Complex** (1836 Sam Houston Ave, ☎ 409-294-1832), which displays 15 acres of Houston memorabilia, including the Steamboat House, his Woodland home, his law office and a comprehensive digest of Houston's accomplishments.

Hidden in the Big Thicket, just east of Lake Livingston, is the **Alabama-Coushatta Indian Reservation** (☎ 800-444-3507 or 409-563-4391), one of only two reservations in the state. (The Tigua in West Texas own the other one.) The Alabama-Coushatta Indians have lived here for more than 150 years and have played important roles in Texas history. Some served in the Confederate Army during the Civil War and, earlier, they assisted Sam Houston in his bid for Texas independence. They welcome visitors and offer a museum, restaurant, craft shop and daily dancing performances. They also have overnight camping and RV accommodations on their 26-acre lake if you'd like to stay longer.

Information Sources

The **Huntsville/Walker County Chamber of Commerce** (☎ 800-289-0389, www.chamber.huntsville.tx.us) can help if you have any other questions.

■ Adventures on Foot

There are four national forests in the Piney Woods of East Texas that total over 675,000 acres. National forests are not to be confused with national parks – by law, the forests must attempt to produce a variety of goods and services, including timber, minerals, wildlife and forage for livestock. Because of this distinction, park managers are actively working the area, harvesting timber, allowing hunting, etc.

The **Sam Houston National Forest** (394 FM 1375 West, New Waverly, 77358, ☎ 888-361-6908, 409-344-6205) weaves its 161,000 acres around the northern edges of Lake Conroe south of Huntsville, then moves eastward, where it reaches the southwestern edge of Lake Livingston and the northern edges of the Cleveland area.

The **Lone Star Hiking Trail** distinguishes itself as one of the longest trails in the state. It meanders a total of 140 miles through Sam Houston, stretching from the western edge of the forest near Richards to FM1725 northwest of Cleveland.

✹ Take Care!

The trail is very primitive and hikers must periodically cross roads and private property. Spring and fall are the best times for the trail. Unless you're acclimated and enjoy the heat, summers are considered a little too hot (and bug infested) to be comfortable. Also, many hikers steer clear of the trail between November 1 and January 1 – deer hunting season. The park is open to deer rifle hunters so hiking is at your own risk.

Overnight camping during hunting season is prohibited. Throughout the rest of the year camping is permitted anywhere along the trail. There are no facilities along the trail, so you'll have to bring everything you need. In conjuction with the main trail, there are five loops, making both overnight and day hikes feasible. Trailheads and parking areas are scattered strategically along the trail to accommodate different starting and stopping points. Be sure to pick up a trail map and talk to park rangers before you begin any extended hike.

All of the following places offer a variety of recreational options.

Stubblefield Lake Campground, on the upper regions of Lake Conroe, is transected by the Lone Star Hiking Trail. Parts of the campground are very open, while other parts are covered by thick vegetation. Fishing on Stubblefield Lake and Lake Conroe is very popular.

Kelly's Pond Campground is much more primitive, with only eight camp sites and no facilities. There are three small fishing ponds directly south of the camp grounds and the Lone Star Trail runs within a mile of

East Texas

the camp to the north. On the far western edge of the forest is the **Little Lake Creek Wilderness Area**, a 3,810-acre parcel that remains undeveloped. There are no shelters, campgrounds, drinking fountains, restrooms or detailed trail maps.

> ### ✳ Take Care!
>
> Only experienced hikers should wander from the Lone Star Trail, which spans this designated wilderness area. You can get lost here, so you should be well provisioned and practiced in orienteering.

See also Lake Livingston State Park, below.

■ Adventures on Wheels

The **Double Lake Mountain Bike Trail**, considered the only one of its kind in the national forests of Texas, winds through the Double Lake Recreation Area for some 8.1 miles. It is challenging enough for an expert, and yet not too difficult for a novice. The trail crosses park roads in three different places, so you must be cognizant of road traffic. Other than that, its just you, other bikers and occasional hikers. Off-roaders appreciate the flat surfaces upon which you can reach high speeds. The forest provides shade that keeps bikers relatively cool.

The Double Creek Campground, built in large part by the CCC in 1937, includes a dining lodge, a picnic shelter, a bathhouse and a nearby 24-acre lake. Stocked with catfish, bass, bream and crappie, the lake boasts a white sand beach and a one-mile trail that follows its shoreline. No gasoline motors are allowed on the lake, just trolling motors and manually powered watercraft. Canoes and paddleboats may be rented at Double Creek's concession stand.

Special areas and trails have been designed for multi-use, including off-road vehicles, horses, mountain bikes and motorcycles. There are almost 70 miles of designated multi-use trails – but they exclude the ecologically sensitive Lone Star Trail.

See also Lake Livingston State Park, below.

■ Adventures on the Water

You'll find solitude a bit closer to town at the **Huntsville State Park** (I-45 south to Park Rd 40, ☎ 409-295-5644), set on Lake Raven. There are at least 11 miles of hiking and nature trails intertwined in the piney woods of Sam Houston National Forest. Fishing and swimming are the recommended water activities – no water-skiing is allowed. You can also rent canoes and paddleboats. The park feels like a perpetual summer camp.

To many, the Blue Lagoon is an early Brooke Shields movie. To East Texans, the **Blue Lagoon** (☎ 409-291-6111) is just short of scuba diving paradise. It is strictly monitored for scuba use only – no swimming or cliff jumping is allowed. However, you can enjoy camping and picnic facilities that surround what they call "The Texas Cozumel."

With 452 miles of forested shoreline, **Lake Livingston** can quench any outdoor need you might have, from camping, to hiking, to swimming and fishing. You can pick your spot along the 52 miles of lake. On the western shore is **Wolf Creek Park** (☎ 409-653-4312) and on the southeastern edge is **Lake Livingston State Park** (☎ 409-365-2201). Both have all of the amenities you might need, plus some. There are close to seven miles of trails within Lake Livingston Park, which is located near the ghost town of Swartwout, a steamboat stop on the Trinity River during the mid-1800s. The trails have multiple uses: 4.4 miles are for hiking, five for mountain biking, 2.5 for horseback riding and 2.7 for nature study.

Guided trail rides have been one of the most popular recent additions. In addition to the normal equestrian tours, **Lake Livingston Stables** (☎ 409-967-5032) offer breakfast and dinner rides. Because the park provides its own horses, visitors are not allowed to bring their own.

The park also provides a swimming pool, boat ramps, screened shelters and a seasonal park store (March to October) with bait, gas and dock facilities.

David Cox, with **Palmetto Guide Service** (☎ 409-291-9602), is one of the few area guides who concentrates solely on Lake Livingston. He'll take you on fishing trips, duck and goose hunts, photo shoots, alligator hunts and night trips.

■ Where to Stay

 Bluebonnet Bed & Breakfast, 1704 Ave O, 77340, ☎ 409-295-2072. $-$$. Large Victorian home on seven wooded acres. The owner calls it the "kick-back" place.

Longhorn House Bed & Breakfast, 1697 FM 1696 W, 77340, ☎ 409-295-1774 or 888-295-1774. While you're on the ranch, you can help feed the animals.

Parker House Bed & Breakfast, 304 N Maple, PO Box 2373, Trinity, 75862, ☎ 800-593-2373, 409-594-3260, www.bbmtview.com/~bbonline/tx/parkerhouse/. $$-$$$. Furnished exclusively with a collection of fine Victorian antiques, the parlor features an ornate 1860s rosewood parlor set. The Cistern Porch offers morning shade in the backyard.

La Quinta Inn, 1407 I-45 North, 77340, ☎ 409-295-6454 or 800-531-5900. $$. Basic amenities, with a pool to boot.

Waterwood National Resort & Country Club, One Waterwood, 77340, ☎ 409-891-5211 or 800-441-5211. $-$$$. Primarily a golf resort, but there is a swimming pool and playground if you're looking for a family adventure. The golf course is rated Number 4 in Texas.

The Whistler, 906 Ave M, 77340, ☎ 409-295-2830 or 713-524-0011. $$-$$$. The Greek Revival mansion turned bed and breakfast is bursting with classic antiques and Old South elegance.

■ Where to Eat

Junction Restaurant, 2641 11th St, ☎ 409-291-2183. Steaks, seafood, chicken and other tasty fare served in a historic landmark.

New Zion Missionary Baptist Church, FM 1374 one mile east of I-45, ☎ 409-295-7394. More than one person claims that this barbecue has helped them find religion. Family-style, all-you-can-eat specials are available.

Conroe

■ History

Conroe is really about Lake Conroe, a jewel of a lake that serves as the recreational refuge of Houston, 40 miles south, and has become a retirement hamlet. Isaac Conroe, who lent his name to the town, operated a lumber mill on the edge of the Big Thicket. He constructed a small tram to connect with the International and Great Northern Railroad. The junction of the two became "Conroe's Switch." Several other railroads decided to lay track through the switch and the small town became a shipping hub.

Conroe went on to enjoy a small oil boom in the 1930s. Though local wells still produce, the boom days have long since passed. Today the laid-back community involves itself in the simpler things of life: bass fishing, boating and sailing. There seem to be a lot of part-timers that make their way to Conroe. They split their time between the big city and the outdoors. And when they retire, they join Conroe on a full-time basis.

■ Touring

Usually, if you're in Conroe, you're lake-bound. But if you do need a break, try the **Crighton Theatre** (235 N Main, ☎ 409-756-1226), built in 1934. This beautifully restored vaudeville theater is now home to stage plays, music performances, opera, ballet and other special events.

The **Heritage Museum** (1506 I-45 North feeder, ☎ 409-539-MUSE) explores Montgomery County's development as a major oil and lumber center. It also offers some snippets of Texas history.

J-Mar Farms (Exit 91 off I-45, ☎ 409-856-8595, 800-636-8595), in addition to its on-site bed and breakfast, there is a petting farm and playground featuring over 200 animals, along with pony rides, fishing and hay rides.

One of Texas' most enduring favorites is the **Texas Renaissance Festival** (FM 1774 between Hwy 105 in Plantersville and FM 1488 in Magnolia, www.texrenfest.com, ☎ 800-458-3435, 281-356-2178, or 409-894-2516). It begins with the fall season and runs for seven continuous weekends (October through mid-November). One of the largest Renaissance festivals in the nation, it enjoys a pristine setting in the piney woods of East Texas. Begin early in the day – there's more than a day's worth of food, arts and crafts and jousting matches.

Another side trip worth taking is to **Montgomery**, 17 miles west of Conroe on TX 105. It was originally the county seat until Conroe outgrew the quaint town. Today it is strewn with antique shops, restored historic homes and white picket fences. The **Montgomery Carriage Service** (☎ 409-597-5786) offers a leisurely carriage ride through historic Montgomery in an authentic horse-drawn carriage.

East Texas

Information Sources

The **Conroe Chamber of Commerce/Convention and Visitors Bureau** (☎ 800-283-6645, PO Box 2347, 77305, http://chamber.montgomery.tx.us) will supply any additional information you might need.

■ Adventures on Foot

There are two state forests to explore close to Conroe. The best-known, **Sam Houston National Forest** (I-45 north to FM 1375, ☎ 409-344-6205), spreads itself across 160,000 East Texas acres. The most accessible spot from Conroe is the **Kaygal Recreation Area**, where there are ample opportunities to hike, bike, camp, fish, boat or go horseback riding. (For more information on the Sam Houston National Forest, see the section on Huntsville, page 233.)

At 1,700 acres, the **W. Goodrich Jones State Forest** (I-45 south to FM 1488, ☎ 409-273-2261) may be a little smaller than Sam Houston, but its beauty is by no means diminished. There's a marked self-guided nature trail as well as opportunities for hiking, biking, swimming and fishing.

■ Adventures on the Water

Lake Conroe (☎ 409-588-1111), with its 22,000 acres of fresh water and its 150 miles of shoreline, is surrounded by the majestic Sam HoustonNational Forest. It was originally created as the water supply for Houston, but has evolved into much more. Fishermen, who prey on Texas and Florida bass, walleye, striped bass, catfish, bream, hybrid perch, and crappie, may use two public ramps on the north end of the lake or one of the lake's eight public marinas to launch their boat. Several of the marinas also offer professional fishing guide services.

Motor boats, jet skis and sailboats usually congregate on the southern end of the lake. There's also public camping and RV facilities.

An authentic 250-passenger sternwheel paddleboat, the *Southern Empress* (Del Lago Resort, ☎ 800-324-2229), churns its way around Lake Conroe, Tuesday through Sunday of every week. The Del Lago Resort also rents out sailboats, pontoon boats and waverunners.

Lake Conroe Fishing Guides

Bass Adventures . . . . ☎ 409-856-8537

Bill Cannan . . . . ☎ 409-594-7645

James Chism . . . . ☎ 713-726.9410

Jim Ford . . . . ☎ 281-429-2023

■ Where to Stay

April Plaza Marina & Motel, PO Box 907, 17742 Hwy 105 W, Montgomery, 77356, ☎ 409-588-1144. $$. Basic rooms right at the marina, which offers a boat launch and bait and tackle shop.

April Sound Resort, 1000 April Sound Blvd, Montgomery, 77356, ☎ 409-588-1101, 800-41ROOMS. $$-$$$$. Accommodations range from villas to condos. There are both an 18-hole and nine-hole golf courses, a tennis center and a marina with boat rentals.

Del Lago Golf Resort and Conference Center, 600 Del Lago Blvd, Montgomery, 77356, ☎ 409-582-6100, 800-833-3078, www.dellago.com. $$$-$$$$. There's a championship golf course, 11 lighted tennis courts, a health spa, saunas, steambath, golf course cottages, private boat slips, sailboat rentals and more. For many, the resort is their entire vacation.

First Fairway at Walden, 13151 Walden Rd, ☎ 409-582-4477. Various condos for rent.

Heather's Glen Bed & Breakfast, 200 East Phillips, 77301, $$-$$$$, ☎ 409-441-6611, 800/66-JAMIE. Jacuzzis for two in the rooms and a full gourmet breakfast. This three-story carriage house rests on over an acre of beautiful gardens and grounds. It's so attractive that professional photographers use it on a regular basis for bridal shots and catalog photos.

Magnolia Blossom Bed & Breakfast, 902 N San Jacinto, 77301, ☎ 409-756-3878. $$$. The rooms open out to a balcony. It's also close to downtown Conroe and within 15 minutes of all the area recreational hotspots.

Villas on the Lake, Hwy 105 W, ☎ 409-447-2728. $$$-$$$$. Time share condos for rent on Lake Conroe near April Sound.

Invernes II at Walden, 13151 Walden Rd, ☎ 409-582-1012. Condo rentals.

J Mar Bed & Breakfast, 11780 Calfee Rd, 77304, ☎ 409-856-8595, $$$. Set on 16 acres, there is a petting zoo, paddleboats, and fishing gear for guests. It's also minutes away from the Texas Renaissance Festival and the Conroe Outlet Mall.

The Landing at Seven Coves, 700 Kingston Cove, ☎ 409-856-5501. Condo rentals and timeshares.

Seven Coves Resort on Lake Conroe, 7041 Kingston Cove, Willis, ☎ 409-856-5162. Condo rentals.

East Texas

TMC Resort Rentals, 14001 Walden Rd, ☎ 409-582-6105. Their offerings run the gamut.

■ Where to Eat

 Banana Bay, Hwy 105 W, ☎ 409-588-6588. It's all-out entertainment. You can drive by car or boat and, once you get here, there's volleyball, dancing, live music and more, plus the food.

The Fisherman's Wharf, 901 N Loop 336 W, ☎ 409-539-4121. Their name gives it away – they cater to seafood lovers.

The Golden Triangle

Beaumont

■ History

You can smell Beaumont's history, literally, the moment you set foot in town. The air is not only laced with the smell of oil, it's sopping with it. But the town began before oil was discovered, with Spanish and French fur trappers arriving in the early 1800s. It then became caught up in the lumber industry.

Spindletop

In 1901, when about 9,000 people called the town home, Beaumont hit pay dirt. Drillers discovered Spindletop, and its bounty spurted 150 feet into the air. No one had yet encountered a gusher like Spindletop and it took some time to figure out how to contain the well. Over a million gallons of oil were wasted. Within a month Beaumont boasted 30,000 residents. Throughout its lifetime, the well has produced over a 100 million gallons of petroleum. Today, the hill that Spindletop sat on is flat – it collapsed when the oil was removed.

While oil remains a lead industry for the town and the area, Beaumont is also an industrial center. Beaumont, Orange and Port Arthur are together called the Golden Triangle, reflecting their economic power as the industrial leaders in East Texas.

■ Touring

Spindletop has been recreated at the **Gladys City Spindletop Boomtown** (Lamar University Campus, ☎ 409-835-0823). You can mosey right back into 1901 and experience the excitement of one of the biggest booms in oil history.

The **Art Museum of Southeast Texas** (500 Main, ☎ 409-832-3432, www.amset.org) is another good start for the entire family, with an extensive mixture of permanent and traveling exhibits.

One of Beaumont's most famous natives is immortalized at the **Babe Didrikson Zaharias Memorial Museum** (I-10 at Gulf exit, ☎ 409-833-4622), which doubles as a visitor information center. She was named Woman Athlete of the Year on six different occasions by the Associated Press and was a pioneer in women's sports. The memorial displays various mementoes from her long and varied career.

Another pioneer who is immortalized at a local museum – although he was not a local resident – is Thomas Alva Edison at the **Edison Plaza Museum** (350 Pine, ☎ 409-839-3089). Edison invented more than 1,000 items, which, of course, included the light bulb. The museum is appropriately in the restored Travis St Power Substation and explores the transformation of the energy industry.

If you're around between Memorial Day weekend and the second weekend in July, you can pick your own blueberries and other seasonal fruit at **Griffin's Farm** (Moore Rd, ☎ 409-753-2247).

Although Beaumont lies a considerable distance north of the Texas coast, its deepwater port on the Neches River ship channel is one of the busiest in the nation, handling millions of tons of cargo each year. You can see the **Port of Beaumont** (1255 Main St, Downtown, ☎ 409-832-1546) in action all day long.

Information Sources

For more information on the Beaumont area, contact the **Beaumont Convention and Visitors Bureau** (☎ 800-392-4401, PO Box 3827, 77704).

East Texas

■ Adventures on the Water

Part of the allure of East Texas is its swampy underground. **Alligator Island** (I-10 west to FM 365, ☎ 409-794-1995) may not sound alluring at first, but it's an incredible (and safe) way to get up-close to the swamp's most ferocious residents. The gator farm has hundreds of alligators at all times, ranging from babies to mammoth creatures. If you're lucky, you can still see "Big Al," 800 pounds of big-jawed excitement.

You can find smaller critters at **Doguet's Crawfish Farm** (1801 E Hwy 90, ☎ 409-752-5105), where they'll let you watch the process of farming crawfish.

■ Eco-Tourism

Birders and nature enthusiasts will enjoy a one-hour tour of **Cattail Marsh** (Tyrell Park Entrance/Babe Zaharias Drive, ☎ 409-866-0023), constructed wetlands with eight miles of levees on 900 acres. Over 375,000 plants, including bulrush, cattail, pickerelweed, arrowhead, smartweed, yellow canna and blue flag iris, are found here.

■ Where to Stay

Grand Duerr Manor, 2298 McFaddin St, 77701, ☎ 409-833-9600. $$. If you slur Grand Duerr, you get "grandeur." They say they're "Beaumont's Bed & Breakfast."

Holiday Inn Beaumont Plaza, 3950 I-10 S, 77705, ☎ 409-842-5995. $$. All of your basic amenities.

■ Where to Eat

Don's Seafood and Steakhouse, 2290 I-10 S, ☎ 409-842-0686. Classic atmosphere and affordable seafood dishes.

Sartin's, 6725 Eastex Freeway, ☎ 409-892-6771. Cajun seafood with lots of style and attitude.

Port Arthur

■ History

As with any town, there are a lot of pieces that make up the whole. But for Port Arthur, almost all of those pieces happen to be water-related. Situated on the shore of the Gulf of Mexico, where the confluence of the Neches River, the Intracoastal Waterway, Sabine Lake and the Gulf all mix together in a grand miasma, Port Arthur's existence and success is tied to its waterways. Commercial fishermen depend on it for obvious reasons. Recreation centers around boating, fishing and sailing. The oil industry finds the city an easily accessible hub.

Despite the city's focus on oil and shipping, it doesn't want you to forget that it was home to people like Janis Joplin and Jimmy Johnson (street names reflect their reverence).

The actual city of Port Arthur is about nine miles inland from the Gulf Coast and was founded in the 1840s under the name of "Aurora." Arthur Stillwell (the "Arthur" in "Port Arthur") had grander visions of the city and revamped it around the turn of the century, dredging a canal up to 25 feet deep.

No sooner had he done that than ocean-equipped ships began to arrive. Oil from Spindletop, up the road in Beaumont, was pumped to Port Arthur, where it was refined and loaded onto ships. Like most of the oil cities in southern East Texas, the pungent smell of refined oil fills the air. Locals call it the "smell of money."

Back in its heyday, Port Arthur whimsically proclaimed that "We Oil the World." Port Arthur also earned a title of "Cajun Capital" as a number of Acadians settled here.

■ Touring

On the historical side, perhaps the most unexpected find is **La Maison Des Acadiens and Dutch Windmill Museum** (1500 Boston, Tex Ritter Park, Nederland Chamber of Commerce, ☎ 409-722-0279), which pays tribute to two of the largest cultural influences in the area: the Cajun and the Dutch. Their inclusion in the Tex Ritter Park, a tribute to the late country singing sensation, is all the more mind-boggling. The Dutch settled in Nederland, on the northern fringes of town, beginning in 1898, and were joined by the Cajuns a few years later.

The **Museum of the Gulf Coast** (700 Proctor, ☎ 409-982-7000) attempts to parcel out all the various aspects that make the area unique. One floor focuses on the Gulf Coast and its colonization. The second floor features special exhibits on the Gulf Coast and area celebrities like Janis Joplin, George Jones, The Big Bopper, Jimmy Johnson, Bum Phillips and Bruce Lietzke. A display of pieces by Port Arthur native Robert Rauschenberg is housed in the Grace Snell Room.

One of the finest and most popular residences is the **Pompeiian Villa** (1953 Lakeshore, ☎ 409-983-5977), which offers tours by appointment. It was built at the turn of the century for the "Barbed-Wire King," Issac Ellwood, who later sold it to James Hopkins. Hopkins in turn sold it to George Craig for a nifty 10% interest in a fledgling company called Texas Company, a precursor of Texaco. If Craig had retained his stock it is estimated that it would be worth close to $1 billion today. The villa also has the nickname of the "Billion Dollar House."

Sabine Pass, just across the Intracoastal Canal fronting the Gulf of Mexico, was the site of one of the most exciting Civil War battles. The **Sabine Pass Battleground State Historical Park** (Hwy 87 south, ☎ 409-971-2451) marks where the event took place and doubles as a state park complete with camping facilities, boat ramp and RV hookups. Confederate forces at Fort Sabine, under the command of a young Houston barkeeper named Dick Dowling, completely stunned Union aggressors by putting up a successful defense and capturing 315 people and two boats.

Pleasure Island (TX 82 over MLK-Gulfgate Bridge, ☎ 409-982-4675) is a work in progress. The 3,500-acre island now includes a marina, lighted fishing pier, yacht club, lakefront park, windsurfing park, disc golf course, residential subdivisions, boat launches, a concert park, and all of the restaurants and bars that go with it. And they're still adding things.

Information Sources

For more information, call the **Port Arthur Visitors and Convention Center** at ☎ 800-235-7822 or visit 3401 Cultural Center Dr., Port Arthur, 77642.

■ Adventures on the Water

Just down the road, **Sea Rim State Park** (Hwy 87 west of Sabine Pass, ☎ 800-792-1112 or 409-971-2559) stretches 5.2 miles along the Gulf of Mexico coast. The park contains both typical sandy beaches and a biologically important zone where the Gulf meets salt tidal marshlands. The marshlands are very fertile feeding grounds for every step in the food chain – which includes bugs and, more specifically, mosquitoes. Insect repellent is a must if you would like to spend time here.

Park officials have made it very easy to see and enjoy the marshlands, with wildlife observation blinds and the **Gambusia Nature Trail**, a boardwalk and canoe trail through the marsh. Airboat tours are also available. Swimming is allowed only off the sand beach – the marshland is populated by alligators.

Guide Services

B&L Charter . . . . ☎ 409-983-5617.

D.G. Guide Service . . . . ☎ 409-736-2126.

Sabine Lake Guide Service & Marshland Birding Tours . . . . ☎ 409-736-3023.

Tomcat Charter, Port Neches, Texas . . . ☎ 409-721-6333.

■ Where to Stay

Aurora B&B, 141 Woodworth Blvd, 77640, ☎ 409-983-4205. $$-$$$. One of the older homes in town, it has views of the ship traffic that traverses the Intracoastal Canal and the activity on Pleasure Island. One of the beds is a Malaysian showpiece and all the chandeliers (three) and wall sconces (five) are hand-cut antiques.

Cajun Cabins, 1800 M.L. King Blvd, Pleasure Island, 77640, ☎ 409-982-6050. $$. They come equipped with a refrigerator, stove and microwave. Available for the night, week or month.

■ Where to Eat

Channel Inn, TX 87, entrance to Sabine Pass, ☎ 409-971-2400. Owned by a commercial fisherman who wanted to branch out. Fresh, fresh, fresh seafood.

Dorothy's Front Porch, 100 Holmes Rd, Nederland, ☎ 409-722-1472. Even with 5,000 square feet to sit visitors, they suggest you make reservations. They serve catfish just about every way possible!

East Texas

Esther's Cajun Seafood and Oyster Bar, TX 87 at Rainbow Bridge, ☎ 409-962-6268. Situated on the Neches River, it's a view with fresh Cajun flair.

Special Attraction

The Big Thicket

There's a place where visitors sit at the crossroads of four states and marvel at their ability to be in so many states at once. The Big Thicket just north of Beaumont provides the same sense, having been called the "biological crossroads of North America" and an American ark.

It is not the size of the thicket that makes it such an anomaly. In fact there are under 300,000 acres left of what was once 3.5 million acres. The diversity of the species and terrains that coexist here are what makes it unusual. Hardwood pines are adjacent to cypress forests, blackwater swamps sit next to meadows, and virgin pine stands alongside southwestern sandhills.

There are 85 tree types and more than 1,000 flowering plants found here. Nearly 300 different types of birds either live here permanently or pass through on their annual migration. Fifty species of reptiles, including a reclusive type of alligator, wander the land.

Encroachment into the Big Thicket occurred relatively late in the drive toward Western colonization. Early Spanish settlers avoided the choking woods, as did Anglo-American colonists, who didn't begin farming the perimeter until the 1820s.

But by the 1850s lumbering had begun. The largesse of the thicket coupled with its stellar variety made it a gold mine. When a narrow-gauge railroad was built in 1876, devastation to natural timberland was ensured.

The 84,000 acres that the preserve encompasses owe their protection to intervention by the national government. During the Great Depression, the government purchased parcels of land from a number of timber companies in an attempt to keep them solvent. Rather than relinquish their holdings later on – much to the logging industry's dismay – they held on to them.

In 1966, Sen. Ralph Yarborough introduced a bill establishing a national park. In 1974, the area was named a preserve by an act of Congress. Preserve status stopped the lumbering, but allows oil and gas exploration, hunting and trapping.

Because of the way in which the land was purchased, the park extends south in a long, thin "strand of pearls," curling northwest after it hits Beaumont toward Jasper and Tyler counties.

Twelve different units make up the Big Thicket National Preserve. The principal tourism office is the Turkey Creek unit, eight miles north of Kountze. Since the preserve is such a delicate mixture of elements, no cars are allowed in beyond designated points.

Information Sources

For information about the Thicket, contact the park superintendent at 3785 Milam, Beaumont, TX 77701, ☎ 409-839-2689 (administrative offices) or 409-246-2337 (information).

Guide Services

Timber Ridge Tours (☎ 409-246-3107) in Kountze will do the planning for you, offering cruises of the Neches River.

■ Hiking

Turkey Creek Unit

Kirby Nature Trail: A great introductory trail that winds through hardwoods and pines. The outdoor loop stretches 2.4 miles, while the inner loop is 1.7 miles long.

Turkey Creek Trail: There are three trailheads for this 15-mile stretch, good for backcountry camping and extended hikes. Check with the visitors center for specific access information.

Pitcher Plant Trail: Meanders through a mixed pine forest before bringing you to the edge of a wetland savanna. Several carnivorous plants, including pitcher plants, can be viewed up close.

East Texas

Hickory Creek Savannah Unit

Sundew Trail: Known for a bright display of wildflowers from late spring through the summer, there is both a one-mile option and a fully handicapped-accessible half-mile trail.

Big Sandy Creek Unit

Beaver Slide Trail: A 1½-mile loop that winds around a series of ponds formed by beaver dams. The trail also permits access to Big Sandy Creek and a number of fertile fishing spots.

Woodlands Trail: There are lots of options here with three different loops of varying length – 5.4 miles, 4½ miles and 3.3 miles. The trail traverses a wide variety of different terrains.

Big Sandy Creek Horse Trail: Designed for horseback riding, all-terrain biking and hiking. The 18-mile round-trip ride goes through upland pine forests before crossing Simons Branch to a forest of basket oak, sweetgum, hornbeam and holly.

Beech Creek Unit

Beach Woods Trail: The one-mile trail leads past a beautiful stand of beech and magnolia.

■ Fishing

Fishing is permitted in all waters; all that's required is a Texas fishing license. Bass, catfish and crappie are the primary fish.

North Texas & the Panhandle

■ The Land

The North Texas that this book depicts is really a marriage of two districts: North Texas blackland prairie and the Texas Panhandle. The cotton that sprouts from the blackland's fertile recesses is some of the finest in the world. Only one other patch of similar terrain exists on earth (it's in Australia).

The Panhandle has been much maligned. Some ungrateful Texans even think it should be given away to Oklahoma. However, that would be a tragic mistake, as it not only contains rich pockets of oil, it hides many of the state's most precious treasures, like the Palo Duro Canyon.

Real Texans live in the Panhandle, with salt-of-the-earth demeanors, steady stares, straight talk and pure souls. You'll want to sit and talk awhile with these folks.

■ History

The Panhandle remained essentially vacant during early American colonization. The Indians seemed to be the only ones who could survive the region's harsh climate and sometimes severe weather. In fact, the Palo Duro Canyon was where the Comanche Indians made their last stand. The Spaniards, Mexicans and French all wandered through, but none stayed – they didn't believe the land to be habitable.

Charles Goodnight claimed the Palo Duro Canyon as his ranch in the late 1800s, beginning the American encroachmenthe, but the Panhandle remains sparsely settled to this day.

Fort Worth and Dallas anchor the eastern edge of the region. While the Panhandle is slow and countrified, these two cities are as metropolitan as Texas gets. Dallas is known for its well-coiffed and well-dressed residents. Fort Worth is known for its immense collection of art. The pair, grandly termed "the Metroplex," move dangerously fast.

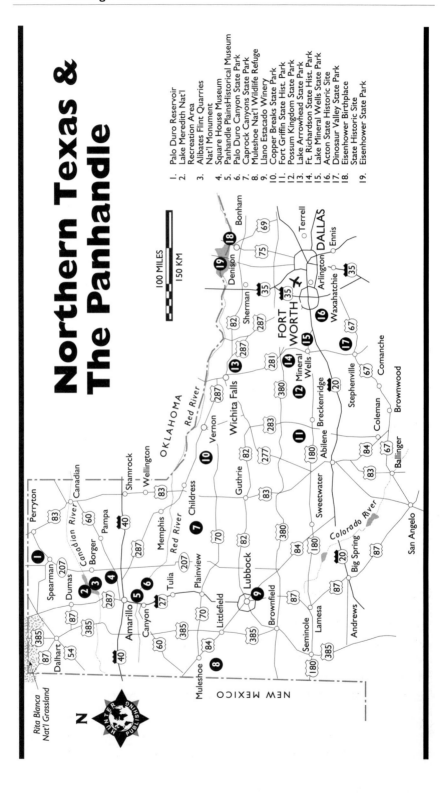

Northern Texas & The Panhandle

100 MILES
150 KM

1. Palo Duro Reservoir
2. Lake Meredith Nat'l Recreation Area
3. Alibates Flint Quarries Nat'l Monument
4. Square House Museum
5. Panhandle PlainsHistorical Museum
6. Palo Duro Canyon State Park
7. Caprock Canyons State Park
8. Muleshoe Nat'l Wildlife Refuge
9. Llano Estacado Winery
10. Copper Breaks State Park
11. Fort Griffin State Hist. Park
12. Possum Kingdom State Park
13. Lake Arrowhead State Park
14. Ft. Richardson State Hist. Park
15. Lake Mineral Wells State Park
16. Acton State Historic Site
17. Dinosaur Valley State Park
18. Eisenhower Birthplace State Historic Site
19. Eisenhower State Park

■ Logistics

Air travel hereabouts centers on the **Dallas/Fort Worth (DFW) Airport**, so that's the easiest place to begin. The airport is a monstrous affair and has been the cause of more than one headache. That's the bad news. The good news is that just about every domestic airline flies here. (Southwest Airlines flies into Love Field, Dallas' other airport. Love Field usually caters to the smaller flights and airlines.) Suffice it to say, you won't have any problems getting here.

To get into North Texas and the Panhandle, you'll probably have to start in Dallas. You can catch puddle-jumpers into Amarillo, Wichita Falls and Lubbock. Other than that, everything is spread out, so make sure you're comfortable with your choice of rental car.

Dallas has been doing some great work with its metro system (**DART**), so if you're not going far, a call to check their routes at ☎ 214-979-1111 is worth a try.

■ Weather & Climate

Weather in the area tends to be agreeable, although the Dallas/Fort Worth region is pummeled regularly by hail. Tornado Alley zips out west of this region, through Wichita Falls and down south. Storms can move quickly, so be prepared. This part of Texas – with its flat, high plains – is also very windy. Which is fine for residents. It blows away the heat and keeps things pleasantly cool.

Dallas

■ History

Created at the crossroads of commerce, Dallas – Big "D" – is a curious mix of a million residents and the hot Texas earth. Unlike its neighbor Fort Worth to the west, which embraces cowboys and country, Dallas prides itself on its conservativism, its religious ethic and its big corporate buildings. It's a white collar town where cut-off shorts earn strange stares and businessmen wear three-piece suits despite 100° weather. Texans might call it snotty; visitors might call it cosmopolitan.

The city has been one of the most visible in Texas. It is accidentally identified as the state capital on more occasions than Austinites would like to admit. But that's because it hit the international spotlight like no

Dallas by night.

other Texas town. It was home to the Ewing gang and their ranch mansion, Southfork, on the *Dallas* TV series. It's still home to the Dallas Cowboys, America's most loved or hated football franchise, depending on whom you ask. It was where Nolan Ryan finished out his spectacular baseball career pitching for the Texas Rangers.

And, unfortunately, no one in this lifetime will forget that it was the city in which President John F. Kennedy said his last words before being gunned down.

The ostentatious spirit for which Texans are known most certainly began early in the state's history. The first settler, John Neely Bryan, built his cabin in 1841 on the banks of the Trinity River and then widely publicized his new "town." Within a year, two more families joined him. When the railroads came to town in 1873, the population soared beyond 7,000.

Early on, Dallas began its social ascension. One of the earliest cosmopolitan influences was brought by François Cantagrel, who formed a utopian society called La Réunion on the bluffs a few miles west of Dallas. He brought around 300 French, Belgian, American and Swiss socialists to his planned community.

The enclave of artists and idealists failed – a result of poor management and placement. Some of the Europeans returned home, but many of the scientists, musicians and writers moved to Dallas, lending the growing town a cultured air.

That Dallas became what it is today – a massive hub for all industries – is a little strange considering it was not as well endowed as many other Texas cities. Galveston and Houston were both natural ports. El Paso was a natural pass both west and south. The Trinity River wasn't even navigable, but that was no matter. Dallas became the biggest inland cotton market in the world and was the largest publishing hub in the South.

Dallas pulled off its biggest coup in 1936 by landing the Texas centennial celebration with a bid of $10 million and a pledge of 242 acres. Much to the chagrin of older cities like Houston and Galveston – which had actually been around in 1836 at the beginning of the centennial – Big D became the perpetual host. President Franklin D. Roosevelt, Ginger Rogers, Shirley Temple, Jack Dempsey and hundreds of thousands of other people attended the worldly celebration. It was estimated that between the Texas Centennial Celebration and 1937's Pan American Exposition, over 13 million visitors walked the streets of Dallas.

While Dallas' first boom was launched by the railroads, subsequent booms (and busts) followed cotton, oil, insurance, real estate, banking and the computer industries. It has become a center for several major corporations, including J.C. Penney, American Airlines, Mary Kay Cosmetics and the Boy Scouts.

The first 7-Eleven convenience store was opened in Dallas on July 11, 1927 (7/11/27). The world's first microchip was created at the local Texas Instruments facility.

■ Touring

Dallas has approximately a million residents. If you include its suburbs and the surrounding area, it has closer to 4½ million, making for a very culturally diverse and rich environment. For more area information, see entries for Arlington, Irving and Grand Prairie, pages 275, 278 and 286, respectively.

Art plays a central role for Dallas, a tangible aspect of the cultured climate Dallas residents strive to preserve. Sculptured pieces and statues of tribute are placed throughout the city.

The **Dallas Museum of Art** (1717 Harwood, ☎ 214-922-1200, www.unt.edu/dfw/dma/www/dma.htm) provides the heart for downtown's arts district that includes 60 acres of cultural attractions. Most of the large traveling exhibits will stop at the DMA. A sculptured outdoor garden and a children's area round out the museum.

Dallas Area

N

1.5 MILES

.93 KM

Northwest Hwy

Garland Rd

Dallas Arboretum

Grand Ave

Ferguson Rd

Thornton Fwy

12

Lake June Rd

Hawn Fwy

Buckner Blvd

White Rock Lake

Military Pkwy

Scyene Rd

175

12

Mockingbird Ln

78

30

Cotton Bowl
Texas State
Fairgrounds

310

Gaston Ave

Greenville Ave

45

Southern
Methodist
Univ

Lovers Ln

75

Corinth St

35E

Dallas Northern Tollway

77

12

Love
Field

35E

World
Trade
Center

Hampton Rd

Blvd

Keist

77

Westmoreland

Ft Worth Ave

Irving Blvd

Trinity River

Singleton Blvd

30

Davis St

Jefferson Blvd

Illinois Ave

183

Airport Fwy

Shady Grove

Dallas-Ft Worth Tpk

12

North Texas & the Panhandle

Former School Book Depository.

The Meadows Museum of Cultures (Southern Methodist University campus, ☎ 214-768-2516), though small, boasts a powerful collection of both Picasso and Diego Rivera, among others.

The downtown district is also home to **Old City Park** (1717 Gano, ☎ 214-421-5141), a small village museum of 37 buildings. Each building, including a schoolhouse, bank and church, was moved to the site from towns across North Texas and restored to their original condition.

Springtime is perfect for a stroll through the **Dallas Arboretum and Botanical Garden** (8525 Garland Rd, ☎ 214-327-8263), 66 acres tucked away just minutes from downtown. The **Jonsson Color Garden** boasts more than 2,000 varieties of azaleas. While spring and summer might be the most exciting times for the gardens, fall and winter are certainly not far behind, with a steady and varying line-up of flowers and foliage.

Also on the grounds is the historic **DeGolyer House**, a 21,000 square-foot Colonial mansion built in 1940 for oil man Everett DeGolyer. Footpaths meander throughout the rolling, manicured lawn and are surrounded by an old English garden.

Perhaps the most visited museum in town, morbid as it may be, is the **Sixth Floor Exhibit** (411 Elm, ☎ 214-747-6660), in the former School Book Depository building where Lee Harvey Oswald allegedly targeted

President John F. Kennedy. Overlooking the site of the assassination, the museum pays tribute to Kennedy.

For three weeks in September and October each year, Dallas plays host to the **Texas State Fair**. Millions attend and the fairgrounds are a permanent fixture for Texans. It's not to be missed if you're in town. The Cotton Bowl serves as the fairgrounds' centerpiece and when the fair isn't in gear, the State Fairgrounds turn into a giant park (Fair Park) with an array of attractions.

The **Cotton Bowl**, a 70,000 seat football stadium, sits idle much of the time, but for most native Texans (and even transplants), it is a football icon for two reasons: the Cotton Bowl game, played on New Year's Day, and Texas-OU weekend. Before the demise of the Southwest Conference (SWC), there was almost always at least one Texas team playing in the Cotton Bowl, usually against some northern team like Notre Dame.

Texas-OU (University of Texas at Austin vs. Oklahoma University) weekend is another milestone in Texas football history. The teams annually meet around the second week of October for one of the oldest collegian traditions. For two days, tens of thousands of students stop traffic and revel in the adopted city.

Some of the largest and most powerful locomotives are at the **Age of Steam Museum** (Fair Park, 1105 Washington, ☎ 214-428-0101). Along with brawny trains come examples of luxury, with Pullman sleeping cars and lounge cars included in the exhibit.

The **Aquarium** enthralls its visitors each day with piranha and shark feedings. But there are also more subtle, subdued marine exhibits, with more than 375 species represented.

Kids will enjoy **Science Park I and II** (Fair Park, ☎ 214-428-5555), which provide hands-on scientific displays and educational features.

The **Hall of State**, a shrine to Texas greats, the **Museum of Natural History**, the **Civic Garden Center** and the **Starplex Amphitheater** round out Fair Park's attractions.

For entertainment there are several pockets of restaurants and bars that are notable. Downtown is host to the **West End Historical District** (bounded by the Woodall Rodgers Freeway, Commerce and Lamar), over 20 blocks of restaurants, shops, bars and offices that is open to foot traffic only. Occupying the original site of Dallas as plotted by John Neely Bryan, the West End includes a three-tiered mall as its focal point. **Dallas Alley**, a $3½ million enterprise, can fulfill your every nightclub dream. With one cover price you have access to country, rock, classic oldies, smoky alternative and dueling sing-along piano music.

Deep Ellum (east of downtown, bounded by Central Expressway, I-30 and Parry at Fair Park, www.deepellumtx.com) has historically provided an alternative to the mainstream crowd at the West End. It flourished during Prohibition with jazz and blues performances. With firm roots in the local black community, the live music here is more original than the covers that usually make up the West End's repertoire. Originally centered on Elm St and nicknamed Deep Elm, the locals turned "Elm" into "Ellum."

A third entertainment option is **Greenville Avenue**, a more recent addition. Most of the road is mercantile, but there are several blocks of trendy bars and restaurants for the college crowds. Parking in these areas is hard to find.

Dallas prides itself on its professional sporting prowess, boasting every type of team you might want to watch. The legendary **Dallas Cowboys** (www.dallascowboys.com) call Texas Stadium in Irving home and play to capacity crowds nearly every home game. Call ahead for ticket information (☎ 972-579-5000). The **Texas Rangers** (☎ 817-273-5100) play to excited crowds at Arlington Stadium. Though the Rangers haven't quite reached the pinnacle of baseball success, they've come close and are widely respected.

The **Dallas Mavericks**, an NBA franchise since 1980, have spent more than their share of time in the basketball cellar. But they still provided an exciting game. You can catch them at Reunion Arena in the heart of downtown Dallas (☎ 972-988-DUNK, www.nba.com/mavericks).

The **Dallas Stars** (www.dallasstars.com) are one of the area's most exciting up-and-coming teams. Texans are excited about hockey and the exuberant crowds you'll encounter at Stars games reflect that.

You can view all of downtown from atop **Reunion Tower** (300 Reunion Blvd, ☎ 214-741-3663), which anchors the western edge of the city's skyline and is the identifiable landmark in photos of downtown. A narrow shaft topped by a spinning restaurant, bar and observation deck, it affords a birds-eye view of Dallas and the Trinity River greenbelt. There's a fee for going on the observation deck and you pay a price for the view if you choose to eat or drink here.

Two of the city's premiere areas, **Highland Park** and **University Park**, are incorporated separately and are packed with mansions and well-manicured lawns. Highland Park was designed by landscape architect Wilbur David Cooke, who also planned Beverly Hills.

North Texas & the Panhandle

✻ Author's Tip

You'll find the most ornate homes along Lakeside Drive.

Swiss Avenue was the most prominent area of town up until World War I. Settled by Europeans in the 1850s, the houses and estates, especially along Swiss and Gaston Avenues, were grand affairs. Most of the houses – many of mansion proportions – fell into decay by the 1960s. However, a preservation effort that began in the 70s continues today. You'll notice great disparities as you wander through the neighborhood, with pockets of grandeur a block away from properties close to condemnation.

The **Belo Mansion** (2101 Ross Ave, ☎ 214-969-7066) sits apart from these other high-end housing districts. Alfred Belo, founder of the *Dallas Morning News*, got to enjoy the mansion he had built for only a year before his death in 1901. Today, the Dallas Bar Association and the Dallas Bar Foundation have their offices in the grande dame, but tours are allowed during certain times. Call for details.

Part of the irony of the *Dallas* TV series (besides the fact that it depicted every Texan as owning an oil well and riding their horse on a daily basis) was that the ranch called **Southfork** (3700 Hogge Rd, Parker, ☎ 972-442-7800) isn't really even in Dallas. It's in Parker, a short drive north of town. Embracing the show that was a hit in 83 different countries, there is a museum, Miss Ellie's restaurant and a Western store. Of course,

Southfork Ranch.

there's also the house and the ranch, complete with longhorns and horses.

■ Adventures on Foot

Within the city's boundaries are two small lakes perfect for joggers. **Bachman Lake** (3500 Northwest Hwy, ☎ 214-670-6266) is ringed by a trail that works for all types of wheels as well, whether they be bicycle, roller skating or blading. There are also areas for soccer, picnics and a playground. The concession area rents out roller skates and paddleboats.

White Rock Lake (8300 Garland, ☎ 214-670-4100) finds itself inundated with 5K-ers, 10K-ers and other runners a majority of the time. Its 12.5K loop is attractive to bikers, as well. Several sailboat clubs regularly hold regattas on White Rock.

White Rock Lake.

Lake Texoma, north of Dallas on the Texas/Oklahoma border, draws visitors from both Oklahoma and Texas. The **Cross Timbers Hiking Trail** hugs over 14 miles of the southern shore. Parts of the trail are atop the rocky ledges that overlook the lake; others snake through a blackjack oak woodland, typical of the Cross Timbers terrain. Considered a moderate hike, it has several places to camp along the way. Juniper Point, Cedar Bayou and Rock Creek Camp have water and other facilities. Five-Mile Camp, Lost Loop Camp and Eagle's Roost Camp are primitive, with no water or conveniences. A permit is required when camping at any of the wilderness camps. They can be obtained at the Corps of Engineers office at Dennison Dam or at the Juniper Point Park entrance. Beware of poison ivy.

Dallas **rock climbers** must venture far outside the city for any naturally occurring challenge, heading out for Mineral Wells or Enchanted Rock. There are several climbing gyms that cater to the misplaced climber. **Stoneworks** (1003 4th Ave, Carrollton, ☎ 972-323-1047) bills itself as the "world's tallest climbing gym" and utilizes seven grain silos to climb inside. Climbs range from 10 to 110 feet and are on a variety of surfaces. In addition to the silos, there are outside routes and a garage used for training. **Exposure Indoor Rock Climbing** (2389 Midway, Carrollton, ☎ 972-732-0307) employs 6,000 feet of vertical, overhanging and slab routes on realistic rock surface.

■ Adventures on Wheels

Cedar Hill State Park's (FM 1382, south of I-20, ☎972-291-3900) mountain biking trails are considered some of the premiere trails in the DFW Metroplex. Located on the eastern edge of Joe Pool Lake south of Grand Prairie, there's a little of everything here. Three trails make up the mixture: **Talala Trail**, three miles; **DORBA (Dallas Off-Road Bike Association) Trail**, 3.2 miles; and the **Baggett Branch Loop**, 10 miles. They've made it easy for you by posting signs that rate the difficulty of different loop options. Believe the signs. There are some steep, tricky creek crossings and some tight tree sections.

> **✳ Author's Tip**
>
> Some portions of the trails take you past Joe Pool Lake. Feel free to take a dip.

Though mountain bikers lay claim to a large portion of Cedar Hill park, they aren't the only ones to enjoy its charms. An eight-mile hiking trail, picnic areas, camp sites and lake access round out the park's offerings.

■ Adventures in the Air

For a true rush, **Skydive Dallas** (☎ 800-688-JUMP, 903-364-5103), an hour northeast of Dallas near Whitewright, will guide you on your first jump or your 1,000th jump. They offer skysurfing, freestyle and freeflight, with training to match.

Farmers Market.

Skydive Today North Texas (☎ 800-425-8375, Gainesville Municipal Airport) and **Skydive Texas** (☎ 817-430-3696) are two more options that provide the same rush for thrill-seekers. Skydive Texas, 15 miles west of Denton, has 320 acres devoted to their skydiving enterprise and also has a restaurant, a bunkhouse, RV hook-ups and camping sites.

If you'd like the rush of flying to last longer than one minute, hot air balloon rides are available throughout the Metroplex.

Airventure Balloon Port (1791 Millard, Suite D, Plano, 75074, ☎ 972-422-0212) schedules flights for every sunrise and sunset of the year, weather permitting. **The Sky's the Limit** (☎ 972-724-0343), headquartered in Flower Mound, takes off from a variety of spots, depending on weather conditions and the clients request.

■ Where to Stay

Adolphus Hotel, 1321 Commerce St, 75202, ☎ 800-221-9083, 214-742-8200. $$$-$$$$. The Adolphus has won just about every possible award. *Condé Nast Traveler* calls it one of the top 10 hotels in the nation. Built by Adolphus Busch of Busch beer fame in 1912, it has everything you could want.

American Youth Hostel, 3530 Forest Lane, ☎ 214-350-4294. $. Always an option for the young.

Bed & Breakfast Texas Style, 4224 W Red Bird Lane, 75237, ☎ 972-298-8586. This service offers a wide variety of accommodations all over town and nearby area lakes.

Courtyard On The Trail Bed & Breakfast, 8045 Forest Trail, 75238, ☎ 214-553-9700; 800-484-6260 pin #0465; www.bbonline.com/tx/courtyard/. $$$. A morning jog is easy; just open your French doors and hit the trail around White Rock Lake. The same doors also lead to the pool and courtyard. For both business travelers (it is equipped with a fax machine) and couples.

Dallas Grand Hotel, 1914 Commerce St, 75201, ☎ 800-421-0011, 214-747-7000. $$$. A full city block, "grand" describes both the hotel's luxury and its size. Located in the business district for easy access.

Hyatt Regency, 300 Reunion Blvd W, 75207, ☎ 800-233-1234, 214-651-1234. $$$$. Adjacent to Reunion Tower (and its acclaimed Antares restaurant, which rotates), it is also steps from the West End entertainment district and the Dallas Convention Center.

Le Meridien, 650 N Pearl, 75201, ☎ 800-543-4300, 214-979-9000. $$$$. Anchoring the Plaza of Americas complex in the middle of the arts district, Le Meridien boasts an award-winning restaurant and indoor ice skating rink. Parking is sometimes difficult.

The Wyndham Anatole, 2201 N Stemmons Freeway, 75207, ☎ 800-WYNDHAM, 214-748-1200. $$-$$$$. This grand hotel boasts over 1,600 units, making it the largest in the Southwest. It has eight restaurants, three pools and 3,000 parking spaces.

Skyline Ranch, 1801 Wheatland, 75241, ☎ 972-224-8055. $$-$$$. Ninety acres of picket fenced fun. There are hiking trails, fishing, horseback riding, carriage rides and green pastures. It seems far away, but the Dallas skyline view is spectacular.

Stoneleigh Hotel, 2927 Maple Ave, 75201, ☎ 800-255-9299, 214-871-7111. $$$. When Hollywood comes to town, Stoneleigh pampers them. Its four-star restaurant, Ewald's, is emblematic of the service you'll find.

Texas Lil's Dude Ranch, PO Box 656, Justin, 76247, ☎ 800-LIL-VILL (545-8455) or 817-430-0192, www.texaslils.com. $$-$$$. For over 20 years, Texas Lil's Dude Ranch has served up fun, food and entertainment in Texas fashion.

■ Where to Eat

Alessio's, 4117 Lomo Alto, ☎ 214-521-3585. Italian cuisine, their veal attracts repeat business.

Arcodoro, 2520 Cedar Springs, ☎ 214-871-1924. Authentic Italian in uptown Dallas.

Arthur's, 8350 N Central Expwy, Campbell Ctr, ☎ 214-361-8833. Pure American cuisine. The sumptuous steaks and delicious salmon are Dallas favorites.

Dick's Last Resort, Ross and Record St, in the West End, ☎ 214-747-0001. Serves up a mess of local cuisine, including ribs, chicken and shrimp. Dick's is loud with nightly entertainment and a generally festive roar.

Ewald's at the Stoneleigh, 2927 Maple – Stoneleigh Hotel, ☎ 214-871-2523. Classic European fare with rich French and continental-style sauces.

Gennie's Bishop Grill, 321 N Bishop in Oak Cliff, ☎ 214-946-1752. Homemade pies follow the real mashed potatoes and greens. It's an inexpensive downtown favorite for lunch only.

The Grape, 2808 Greenville, ☎ 214-828-1981. Upscale New American cuisine.

Hard Rock Café, 2601 McKinney Ave, ☎ 214-855-0007. Like most of the Hard Rock's counterparts, it's big on ambiance, not necessarily on food. In the same vein, there is also a **Planet Hollywood** in town (West End, ☎ 214-749-7827).

La Valentina de Mexico, 14866 Montfort, ☎ 972-726-0202. Rated as one of the best Mexican restaurants in town.

Nana Grill, 2201 Stemmons – Wyndham Anatole Hotel, ☎ 214-761-7479. Lots of choices, from seafood and chicken to lamb, steak and veal.

Mansion on Turtle Creek, 2821 Turtle Creek in Oak Lawn, ☎ 214-526-2121. The Mansion is almost always included on the "Best of Dallas" lists for its Southwestern cuisine. Located in the hotel of the same name.

Momo's Italian Specialties, 9191 Forest Ln, ☎ 972-234-6800 and 8300 Preston Center Plaza, ☎ 214-987-2082. First generation Italian, courtesy of the Gattini family, who left their homeland just over a decade ago. Momo's, which derived its name from Pappa Gattini's native nickname, is as authentic and delicious as you'll find anywhere. Everything's big, relatively inexpensive and unforgettable. It's also BYOB. Try Momo's Special – it's one of the author's personal favorites.

Mr. Sushi, 4860 Beltline, Addison, ☎ 214-385-0168. An alternative to the Tex-Mex and barbecue that permeates the state. The Japanese cuisine here is great; its sushi bar has been called exceptional.

Pierre's By The Lake, 3430 Shore Crest Dr, ☎ 214-358-2379, www.dallasdinesout.com/restrant/p/pierres/pierres. With an elegant steak and seafood menu served next to Bachman Lake, Pierre's is in a classic home. There's plenty of room, though, with banquet seating and a lake-front patio.

Razzoo's Cajun Café, 13949 N Central Expwy, ☎ 972-235-3700 and 3712 Towne Crossing, ☎ 972-686-9100. If you like hot and spicy, this is a perennial favorite.

Riviera, 7709 Inwood Rd, ☎ 214-351-0094. This romantic, intimate place will captivate you with Mediterranean and French dishes that have earned them lots of stars. They serve only dinner and reservations are recommended.

Sonny Bryan's Smokehouse, 2202 Inwood, ☎ 214-357-7120. Not much has changed here for many years. Food starts at 10 am and lasts until it runs out. Seating is in one-armed school desks and limited. Locals can't get enough of it.

Star Canyon, Cedar Springs at Oak Lawn – The Centrum, ☎ 214-520-7827, www.starcanyon.com. Offering "New Texas Cuisine," they can also teach you how to cook and offer some of their secret recipes (including a cowboy coffee blend) for sale.

Stoneleigh P, 2926 Maple Ave, ☎ 214-871-2346. Part of the exquisite hotel, the restaurant has been rolling along for over 20 years. Includes an incredible juke box and patio seating.

Uncle Julio's, 4125 Lemmon Ave, ☎ 214-520-6620; 7557 Greenville Ave, ☎ 214-987-9900; 16150 Dallas Parkway, ☎ 972-380-0100. Readers' polls in the local papers name Julio's as the number one Tex-Mex restaurant in the city. Their swirl margaritas may be one reason why.

Y.O. Ranch, 702 Ross Ave, ☎ 214-744-3287, www.dallassites.com/yoranch. From prairie fire nachos to a foot-long enchilada to top sirloin, the Y.O. offers a blend of Mexican, chuckwagon and prairie fare.

Fort Worth

■ History

The man for which the city is named – William Jenkins Worth – doesn't stir many historians' memories. He fought in the War of 1812 and the Florida Seminole Indian War and died inauspiciously of cholera in 1849, the same year that Camp Worth was established. Fort Worth (having moved from camp to fort status) was abandoned by the army, but by then settlers had come to join the post.

Area residents took over the empty buildings and barracks – a stable became the town's first hotel. The Civil War brought economic hardship, but cattle carried prosperity to the humble city, though it wasn't without a little competition.

The Chisholm Trail ran east of town between Dallas and Fort Worth; the Western Trail passed to the west between Fort Worth and Fort Griffin. Fort Worth became a supply hub, representing the last chance for cattle drivers to provision before heading north.

The time of the trail ended with the invention of barbed wire and the efficiency of shipping by rail. Again, Fort Worth took advantage of its location and became a shipping hub for beef processing. The Fort Worth Stockyards rose overnight to become the fifth largest such center in the nation. Between 1902 and 1912 over 16 million head of cattle passed through the stockyards.

The population of Fort Worth reflected the change, growing from 27,000 in 1900 to 73,000 in 1910 to 105,000 in 1920. With such a heavy investment in cattle and cowboys, it comes as no surprise that Fort Worth was a rowdy place, strewn with colorful gunfights and eccentric characters.

✺ Did You Know?

Butch Cassidy (George Leroy Parker) and his Wild Bunch tried to lay low in Fort Worth for awhile but had to take off after police recognized a picture of the bunch that was proudly displayed in a photographer's window.

Chief Quanah Parker stopped regularly in Fort Worth on business, staying at the Pickwick Hotel, a first-class affair. The stockyards eventually faltered as the cattle business moved farther west.

Fort Worth turned to oil (which was found nearby), the defense industry and aviation. Today, both General Dynamics and Bell Helicopter design and build airplanes here.

Fort Worth is the maligned step-sister of Big D. Joined at the hip with one of fastest growing areas in the nation, it is part of what has been termed the "Metroplex," a grand moniker than encompasses Fort Worth, Dallas and the dozens of smaller communities that surround the two cities. Boundaries between Metroplex members are obsolete. A sign will tell you when you've left one town and entered another. Fort Worth, with all the mad growth of the Metroplex, somehow got thrown out of the limelight and earned the reputation as the "hick" in the family. Perhaps there are a lot of pick-ups and Stetsons around town, but Fort Worth is a cultural jewel that has somehow preserved a slower pace and a family atmosphere. Its downtown has been recreated and its art district has been deemed one of the finest in the nation. Not bad for a cow town.

The town's cultural appetite is unparalleled for its size of just under 500,000 residents. Among the town's favorite artists is Van Cliburn, the legendary pianist who won the first Tchaikovsky Competition in Moscow, along with the hearts of millions, at the age of 23. The Annual Van Cliburn International Piano Competition began at Fort Worth in 1962 – Cliburn moved to Fort Worth in 1986, reviving his career the next year. People move mountains to get tickets for Cliburn's recitals.

■ Touring

Fort Worth is certainly an odd combination of cow town and culture – a pristine jewel that refuses to leave its country background. For a taste of the country head toward the **Fort Worth Stockyards** National Historic District (visitor information at 130 East Exchange Ave, ☎ 817-624-4741, www.stockyardsstation.com), a 125-acre hodgepodge of dining, shopping, entertainment and night life.

The centerpiece of the stockyards is **Billy Bob's Texas**, the world's largest honky-tonk (2520 Rodeo Plaza, ☎ 817-624-7117), an original piece of the yards. The bull-riding arena first served as an auction ring; the slop-

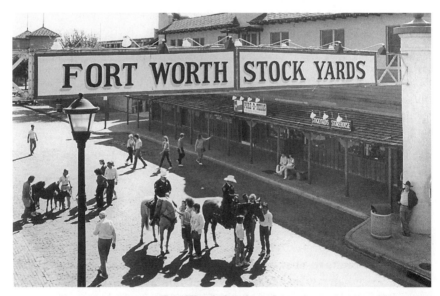

Fort Worth Stockyards.

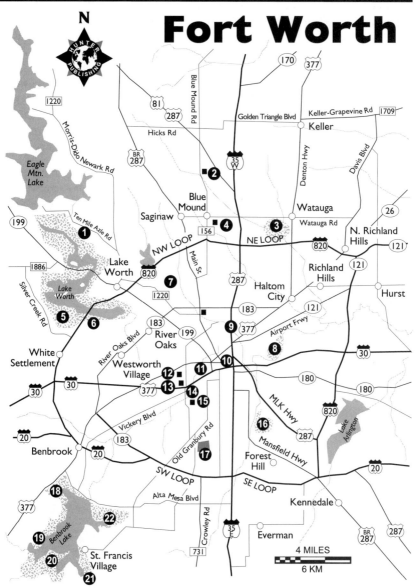

Fort Worth

N

1. Fort Worth Nature Center & Refuge
2. US Bureau of Engraving & Printing
3. Buffalo Ridge Park
4. Stockyards / Visitor Center
5. City Park
6. Marion Sansom Park
7. Buck Sansom Park
8. Gateway Park
9. Sycamore Park
10. Convention & Visitor Bureau
11. Trinity Park
12. Will Rogers Memorial Center
13. Botanic Gardens
14. Forest Park
15. Fort Worth Zoo
16. Cobb Park
17. Rosemont Park
18. Dutch Branch Park
19. Holiday Park
20. Mustang Park
21. Rocky Creek Park
22. Longhorn Park

ing floor, perfect today for concert seating, was originally constructed to allow runoff from the cattle pens.

While Billy Bob's is a bar at heart, boasting some of the finest in country entertainment, you don't have to be country or a drinker to enjoy the monstrous center. There's professional bull-riding every Friday and Saturday night, an arcade, a number of dance floors, a restaurant and an impressive Walk of Fame.

The **Stockyards Museum** (Livestock Exchange Building, ☎ 817-625-5087) does its best to preserve both what the Stockyards meant for its community and what the Wild West meant for the world. Exhibits include everything from household items to staff photographs of Stockyard personnel from the 1930s. A Native American exhibit emphasizes Quanah Parker, a Fort Worth regular.

March through October, the kids (and young-at-heart adults) will get a kick out of the **Stockyard Amusement Park**, the only Western theme amusement park of its kind that includes a 1932 carousel and a champion bronc and bull ride.

The **Cowtown Coliseum** (121 E Exchange Ave, ☎ 817-625-1025), built in 1907, hosted the world's first indoor rodeo in 1918 and has been action-packed ever since. There's a rodeo on Saturday nights from April to September.

If you're interested in wetting a thirsty whistle, the **White Elephant Saloon** (106 E Exchange Ave, ☎ 817-624-1887) can please any palate. It has been around for over 100 years and was once a haven for gamblers and gunfighters. One national magazine (*Esquire*) included it in its list of top 100 US bars.

✳ Did You Know?

According to legend, Bonnie and Clyde once hid out at the **Stockyards Hotel,** which boasts 52 rooms.

There are dozens of other shops and buildings to peruse in the Stockyards; a unique way to capture a bird's-eye view of the area is to take a ride on the **Tarantula** (Depot at Stockyards Station, ☎ 817-625-7245), an 1896 steam train that tours the historic district.

About three miles south of the Stockyards, you'll find some of the best art collections and museums in the state. Amon Carter, oilman and publisher of the *Fort Worth Star-Telegram*, arguably has had the most influence on Fort Worth through the **Amon Carter Museum** (3501 Camp

Bowie Blvd, ☎ 817-738-1933), which was originally endowed to showcase his collection of work by Frederic Remington and Charles Russell. It has since expanded its scope and boasts pieces by Georgia O'Keeffe, Winslow Homer, James McNeill Whistler and Mary Cassatt. There are also over 250,000 photographs, including works by Ansel Adams, Alfred Stieglitz and Richard Avedon.

The **Kimbell Art Museum** (3333 Camp Bowie Blvd, ☎ 817-332-8451) has been deemed "America's best small museum" and features work by world-renowned artists like Rembrandt, Gauguin, Cezanne, Picasso and Matisse. Kimbell was another area patron who made his fortune in oil and grain. The building itself is a work of art, using natural light and aesthetic space to embrace its works of art.

The **Modern Art Museum** (1309 Montgomery St, ☎ 817-738-9215) was actually the first museum around, created by a group of women in 1892 who wanted to bring a little culture to their town. It has moved around (and changed names) a few times, but is currently located in the arts district, with works by Picasso, Andy Warhol, Jackson Pollock and Mark Rothko.

The entire family can appreciate the **Fort Worth Museum of Science and History** (1501 Montgomery St, ☎ 817-732-1631), the Southwest's largest science and history museum. Hands-on exhibits include the popular Dino Dig, where visitors can become paleontologists for the day and take home their fossil finds. An 80-foot Omni Theater and the Noble Planetarium top off the entertainment.

The **Fort Worth Botanic Gardens and Japanese Garden** (3220 Botanic Garden Dr, ☎ 817-871-7689) are the oldest in Texas, thriving with exotic flora and smells of over 2,000 different plants. A fragrance garden was created especially for the blind, but it can be enjoyed by all. Seasonal plants bloom throughout the year, but springtime brings the most color and excitement.

The **Fort Worth Zoo** (1989 Colonial Parkway, ☎ 817-871-7050) provides perpetual excitement, with over 5,000 exotic and native species represented. It has been voted by several sources as one of the best zoos in the nation. If you're trying to pick a zoo in North Texas, pick Fort Worth (San Antonio is the other notable Texas zoo). Designers have gone out of their way to make the grounds lush and enjoyable – more park-like and peaceful than most medium-sized zoos.

The **Log Cabin Village** (2100 Log Cabin Village Lane, ☎ 817-926-5881) is a step back into frontier life. Costumed pioneers tend to their daily chores on the 2½-acre living museum.

Tarrant County Court House, near Sundance Square.

The culture extends even further into the downtown district. The **Sid Richardson Collection of Western Art** (309 Main St, Sundance Square, ☎ 817-332-6554) is little known, but a great collection of works by Frederic Remington and Charles Russell. Most of the pieces were purchased by oilman Sid Richardson, who had a friendly art-collecting rivalry going with Amon Carter. Fort Worth residents culturally prospered when the two wealthy oil barons' healthy art battle turned into philanthropy.

The **Cattleman's Museum** (1301 W Seventh, ☎ 817-332-7064), a cross between highbrow and cowboy, provides the legends and lore surrounding the Texas range. Photographs of legendary cowboys like Charles Goodnight and Richard King are just pieces of the history of ranching and cattle in Texas. A collection of famous cattle brands, including some that belonged to Lyndon Johnson and John Wayne, are on display, along with interactive exhibits and films.

Sitting demurely next to a downtown glass skyscraper (it's a skyscraper by Fort Worth standards) is **Fire Station No. 1** (2nd and Commerce, ☎ 817-732-1631), which offers 150 years of Fort Worth history. Displays in the 1873 fire-station-turned-city-hall, trace the path from frontier outpost to cattle hub to aerospace center.

One of Fort Worth's finest modern accomplishments has been the complete revitalization of its downtown into a cultural hotspot. **Sundance Square** (Between Throckmorton and Calhoun from 2nd to 5th), named for the Sundance Kid who, along with partner Butch Cassidy, used to hide out nearby, is 14 blocks worth of shopping, live theater, museums, dining and nightspots.

One of the most attended theaters is the **Caravan of Dreams** (312 Houston St, ☎ 817-877-3000), a combination theater, nightclub and rooftop grotto bar. Non-traditional plays and performers are the norm, but the Caravan routinely lands internationally-acclaimed acts.

The newest addition to the cultural mix in Fort Worth is the **Nancy Lee & Perry R**. **Bass Performance Hall** (☎ 817-212-4200), considered the "last great performing arts hall built in the 20th century." The $60 million entertainment mecca will anchor Sundance Square, contributing world-caliber performances. Another anchor – but of a slightly different genre – is the **Texas International Speedway** (☎ 888-FW-SPEED). The 150,000-seat sports track is the second largest sports facility in the world and the only one to offer dual-banked turns, which allows both Indy-style racing and NASCAR Winston Cup stock car events.

Until just recently, **Thistle Hill** (1509 Pennsylvania Ave, ☎ 817-336-1212) sat in a sad state of entropy. But Fort Worth preservations have restored this 1903 mansion, built by oil baron W.T. Waggoner for his daughter Electra as a wedding present. Only the finest was allowed (Electra made shopping history by becoming the first customer to spend $20,000 in one day at Nieman Marcus) and the present-day restoration adheres to the house's grand past. With a horseshoe-shaped staircase and opulent Tiffany-style windows, there are 18 rooms to wander through.

Wine devotees will enjoy a trip out to **La Buena Vida Vineyards** (TX 199 northeast, five miles past Lake Worth, ☎ 817-237-9463) for tasty samples of their signature port and red and white wines. You can tour the nearby winery by appointment.

Information Sources

To get more information on Fort Worth call the local **Convention and Visitors Bureau** at ☎ 800-433-5747 (415 Throckmorton St., 76102, www.fortworth.com). You can also try a few Web sites for local flavor and pertinent information, such as www.introfortworth.com and http://cityview.com/fortworth.

■ Adventures on the Water

Lake Worth (TX 199 northwest nine miles and follow signs, ☎ 817-870-7000) is a convenient city-owned park that offers 3,560 acres of water sports and facilities for picnicking, walking and lounging. The ***Queen Maria*** river boat (☎ 817-238-9778) can be chartered by groups.

Just north of Lake Worth lies **Eagle Mountain Lake**, an area marked by solitude and beautiful sloping hills juxtaposed with steep canyon walls. The large basin at its southern end attracts a number of sailors and is home to the Fort Worth Boat Club, a very active private marina that hosts races and pleasure cruises year-round. Fishermen find the narrow fingers that feed the lake and wind north great for catching a variety of fish. There are lots of ways to get to the lake (which also serves as the city's water supply), so call the **Fort Worth Convention and Visitors Bureau** (☎ 800-433-5747) with specific needs.

■ Adventures on Horseback

 Benbrook Lake (US 377 southwest 12 miles), in southwest Fort Worth on the Clear Fork of the Trinity River, offers a wide variety of activities. Chief among them is horseback riding – the west side of the lake is laced with over seven miles of horseback and hiking trails. The trails traverse a variety of terrains, including flat, open prairie, rolling hills, steep inclines and thick woods. While the trail hugs the Benbrook shore, you'll be rewarded with periodic panoramic views of the lake. There are hitching posts along the path, watering stops and stables. Call the reservoir manager (☎ 817-292-2400) for more information.

Six parks dot the lake's shores, offering swimming, fishing, boating, water-skiing, hiking, picnicking and camping. The **Pecan Valley Golf Course** meets the northern edge of the lake.

■ Adventures on Wheels

 The Trinity River is edged with a paved biking trail that runs for miles. You can rent bikes, rollerblades and paddleboats at **Heritage Park** (☎ 817-293-4355), which serves as a kind of focal point for the riverfront trail.

Kids can enjoy what is billed as the longest miniature train ride in the world in Forest Park. The **Forest Park Train Ride** (University Drive at Fort Worth Zoo, ☎ 817-336-3328) carries its occupants five miles along the Trinity River. The $1 admission fee is more than worth it.

Visitors come to the **Lyndon B. Johnson National Grasslands** for various reasons. The 20,000-acre park northwest of Fort Worth near Decatur (140 US 287, PO Box 507, Decatur, 76234, ☎ 940-627-5475) attracts hikers, birders, horseback riders, mountain bikers, road bikers, campers and fishermen.

Birders come to observe the fall and spring migrations of waterfowl, including geese, ducks, cranes, egrets and herons. The broad prairies are tailor-made for horseback riders. During portions of the year, cattle grazing is allowed, so watch out for roaming herds.

Mountain bikers have been the most recent group to fall in love with the grasslands' grandeur. The trails, which are also used for an equestrian endurance course, consist of two loops, one 15 miles long and the other 30 miles long. The trails are single and double track, with a few sandy sections. There are other trails created by area cattle. Bring your map (and your compass) – this is considered a real adventure by area bikers.

■ Where to Stay

 Azalea Plantation Bed & Breakfast, 1400 Robinwood Dr, 76111, ☎ 817-838-5882. $$-$$$. The large plantation-style home is only 10 minutes from downtown Fort Worth. Springtime is lovely, with a huge crop of colorful azaleas filling out the grounds.

Green Oaks Park Hotel, 6901 West Freeway, 76116, ☎ 800-772-2341, 817-738-7311. $$-$$$. All the amenities you could ask for, including a pool and large restaurant. You can either play on two lighted tennis courses or go to the golf course adjacent to the hotel.

Miss Molly's Hotel/Bed & Breakfast, 109½ W Exchange Ave, 76106, ☎ 800-99-MOLLY, 817-626-1522. $$-$$$. Located in the Stockyard District, they have opened up eight historic rooms to visitors, complete with iron beds, antique quilts and claw-foot tubs.

Radisson Plaza Fort Worth, 815 Main St, 76102, ☎ 800-333-3333, 817-870-2100. $$$-$$$$. With over 500 rooms, two restaurants and seating for 14,000 attending meetings, the Radisson is a business hub.

Stockyards Hotel, 109 E Exchange Ave, 76106, ☎ 800-423-8471, 817-625-6427. $$-$$$. For pleasure and business travelers. The 1906 hotel has been restored to its original splendor, with custom oak furnishings.

Texas White House B&B, 1417 Eighth Ave, 76104, ☎ 800-279-6491, 817-923-3597. $$-$$$. Three quaint bedrooms in the heart of downtown. They provide fresh flowers and bubble bath. Breakfast is whenever and wherever you would like it.

Worthington, 200 Main St, 76102, ☎ 800-433-5677, 817-870-1000. $$$$. Another mega-hotel with all the trimmings. Its top floors offer an incredible view of the city.

■ Where to Eat

 8.O. (Eight-O), 111 E Third St, ☎ 817-336-0880. You might not expect something this trendy (and health-conscious) in downtown Fort Worth. Massive murals cover the walls. Happy hour drinks are ornate and the yuppies come here after work.

Angeluna Restaurant, 215 E Fourth St, ☎ 817-334-0080. "Contemporary global" cuisine brought to visitors by Joe Cosniac, owner of the famed Mezzaluna restaurant in Aspen, CO. It derived its name from the majestic 50-foot trumpeting angel that adorns the Bass Performance Hall, overlooking the restaurant.

The Balcony of Ridglea, 6100 Camp Bowie Blvd, ☎ 817-731-3719. Jacket and tie are suggested for dinner, which should tell you something about the continental cuisine's elegance. Piano music makes Friday and Saturday nights romantic interludes.

Booger Red's Saloon & Restaurant, 109 E Exchange Ave, Stockyards Hotel, ☎ 817-625-6427. Don't let the name fool you; there are other things on the menu. Groups of up to 65 can pull up a saddle (they double as bar stools) and enjoy standard Southern fare that includes burgers, steaks and several chicken-fried options.

Café Aspen, 6103 Camp Bowie Blvd, ☎ 817-738-0838. Pasta, chicken and fish served up "contemporary American-style."

Campo Verde, 7108 Hwy 80 W, ☎ 817-731-1052. Primarily Tex-Mex, but you have to try the fajitas. They're made out of rattlesnake, ostrich, elk, buffalo or alligator, depending on your taste (they also have the traditional beef and chicken fajitas).

Cattlemen's Steak House, 2458 North Main St, ☎ 817-624-3945, www.cattlemenssteakhouse.com. If you like their juicy steaks, you can have them air-mailed home through their mail order business. This Stockyard icon has been around almost half a century.

Edelweiss German Restaurant, 3801A Southwest Blvd, ☎ 817-738-5934. Singing along with the oompah bands is contagious. You'll love all the traditional German dishes, from sauerbraten to schnitzel.

J&J Oyster Bar, 612 University Dr, ☎ 817-335-2756. Oysters are their specialty, but all types of seafood are offered.

Joe T. Garcia's Mexican Dishes, 2201 N Commerce St, ☎ 817-626-4356. A hoppin' Mexican restaurant; reservations are recommended for large groups. There are no menus, but the regular dinner (two enchiladas, two tacos, two nachos, and all the fixings) should satisfy anyone.

Macaroni Grill, 1501 S University Dr, ☎ 817-336-6676. Northern Italian – even though it's a chain, it's still great.

Mi Cocina, 509 Main St, Sundance Square, ☎ 817-877-3600. Neighborhood Tex-Mex known for their mambo-taxi margaritas.

Picchi-Pacchi Italian Restaurant, 512 Main St, Suite 106, ☎ 817-870-2222. Pasta and New York-style pizza.

Razzoo's Cajun Café, 4700 Bryant Irvin Rd, ☎ 817-292-8584. For the Cajun palate, this is a local favorite.

Rodeo Steakhouse, 1309 Calhoun St, ☎ 817-332-1288. Steaks, burgers and seafood.

Water Street Seafood Co., 1540 S University Dr, ☎ 817-877-3474. Casual setting serving up sumptuous seafood.

Williams Ranch House, 5532 Jacksboro Hwy, Sansom Park, ☎ 817-624-1272. Tender steaks and tasty barbecue are their specialties.

Arlington

■ Touring

Not only is Arlington the "Midway of the Metroplex," many children consider it the fun center of the universe. Amusement parks dot the landscape. The short list of theme parks includes Air Combat, Six Flags Over Texas, Hurricane Harbor and Mountasia Fantasy Golf. Baseball-lovers consider it a center of the universe as well, with the Texas Rangers playing all of their home games at the Ballpark in Arlington.

It is treated as a suburb of Dallas – the boundaries that separate the Metroplex are vague at best – but with 270,000 residents it is a large city on its own.

The **Arlington Historical Park** (621 W Arkansas, ☎ 817-460-4001) provides some historical context to the area. What began as a plantation now includes two log cabins, a one-room schoolhouse and a rustic barn, thanks in large part to the Fielder Foundation, which has moved several historic buildings to the site.

The **Fielder Museum** (1616 W Abram, ☎ 817-460-4001), housed in James Park Fielder's 1914 two-story farmhouse, was one of the first buildings in the area to enjoy indoor plumbing. Today the house plays host to both traveling exhibits and a permanent collection of period pieces, early photographs of Arlington and a century-old barbershop.

While the art of sewing has become more and more obsolete among the urban sprawl of the US, it hasn't been forgotten at the **Antique Sewing Machine Museum** (804 W Abram, ☎ 817-275-0971). An 1858 Wheeler-Wilson is the oldest piece on display, for those who are in the know about the sewing revolution. For those that don't know, there are over 100 other pieces to check out.

For a thick slice of American pie, catch a **Texas Rangers** game at Arlington Stadium (Exit FM 157 from I-30, ☎ 817-273-5100, www.texasrangers.com and www.ballparks.com/baseball/american/bpkarl.htm). With about 80 home games a year, you have a 50/50 chance of catching a game during the season.

Baseball fans will also enjoy the **Legends of the Game Baseball Museum** (1000 Ballpark Way), which features baseball uniforms, balls, equipment, baseball cards and photographs depicting the history of the sport.

Exhibits include items from the Texas League and the Negro League. The Learning Center features interactive exhibits on baseball and explains how the sport is related to fields such as science, math, history, geography and literature. A 225-seat auditorium features films and videos.

Six Flags Over Texas (2201 Rd to Six Flags, ☎ 817-640-8900, www.sixflags.com/dallas/index.htm), named for the six different political entities that governed Texas, is 205 acres of breath-taking rides, souvenirs, tasty carnival food and fun. The Texas Giant, a 143-foot wooden roller coaster, may be the star, but revelers enjoy more than 100 rides.

✴ Author's Tip

Over 2½ million visitors pass through Six Flags' gates each year – a good indication of how busy things can get. Your best bet is to go during the week to beat the weekend crowds.

Six Flag's seasonal sister, **Hurricane Harbor** (1800 E Lamar, across I-30 from Six Flags, ☎ 817-265-3356), is open daily between May and Labor Day and weekends only before and after the season (mid-April through September). You can play hard on 23 different slides or just laze in its three pools and around Lazy River. Family picnics are welcome, but no glass or alcohol are allowed.

Air Combat (921 Six Flags Drive, ☎ 817-640-1886, www.themetro.com/aircombat) allows thrill-seekers the feel of flying military aircraft in hydraulic-motion flight simulators. Pilots must go through ground school and suit up in full gear. Reservations are required and the simulation takes around 1½ hours.

Information Sources

Call the **Arlington Convention and Visitors Bureau**
(☎ 800-772-5371, 1250 E Copeland, Suite 650, 76011,
www.arlington.org) for information.

■ Adventures on the Water

City-owned and -run **Lake Arlington** is relatively small at
2,275 acres, but has plenty of room for boating, sailing and fishing. You can access the lake through two parks: Arkansas Lane
Park (6300 W Arkansas) and Bowman Springs Park (7001 Poly Webb
Rd).

■ Where to Stay

Ball Park Inn, 903 North Collins, 76011, ☎ 817-261-3621. $-
$$. Restaurant, cocktail lounge, outdoor swimming pool and ex-
ercise facilities. Within two miles of Six Flags Over Texas, Hur-
ricane Harbor and The Ballpark in Arlington.

Country Suites by Carlson, 1075 Wet 'n Wild Way, ☎ 800-456-4000,
817-261-8900. $$-$$$. Right in the middle of fun-ville, they've got all the
basic amenities.

Holiday Inn Arlington, 1507 North Watson Rd, 76006, ☎ 800-465-
4329, 817-640-7712. $$-$$$. Everything you might need, along with live
entertainment and both indoor and outdoor pools.

Sanford House, 506 North Center St, 76011, ☎ 817-861-2129.
www.thesanfordhouse.com. $$$-$$$$. French country-style frame
house with seven rooms for rent. There's a library up the spiral stair-
case, a cozy parlor complete with fireplace, an outdoor pool and gardens
that include gazebos and a fountain.

■ Where to Eat

Humperdinks Bar & Grill, 700 Six Flags Drive, ☎ 817-640-
8553. Also featuring Big Horn Brewery. You're surrounded by
TVs.

J. Gilligan's Bar & Grill, 400 East Abram, ☎ 817-274-8561. It's an old-
timer, having served up dinner and lunch since 1979. Live entertain-
ment each night.

Trail Dust Steak House, 2300 E Lamar Blvd, ☎ 817-640-6411. Juicy steaks and other delectables are the norm. You can work it off afterwards with live country music – there's lots of room for dancing.

Irving

■ History

The two men that settled Irving, J.O. Shulze and Otis Brown, were big fans of author Washington Irving. So it made sense that they named their brainchild for him. After buying up a large chunk of land that included a watermelon farm in the early 1900s and donating a portion of it to the railroads, Shulze and Brown sold town lots for $50 each.

Their town grew slowly but steadily, always in the shadow of Dallas, just to the southeast. In 1950 there were still just over 2,500 residents. But by the 1970s Irving hit its stride and burgeoned – 1971 marked the opening of Texas Stadium (home of the Dallas Cowboys) and 1973 saw the Dallas/Fort Worth International Airport land on the city's western door. Now Irving boasts more than 150,000 residents.

The big news, of course, is the Dallas Cowboys, the nation's most loved and hated professional sports team. The image of Tom Landry beneath his stoic hat and demeanor is indelibly etched into every fan's mind.

■ Touring

 Even if you don't follow football, it's hard not to follow the rises and falls of a team that is somehow perpetually makes news. Some of the greatest football moments have occurred in **Texas Stadium** (2401 E Airport Freeway off TX 183), the 64,000 seat home of the Cowboys. Tours of the stadium are given each day, depending on planned events. In one hour you'll go through their locker rooms, the players' tunnel, the press box and several private suites. Reservations are required. For ticket and schedule information, ☎ 972-579-5000.

The **Byron Nelson Golf Classic**, a popular PGA stop, is played annually in Irving at the Four Seasons Resort and Club (4150 N MacArthur Blvd, Las Colinas, ☎ 972-717-0700 for ticket information).

Las Colinas is considered one of the premiere planned communities in the nation. Designers filled the 12,000-acre site with parks, green belts, luxury housing, retail shops and everything else to make this city-within-a-city self-sufficient.

There are several ways to see the Urban Center, located in the southeast portion of the Las Colinas. The **Mandalay Canal** (Las Colinas Blvd and Mandalay Dr, ☎ 972-556-0625) is lined with trees, cobbled walkways, restaurants and shops. **Venetian water taxis** can ferry you among the points that interest you. You can also pilot your own boat for an hourly fee. Las Colinas also relies on a **monorail** system to whisk residents around a 5½-mile track.

Texas' own slice of Hollywood is encased at the **Movie Studios at Las Colinas** (☎ 972-869-FILM, www.studiosatlascolinas.com), a motion picture and television production center. It has hosted movies such as *Robocop, Problem Child, JFK* and *Leap of Faith*. A tour of the facilities showcases sets, props and other movie memorabilia and includes a ticket to the National Museum of Communications.

Information Sources

You can reach the **Irving Chamber of Commerce/ Convention and Visitors Bureau** at ☎ 800-247-8464 (3333 N MacArthur Blvd., Suite 200, 75062, www.irvingtexas.com).

■ Where to Stay

Four Seasons Resort and Club, 4150 N MacArthur Blvd, 75038, ☎ 800-332-3442 or 972-717-0700. $$$$. Two full golf courses spread out along its 400 acres, including the Tournament Players Course that hosts the Byron Nelson Classic PGA tour event.

Harvey Hotel DFW Airport, 4545 W Carpenter Freeway, 75063, ☎ 800-922-9222, 972-929-4500. $$$$. The rooftop indoor/outdoor pool tops off this luxury stop.

Omni Mandalay at Las Colinas, 221 E Las Colinas Blvd, 75039, ☎ 800-843-6664 or 972-556-0800. $$$-$$$$. Set in the heart of the Las Colinas Complex, adjacent to Lake Carolyn and the Mandalay Canal, it is pure luxury.

■ Where to Eat

Café Cipriani, 220 E Las Colinas Blvd, ☎ 972-869-0713. Celebrities are often spotted at this bastion of fine Italian dining. It's expensive, but that's the price you pay for exquisite food.

Pappadeaux Seafood, 10428 Lombardy Lane, Dallas, ☎ 214-358-1912. That it's a chain should not deter you. Some of the finest seafood you'll find in Texas.

Via Real Gourmet Mexican Restaurant, 3591 N Belt Line, ☎ 972-255-0064. Standard Mexican fare, along with some inventive and delicious concoctions.

Grapevine

■ History

Grapevine finds itself in a strange, enviable situation. It's truly a small town (30,000 residents) with big amenities literally at its doorstep. It sits right in between Dallas and Fort Worth on the northern edge, with DFW Airport falling within its city limits.

Established in 1844, a year before Texas attained statehood, Grapevine took its name from the naturally abundant tart, mustang grape that flourished in the area.

Over 75 historic structures have been preserved here. A walking tour downtown – with its town square, white-washed gazebo and green sloping lawns – will take you back a few decades when things moved at a different pace.

■ Touring

Stop by the **Grapevine Convention and Visitors Bureau** (One Liberty Park Plaza, 76051, ☎ 800-457-6338, or 817-481-0454, www.ci.grapevine.tx.us) for a map of all the downtown historical sites, including the **Torian Log Cabin** in Liberty Park, one of the oldest buildings in the county.

The **Grapevine Opry** (308 S Main, ☎ 817-481-8733) has long been an anomaly, featuring talents like Willie Nelson and the Judds when they were still unknown. The famous still revisit their old stomping ground on occasion and shows are performed every Friday and Saturday night.

Wineries have cultivated the area's natural flora. You can start your tour of Grapevine's splendid grapes right after landing at the DFW Airport. **La Bodega Winery & Tasting Room** (Terminal 2E, Gate 6, DFW, ☎ 972-574-1440), the first-ever winery and tasting room in a major airport, shows true Texas hospitality by offering wines from select Texas vineyards in addition to their own label.

La Buena Vida Vineyards (416 East College St, ☎ 817-481-9463) prides itself on being Grapevine's first winery and tasting room and Texas' oldest continuous producer of champagne. Their vineyard produces a Cabernet Sauvignon, Chenin Blanc, Johannisberg Riesling, Sauvignon Blanc, Texas Blush, Mead and Texas Vintage Port. Their downtown location includes a winery museum, fountains, an herb garden, and native Texas gardens. Call to make appointments to tour the actual vineyards in Springtown.

You can stroll the grounds at **Delaney Vineyards** (2000 Champagne Blvd, Hwy 121 at Glade Rd, ☎ 817-481-5668), which just planted its roots in 1992. Among their offerings are a Pinot Noir, a Chardonnay and a Cabernet Franc. Delaney even offers up its barrel room for special events.

Grapevine celebrates its grape-laden background twice annually: at the **New Vintage Festival** during the third weekend in April, and at **Grapefest**, the second weekend in September. Grapefest is the state's oldest and largest wine festival and annually attracts upwards of 80,000.

If you're a golfer, you might want to consider an extended stay in this small enclave. Three championship public golf courses – one designed by legendary Byron Nelson – call Grapevine home. The **Grapevine Municipal Golf Course** (3800 Fairway Dr, ☎ 817-481-0421) is the Nelson creation, and the **Hyatt Bear Creek Golf and Racquet Club** (W Airfield Dr, ☎ 972-615-6800) offers two 18-hole courses over 335 acres of rolling hills.

Information Sources

Both the **Grapevine Convention and Visitors Bureau** (☎ 800-457-6338, One Liberty Park Plaza, 76051) and the **Chamber of Commerce** (☎ 817-481-1522, PO Box 368, 76099) can provide visitors with more information. The town also maintains a Web site at www.ci.grapevine.tx.us.

■ Adventures on the Water

 One mile north of downtown is **Lake Grapevine** (northeast on TX 26, ☎ 817-481-4541, http://155.84.88.67/grapevine) considered the fourth busiest lake in Texas, with more than four million visitors a year. The lake has 146 miles of shoreline and offers a prime windsurfing, sailing and fishing area for North Texans. Included in the extensive park system are public tennis courts, baseball and softball diamonds, football and soccer fields, jogging and biking trails, a swimming pool, playgrounds and picnic facilities.

Fishermen are rewarded with black bass, catfish, crappie or white bass. Some of the best areas to fish are near the dam (where it is aerated), at Twin Coves and near the stumps in Marshall Creek. Every so often, dead Christmas trees are put in the water to provide fish shelters – the office can give you a map detailing the most current conditions.

The lake also offers public hunting and overnight camping facilities.

■ Adventures on Wheels

 By several accounts, the **Northshore Trail** (for directions call ☎ 817-481-4541; trail conditions, 817-481-3576), which runs along the northern shore of Lake Grapevine, is one of the most used trails in the entire Dallas/Ft. Worth Metroplex. Stretching west from Rock Ledge Park through Twin Coves Park, it's almost a 20-mile round-trip, just over nine miles each way. The eastern portion is less technical and good for intermediate and novice mountain bikers. The western edge is more of a challenge with several "rock gardens" that add spice.

There are trailheads in Rock Legde, Murrell and Twin Coves parks.

Knob Hills Trail, on the west end of the lake, traverses prairie and bottomland of Denton Creek. Though it's less rocky than the Northshore, it's still a challenge. Spring's wildflower display along the trail is memorable.

> ### ☀ *Take Care!*
>
> Make sure to dodge the cacti and the occasional lost steer.

Off-road vehicles are welcome on **Marshall Creek Park's** 250 acres of challenging terrain. Park engineers have gone out of their way to provide a variety of trail conditions, including some extremely steep hills. They recommend extreme caution.

■ Adventures on Horseback

Lake Grapevine has gone through great pains to offer a variety of options to equestrians who bring their own horse. They have also instituted a strict park rule: No horses on bike trails, no bikes on horse trails. The **Walnut Grove Horse Trail**, which follows the southwestern edge of the lake, is divided into an upper woodland trail and a lower shoreline trail. There are no facilities on the 10-mile trail, but you can water your horse in Lake Grapevine.

Cross Timbers and **Rocky Point** are the other two horse options. (All of these trails are also open to pedestrian traffic.) Cross Timbers winds five miles along the lake's northwestern edge through a brilliant array of wildflowers (in the spring and summer) and birds. Rocky Point is shorter (three miles). It takes riders along the bluffs overlooking the lake.

■ Where to Stay

Hyatt Regency DFW, International Parkway inside DFW Airport, ☎ 800-233-1234 or 972-453-1234. $$$. Everything you could ask for plus a complimentary health spa, racquetball courts, indoor and outdoor tennis, four restaurants and 24-hour airport transportation. Two 18-hole golf courses are just five minutes away.

DFW Lakes Hilton, 1800 Hwy 26E, 76051, ☎ 800-645-1019, 800-445-8667. $$$. Decked out with all amenities on 40 wooded acres and includes add-ons like fishing in a private lake and a jogging trail.

The Terraces, 2200 W. Airfield, DFW Airport, 75261, ☎ 972-453-0600. $$$-$$$$. Facilities include fitness equipment, workout area, jogging trail, basketball, racquetball courts, softball field and outdoor tennis courts.

1934 Bed & Breakfast, 322 E. College St, 76051, ☎ 817-251-1934. $$. Completely restored and located in Grapevine's historic College Heights district. Breakfast included.

■ Where to Eat

Joe's Crab Shack, 201 Hwy 114 West, ☎ 817-251-1515. It's a chain, but it's also festive and fun, with great seafood choices.

Julia's Antiques and Tea Room, 210 N Main St, ☎ 817-329-0622. A lovely lunch spot while you're enjoying downtown Grapevine.

Little Pete's, Twin Coves Marina, Grapevine Lake, ☎ 972-724-1032. If you're at the lake, it's your best bet. They serve breakfast, lunch and dinner.

Willhoite's, 432 S Main St, ☎ 817-481-7511. They're big on buffets. Try the Sunday buffet; there's more than enough to choose from.

Other Dallas Communities

The Dallas/Fort Worth Metroplex is much more than just Dallas and Fort Worth. The small towns that once sat on their own and have been engulfed by a thriving economy and spreading populace still retain their individual local flavors. Arlington, Irving and Grapevine were among the larger ones, but other smaller communities should not be forgotten.

Among them are Addison, Carrollton, Denton, DeSoto, Duncanville, Farmers Branch, Garland, Grand Prairie, Lewisville, Mesquite, North Richland Hills, Plano and Richardson.

■ Addison

Addison (☎ 800-ADDISON), directly north of Dallas, is a gentle mixture of shopping, dining and hotel accommodations, all within a five-mile radius. Three malls – the Galleria, Prestonwood and Valley View – make shopping an easy task. The **Cavanaugh Flight Museum** (4572 Claire Chennault, ☎ 972-380-8800) displays aircraft from World Wars I and II and the Korean War, including a Spitfire, a MIG 15 and a P-51 Mustang. They also boast one of the largest signed print art collections in the South.

■ Carrollton

The town square of Carrollton, also north of Dallas, is still adorned with a traditional gazebo, an indication of the small town that is now a community of more than 84,000. Antique shops and other eclectic boutiques surround the square in Old Downtown, making for a pleasant afternoon stroll. The **A.W. Perry Homestead Museum** (1509 Perry Rd) was restored as a part of a bicentennial project. Turn-of-the-century furnishings and tools give visitors a great look back in time.

■ Denton

Denton (☎ 940-382-7895) has somehow retained a sense of boundary, even though the Metroplex is encroaching at a rapid pace. You actually feel you're in a different town. Denton, home of the University of North Texas (UNT) and Texas Woman's University (TWU), retains a very cultured atmosphere. UNT is famous for its musical students and the nightlife in town reflects their influence.

The **Denton County Courthouse** (110 W Hickory, ☎ 940-383-8073), built in 1895 and considered one of the most picturesque buildings in the area, also houses a historical museum that depicts city and country life. Across the street is **Evers Hardware** (109 W Hickory), complete with displays that were constructed when the store was opened more than a century ago. **Silk Stocking Row** (W Oak St) is brimming with refurbished Victorian cottages that were built before the turn of the century.

Denton is close to several lakes, including **Ray Roberts Lake** (I-35 north to Sanger, FM 455 east), with **Isle du Bois State Park** on the wooded south edge of the lake. A 12-mile trail in the park can be used for hiking, biking and horseback riding. There are also facilities for overnight camping, in addition to boating, swimming and fishing.

■ DeSoto

The frantic pace of the big city is something DeSoto (☎ 972-224-3565) residents say they don't have to worry about. They boast clean living with family celebrations and traditional entertainment – parks, pools and water recreation.

■ Duncanville

Duncanville (☎ 972-780-5099) has attained a type of yuppie status. Family-oriented and enjoying a pleasant amount of wealth, Duncanville children can be seen doing every type of organized sport on a Saturday or Sunday afternoon, from soccer to baseball to softball to tennis. The community also is just minutes from **Joe Pool Lake**, a recreational mecca.

■ Garland

Garland, which began as a farming community, sits on the western edge of **Lake Ray Hubbard**, a big draw for boating, sailing and fishing. The *Texas Queen* (☎ 972-771-0039), a 105-foot paddle wheeler, offers dinner cruises along the lake, taking off from Elgin Robertson Park.

■ Grand Prairie

One of the biggest attractions in Grand Prairie (☎ 972-263-9588) is the **Palace of Wax & Ripley's Believe It or Not** (601 E Safari Parkway, ☎ 972-263-2391). Galleries of life-like wax figures can make even the most cynical of visitors take a second glance. The Ripley's exhibits include a piece of straw blown through a telephone pole during a Texas tornado and a series of shrunken heads.

Another popular stop is **Traders Village** (2602 Mayfield, one mile north of I-20), a weekend flea market that attracts upwards of 1,500 vendors and stretches across 106 acres. Thirty-two restaurants round out the activities that include more than just bargain hunting.

■ Lewisville

Lewisville (☎ 800-657-9571) finds itself in an enviable spot, nestled along the southern shore of gigantic **Lake Lewisville** and the northern shore of **Lake Grapevine**. It is a water paradise. Lake Lewisville seems to be one of the most used lakes in America. A summer holiday will attract literally thousands of boaters.

✳ Take Care!

Use caution during busy seasons; it is also known as a party lake, which is usually fine but can prove hazardous when speeding boats are involved.

■ Mesquite

The name Mesquite fits well with some of the old-fashion, rustic events that take place here. Among them are the **Mesquite Championship Rodeo** (118 Rodeo Dr, Mesquite Arena, ☎ 972-285-8777) every weekend, April through September. There's bull-riding, calf roping, steer wrestling and all types of entertainment, plus a barbecue pavilion for the hungry. It's been operating since 1958 and enjoys a steady stream of visitors.

■ Plano

Plano is another of the yuppie enclaves. It is dotted with good restaurants and luxury accommodations. The historic downtown district boasts more than 40 unique shops that attract treasure hunters from around the state. It is also home to the infamous **Southfork Ranch** (3700 Hogge Road, Parker – just outside of Plano, ☎ 972-442-7800), the Ewing family's estate in the *Dallas* serial TV show.

■ Richardson

Owens Country Sausage, one of the most visible family brands of sausage around, made their start in Richardson (☎ 972-234-4141). The **Owens Spring Creek Farm** (1401 E Lookout Dr, ☎ 972-235-0192) includes some of the tools used by the Owens family back when they began their business in 1928. The farm-turned-museum also boasts a true country kitchen, the original butcher shop and a country store.

Granbury

■ History

The theory that great things come in small packages holds true in Granbury, 35 miles southwest of Fort Worth. They've been able to preserve their small town with the convenience of big town amenities just up the road and without a large-scale threat of encroachment. It's about good small-town hokey fun – fishing all day and rocking on the porch swing at night while chatting with neighbors.

The town began in 1854 and became prosperous when the railroad ran through in the late 1880s. The buildings from this heyday still stand. After decades of deep decline, the 1970s brought rejuvenation and interest in preserving the town's natural wonders and spirit. Today it is a recreational safety valve for Metroplex residents who need an escape from the city and it has become a tourist attraction.

■ Touring

As in most small towns, activity begins around the town square. The Granbury courthouse town square was the first place in Texas to be listed on the National Register of Historic Places. More than 50 specialty shops, boutiques and restaurants – many housed in 1880s historic buildings – are now clustered in the lively area.

The **Granbury Historic Railroad Depot** (109 E Ewell, ☎ 817-573-5548) hasn't changed much since it was built in 1914 – a true representation of early rural Texas. Group tours are available. The **Jail and**

Granbury.

Hood County Historical Museum (208 N Crockett, ☎ 817-573-5135), a jailhouse-turned-museum since 1978, still has an original cell block and hanging tower. There's also a collection of artifacts tracing both the city's and the county's history.

A trip to the **Granbury Cemetery** (N Crockett and Moore) might seem on the wrong side of morbid, but it is also an education. Jesse James was laid to rest here, as was General Hiram Granbury (Granberry), a commander of the Civil War Texas Brigade who lent his name to the community.

The **Granbury Opera House** (116 E Pearl, ☎ 817-573-9191), originally built in 1886, then restored and re-opened in 1975, sat empty for over six decades before its rebirth. It's now a cultural and social center, boasting musicals, plays and dramas almost year-round. It draws visitors from around the region and plays to capacity crowds.

For just as much entertainment and a touch of fresh air, take your lawn chair to the **Brazos Old-Fashioned Drive In & Cinema** (1800 W Pearl, ☎ 817-573-1311), where you can sit beneath the stars and soak in some family entertainment in an authentic '50s drive-in.

The area surrounding Granbury is famous in dinosaur circles for its abundant and well-preserved traces of the earth's earlier tenants. The **Creation Museum** (FM 205 west of Glen Rose, ☎ 254-897-3200) was founded in 1982 by archeologist Carl Baugh to examine both scientific and religious evidence of man's and dinosaur's early presence. **Dinosaur Valley State Park** (FM 205 west of Glen Rose, ☎ 254-897-4588) is touted as having some of the best preserved dinosaur tracks in Texas. In addition, there are facilities for camping, hiking and picnicking.

Most everything is within walking distance or a short drive from town, but the **Tarantula Train** (☎ 800-952-5717, 817-625-RAIL) will ferry you between Fort Worth and Granbury across the Texas prairies. For a local tour, try the **Yellowstone Kelly Tours** (6321 Carter Rd, ☎ 817-573-2198), which depart from the courthouse on Friday, Saturday and Sunday in a 1925 Yellowstone Park tour bus.

✷ Did You Know?

Elizabeth P. Crockett, the second wife of Davy Crockett, moved to Acton after her husband's death at the Alamo. Her gravesite is memorialized at the Acton Cemetery.

Just up the road, you'll find the **Acton State Park** (two miles north on Farm Rd 4), the smallest state park in Texas. Bluebonnets flourish here in the springtime.

Information Sources

Call the **Convention & Visitors Bureau** (☎ 800-950-2212, 817-573-5548) for the most current information.

■ Adventures on the Water

 Much of Granbury's attraction is in its close relationship with the verdant river valleys that flow through the area. A crook in Lake Granbury wraps itself around downtown, giving almost every store, restaurant and hotel a lake view.

Lake Granbury (☎ 817-573-3212/1407), all 33½ miles of it, is a favorite with water lovers of all kinds. Water-skiers wake at dawn to play on its calm long stretches. Fishermen hunt down black bass, catfish and stripers in all the lake's crannies. There's also canoeing and swimming in the four parks operated by the Brazos River Authority.

Fishing Guides

Dale's Fishing Guide Service . . . . ☎ 817-279-8747

Granbury Fishing Guide Service . . . . . ☎ 817-326-5900

McKelvey's Marina Boat Rentals & Public Fishing
. . . . ☎ 817-573-3698

Mr. Whisker's Fishing Guide . . . . ☎ 817-326-5719

Jim Wann Fishing Guide . . . . ☎ 817-573-4854

Davis Catfish Ponds (4210 Waples West Ct, ☎ 817-279-0765) provides both a stocked tank (Arkansas catfish) and a fishing pole.

Just south of town, you'll find another watering hole of note. **Squaw Creek Reservoir** (2300 Coates Rd off Hwy 144 south, ☎ 817-573-7053, 279-1657) comes complete with scuba diving, fishing, boating and camping. There's even an imported sandy beach.

A navigable and popular portion of the **Paluxy River** borders the southern edge of Granbury. There are a variety of rock shelves, chutes and falls for tubing adventurists. Because much of the land surrounding this portion of river is privately owned and subject to change (they could put up fences, etc.), talk to a local outfitter before you plan anything.

The first put-in is at Highway 67. The last place to get out (4.8 miles later) before the Paluxy joins the Brazos River is the Tres Rios campground (☎ 254-897-4253). Tres Rios also offers rentals and shuttles and can probably answer your questions about current river conditions. They also outfit Squaw Creek and the Brazos River.

■ Where to Stay

The Lodge of Granbury, Lake Granbury, 400 E Pearl, 76048, ☎ 817-573-2606. $$-$$$. Fully equipped condominium units with kitchens. There's room for meetings, a pool, hot tub, tennis courts and a restaurant. There's also a dock out back and facilities to launch your boat.

The Nutt House Hotel & Dining Room, 121 E Bridge, 76048, ☎ 817-279-9457. $-$$$. A gentle mix of quaint historical (and affordable) rooms complete with homemade quilts, and four-star food from Hennington's Café. The chef's table (five stars) will prepare a special menu just for you. On the square and a block from the lake, you don't need anything but your two feet.

Plantation Inn On Lake Granbury, 1451 E Pearl, 76048, ☎ 800-422-2402, 817-573-8846. $$. Each room comes equipped with a refrigerator and coffee server. Free continental breakfast each morning. Overlooks the lake (but no access), with some rooms offering panoramic views.

Anna Bell's Victorian Rose B&B, 404 W Bridge, 76048, ☎ 800-430-ROSE, 817-579-7673. $$. With three rooms, they offer a full breakfast and are just a few blocks from the town square.

Arbor House Bed & Breakfast, 530 E Pearl, 76048, ☎ 800-641-0073, 817-573-0073, http://207.22.198.29/~arbor/. $$-$$$. Some of the seven rooms are equipped with marble jacuzzis. Many of the windows look out over Lake Granbury.

The Captain's House B&B, Lake Granbury, 123 W Doyle, 76048, ☎ 817-579-6664. $$$. An 1874 Queen Anne Victorian house with lake access and a large balcony overlooking the lake. They serve both breakfast and lunch.

The Cottage, 204 S Travis, 76048, ☎ 817-579-6664. $$$. An unhosted B&B in a 1920s bungalow – it's three blocks from the square and children are welcome.

The Dabney House B&B, 106 S Jones, 76048, ☎ 817-579-1260. $$. A country manor within walking distance from the town square. They stock the parlor with movies and the comfortable porch is a relaxing retreat.

The Doyle House B&B, Lake Granbury, 205 W Doyle, 76048, ☎ 817-573-6492. $$$. They've got the best view of the lake, but you have to reserve early for one of only three rooms. The house backs up to the lake and has a fishing pier for their guests. Children are welcome.

Elizabeth Crockett B&B, 201 W Pearl, 76048, ☎ 817-573-7208. $$-$$$. "Very cozy" is the way many guests describe this place. The 1880 Queen Anne home offers four rooms.

The Iron Horse Inn B&B, 616 Thorp Springs Rd, 76048, ☎ 817-579-5535, www.ironhorseinn.com. $$-$$$$. With 7,000 square feet, it still feels like a cattle baron's mansion. It's the largest historic home in town and boasts a shady porch with century-old live oaks and pecan trees.

Lambert Street Guest House, 215 S Lambert St, 76049, ☎ 817-326-2611. $$$-$$$$. Unhosted, there are two units in this 1930s-style B&B. Its two units are very private and perfect for honeymooners. Each unit is a house in itself and sleeps four people. Two blocks from downtown.

Oak Tree Farm B&B, 6415 Carmichael Ct, 76049, ☎ 800-326-5595, 817-326-5595. $$-$$$. They've got four rooms out in the country on 25 acres. The hosts serve breakfast as well as entertainment, performing skits in the morning. Their guests come back repeatedly.

Pearl Street Inn B&B, 319 W Pearl, 76048, ☎ 888-PEARLST, 817-579-7465. $$-$$$. There are five rooms in this antique-filled home. Ask about the Enchanted Evening package.

■ Where to Eat

Hennington's Texas Café at the Nutt House, 121 E Bridge, ☎ 817-573-8400. It's one of the few restaurants in town that garners stars – and lots of them. The eclectic menu boasts some of the finest entrées around. The chef's table will be the highlight of your evening.

Niester's German Restaurant Deli & Bakery, 4426 E Hwy 377, ☎ 817-573-0211. All the German food you could want (or pronounce). Try the creamy potato soup – it keeps the locals coming back.

Rinky-Tink's Sandwich & Ice Cream Parlor. On the square, 108 N Houston, ☎ 817-573-4323. It's old-fashioned fun with good low-key food and ice cream to top it off.

Mineral Wells

■ History

The well that a local judge dug under his cabin in the late 1870s did little for his family, who found the water undrinkable. But when his wife, suffering from rheumatism, gave the foul-smelling liquid a second try, she swore it made her feel better. Rumors of the water's supposed medicinal value spread like wildfire and Mineral Wells was established soon after. One story went that a woman – considered crazy by the townspeople – was cured by the water. That's when the "craze" hit town. There was a Crazy Hotel, Crazy Park and the Crazy Theater, among others.

By 1920, on the verge of the Great Depression, 400 wells had been tapped and were touted worldwide. People flocked to the city to drink and bathe in its waters. When the town's popularity peaked during the Depression, over 150,000 visitors had come during a single year.

The Baker Hotel

Built at a cost of $1.2 million, the Baker still dominates the city's skyline, though its 14 stories and 450 rooms are vacant today. Among its guests were Marlene Dietrich, Clark Gable, Judy Garland, Audie Murphy and the Three Stooges. It was one of the nation's most lavish hotels and nightly entertainers included Herby Kay, Paul Whiteman and Lawrence Welk.

The 1960s brought change. A developing economy and social changes shifted the populace away from enterprises like the Baker Hotel. When the Federal Drug Administration stepped in and told the mineral water purveyors in town to stop their claims for the water, the last nail in the coffin was driven. Several efforts to restore the hotel have failed.

The other hotel built during Mineral Wells' opulence, the Crazy Water Hotel, is now a retirement home.

Modern-day testing found traces of lithium in several of the wells, which could support "feel good" claims.

Today there is little left of the mineral-crazed town that once was. Remnants remain but a quiet ruralness has crept in, leaving the town with just the façades of its past.

■ Touring

Since the trendiness of Mineral Wells faded away, there has been little growth to the town of 15,000, which serves as a way-station for West and North Texas. The seventh story of the **Crazy Water Hotel** (North Oak St at 3rd, ☎ 940-325-4441) has the perfect bird's eye view of Mineral Wells and beyond. Though it's currently a retirement home, management generously shares the view with visitors. The Palo Pinto Mountains, to the north, serve as the town's backdrop.

You can also visit the **Baker Hotel** (201 E Hubbard St) for a glimpse of the past.

Try some of Mineral Wells' famous waters at the **Famous Water Company** (209 NW 6th St, ☎ 940-325-3853), a throw-back to the bygone era. Founded in 1913 by Edward P. Dismuke, it is the only remaining water well in operation.

The **Palo Pinto Museum** (5th and Elm, ☎ 940-659-3781) is small, but still does a good job of preserving the area's unique history. It's open only a few hours each weekend, so call ahead to confirm they're open or to make an appointment.

Information Sources

Call the **Mineral Wells Chamber of Commerce** (☎ 800-252-6889, PO Box 1408, 76068, www.wf.net/ ~mwcc/) for more information.

■ Adventures on the Water

Lake Mineral Wells State Park (Route 4, Box 39C, ☎ 940-328-1171, reservations 512-389-8900) was built in the 1930s by the Civilian Conservation Corps to control flooding and provide drinking water. **Rock climbers** and **rappelers** find the unique geological formations surrounding the 3,000-acre lake to their liking. (All climbers must check in at headquarters for safety purposes.)

The park also offers fine fishing and boating, including canoe and paddleboat rentals. Skiing, jet skis and tubing are not allowed on the calm waters. A total of 21 miles of trails, designated for backpackers, horseback riders (BYO horse), mountain bikers and hikers, allow a great look at the park's terrain. Five fishing piers (one lighted) offer possibilities for bass, catfish and crappie.

Lake Palo Pinto (☎ 940-769-2911, marina), about 12 miles west of town, hasn't been developed like many of Texas' lakes. It offers a peaceful day with few interruptions from camping, fishing and boating.

The jewel in this regions' recreational arsenal is without a doubt **Possum Kingdom Lake State Park** (North of Caddo on Park Rd 33, ☎ 940-549-1803), with water so clear that scuba divers flock to its 150-foot-deep depths. The actual lake covers over 20,000 acres and includes 310 miles of shoreline, with the state park, on the south shore, offering cabins, boat ramps, canoe and paddleboat rentals, a 300-foot lighted pier, superb hiking trails and a small but pleasant beach. Restaurants and marinas dot the shoreline.

> The Brazos River has been an icon to Texans for centuries. John Graves is perhaps the river's most prolific admirer. In his most acclaimed novel, ***Goodbye to a River,*** he weaves the history of Texas into his solitary canoe trip down the Brazos. He puts in west of Dallas, ultimately reaching the Gulf of Mexico. In 1962 Texas dammed the Brazos to create a system of recreational lakes, erasing the remaining vestiges of a proud and powerful river that was its own pioneer. If you truly want to appreciate the Brazos, read Graves' book.

Today, you can still canoe the Brazos, but you just must do it in parts. One such part is between Lake Possum Kingdom and Mineral Wells, almost a 40-mile stretch. The water is cool as it comes from the bottom of Possum Kingdom. Shade is hard to come by, so try to go during mild seasons. Plan on spending two to four days canoeing.

Outfitter

Rochelle's (Rt. 1, Box 119, Graford, 76449, ☎ 940-659-3341, 940-659-2581) is an outfitter with a firm handle on this section of the river. Located at the mid-point of the 38 miles, they provide canoe rentals, shuttle service and primitive camp sites.

■ Where to Stay

HOJO Inn, 2809 Hwy 180 W, 76067, ☎ 800-IGO-HOJO, 940-325-3377. $-$$. Standard amenities with family rooms (triple beds) available.

Ramada Limited, 4103 Hwy 180 E, 76067, ☎ 800-2RAMADA, 940-325-6956. $$. Standard amenities with free executive continental breakfast.

■ Where to Eat

El Paseo, 2801 Hwy 180 East, ☎ 940-325-7262. Standard Tex-Mex, with fajitas and the locals' favorite, chicken enchiladas.

Palace Tearoom, 113 North Oak, ☎ 940-325-9508. They serve lunch only Monday through Friday, but are open by reservation during the evenings and on Saturdays.

Wichita Falls

■ History

If you're going to have "falls" in your name, you'd better have some falls. That's what city planners concluded before constructing 54 feet of waterfalls that cascade down three tiers. The original falls – all of five feet high – had disappeared almost a century ago because of flooding and the damming of the Wichita River.

Certificates for the land that Wichita Falls occupies sat in John C. Scott's trunk for nearly two decades before seeing the light of day. Scott had apparently won the land titles in an 1837 New Orleans poker game and didn't see much use for them. His family did, though, especially when they heard that the railroad would be coming through.

By the 1900s, the town they plotted was prosperous, with over 100 merchants, 21 of which were saloons, earning the town the nickname of "Whiskey Falls."

Wichita Falls' fate as an area hub was sealed in the next decade with the discovery of oil. Oil-related industries, along with manufacturing, agribusiness and military, remain core industries in the town that considers itself the "Buckle of the Sun Belt."

Along with the tremendous amounts of sunshine, Wichita Falls also falls smack dab in the middle of America's tornado alley. It has survived at least two devastating twisters, one of which (April 10, 1979) killed 42, injured 1,700 and caused more than $400 million in damage as it ripped through some 3,000 homes.

Most residents can give you first-hand accounts of the twisters they've seen. But they take the wind-whipped threats in stride – having scoped out the safest places. They calmly evacuate themselves to area cellars and bathtubs (if you put a mattress over the tub, you're a lot less likely to be swept away) when the need arises.

In 1998 Wichita Falls made national news when the Dallas Cowboys chose the city for the site of their summer camp. Cowboy fans from around the world migrated to town for the hot summer months.

■ Touring

 The **Texas Ranch Roundup** (☎ 940-692-9011), usually mid-August, features 12 of the largest and most prestigious ranches in Texas competing in eclectic events that reflect daily ranch work. The calf milking (into a long-neck beer bottle) is a crowd favorite. The ranch cooking contest and evening dance round out the events. You'll see more Stetsons, boots and Wranglers in one arena than you've probably ever seen before.

> **✴ Author's Tip**
>
> Drink water beforehand because, unless a fluky cold front comes through, it'll be hotter 'n hell.

Purists might find the **Wichita Falls Waterfall** (adjacent to I-44 south coming into town from the north) a little contrived, to say the least. But what else is a town to do? A pump recirculates 3,500 gallons a minute. There are also four miles of walking trails that wind along the Wichita River and connect with **Lucy Park** (off Seymour Hwy at Sunset, ☎ 940-

761-7490), a 170-acre affair complete with Lucy Land playground, duck ponds, prime picnic areas, jogging trails and a public swimming pool

The **Kell House Museum** (900 Bluff St, ☎ 940-723-0623), a national and state historic landmark, has been restored to its original grandeur, with original Kell family furnishings. A one-hour guided tour takes visitors through a series of period pieces, including a baby grand piano and seven different fireplaces.

The first map of America made in America itself is at the **Wichita Falls Museum and Art Center** (#2 Eureka Circle, ☎ 940-692-0923), the town's largest museum. Among its permanent collection is the *Boston Massacre* by Paul Revere. There's also a planetarium and laser shows for the action seekers.

If nostalgia for the original frontier directs your thoughts, visit the **Railroad Museum** (501 8th St, ☎ 940-692-6073) on the site of the former Union Station house. There are 11 vintage railcars from sleepers to coaches to cabooses. There are also interpretive exhibits and artifacts from railroad history.

If your nostalgia leans more toward the booming oil industry, go north to Burkburnett and visit the **Trails and Tales of Boomtown, USA** (West 3rd in Burkburnett, ☎ 940-569-3304, or 569-0460), which recalls the days of the Oil Boom with a visit to an oil field, outdoor oil museum and a video for those who don't want the guided tour. Burkburnett had its 10 minutes in the spotlight in 1941 when Clark Gable played in the hit movie *Boom Town* based on the area.

One of the most recent trends in Wichita Falls is toward antique sales. A very strong antique association has been promoting area stores for their immense selection and fair prices. Collectors from Dallas/Ft. Worth make the trek to the smaller town to find better deals. Try the **Mansion Antique Shop** for some of the most interesting pieces.

Information Sources

Call the **Wichita Falls Convention and Visitors Bureau** (☎ 940-723-2741) for more specific information.

■ Adventures on Wheels

The **Hotter 'N Hell Hundred** bicycle race is aptly named, as the August heat is often suffocating. But Wichita Falls thinks that's just the point as they invite thousands to test their skills

298 ■ Wichita Falls

against the 100°-plus temperatures. Serious bikers attempt the 100 miles of flat terrain. Recreational riders can try 50- or two-mile stretches or either 100- or 10-kilometer rides. The race is surrounded by an entire weekend of festival activities.

■ Adventures on the Water

It's a little murky, but if you like fishing, **Lake Arrowhead State Park** (18 miles southeast on FM1954, ☎ 940-528-2211) has got more nooks and crannies for fish to hide out than you can shake a fishing pole at. The actual lake covers 13,500 acres, with 106 miles of shore. The lake was created on top of an old oilfield; derricks still stand all over the lake and are prime fish hangouts. There are also tree stumps hiding beneath the water in some of the shallow spots, so keep to the middle if you're water-skiing and boating. There are facilities for overnight camping, as well as nature trails.

■ Where to Stay

Comfort Inn, 1750 Maurine St, 76304, ☎ 940-322-2477. $$. Close to Sheppard Airforce Base.

Inn by the Falls, 100 Central Freeway, 76305, ☎ 940-761-6000. $$. Executive business center located next to the Falls.

Harrison House Bed & Breakfast, 2014 11th St, 76301, ☎ 940-322-2299. $-$$$. Historic home furnished with antiques and period pieces. Four bedrooms including a honeymoon suite. The lush grounds and living area are perfect for weddings or other less formal occasions.

Holiday Inn Hotel & Suites, 401 Broad St, 76301, ☎ 940-766-6000. $$$. Lush tropical atrium surrounded by 240 rooms. There's also an indoor pool, nine-hole putting green, gameroom, bar, restaurant and health club.

Ramada Limited, 3209 NW Freeway, 76305, ☎ 940-855-0085. $$. Standard amenities, adjacent to an 18-hole golf course.

■ Where to Eat

Dyer's Barbecue, 2927 Southwest Parkway, 76308, ☎ 940-696-3300. Some of the best barbecue in town.

McBride Land & Cattle Co, 501 Scott, ☎ 940-322-2516. Mesquite-grilled steaks made for real Texans. The McBride family has been a Wichita Falls fixture for as long as anyone can remember. The family also runs the Pioneer.

Secret Garden Tea Room, 700 8th St, ☎ 940-767-5570. Garden setting in the Somewhere in Time antique mall. Food ranges from gourmet American to vegetarian. They serve lunch only.

Pioneer Restaurants El Gordos, 513 Scott Ave, ☎ 940-322-6251. The most famous of the area's restaurants. Serves up steaks, Tex-Mex, etc.

Stanley's Barbecue, 2703 Avenue U, 76308, ☎ 940-692-8561. Stanley has been around Wichita for quite some time now doing what he does best.

Zocalo's, 2510 Mallard Dr, ☎ 940-692-9914. Some of the finest Mexican food in town. You can easily see owner Marty McBride's allegiance to the University of Texas – burnt orange mementos cover the walls.

Archer City

When you step into the **Booked Up** book store in Archer City (Main St, ☎ 940-574-2511), there are two things surely on your mind. How in the world does a town of under 2,000 support an enterprise of this size, and where in the world do you start? There are, of course, other questions. Can I touch the signed copy of Truman Capote's *Breakfast at Tiffany's?* Is that a Frank Dobie original? Can I sit on the floor while I thumb through the hundreds of thousands (300,000 and growing) of used Texana books? Where is the staff to this massive affair?

If you are a book lover, Booked Up, the dream-child of Larry McMurtry, is a day's adventure at least. The reclusive, prolific Pulitzer prize-winning McMurtry grew up in this small town 22 miles south of Wichita Falls and has come home to share his wealth of knowledge with this working community.

✻ Did You Know?

Although you may not have actually set foot in Archer City, you've been here. Both *The Last Picture Show* and *Texasville* were filmed here and based on McMurtry's life in the small Texas town he named "Thalia."

In graduate school McMurtry wrote one of his finest works, *Horseman Pass By*, which became the movie *Hud* and the springboard for Paul

Newman's career. He is also known worldwide for other works, including *Lonesome Dove* and *Terms of Endearment*.

His relationship with Archer City has at times been estranged. McMurtry made a mad dash from his small-town roots, with stints in Houston and Washington DC and places with lots of dazzle and lights. His seeming distaste for his hometown left residents sore. They'd rather some other city be portrayed with the smallness that surrounded many of his characters.

But all of that seems to have passed as McMurtry has made peace with his town and come home in a permanent sense. In 1997 he announced that he would write one more novel following the publication of *Comanche Moon*, and would concentrate his efforts on Booked Up, among other things, a sprawling store that spreads through several buildings and across the street.

■ Touring

 In the touristy sense, Archer City might as well be McMurtryville. But that's not meant as a detraction; there is a palpable feeling of Texas along Archer City's streets. You'll know you're there when you see the majestic courthouse just past the four-way stop sign. You don't need any kind of map to get around – just find a parking spot and start walking.

The **Royal Theater**, which became a pop icon as the burnt out movie house in *The Last Picture Show*, remained charred until just recently, when native actor Abby Abernathy decided to rebuild the structure into a 28,000-square-foot, four-level facility to host acting, film-making and play-writing seminars. The original theater, which was abandoned after a balcony fire in 1965, was only 2,500 square feet. The new digs are scheduled to open in June of 1998. You can contact the re.bu.r.th effort (Rebuilding the Royal Theater) by calling ☎ 800-853-0238 for a status report.

Remember the **Dairy Queen** that played such a prominent role in the lives of Jacey Farrow (Cybill Shepherd) and friends in *The Last Picture Show*? It's still there and just about the only place where you'll find fast food in a 20-mile radius. The curtains, courtesy of the movie set, were still up last time we dropped by.

And, of course, there's **Booked Up** (Main St, ☎ 940-574-2511), which previously operated as the Blue Pig Bookstore. You can't miss it, nor would you want to.

The **Archer County Historical Museum** (400 W Pecan, ☎ 940-574-2489) houses an assortment of frontier and pioneer pieces.

Information Sources

You can get more information from the **Archer City Chamber of Commerce** (☎ 940-574-CITY, 2489, P.O. Box 877, 76351-0877) or visit their Web site at www.archercity.org.

Abilene

■ History

The third time proved the charm for the settlement of Abilene, which borrowed its name from a town with the same name in Kansas. First Buffalo Gap, built off a natural divide 10 miles south, sprang up. Second, 14 miles north of present-day Abilene, Fort Phantom Hill, originally called "Post on the Clear Fork of the Brazos," was established. (It was actually situated on Elm Creek). The post was plagued by poor water and lumber resources and was abandoned in 1854. In 1871 it rose from the ashes, but again it floundered and fizzled out.

Abilene arose between the two failed towns. The railroad came through in 1881, insuring its longevity and Abilene quickly became an agricultural hub (it later added oil servicing to its resume, though it has virtually no oil). Its early years were marked by outright lawlessness. However, as the town progressed so did its position as an active part of the Bible Belt.

Earning a reputation as the buckle of the Bible Belt, Abilene now has three church-affiliated colleges, Abilene Christian University, Hardin-Simmons University and McMurray University.

■ Touring

The **Museums of Abilene/Grace Cultural Center** (102 Cypress St, ☎ 915-673-4587, www.abilene.com/moa) serve as one-stop shopping for visitors on a museum hunt. Housed in the old magnificent Mission-style Grace Hotel, built in 1909 for weary railroad passengers, the Museums of Abilene include the Art Museum, the Historical Museum and the Children's Museum.

The close proximity of the three independent, yet interlocking, attractions makes it a family favorite. While the kids enjoy hands-on adventure, parents can choose from a variety of permanent and traveling fine art exhibits.

Historical adventures of the outdoor variety are just north and south of town. The **Fort Phantom Hill Ruins** (FM 600, 14 miles north) are the last remaining pieces of what used to be a fort for five US Army infantry units. Today it's just a few buildings and a dozen chimneys. The ruins are on private property, but the landowner has kept them open to the public for free.

A jaunt south of town to the **Buffalo Gap Historic Village** (see *Buffalo Gap*, page 304) is another living history lesson. A large cluster of original frontier buildings has been collected and restored for a palpable representation of early Texas life.

The **Abilene Zoo** (TX 36 at Loop 322 in Nelson Park, ☎ 915-673-WILD, 915-676-6085, camalott.com/abilene/zoo) is not your typical medium-sized town zoo. As one of the five largest in the state, it cares for more than 800 animals representing over 200 species.

Educational exhibits allow visitors comparative study of West Texas and Southwestern species with those of Africa and Madagascar.

Nelson Park, home of the zoo, is a perfect place for all your leisure time. Rent a paddle boat for the full Sunday afternoon experience.

The **Linear Air Park** at Dyess Air Force Base (☎ 915-696-5609 or 696-2196, www.dyess.af.mil) houses 31 planes from World War II, the Korean War, the Vietnam War and Operation Desert Storm. Dyess is the home and sole training center for the B-1 Bomber. You must stop at the base entrance for permission to enter.

On a rainy day, you'll enjoy the **Paramount Theatre** (352 Cypress, ☎ 915-676-9620) built in the 1930s and now used for classic films and other special events. Stars and clouds float above the interior, built to resemble a courtyard.

Information Sources

The **Abilene Convention and Visitors Bureau** can be reached at ☎ 800-727-7704 (1101 N. First, 79601, www.abilene.com/visitors).

North Texas & the Panhandle

■ Adventures on Foot

Abilene State Park (16 miles SW of town on FM 89, Buffalo Gap, ☎ 915-572-3204, reservations 512-389-8900) covers 621 acres along Elm Creek and once served as a resting place for the Comanches.

Now there's modern camping and recreational facilities intermingled among 4,000 native pecan trees. Hiking and walking trails will keep you on your feet. Buffalo and longhorns can be found near the park at Lake Abilene, where there is fishing and picnicking until sundown every day.

■ Adventures on Horseback

You can also enjoy some horseback riding at the **Double J Horse Ranch** (6950 West Lake Rd, ☎ 915-675-0945). Experience real old-time Texas.

■ Adventures on the Water

Although Fort Phantom no longer exists, **Lake Fort Phantom** (off FM 600, 10 miles NE, ☎ 915-676-6217) is alive and well, with more than 4,200 acres and 29 miles of shoreline. Fishermen flock to the lake for walleye and crappie, but other outdoor enthusiasts can also enjoy the site, which offers primitive camping, a swimming area, marinas and a public boat ramp.

■ Where to Stay

Blue Willow Bed & Breakfast, 435 College Dr, 79601, ☎ 915-677-8420. $$. Two-story studio apartment with fireplace.

Bolin Prairie House Bed & Breakfast, 508 Mulberry, 79601, ☎ 915-675-5855. $-$$. Four rooms in a 1902 home furnished with antiques.

Embassy Suites, 4250 Ridgemont Dr, 79606, ☎ 915-698-1234 or 800-EMBASSY. $$-$$$$. Large hotel amenities along with a full breakfast.

Myrtle Ranch, 102 CR 146, Ovalo, 79541, ☎ 915-554-9152 or 554-9153. www.abilene.com/myrtleranch. $$-$$$$. If you're a hunter, you might want to check out the facilities on this 7,300-acre spread replete with white-tailed deer.

The Mulberry House Bed & Breakfast, 1042 Mulberry, 79601, ☎ 915-677-7890. $$-$$$. Former home of Bob Wills, country music star, many of the rooms are named and decorated for different Wills hits. There's a lovely garden area and a swimming pool for the hot summer months.

■ Where to Eat

Cahoots Catfish & Oyster Bar, 301 S 11th St, ☎ 915-672-6540. The all-you-can-eat fish platters attract the hungry. They'll also give you the "whole cat," if that's what you want (bones and all).

Towne Crier Steakhouse, 818 E Hwy 80, ☎ 915-673-4551. Your standard steak-and-potato kind of Texas restaurant.

Zentner's Daughter Steak House, 4358 Sayles Blvd, ☎ 915-695-4290. They have a variety of things on the menu, but it would be a shame to miss one of their steaks.

Buffalo Gap

■ History

Ten miles south of Abilene, Buffalo Gap appears just a dot on the map – a town with an interesting name that just happens to be on the way to the big city. But you'd be remiss not to stop in this small enclave of history and taste the rich essence of Texas tradition.

Ironically Abilene owes its existence to Buffalo Gap, a natural divide that migrating buffalo followed during their annual fall forage south and return north in the spring. Hunters found it convenient and pleasant stalking ground. Ranchers also used the gap to drive longhorns north to the Western Trail. A small settlement grew up and in 1878 it became the county seat, a position it has since given up to Abilene.

The small, yet interesting, town never enjoyed mainstream success. To its 500 residents that matters little. It has become a favorite tourist stop for two reasons: Dr. R. Lee Rode and Tom Perini.

■ Touring

Dr. Rode, an avid historian, recreated history with the continuous restoration of the **Buffalo Gap Historic Village** (FM 89 to Elm St, ☎ 915-572-3365) a frontier complex complete with a railroad depot (built in 1881), the first Taylor County Courthouse and Jail (1879), a Nazarene church built just after the turn of the century and a blacksmith shop. While he owns and maintains the living history lesson, he has shared them with the public. If you're even close to Buffalo Gap or Abilene, the village is well worth a detour.

■ Where to Eat

 Bar-B-Que Barn, Buffalo Gap, ☎ 915-572-3552. If you're not in the mood for a Perini steak while you're in Buffalo Gap, try the brisket and German sausage here.

Lola's Mexican Food Café, Buffalo Gap, ☎ 915-572-3731. You'll be treated like family at this small, family affair. Reservations are recommended to land one of the few tables. BYOB.

Perini Ranch Steakhouse, FM 89 W, State Park Rd, ☎ 915-572-3339. You absolutely can't miss this place. Perini, who spent the first part his life in the saddle with his cow-calf operation, noticed early on that he was spending more and more time at the chuck wagon – and was enjoying it. In 1974 he began a catering business with his cowboy brand of tenderloin and ranch fare. Perini has been so successful with his venture that Perini Ranch has been transformed into the **Perini Ranch Steakhouse**.

A humble ex-hay barn off a dirt road, the steakhouse is a throwback to a family experience of yesteryear. Children ramble among the tables on the lush grass playing games and capturing lightning bugs, while parents listen to the sounds of the country at its red-check table-clothed tables.

The embrace that Perini has received from the world is deserved, although it surprised the cowboy cook and he has changed little since the business began. His culinary skill has taken him as far as Japan, where he served as an ambassador for the Texas beef industry. It has taken him to New York, where he has been invited on more than one occasion to cook with the world's finest chefs. And it has taken him to the Texas capital, where Gov. George Bush III had him cater his personal shindig.

But that's only the tip of the iceberg. *The New York Times*, calling his beef tenderloin "spectacular," named Perini's wares one of the best mail-order gifts in 1995. The mention put Perini on the map, as well as in the prestigious Neiman Marcus catalog and on the cover of *Texas Highways*, a long-standing Texas travel magazine. His success has snowballed. But even more important is his unwavering commitment to the food. It is unchanged and charming, like Perini himself, a 50-something rancher who dons his cowboy hat daily, talks with a broad southern drawl, and still returns his own phone calls.

You'll find the steakhouse off Ranch Rd 89 (make sure you don't split onto RR 613), marked by a sign (☎ 915-572-3339). Reservations are recommended, especially on summer weekends when there is a spectacular buffet special. If you can't come by, you can sample some of the menu from his mail order catalog (☎ 800-367-1721).

Post

■ History

C.W. Post, cereal magnate extraordinaire, was a nervous man, and in learning to cope with his nervous disorders, Post set out on a life of experimentation. The Illinois native first visited Texas during several hunting trips in the 1890s. He quickly became smitten with "chicory coffee," a cowboy concoction made of wood berries and chicory. Fiddling with the treat's recipe a bit, Post came up with non-caffeinated Postum. By 1894 he had built a small factory near Battle Creek, Michigan to produce his increasing stable of offerings. Soon there were Post Toasties and Post Bran. Grape-Nuts came about in 1897 and Post's place in cereal history became permanent.

In 1906 he moved to Texas and purchased a 250,000-acre ranch. Post City, the cereal-maker's envisioned utopia, was put on the map. He strategically settled his new city, mapping out 160-acre homesteads and effectively colonizing the town with 1,200 families. He refused to sell land to speculators and forbade the sale of liquor.

He also enforced sanitary codes and built a hotel, cotton gin, sanitarium and textile plant. It was the ultimate example of a planned community.

But Post, still nervous, was concerned about the lack of rainfall. After reading about rain following cannon battles, he began a three-year, $50,000 experiment setting off blasts around town. He claimed success, yet records indicate no difference in rain levels from previous years.

In 1912, following a blast, hail dropped from the sky, ruining the community's crops. Post, never having achieved peace of mind, left soon after.

In 1914, while in California, he committed suicide.

■ Touring

 However troubled Post's life might have been, his memory lives on in a town that not only bears his name, but was molded by his hand.

The hotel that Post built, the Algerita, now houses the **Algerita Art Center** (129 West Main), a collection of area artists' work.

Though Post never succeeded in his utopian society, the town enjoyed moderate success. One of the first movie theaters in West Texas opened here in 1920 – the **Garza Theatre** (226 East Main, ☎ 806-495-4005). By 1929 it adapted itself for sound, moving beyond the silent pictures. By 1960 it had closed, but a local group renovated and reopened the theater in 1986, using it for live performances. If you drop in on a play or musical, you will usually also find a fine barbecue dinner waiting.

A collection of area lore has been assembled at the **Garza County Museum** (119 North Ave), with Indian, cowboy and pioneer artifacts.

The town of Post (around 4,000 population) is settled on the southeastern edge of the Great Plains at the foot of the magnificent Cap Rock, a range of flat-topped mountains that mark the boundary of the Llano Estacado, or "staked plains." The **Llano Estacado Tourist Marker** (US 84, six miles south) is a sign in front of a great view of the plains, providing a detailed explanation of the extraordinary geography of the staked plains and the Cap Rock escarpment.

Information Sources

You can get more information about the historic town of Post from their **Chamber of Commerce** (☎ 806-495-3461, PO Box 610, 79356). The city maintains a Web site at www.posttx.com.

Lubbock

■ History

Contemporary Lubbock is young by Texas standardsu, but on the world's scale it is much older. Archeological evidence suggests that mankind roamed the area more than 12,000 years ago during the Clovis Period. More recently, Native American Indians followed the buffalo through these fertile hunting grounds.

Yellow House Canyon, named for the yellowish walls (in present day Mackenzie State Park), was called Cañon de Rescate, Spanish for "Canyon of Ransoms." Certainly, settlement in Indian and buffalo territory came at a high human cost and, as a result, the frontier remained wild and uninhabited until close to the 1900s, when the buffalo began to dwindle.

The actual town of Lubbock, named for Tom S. Lubbock, a Texas Ranger and Confederate officer, began as two competing developments. Monterey was settled south of the canyon; Old Lubbock was settled north of the canyon. In 1891 the towns consolidated, moved to yet a third location and became Lubbock.

Despite the elements – wind, fire and drought – Lubbock made steady headway and grew into one of the Panhandle's only hubs. It began its preoccupation with morality early on; except for one saloon, the town was "dry" even in the early days. And soon enough that one saloon owner was persuaded to close the doors and pursue a different career.

Lubbock remains dry today – residents mosey out to the city limits to buy their liquor. (You can buy liquor in restaurants and bars, but not retail stores.)

The terrain is still brutal. Dust storms can be blinding and trees are few and far between. However, Lubbock retains its role as an agribusiness center, growing cotton, cattle, grain and oil, among other crops. Wine has been the most recent agricultural introduction and is flourishing beneath the hot, dry South Plains sun. Texas Tech University, a sprawling affair, has become one of the leading public universities in the state.

Buddy Holly et al.

Rough and basic though Lubbock might seem, one of its finest products has been its musical talent. Buddy Holly (who inspired the Beatles) was perhaps the most renowned of an incredible string of creative pioneers who hailed from this dusty city. On Feb. 2, 1959, Holly's plane went down near Mason City, Iowa, killing Holly, Ritchie Valens and the Big Bopper. Lubbock grieved deeply for its favorite son and a bronze statue commemorates his life. Holly's perennial hits include *Peggy Sue, That'll Be the Day* and *It's So Easy*.

Other musicians who have honed their young talents here are Roy Orbison, Valens, Waylon Jennings, Joe Ely, Mac Davis, John Denver, Tanya Tucker, Jimmie Dale Gilmore, the Gatlin Brothers and Butch Hancock.

■ Touring

 Music is truly an international language – the worldly crowds that visit the memorial to Holly at the **Buddy Holly Statue and Walk of Fame** (8th and Ave Q, at entrance to Civic Center) reflect that much. His likeness stands over eight feet high and weighs in at 2,500 pounds. Other West Texans honored include Waylon Jennings, Mac Davis and Jimmie Dean.

If you're a died-in-the-wool Holly fan, you'll want to visit his gravesite at the **Lubbock Cemetery** (east end of 34th St). While it's no ornate mausoleum, visitors find the flat stone decorated with only a guitar and musical notes a somber experience.

The **Ranching Heritage Center** (4th and Indiana, ☎ 806-742-2498, http://interoz.com/lubbock/ranch) provides visitors with over 14 acres of pure ranching experience. More than 100,000 people venture here each year to tour the 30 buildings that have been collected and restored. The buildings follow the evolution of ranching from the one-room cabins of early trail drivers to stylish Victorian ranch houses at the turn of the century. There's a blacksmith shop, a log cabin, a schoolhouse relic, a train depot and a bunkhouse.

Many of the structures came from famous area ranches – like the Matador, XIT and King Ranch – that played instrumental roles in the development of the ranch and the ranching culture.

The evolution of the Texas ranch is a study of American history, from the slaughter of the buffalo, the conquest and defeat of the American Indians, to the creation and utilization of barbed wire and the windmill. Displays and exhibits present this history in fascinating detail.

Exhibits and demonstrations range from candle-dipping (a hands-on proposition) to sheep-shearing and breadmaking. There's quilt making, branding and special events presented by costumed volunteers. There's also a large collection of wagons, branding irons, saddles and Western art.

One of Lubbock's newest adventures is in the world of wine making. While its first harvests were not as tasty as Napa Valley's, many of the local wineries have made substantial strides and are considered on a par with the California labels. The warm, dry days followed by cool nights are perfect for grape growing.

Llano Estacado (FM 1585 east 3.2 miles, ☎ 806-745-2258) is the area's oldest winery and most celebrated. They offer complimentary tours and tastings througout the day. For a complete wine tasting tour, you can also visit **Pheasant Ridge** (in New Deal, ☎ 806-746-6033), a European-style winery that specializes in a select few varieties, and **Cap Rock** (Hwy US 87 S & Woodrow Rd, ☎ 806-863-2704), a popular place for special events.

Texas Tech University (W Broadway and University), which took on the Texas axiom that if you've got room you might as well spread out, is a grande dame of campuses, with 1,837 acres. Students at times rely on their cars to get them from class to class. The campus welcomes visitors – just stop at a kiosk and ask for a visitors permit.

The **Texas Tech Museum and Moody Planetarium** (4th and Indiana, ☎ 806-742-2490) keeps a lot of things out of sight for academic and research purposes, but it still hosts a wide variety of public displays from Pre-Columbian to early Texas. The museum also boasts a large collection of Mexican Indian costumes and historical fashions.

For night life and entertainment, check out the **Depot District** (19th St and IH-27), a conglomeration of unique restaurants, live music and bars. The **Depot Restaurant** specializes in steaks and prime rib; the 19th Street Warehouse, is known for its live music; the **Depot Beer Garden** offers an outside spot to enjoy starry nights. There's also **Stubb's Barbecue** and the **Hub City Brewery**, two excellent dining choices.

■ Adventures on Foot

Lubbock Lake is a misnomer – there hasn't been a lake here for quite some time. But the **Lubbock Lake Landmark State Historical Park** (Loop 289 & Clovis Rd, ☎ 806-741-0306) is here for good. Considered to be the only archaeological spot in North America with artifacts from all of the Southern Plains cultures, many of its finds date back 12,000 years. They've also uncovered remains of bison, mammoth, camel and a six-foot armadillo. There's a three-quarter-mile trail through the excavation area and a three-mile trail through the park grounds. An interpretive center contains life-size replicas of what archeologists have found here.

North Texas & the Panhandle

For a real "taste" of the outdoors, visit the **Apple Country at Hi Plains Orchards** (Hwy 62/82, four miles east of Idalou, ☎ 806-765-6772), an orchard with 5,500 trees, featuring pick-your-own apples and vegetables (July-Oct). There's also a gift shop, bakery, tearoom, meeting and party facility, cider production, wedding gazebo, coordinator and caterer.

■ Adventures on the Water

Only historical remnants remain of the ocean that once covered the South Plains. **Buffalo Springs Lake** (five miles east of Loop 289 on East 50th, ☎ 806-747-3353) offers fishing, skiing, picnics, camping, nature trails, horseshoe pits, volleyball courts and a beach area with water slides year-round. There is also a party house for rent, a restaurant and a marina complete with boats for tours and rental.

■ Where to Stay

Country Place B&B, 160th St and Upland, 79401, ☎ 806-863-2030, $$-$$$. A five-room getaway serving a full gourmet breakfast and with a lap pool and hot tub.

Four Points Hotel by ITT Sheraton, 505 Ave Q, 79401, ☎ 806-747-0171, http://interoz.com/lubbock/fourpt.htm. Complete with restaurant, atrium bar and indoor heated pool.

Lubbock Inn, 3901 19th St, 79401, ☎ 800-545-8226, 806-792-1319, http://interoz.com/lubbock/hotels/inn.htm. Restaurant, lounge, meeting and conference accommodations and complimentary transportation.

Woodrow House Bed and Breakfast, 2629 19th St, 79401, ☎ 806-793-3330, www.woodrowhouse.com. $$. Seven guest rooms available, all with private baths, and a full complimentary breakfast. Just across from Texas Tech University.

■ Where to Eat

Jazz: A Louisiana Kitchen, 3703 C. 19th St, ☎ 806-799-2124. Hot and spicy Cajun that'll please most palates. They also serve up lots of live jazz and blues music.

Skyviews, 1901 University, ☎ 806-744-7462. You're pampered (or experimented on, depending on how you look at it) by Texas Tech schools in the restaurant, hotel and institutional management program. Menu and times vary, so call ahead. It has a great view of town.

Hub City Brewery Menu, 1807 Ave H, ☎ 806-747-1535, http://interoz.com/lubbock/brew.htm. An eclectic mix of brew-pub and restaurant with daily choices.

Amarillo

■ History

Amarillo was a center of commerce long before it was officially a town. Conveniently located on the edge of the buffalo frontier, the settlement, known as "Ragtown," grew into a large supply depot and shipping point dotted with hide huts and transitory housing. The Fort Worth & Denver City Railroad made things official in 1887, choosing a site named Oneida to develop into a commercial port. Oneida, which bordered Ragtown and was the brainchild of Henry B. Sanborn, immediately had its name changed to Amarillo, the Spanish word for "yellow" and the color Sanborn chose to paint every building in his settlement.

Amarillo grew to be the biggest transfer point for cattle in the New World, taking in 100,000 cows each year and shipping them out to destinations like Fort Worth. The cattle – the average stay for each cow being around two weeks – left the town mired in muddy, smelly sludge. Sanborn, who owned the Frying Pan Ranch northwest of town, insisted that the town move to higher and dryer land, even offering $40,000 and a large chunk of land to entice a move.

The town bit on the offer – after an especially muddy 1889 – and moved to a more hospitable location. After farmers near Hereford tapped into the Ogallala aquifer, the landscape of Amarillo changed from premiere grazing land to rich farming soil suitable for growing grain. Grain could fatten up the cattle much faster than the grasses that previously were grown and instead of shipping the cows off to auction in Fort Worth, Amarillo became an auction hub. At the end of World War II, 85% of Texas' cattle were carted into the Panhandle for auction. The town's commerce grew beyond cattle to include cotton and oil and today it is the world's leading producer of helium.

Amarillo's dependence on and relationship with the land it occupies is obvious. Its residents are proud of their cowboy heritage – boots and Stetsons are not only commonplace on the streets of Amarillo, they are well-worn. It is a hard working town. The tanned and wrinkled faces you encounter will most likely have stories to tell.

Palo Duro Canyon.

Country music fans are familiar with Amarillo, even if they've never set foot in it. George Strait has been crooning *Amarillo By Morning* for decades.

If you're in Amarillo, or even close, you owe it to yourself to see the **Palo Duro Canyon**, the second largest canyon in the nation. See page 320 below to find out more about the beautiful oasis that was home to the Indians of the plain until their demise.

Palo Duro's buddy, **Caprock Canyons State Park**, is just a tad further and is another can't-miss experience. See page 321 for more information.

■ Touring

Amarillo still relies on the weekly cattle auctions to drive area commerce. More than $130 million changes hands for 600,000 cattle each year at the **Amarillo Livestock Auctions** (100 S Manhattan, ☎ 806-373-7464, held every Tuesday). Visitors are welcome to witness the state's largest livestock auction.

Quarter horses, the first American breed and still the mount of choice for cowboys, are paid tribute at the **American Quarter Horse Heritage Center & Museum** (2601 I-40E at Quarter Horse Drive, ☎ 806-376-5181). Registered at the headquarters are more than 2½ million quarter horses throughout the world, with Texas claiming 369,000 of that number. The exhibits range from a hands-on area for youngsters to a theater featuring historical video and spectacular vintage rodeo footage.

Despite their surroundings, several early Amarillo settlers brought splendor to their corner of the world, importing the world's finery to their homes. The **Harrington House** (1600 S Polk, ☎ 806-374-5490) is a little particular about its visitors. You're only allowed to wear low, broad-heeled shoes. You must make reservations and only four are allowed at a time (no one under the age of 14). But if you qualify for the tour, you're in for a treat. Built in 1914 and acquired in 1940 by the Harringtons, a notable local family, the neoclassical mansion is a study of historical grandeur and luxury.

The **Lee and Mary E. Bivins' Home** (1000 S. Polk, ☎ 806-373-7800), at the Amarillo Convention and Visitors Center complex, is less discriminating with its guests, and offers a splendid step back in time. The Junior League maintains this Georgian Revival three-story house built in 1905 by Lee Bivins, an area pioneer.

The Harringtons lent their name to the **Don Harrington Discovery Center and Planetarium** as well (1200 Streit, Amarillo Medical Center Complex, ☎ 806-355-9547). It's a perfect place for kids who like science, but couldn't care less for school. You get to do your hands-on science project, but you don't have to write a report on it afterwards. Meant for children of all ages, this science museum includes the Exploration Gallery, the Construction Zone (architectural elements), Kidscovery (for ages 2-6) and a planetarium that can propel you through space.

Opposite the Discovery Center is the **Helium Monument** (1200 Streit, ☎ 806-355-9547), built in 1968 to celebrate the discovery of helium a century before. The helium atom/time capsule is scheduled to reveal its contents, more than 4,000 items, throughout the next century – in 2018, 2068 and 2968. Perhaps the greatest find in 2968 will be a savings account passbook containing $10, which will have drawn 4% interest over the next millennium. By 2968 it will be valued at over one quintillion dollars.

Some of Georgia O'Keefe's work is on display at the **Amarillo Art Center** (2200 S. Van Buren, Amarillo College Main Campus, ☎ 806-371-5050), designed by the same man (Edward Stone) as the Kennedy Center. With a theater, a sculpture garden and an amphitheater, there's no shortage of entertainment here. The art museum's permanent display delves deeply into 20th-century work, including pieces by Elaine de Kooning, Jack Boynton, Franz Kline and Fritz Scholder in addition to

O'Keefe. There's also a collection of photographs taken during the '30s and '40s and a contemporary collection of cowboy photos taken by Martin Schreiber.

Getting around has changed quite a bit over the last century, shifting from a dependence on the horse to a reliance on horsepower. The **Sterquell Collection** (812 S Polk, ☎ 806-372-7500) chronicles these changes in mankind's mode of transportation with an array of vehicles that predate the automobile. The collection includes close to 50 horse-drawn carriages, a photographer's wagon, a hearse, farm vehicles, sleighs and more.

Cadillac Ranch

West of Amarillo
On the I-40 side
No way to miss it
For a Cadillac Ride
Walk through the gate
And listen to the sound
Of ten fifty Cadillacs
Planted in the ground.

Out on Route 66
There's something going on
Something in the water
Something in the song
Lullabye of birdland
Rocking to the sound
Of ten fifty Cadillacs
Planted in the Ground

When you go to Texas
Give it a chance
Take me back down to Cadillac Ranch
Kick off your shoes
If you know how to dance
Take me back down to Cadillac Ranch

People gonna say
What does it mean?
A monument
to the American Dream
It doesn't mean a thing
If you don't hear the sound
Of ten fifty Cadillacs
Planted in the Ground.

John Stewart

Perhaps one of Amarillo's most famous and enduring images – and Texas', for that matter – is the display at Cadillac Ranch, west of town on I-40 and formerly Route 66, the road of legend. Ten Cadillacs nosedive in a wheat field, planted all the way up to their windshields and stacked one in front of the other.

They've become the symbol of the eccentric Texan. Texas has created an aura around the world of unabashed quirkiness and of co-existence with the wild earth. The Cadillac Ranch, brainchild of eccentric Stanley Marsh III, has become a pop icon since it was sown in 1974. No photography collection of the state is complete without a shot of the Ranch. And you don't have to look hard to find it. Just pay attention as you head west and it will hit you smack dab in the middle of the forehead, 10 classics sitting at attention in the middle of nowhere.

■ Adventures on Foot

 Perhaps the best way to experience the Texas Panhandle and the life of the Texas cowboy is to stop by one of several area ranches that have opened their gates to visitors.

The most notorious of the cowboy events is the **Cowboy Morning & Cowboy Evening** (Figure 3 Ranch at Palo Duro Canyon, ☎ 806-944-5562 or 800-658-2613). Horse-drawn wagons greet visitors at the ranch gates, carting them to the edge of the Palo Duro Canyon – a spectacular and relatively undiscovered landmark nearly as big as the Grand Canyon – before serving you a cowboy meal. You get to choose either the morning or evening hours. For breakfast, there are biscuits with gravy, flapjacks, eggs and steak. For dinner, there is steak with all the fixings. All cooked over a campfire.

Cowboy Morning.

Creekwood Ranch hosts an Old West Show and Chuck Wagon Supper (eight miles south on FM 1541, ☎ 800-658-6673, 806-356-9256), complete with cowboys and Indians and a peek into the past. Reservations are required. Ranch hands will deliver you to the campsite in horse-drawn wagons.

If you're looking for a little more simplicity, try **Thompson Memorial Park** (US 87 north, between 24th and Hastings). Its amenities include two lakes, 36 holes of golf, an Olympic-size swimming pool, ball fields, Storyland Zoo and Wonderland Park. What remains of the 610-acre spread is perfect for picnicking, lounging and any other activity a family might enjoy.

About 36 miles northeast of town you'll find **Cal Farley's Boys Ranch** (FM1061 to US 385 to Spur 233, ☎ 806-372-2341), a historic refuge for orphaned boys. Farley, a former prizefighter, established the ranch in 1939 and the self-contained community has been nurturing young men ever since. Each year the ranch hosts the **Boys Ranch Rodeo** (Labor Day), which draws more than 10,000 spectators from all over the state. All of the more than 400 residents of the orphanage participate in some way. If you'd like to visit the ranch, call first and arrange a time, as the boys are also full-time students.

At the Boys Ranch you'll find **Old Tascosa**, a boom town gone bust. Originally part of the Wild West, it saw the likes of Billy the Kid and Pat

Garrett. The old courthouse serves as a museum, documenting the town's wild and brief existence.

■ Adventures on the Water

 Even if you might think the Texas Panhandle is only tumbleweeds and flat expanse (there's a lot of truth to that), **Lake Meredith National Park** (☎ 806-857-3151) will make you think again. Created by damming the Canadian River, Lake Meredith is two miles wide in some places and 14 miles long. Eight recreational areas dot its shores, and there's ample room to sail, ski, swim, fish, float and tan. There's also tennis and golf. Make sure you pick up provisions before you get there; that way you can enjoy an overnight camp along one of the surrounding bluffs.

On the south edge of Lake Meredith, rockhounds and archeology buffs will enjoy **Alibates National Monument** (☎ 806-857-3151 for details), a relatively undeveloped site that houses an ancient flint quarry. Flint from this area was distributed across the plains by Indians and farmers, used for tools and weapons. The flint is unique for its brilliant colors, shaded with streaks of blue, black, maroon and orange. Buffalo bones have been found en masse at nearby pits and a village, complete with pictographs, was excavated back in the late 1930s. Ranger-led tours are free. There's also a wealth of good hiking.

■ Where to Stay

Big Texan, 7703 I-40E, 79103, ☎ 800-657-7177 or 806-372-5000. $-$$. If you're going to eat a 72-ounce steak at their restaurant, you might need a bed close by. Accommodations are standard, but the Texas-shaped heated outdoor pool is sure to be a great kid pleaser.

Ambassador Hotel, 3100 I-40W, 79102, ☎ 806-358-6161. $$$. The finest hotel in town, with 266 rooms, a sauna, exercise room, free continental breakfast and other luxuries. There's also a concierge floor and two restaurants.

Auntie's House Bed & Breakfast, 1712 S Polk St, 79102, ☎ 806-371-8054, www.auntieshouse.com. $$-$$$. There are two rooms in the front house and the Enchanted Cottage out back. Among the special treats here are evening snacks, bicycles built for two, and a lovely hot tub. Cottage guests are waited on hand and foot, with everything from complimentary wine and champagne to breakfast.

Galbraith House: A Bed & Breakfast Inn, 1710 S Polk St, 79102, ☎ 806-374-0237. $$. Traditional bed and breakfast.

Martha's Midtown Bed & Breakfast, 2005 S Jackson, 79109, ☎ 806-374-2689. $$. Private baths and entries in country-Victorian home. Breakfast is whenever you want it.

Parkview House Bed & Breakfast, 1311 S Jefferson, 79101, ☎ 806-373-9464. $$-$$$. Just six blocks from the historic district, there's a beautiful garden to enjoy, along with a hot tub, a big front porch and comfortable hammock.

Historical Hudspeth House Bed and Breakfast Inn, 1905 4th Ave, Canyon, 79015, ☎ 806-655-9800 or 800-655-9809, www.hudspethinn. com. $$-$$$. Five of the eight rooms come with fireplaces. It's covered with trees and the house boasts big, open porches.

Christina's Casa De Paz Bed & Breakfast, 16600 FM 2186, 79119, ☎ 806-359-8509, 888-231-1712. $$. Just five miles away from Amarillo, Christina makes both breakfast and dinner for her guests. She specializes in Mexican food, making her own tortillas and salsas.

■ Where to Eat

Big Texan Steak Ranch, 7701 I-40 East, ☎ 806-372-6000. This is no ordinary restaurant. The 72-ounce steak dinner (with salad, shrimp cocktail and potato) is free if you can finish it in an hour. Their gift shop includes everything from Texas-size fly swatters to stuffed rattlesnakes. Hors d'oeuvres include calf fries (mountain oysters), rabbit, buffalo and rattlesnake.

Back to Eden Restaurant and Deli, 2425 I-40W, ☎ 806-353-7476. Sophisticated and mouth-watering salad bar that also offers smoothies and hot deli dishes.

Calico Country, 2410 Paramount, ☎ 806-358-7664. If it's animal for eatin', then Calico Country will probably have it available chicken-fried. They even chicken-fry some of the vegetables. If you're not worried about your cholesterol, you can't pass it up.

Country Barn Steak House, 1805 Lakeside Dr, ☎ 806-335-2325. With a little music and a little two-stepping, the Country Barn boasts traditional Texas fare.

Stockyard Café, 100 S Manhattan, ☎ 806-374-6024. If you're going to be at the stockyards anyway, don't go out of your way for a meal. Hang out with the working bunch and enjoy the fresh pie that is most likely homemade.

Big Texan.

Tacos Garcia, 1412 Ross, ☎ 806-371-0411. Their simple food – soft tacos and chili rellenos – make this restaurant a favorite with the locals.

Special Attractions

■ The Palo Duro Canyon

If the Grand Canyon qualifies as one of the Seven Wonders of the World, the Palo Duro Canyon can't be far behind. Isolated among the vast plains of the Panhandle and the central plains, its mouth gapes open, exposing a colorful congestion of formations in a land otherwise as flat as a tortilla.

The canyon, created by wind erosion and water erosion from the Prairie Dog Town Fork of the Red River, delves down some 800 feet and traverses 110 miles, exposing layers of earth that span 200 million years of geological time.

If you were standing far away – and you were a little ignorant – you might not even see it if you didn't look down. But then you would miss the second largest canyon in America. The Palo Duro Canyon is one of Texas' best kept secrets, even from Texans. They've probably heard about it, but its isolation has kept all but the adventurers away. It could conceivably take a Texan longer to get to the Palo Duro than it could take a Californian.

It was the site of the Comanche's last stand against US troops, led by Quanah Parker, before they were forced onto an Oklahoma reservation. Before their loss, the Comanche used the canyons as a refuge, as did rogues, cowboys and other misfit outfits.

Most of the Palo Duro Canyon is off-limits to visitors because it is pri-vately-owned. While that may not sound great, it insures the canyon's longevity.

You can access the canyon through the **Palo Duro Canyon State Park** (☎ 800-792-1112 or 806-488-2227, 512-389-8900 for camping and cabin reservations), 30 miles southeast of

Palo Duro Canyon Lighthouse.

Amarillo off Hwy 217. There are facilities for camping, backpacking, horseback riding and biking. The **Goodnight Trading Post** (☎ 806-488-2231) provides a hodgepodge of services, from mountain bike rent-als to guided tours to catered meals. The **Goodnight Riding Stables** (☎ 806-488-2231) can give you more information on trail rides.

The epic musical *Texas* is undeniably the biggest attraction in the Palo Duro, having honed in on audiences for more than 30 years. How can you miss when a colorful canyon is your backdrop? The story line is a bit pre-dictable – the retelling of how the region was settled and the tension be-tween cowboy and farmer and Indian. But the stirring sets and dancing, topped off with a fireworks display, keep audiences enthralled year after year. Call ☎ 806-655-2181 for times and reservations.

■ The Caprock Canyons

The Caprock Canyons are even less known than the Palo Duro, yet they lie just a few miles south and east, just west of Quitaque (pronounced "Kitty-Quay"). They don't have a grandiose, nightly production, nor do they have the same enclosed basin vantage that most canyons possess. Rather, they mark the transition between the Llano Estacado (high plains) and the rolling plains to the south, with deep, jagged breaks. A herd of buffalo, offspring of the area's original herd, wander beneath the rugged canyon walls.

Because it does not have mainstream attractions, there is solitude here. Many consider it the better of the canyons because you can truly get away and become engulfed by the varied terrain. Mountain bikers are more than challenged and equestrians have their own campground with corrals and a parking area meant to accommodate horse trailers.

Caprock Canyons Outfitters

The **Caprock Canyons State Park** (☎ 806-455-1492) can organize your adventure. The **Big C Trading Post** (☎ 806-455-1221) rents mountain bikes, canoes and paddleboats. They'll also shuttle you to both ends of the Caprock Canyons Trailway so that you can enjoy the entire trip and not worry about the return journey.

▪ Where to Stay

 Palo Duro National Park Cabins, ☎ 800-792-1112 for information. $$. Two primitive cabins, sleeping four each, stand on the canyon rim. They're inexpensive if you can get a reservation.

Hudspeth House B&B, 1905 4th Ave, Canyon, 79015, ☎ 806-655-9800 or 800-655-9809, www.hudspethinn.com. $$-$$$. Five of the eight rooms come with bedroom fireplaces. It's covered with trees and boasts big, open porches.

Country Home, 8th St, Canyon, 79015, ☎ 800-664-7636, 806-655-7636.

The Rails to Trail Lodge, Caprock Canyons State Park, ☎ 806-455-1344. $$. Three miles to Caprock State Park, it's the closest lodging to the park.

Quitaque Quail Lodge, Hwy 86, Quitaque, 79255, ☎ 806-455-1261. $$-$$$. Spread over 37 acres, this lodge is an adventure in itself. After you enjoy the canyons, you can play in their pool or on their tennis courts.

Hotel Turkey, 3rd and Alexander, Turkey, 79261, ☎ 806-423-1151, www.llano.net/turkey/hotel. $$-$$$. Hotel Turkey was built in 1927 to provide lodging for railroad travelers and salesmen, and has continued to operate since that time. Refurbished between 1989 and 1996, it now operates as a bed and breakfast and as a living museum.

Charles Goodnight, 1836-1929

While many might argue that the incredible Palo Duro Canyon is God's country, historians and locals might waiver a little in their opinion. This was, is, Charles Goodnight country. There's the Goodnight Trading Post and the Goodnight Riding Stables. The Panhandle town where he died in 1929 bears his surname. There are also thousands of enthusiasts, eager to breathe in the days of the Wild West, waiting to eat from chuck wagons, a Goodnight invention that palpably changed the frontier.

Larry McMurtry's Pulitzer-Prize-winning *Lonesome Dove* pays tribute to Goodnight. Captain Call, the reticent and sharp Texas Ranger, is Goodnight's soul. And like Goodnight, Capt. Call was an honorable man. Both Goodnight and his fictional counterpart return their best friends' bodies to Texas for burial.

Goodnight, born in Illinois in 1836, moved to Texas at age 10 and joined the Texas Rangers in 1857. He served the Confederacy during the Civil War and, on his return, took part in a state-wide cattle round-up of roaming herds. His search for a market for the cattle led to a partnership with Oliver Loving, an older rancher who ran a variety of enterprises in East Texas.

The pair then blazed a trail between Belknap, Texas and Fort Sumner, New Mexico, creating the Goodnight-Loving Trail, a stretch that had been little traveled by herds because of its lack of water.

Over time, traffic on their trail picked up, and Goodnight, after Loving's untimely death at the hands of local Indians, expanded its reach to Granada, Colorado.

In 1876 Goodnight tried his hand at a homestead, teaming up with an Irish investor on a ranch near the Palo Duro Canyon. Quickly, the ranch amassed more than a million acres and 100,000 cattle. He sold his ranch late in life, but never slowed. He spent the remainder of his time investing in Mexican mining operations and giving movie production a shot.

His movie didn't quite light up the screens. No one was interested in the real life cowboy that Goodnight portrayed. Goodnight's film didn't have any gun fights, the Indians were often civil and there were no bandits or saloons.

"All in all, my years on the trail were the happiest I ever lived. There were many hardships and dangers, of course, that called on all a man had of endurance and bravery. But when all went well, there was no other life so pleasant. Most of the time we were solitary adventurers in a great land as fresh and new as a spring morning."

West Texas

Texans have to answer a lot of ridiculous questions. About the horse they ride to school and the oil derrick in the back yard. Where they find water to bathe in, let alone swim in. And while the questions might offend the sensibilities of an Austinite or Houstonian, you might just find a West Texan who can tell you straight-faced about how much easier it is at times to ride the horse to his neighbor's house than fire up the pickup.

■ The Land

West Texas is the myth that surrounds the name "Texas," the backdrop for John Wayne and all his stoic crassness. Its varied and harsh topography has shaped a world – with a little help from Hollywood – that believes Texans all chew on straw and are most comfortable astride a mount.

West Texas – the Trans-Pecos region – while rich in history and character, is sparse in terms of population and vegetation. Several counties boast more square miles than residents. And the Chihuahuan Desert, which covers 175,000 square miles of Mexico and the US, claims 30,000 square miles of the Trans-Pecos.

■ History

Experts believe it was only about 4,000 years ago that all of the region was covered by leafy woodlands, making it a relatively young desert.

Up until 1850 no one could really claim West Texas as their own. New Mexico, Chihuahua and Mexican Texas all claimed parts, but the sparseness of the territory and presence of violent Apaches and Comanches kept much of it from being settled. In 1848 Texas finally began its colonization of the area. Railroads brought the first economic boom; oil the second.

On May 28, 1923, the Santa Rita oil well hit pay dirt, changing irrevocably the face of West Texas. Although the area was still susceptible to the busts that follow the booms, much of the Permian Basin still relies on oil as its mainstay.

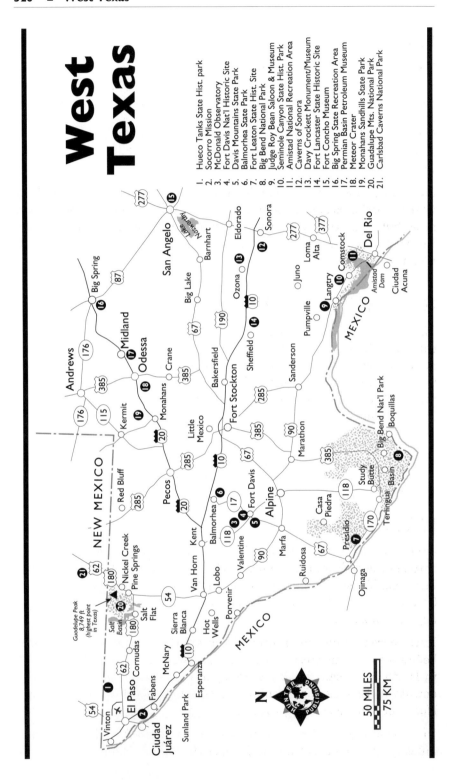

West Texas

1. Hueco Tanks State Hist. park
2. Socorro Mission
3. McDonald Observatory
4. Fort Davis Nat'l Historic Site
5. Davis Mountains State Park
6. Balmorhea State Park
7. Fort Leaton State Hist. Site
8. Big Bend National Park
9. Judge Roy Bean Saloon & Museum
10. Seminole Canyon State Hist. Park
11. Amistad National Recreation Area
12. Caverns of Sonora
13. Davy Crockett Monument/Museum
14. Fort Lancaster State Historic Site
15. Fort Concho Museum
16. Big Spring State Recreation Area
17. Permian Basin Petroleum Museum
18. Meteor Crater
19. Monahans Sandhills State Park
20. Guadalupe Mts. National Park
21. Carlsbad Caverns National Park

■ Logistics

You'll need a car if you're traveling through West Texas. The highway stretches ominously through towns that are a whole gas tank apart in some areas. Pay close attention to your car's maintenance (belts, hoses, etc.) and watch your fuel gauge. If you get stuck, it could be a while before help arrives. Truckers that regularly traverse I-10 and I-20 usually serve as good Samaritans, either offering their own help or calling in for help, but you'll still be a little put out.

Most of the towns are too small for standard airplane service, with El Paso being the exception. Commuter planes fly into the Midland/Odessa area, but that still leaves the vast majority of the area inaccessible. Buses and trains are other options, but you'll have to be on their schedule, not your own.

■ Weather & Climate

The weather is more varied than you might think. Summers are historically hot, there's no way around that. But summer nights can be cool above the desert floor. Winters are mild, on average, but can be wicked when a Canadian front blows through. Storms can quickly sweep the area, so keep an eye out. Afternoon thunderstorms regularly form during late summer.

West Texas

El Paso

■ History

Juan de Onate, a wealthy conquistador, wasn't the first explorer to pass through the El Paso area, but in 1598 he was one of the first to lead a large exhibition. With over 500 colonists, Onate began his journey in Santa Barbara, Chihuahua and crossed the Rio Grande near present-day San Elizario.

It was here that he and his group celebrated Thanksgiving two decades before the Pilgrims crossed the Atlantic, considered the first such event in North America. On May 4 he again crossed the Rio Grande near downtown El Paso, christening the crossing as "El Paso del Rio del Norte" or "the pass across the northern river."

Onate continued his journey all the way to Santa Fe. His path, 1,600 miles long, became El Camino Real, or the "King's Highway." For over

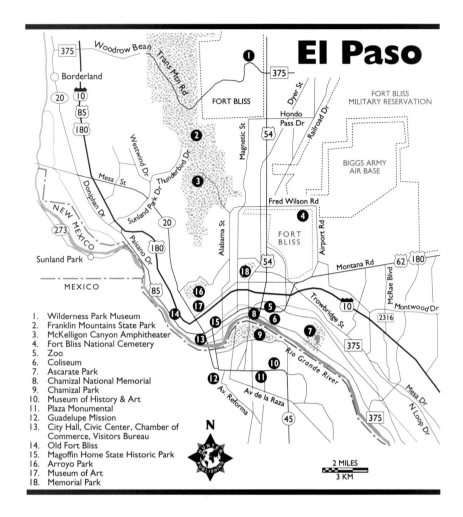

El Paso

1. Wilderness Park Museum
2. Franklin Mountains State Park
3. McKelligon Canyon Amphitheater
4. Fort Bliss National Cemetery
5. Zoo
6. Coliseum
7. Ascarate Park
8. Chamizal National Memorial
9. Chamizal Park
10. Museum of History & Art
11. Plaza Monumental
12. Guadelupe Mission
13. City Hall, Civic Center, Chamber of Commerce, Visitors Bureau
14. Old Fort Bliss
15. Magoffin Home State Historic Park
16. Arroyo Park
17. Museum of Art
18. Memorial Park

200 years, the path remained well-traveled by explorers, merchants and other adventurers.

While Onate's travels laid the groundwork for El Paso, it wasn't until the mid-1600s that the region really saw more colonization, when a mission, Nuestra Senora de Guadalupe, was built. Located in what is today the main plaza of Juárez, it became a primary resting point along the King's Highway. In 1680 a permanent group of Christianized Tigua Indians and Spanish priests landed at the mission, having fled New Mexico in the Pueblo Revolt.

El Paso played no role in the Texas Revolution. It wasn't until Texas entered the Union and the question of a southern boundary arose that El Paso's fate was sealed. The Treaty of Guadalupe Hidalgo, which ended the Mexican War in 1848, named the Rio Grande River the dividing line between Mexico and Texas.

Ironically at the time, the southern half of the settlement in Mexico retained the name El Paso del Norte. To the north, on the US side, the Texas city went through a series of names, including Magoffinsville and Franklin, both for prominent locals. It later settled on El Paso.

El Paso del Norte was renamed in 1888 to honor Mexican President Benito Juárez, who ran his regime from the city and was responsible for ousting the French in 1866 and executing Maximilian. Ciudad Juárez, the city's full name, is most often shortened to just Juárez.

Though the unrest between neighboring countries had been settled, the Wild West was just beginning to flourish, with El Paso, a town of 700, to become one of the wildest and wooliest cities of them all. The river pass that led settlers to its banks in the 1500s served as protection for outlaws and Indian raiders. When the final stretches of the Southern Pacific Railroad passing through the fledgling town were finished in 1881, the population skyrocketed.

Many described the town as "one big brothel." The town earned several nicknames: the Tenderloin, the Zone of Toleration and the Reservation. Attempts to reform the area's prostitution cleaned up about 20% of the town, leaving prostitutes in the other 80%.

Billy the Kid, Wyatt Earp, Bat Masterson and John Wesley Hardin roamed the streets.

John Wesley Hardin

Hardin, gunslinger of legend, drifted to El Paso after spending 15 years in a Huntsville prison. While incarcerated he had earned his law degree, and in El Paso, he put up his shingle. But his errant ways were still intact.

Helen Beulah Mroz was one of the first people to approach Hardin for legal services, wanting him to help her husband, who was accused of hog rustling in New Mexico. Hardin decided he would rather have Beulah than the case and conspired with El Paso lawmen to lure the husband into Texas and then have him killed. His relationship with Beulah didn't last – she left him after he beat her. Hardin was killed in the Acme Saloon in 1895 and is buried downtown in Concordia Cemetery, one space over from Martin Mroz, Beulah's late husband.

El Paso is more about Mexico and its Spanish heritage than skyscrapers and US mega-status. It is considered one with its sister to the south, Ciudad Juárez. It often feels isolated from its own state – closer to the capitals of New Mexico, Arizona and Chihuahua than to the other cities of Texas. It is also the only Texas city in the Mountain Time Zone – throwing normal business activity off by an hour. It gets even crazier during daylight savings, when El Paso observes the change, while Juárez does not.

Its food borders on New Mexican, rather than the Tex-Mex the rest of the state prefers. New Mexican cuisine borders on too-hot-for-visitors, relying heavily on very spicy peppers, including jalapeños. Tex-Mex, though spicy, is a bit heavier, using thick, rich sauces, beans, cheeses, sour cream and guacamole.

Mexican cobbled streets are commonplace, though often disguised by a thin layer of asphalt. You're more likely to hear Spanish than English in many places – a quick radio scan will tell you as much.

El Paso is now a hub of activity for both the military and for *maquiladoras* (factories run by US companies), who use the city as an entry point for their Mexican enterprises. If you like sun, El Paso is your place, boasting that it is the sunshine capital of the state. Sitting amid a desert, El Paso sees more extreme temperatures than many of its neighbors. But the natives will tell you with a smirk that it's dry heat, which gives some consolation.

Rosa's Cantina

Out in the West Texas town of El Paso
I fell in love with a Mexican girl
Nighttime would find me at Rosa's Cantina
Music would play and Faleena would whirl.

This song by country singer Marty Robbins, inspired by a brief glimpse of an obscure cantina seemingly on the edge of the world, is what many remember about El Paso. It is what brings travelers from Australia and Europe to Rosa's Cantina in the middle of nowhere on Hwy 80. While the song was inspired by a moment and written in a heartbeat, its lyrics are indicative of the spirit of the town that lies at the westernmost point of Texas, flush with the Rio Grande.

■ Touring

Rosa's Cantina (3454 Doniphan West, ☎ 915-833-0402) has been close to shutting down for several years, so there's no guarantee it'll be around in the future. What used to be a busy area has seen traffic tailing off as new, more efficient thoroughfares take their place in El Paso. It's not much to look at but you can enjoy good karma and food.

Although El Paso isn't known to be artistically oriented, a wide array of museums dot the area. **The Americana Museum** (5 Civic Center Plaza, ☎ 915-542-4511) has dedicated itself to the study of American and Pre-Columbian history, with a substantial portion of its permanent work centered around the pottery of the region. They also host eight to 10 traveling shows a year.

The **Bridge Center For Contemporary Arts** (127 Pioneer Plaza, ☎ 915-532-6707), a non-profit gallery, focuses on contemporary and experimental art by both emerging and nationally recognized artists.

The US Border Patrol has played a significant role in El Paso's tumultuous past – from the days of classic gunslingers to today as one of the busiest border crossings. The **Border Patrol Museum** (4315 Transmountain Rd, ☎ 915-759-6060) includes displays of airplanes and vehicles used by the patrol, surveillance equipment, confiscated items and more.

The **Camino Real Paseo Del Norte Hotel** (101 S El Paso St, ☎ 800-769-4300, 915-534-3000) may not be an official museum, but you shouldn't miss it. Originally built in 1912 and listed on the National Historical Register, the hotel has hosted notable guests like Pancho Villa, President William Taft and "Blackjack Pershing." The 80-year-old Tiffany glass dome, once gracing the hotel's lobby, is now the showpiece of the exquisite Dome Bar.

Two other museums of interest are the **El Paso Museum of Art** (1211 Montana, ☎ 915-541-4040), which displays both European and American masterpieces, along with Mexican Colonial art, and the **El Paso Museum of History** (12901 Gateway West, ☎ 915-858-1928), which began as the Cavalry Museum. It has since changed its role to tracing the history of El Paso and the colorful parts that Indians, conquistadors, vaqueros, cowboys and cavalrymen played in settling the Southwest. The museum, because of its start, is still rich with exhibits of weapons, uniforms and saddles.

Another place to trace the history of the Southwest is at the **Centennial Museum** (Wiggins and University, University of Texas El Paso campus, ☎ 915-747-5565, www.utep.edu/museum), built in 1936 as part of the state's centennial celebration. Among other things, there are over 600 glass plate negatives from the late 1800s depicting Southwestern life throughout the region. There are also rotating collections of photographs, folk art and paintings on the human and natural history of the region.

If you're already at the museum, you will definitely enjoy the **University of Texas at El Paso's** campus. What began in 1913 as the State School of Mines and Metallurgy is now a part of the UT system, boasting six colleges and a graduate school program. The architecture, reminiscent of the lamaseries in the Himalayan kingdom of Bhutan, is the only example of its kind in the Western Hemisphere. Apparently, the wife of the first dean, who was charged with some of UTEPs construction, saw pictures of Bhutan in a 1914 issue of *National Geographic* and was inspired.

The **Chamizal National Museum and Memorial** (800 S San Marcial, ☎ 915-534-6668) commemorates the peaceful settlement of a Texas/Mexico border dispute after decades of disagreement. It is built on the land that became part of the US. Displays and films trace the history of the dispute and artwork from both Mexico and the US are on exhibit. A 500-seat theater, used frequently for special events, acts as the centerpiece for the complex.

Indian Cliffs Ranch (I-10 east 30 miles, north on FM 793, ☎ 915-544-3200) is as much contrived as it is historical, offering a full day's adventure with trail rides and overnight accommodations in Fort Misery, a frontier fort replica. There's also an Indian maze, movie sets, the Fort Apache playground for kids and hay rides on Sunday. Dinner at **Cattleman's Steakhouse** (☎ 915-544-3200, www.CattlemansSteakHouse.com), an El Paso favorite, rounds out the activities.

John Wesley Hardin, after meeting his match, took up residency at the **Concordia Cemetery** (north of IH-10, Hwy 54 intersection), El Paso's version of "Boot Hill." His grave lies among those of other pioneers, lawmen and outlaws.

The military today serves as one of El Paso's largest employers. **Fort Bliss** (Slater Rd, ☎ 915-568-4505/4601), the largest air defense center in the world, was originally founded in 1849 to keep the Indians in check and was named after Lt. Col. William Wallace Smith Bliss. It has had to move on five occasions – the fickle Rio Grande kept changing course and sending the camp underwater. The last move was instigated by the railroad barons, who used their influence to lay track smack dab through the middle of the installation.

There are four museums on base, including the **Fort Bliss Replica Museum** (Building 600, ☎ 915-568-4518), which displays adobe models of Fort Bliss as it looked in 1854, and the **US Army Air Defense Museum** (Building 5000, ☎ 915-568-5412), which traces the histories of different weapon systems.

Thoroughbreds and quarter horses run October through May at **Sunland Park Racetrack** (Sunland Park Dr west five miles off I-10, ☎ 505-589-1131), with inter-track wagering mid-May to October at Sunland Park in New Mexico.

A 27-foot-high replica of Christ adorns a 4,500-foot peak just across the border in New Mexico. **Sierra del Cristo Rey** (Sunland Park exit off I-10 to Doniphan) inspires thousands of pilgrims to hike the 2½-mile trail to its base. Carved of Cordova cream limestone, the figure is just like the one that looks out over Rio de Janeiro, Brazil.

✳ Take Care!

Authorities warn visitors not to make the ascent of Sierra del Cristo Rey in small numbers – thieves have been known to stalk hikers along the mountain's paths.

Perhaps the truest representation of El Paso's, and the Southwest's, heritage, can be enjoyed by visiting the **Tigua Indian Reservation** (119 S Old Pueblo Rd off Alameda). Operating what they deem a "living history pueblo," the Tigua tribe, which fled New Mexico in the Pueblo Revolt of 1681 and numbers around 600 residents, shows visitors aspects of their daily life, including dancing, cooking and pottery-making. The **Ysleta Mission** (☎ 915-859-9848) was founded the same year the Tigua came to El Paso. Floods and fires have periodically destroyed the actual church. The current church was built in 1908. When it was christened, the mission lay to the south of the Rio Grande. Over time the riverbed migrated south of the mission, landing it in Texas territory.

Several other Spanish missions grace the upper regions of the Rio Grande Valley and are older than the better-known missions in California and the Baja.

Nuestra Senora de la Concepcion del Socorro is another mission gained when the Rio Grande changed its course. Established in 1682 by the Piros, Thanos and Jemes Indians, the mission was moved early on when a group of Indians threatened to revolt.

Daily mass still takes place at the **San Elizario Presidio Chapel** (FM 258 south). A latecomer (established in 1777) compared to its sister missions, the chapel was originally used by the Spanish military and government.

Tour Operator

An easy way to explore all of the missions, including the Tigua Reservation, is to catch a **Mission Tour** (departs from Civic Center, ☎ 915-544-0062 for details), which visits all of the missions, allowing time at each for the myriad activities.

Information Sources

For more information on El Paso and the areas surrounding the city, call the **El Paso Convention and Visitors Bureau** (One Civic Plaza, ☎ 800-351-6024, 915-534-0696, www.elpasocvb.com). Or contact the **El Paso Civic, Convention and Tourism Department** (☎ 800-351-6024, One Civic Center Plaza, 79901, www.elpasocvb.com). Other sites that may guide you during your visit include www.elpasotexas.com and www.citi-guide.com/ep-index.htm.

■ Mexico

For a real taste of El Paso you should cross the border and envelope yourself in a different culture.

✳ Take Care!

While El Pasoans do consider El Paso and Juárez one city, remember that Juárez is a foreign country with a foreign government and police system that do not answer to your local congressman. If you don't respect their laws, you could find yourself in a heck of a bind.

Traditional bullfights are held in the spring and summer at the **Plaza Monumental Bullring** (Paseo Triunfo de la Republica #4630, one block from the Rio Grande Mall). Matches last about two hours. On hot days pay extra for tickets on the shady side of the arena – it will be worth it. Tickets can be purchased at the **International Hotel** (113 W Missouri, ☎ 915-544-3300) in downtown El Paso and transportation from El

Paso can be arranged through **Rancho Grande Tours** (☎ 915-771-6661).

Greyhound racing at the **Juárez Racetrack** (off Av. 16 de Septiembre, east of bullring) is billed as some of the best in the world. The racetrack, considered the Taj Mahal of tracks because its grandstand is enclosed and air-conditioned, is open year round, Wednesday through Sunday.

■ Adventures on Foot

World-class rock climbers flock to **Hueco Tanks State Park** (32 miles northeast of El Paso on Hwy 62, ☎ 915-857-1135, www.tpwd.state.tx.us/park/hueco), named for the large rock basins (huecos, pronounced "way-coes") that have collected rainwater for thousands of years and provided sustenance for natives and travelers.

Apaches, Kiowas and Comanches were all drawn to the area, leaving behind pictographs, some dating back to an estimated 1500 BC. Experts believe there are about 2,000 different pictographs scattered among the rocks and caves of the 860-acre park.

Rock climbers find the small huecos, which were used as water-saving devices for the Indians, perfect for hand and foot-holds. The winter months, October to May, are usually the best; the Chihuahuan Desert can make the stones painfully hot during peak summer hours.

The park is criss-crossed with official and unofficial trails – don't feel obligated to follow the suggested hiking routes. It's difficult to get lost here. You don't have to be a climber to appreciate Hueco Tanks. Other options include picnicking, camping, hiking and studying the 2,000 pictographs. There's also an old ranch house (now an interpretive center) and the ruins of a stagecoach station. Guided tours are available on weekends.

The **Franklin Mountain State Park** (☎ 915-566-6441) is a relatively new addition to El Paso, even though the city surrounds the mountain range on three sides. All 37 square miles of it

Franklin Mountain State Park.

are within the El Paso city limits. While the mountains are not huge, they afford an exquisite view of El Paso, Juárez and deep into Mexico. Indians that inhabited the range for more than 122,000 years before being forced out by American colonization, left colorful pictographs as historical footnotes. You can enjoy these Indian artifacts along 22 miles of equestrian trails, 51 miles of mountain bike trails and 52 miles of nature trails. Camping permits can be obtained at the park.

Two favorite hiking trips are to the north: **Mount Franklin** peak and **Anthony's Nose**, the second highest peak in the range that curiously resembles a facial profile. Both are very strenuous climbs and should not be attempted by the unprepared or out-of-shape.

McKelligon Canyon (McKelligon Rd off Alabama, ☎ 915-565-6900) is located on the north side of El Paso and in the middle of the Franklin Mountains. A sheer cliff acts as the backdrop for a natural amphitheater where **Viva! El Paso** is routinely staged, a summer drama that traces El Paso's heritage through its blend of Spanish, Mexican, Indian and Western colonization.

■ Where to Stay

Camino Real Paseo del Norte Hotel, 101 South El Paso St, 79901, ☎ 915-534-3000, 800-769-4300, www.caminoreal.com. $$$-$$$$. This landmark hotel, built in 1912, has been completely refurbished and includes two restaurants, a lounge, a disco and an outdoor heated pool. (Some executive suites top $900/night.)

Cowboys & Indians Board & Bunk, 405 Mountain Vista, Santa Teresa, NM, 88008, ☎ 505-589-2653, www.softaid.net/cowboys. $$. Located 25 minutes from downtown El Paso, just in New Mexico. A Western hacienda with four guest rooms, each with private baths and patios, queen-size beds, coffee makers and outside entrances. Served up with a full breakfast.

Fort Bliss Inn, 1744 Victory Lane, 79916, ☎ 915-565-7777. $. Basic amenities next to Fort Bliss.

Hilton Hotel, 2027 Airway Blvd, 79925, ☎ 915-778-4241, 800-742-7248, www.kvia.com/ephilton.htm. $$-$$$$. Luxury amenities, including a health club with sauna and Jacuzzi and free daily newspaper. Executive facilities include hors d'oeuvres and private exercise rooms.

La Hacienda Airport Inn, 6400 Montana Avenue, 79925, ☎ 915-772-4231, 800-772-4231. $-$$. Centrally located just a mile from the airport, they offer all modern and standard amenities.

Sunset Heights Bed & Breakfast, 717 W Yandell Dr, 79902, ☎ 915-544-1743, www.SunsetHeights.com. $$-$$$$. The Victorian-style 1905 B&B sits in the city's Sunset Heights Historic District, a turn-of-the-century charmer. The third story can be used for conferences and breakfasts ranging between five and eight courses. There's also a swimming pool and outdoor fireplace.

■ Where to Eat

 Avila's, 10600 Montana and 6232 N Mesa, ☎ 915-598-3333, 915-584-3621. Serving hearty Mexican food for 40 years to the people of El Paso, these two restaurants are still family-owned and -operated. Everything is wonderful.

Billy Crews, 1200 Country Club Rd, ☎ 505-589-2071. Don't let the "Billy" deceive you. Billy Crew's has been famous for fine dining since 1956. It has been ranked as one of the top 10 steakhouses in the US by *Wine Spectator* magazine and boasts over 1,500 wine choices.

The Bistro, 7500 N Mesa in the Promenade Center, ☎ 915-584-5757. Offering what they call "creative cuisine," the menu includes fresh seafood, a unique steak selection, poultry, pasta and great weekly chef's specials.

Café Central, 109 N Oregon (One Texas Court), ☎ 915-545-CAFE, www.kvia.com/cafecent. The baby grand sets the mood. The menu changes, but is likely to include continental, Northern Italian and grilled dishes.

Casa Jurado, 226 Cincinnati (near UTEP), ☎ 915-532-6429 and 4772 Doniphan, ☎ 915-833-1151. Try one of the six different enchilada dishes or the mango margaritas.

Cattleman's Steakhouse, 35 minutes east of downtown, I-10 east to the Fabens, north five miles, ☎ 915-544-3200, www.Cattlemans SteakHouse.com. It's not just dinner (though it has consistently been voted the best steakhouse and restaurant in El Paso); it's also a movie set, a roving longhorn herd and an unforgettable experience.

Delhi Palace, 1160 Airway, ☎ 915-772-9334. In a town that embraces Mexican food with a death grip, the Indian cuisine can lend balance to your stay. Great vegetarian specialties.

Doc's Bar-B-Que, 9511 Viscount, ☎ 915-593-DOCS. You can enjoy Doc's delicious barbecue on their home turf or at the Viva El Paso Production that takes place in McKelligon Canyon during the summer.

Doña Lupe Café, 2919 Pershing, ☎ 915-566-9833 or 564-9467. For over 45 years, and since 1978 at this location, Lupe Armijo has prepared all her meals from the freshest ingredients. Her signature chile sauce and chile rellenos keep business brisk.

Great American Land & Cattle Co, 7600 Alabama, ☎ 915-751-5300 and 600 Valley Chile Rd, I-10 at the Anthony on the TX/NM state line exit, ☎ 915-886-4690, www.grtamerican.com. Everything's served "family style," from two-lb T-bones to top sirloin and chicken-fried steak.

Griggs Restaurants, 9007 Montana Ave, ☎ 915-598-3451. For a change of pace, try the hotter New Mexican cuisine that Grigg's has been serving up for over 50 years.

Michelino's Italian Restaurant, 3615 Rutherglen, ☎ 915-592-1700. Standard Italian fare that has been recognized throughout its 20 years as some of the best in El Paso.

Renelli's Italian Gourmet Bistro, 7500 N Mesa in the Promenade Center, ☎ 915-585-9562, www.citi-guide.com/renellis. Northern Italian cuisine with a Mediterranean twist. Gourmet pizzas are baked in their wood-burning stove.

Shogun Japanese Restaurant, 1201 Airway Blvd, ☎ 915-775-1282. Reservations are recommended at El Paso's first Japanese restaurant, which now includes a sushi bar. The chefs perform inches away.

The State Line, 1222 Sunland Park Dr, one mile south of I-10, ☎ 915-581-3371. El Paso natives take their guests here for a step back in time and what they claim are the best beef ribs in town. There are all-you-can-eat platters for the indecisive and the hungry.

The Northern Reaches

Pine Springs

■ History

Pine Springs, close to nowhere, with a population just over 5,000, saw its heyday back in the mid-1850s when it was a station stop on the Butterfield Overland Mail Route. Crumbling ruins are left to mark the town's lively history.

Pine Springs, for which the town is named, flowed freely for Indians and passengers on the Overland trail. However, in 1931 an earthquake shifted a local fault line and the spring ran dry.

■ Adventures on Foot

For all its smallness, Pine Springs is the last stop before the Guadalupe Mountains National Park and it is just across the border from New Mexico's famous Carlsbad Caverns.

The **Guadalupe Mountains National Park** (Hwy 62, one mile east, ☎ 915-828-3251, www.aqd.nps.gov/grd/parks/gumo) is the centerpiece for the majestic mountain range that rises from the desert like a mirage. The range's barren, arid outer stretches keep its forested interior hidden from the observer. Once within its confines, you'll find rich pockets of ponderosa pine, aspen, maple, madrona and mountain juniper. You are as likely to spot an elk or fox as you are a coyote.

The highest point in Texas – at 8,749 feet – is contained in the Guadalupe Mountains on Guadalupe Peak.

> ## ✳ Take Care!
>
> The first thing you need to do before attempting any kind of Guadalupe Mountain adventure is get yourself prepared. Facilities and services are extremely limited near and in the park. The nearest gas and service stations are 30 miles west or 35 miles east. You'll need to stock up on food as well.

More than 80 miles of trails offer hiking, backpacking and horseback riding (there are some limitations for horses). There are 10 backcountry campgrounds – to really get the flavor of the Guadalupe Mountains, you'll want to go far into the interior.

More than a half of the park's 86,000+ acres is designated wildnerness – which means there's no development. It is where, according to the 1964 Wildnerness Act, "man himself is a visitor."

The **Guadalupe Peak Trail** is considered a strenuous day hike, but it lands you on the highest peak in Texas. On a clear day, the 8.4-mile round-trip will be well worth the view. Be sure to watch out for quickly approaching thunderstorms and high winds.

The **Bowl Trail**, at 9.1 miles round-trip, is another strenuous day trip, taking you through a conifer forest that has been recovering since a 1990

El Capitan, Guadalupe Mountains National Park.

wildfire ravaged pieces of the bowl. There are many more trails to explore. Stop by the ranger station to pick up trail guides and get up-to-date information.

✱ Take Care!

The park service recommends only experienced and well-equipped hikers take on the strenuous trips. A backcountry permit is required for all overnight trips.

While **Carlsbad Caverns National Park** (US 62 north 35 miles, ☎ 505-785-2233) isn't actually in Texas, it's close enough for Texans to enjoy on a regular basis. Don't miss an opportunity to see some of the world's most breathtaking caverns.

Pecos

■ History

Pecos was originally a stop on the Texas & Pacific Railroad line and quickly earned a reputation for rowdy cowboys and gun slinging lawmen. Outlaw Clay Allison, who terrorized people in Texas and New

Mexico, tried to settle in Pecos in 1880 and become a rancher. A year later he was killed when he fell off his wagon, a wheel crushing his head.

▪ Touring

Allison is buried in the **West-of-the-Pecos Museum and Park** (120 E 1st St, ☎ 915-445-5076), which is intent on preserving the Old West. The Orient Hotel, built in 1904 and touted in its time as "the best hotel between Fort Worth and El Paso," is the cornerstone of the complex that boasts over 30 rooms filled with exhibits about Texas life ranging from forms of transportation to a hanging tree. There's also substantial material about the rodeo. Pecos claims to be home to the world's first rodeo. On July 4, 1883, cowboys from area ranches got together for some steer roping and bronc riding to decide who was the superior ranch hand. Pecos hosts a rodeo every Fourth of July, the **West of the Pecos Rodeo** (☎ 915-445-2406), reenacting the 1883 historic event, though they've added crowd-pleasers like the wild cow milking contest and the wild mare race.

Maine lobster, Swiss cheese, Pecos cantaloupe? It may sound a little far-fetched for a town just over 10,000 in population and tucked away in West Texas hundreds of miles from anywhere. But if you know canteloupe, then you know Pecos is home to some of the finest. In the middle of the harvest (late July to September) there's even a festival to honor the almighty canteloupe. Up to 13½ million cantaloupes are shipped across the nation each year. Their special sweetness is credited to a combination of hot sun, dry air and alkaline soil.

Information Sources

For more information call the **Pecos Chamber of Commerce** (111 S Cedar, PO Box 27, 79772, ☎ 915-445-2406). Visit www.texasusa.com/pecos for an on-line view of Pecos events and offerings.

▪ Where to Stay

Quality Inn, 4002 S Cedar, 79772, ☎ 800-332-5255, 915-445-5404. $$. All amenities are included in the 96-room hotel, with a restaurant and outdoor pool.

■ Where to Eat

 The Jersey Lilly Steakhouse, 500 S Cedar, ☎ 915-445-7458. It takes its moniker from Lillie Langtry, the Jersey Lily, serving up steaks and Mexican fare.

"West of the Pecos"

Much of Texas lore hinges on the phrase "West of the Pecos." Pecos, Texas hosts a West of the Pecos Rodeo. Judge Roy Bean of Langtry claimed to be the "Law West of the Pecos."

The Pecos River demarcated the invisible line between civilization and frontier. If you were to cross the Pecos and travel west, you would be going into lawless territory. The brackish, alkaline river that starts over 200 miles into New Mexico before winding through West Texas, dumps itself into the Rio Grande just east of Langtry.

A common phrase at the time, to "Pecos" someone, meant to kill a person and then dump the body in a river.

Today, the Pecos River barely resembles its former self. Its wildness has been lost through both damming and agricultural draining.

Monahans

■ History

Created as a water stop by the Texas & Pacific Railroad back in 1881, the tiny community of Monahans' lifeblood is oil and gas.

> ✸ *Did You Know?*
>
> In order to take full advantage of all the oil in town, residents drill at a slant to get at all those hard-to-reach places beneath area buildings, including city hall and the courthouse.

Monahans owes its name to John Thomas Monahans, a surveyor for Texas & Pacific, who found water – a commodity in that part of the state – beneath its arid surface. Today the town serves as an oil and cattle financial center for more than 800 square miles.

Monahans Sandhills State Park.

■ Touring

The **Monahans Sandhills State Park** (I-20 east to Park Rd 41, ☎ 915-943-2092) is an anomaly, boasting two distinctly different features within its 3,840-acre site. Sand dunes, some up to 70 feet high, are buffeted by one of the nation's largest oak forests. The oak trees – Harvard oaks – aren't standard fare, though. They seldom grow over three feet high, while their roots meander 90 feet below the earth's surface. So if you're expecting the Redwood Forest, you'll be disappointed.

The acorns that the forest of oak produce support the desert wildlife. Visitors will find exhibits at the park headquarters that document the types of animal and plant life, as well as the historical, geological and archeological make-up of the sandhills area.

For the adventurer, rent a disk for **sandsurfing** on the park's many dunes. There are RV hookups, camping sites and a picnic area.

The dunes contained in the park are just a small portion of a sandy oasis that stretches 200 miles north into New Mexico.

During the midday heat, visit the **Million Barrel Museum** (US 80E at Leon, 1½ miles east of town, ☎ 915-943-8401). Built around a hole in the ground, the museum might sound like a sleeper. But the hole played a significant role in the area's oil heyday. Shell Oil built the hole – a 522 x

425-foot oil tank – in 1928 when a nearby gusher was flowing wildly and storage space was needed.

The monstrous tank helped, but it began to leak. It was abandoned when pipelines were developed. In addition to schooling visitors on the oil industry, the museum includes exhibits on the railroad and area agriculture. Several buildings in the complex are of special interest: the area's first county jail, a 5,000-seat covered amphitheater and the Holman Hotel, a Texas Historic Landmark built in 1904 that catered to the Monahans-Fort Stockton Stage Line in the early 1900s. The museum is considered one of the better oil museums in the country.

The **Rattlesnake Bomber Base Museum** (Pyote, 15 miles west of town, ☎ 915-389-5691) is not about rattlesnakes but bombers. During World War II the small base was a major B-17 and B-29 training facility and was home, at one point, to the *Enola Gay*, the famous bomber that dropped the first atomic bomb on Hiroshima.

The museum is within a county park that offers swimming, a three-hole golf course, tennis and overnight camping.

Information Sources

Call the **Monahans Chamber of Commerce** (☎ 915-943-2187, 401 S. Dwight, 79756) for more information.

■ Where to Stay

Best Western Colonial Inn, IH-20 at TX 18, ☎ 800-528-1234, 915-943-4345. $-$$. Over 90 rooms, with a restaurant and outdoor pool.

Howard Johnson Motel, 806 I-20W, ☎ 800-446-4656. $$. Amenities include free newspaper and coffee and an outdoor heated pool.

■ Where to Eat

Leal's Restaurant, 114 W Sealy Ave, ☎ 915-943-6870. Serving Tex-Mex for over 15 years, it's one of the town's mainstays for lunch and dinner.

K-Bob's Steak House, 901 S Stockton St, ☎ 915-943-7498. It's a chain, but it still serves up good Texas steaks and burgers.

Odessa

■ History

The Permian Basin – 250 miles wide and 300 miles long – was formed during the Permian Period, about 280 million years ago. It began as a sea filled with marine life and plants. As it dried up, the decaying plants and animals formed the basis for the giant pools of oil and gas that are found today.

Early settlers knew little about the land they chose to call home, culling only its top layers and establishing farming and cattle trades. It wasn't until the 1920s, 40 years after the railroad made Odessa a permanent stop on its trek across Texas, that oil was discovered and Odessa's course took a sharp turn. Experts believe the city of 90,000 contains more oil field apparatus than any other city in the world.

The fairy tale version of how Odessa got its name includes an Indian princess who wandered into the nearby railroad camp. The more accepted version suggests that Russian workers laying track for the Texas & Pacific Railroad chose the name because it looked much like the area of their homeland in the Ukraine with the same name.

■ Touring

 While Midland serves as the administrative arm of the Permian Basin, Odessa is its heart, providing service, the work force, transportation, supplies and manufacturing for the Basin that produces nearly 20% of the nation's crude oil, natural gas and other gas liquids.

Despite its reputation as a roughneck capital, Odessa has taken great pains to maintain a wide-ranging array of cultural activities.

The **Art Institute for the Permian Basin** (4909 E University, Permian Basin campus, ☎ 915-368-7222) showcases work by both regional artists and traveling exhibits. Many of its works, called "ultramodern" by some, will surprise you if you're expecting traditional Southwestern art. Its gentle mix of old and new keeps the Institute a modern force inline with big city artistry.

The **Presidential Museum** (622 N Lee, ☎ 915-332-7123) is another anomaly in this oil town, as the only museum in the nation dedicated exclusively to the President's office, including the study of constitutional government and the elective process. The Dishong collection accents the aura of the First Lady, with miniature replicas of each one in her inaugural gown. There's also campaign trivia, historical documents and the John Ben Sheppard Library of the Presidents.

Shakespeare lovers will be happy to find a bastion for the famous playmaker at the **Globe of the Great Southwest Theatre and Anne Hathaway Cottage** (2308 Shakespeare Rd, Odessa College, ☎ 915-332-1586). The replica of the Globe Theatre plays host to Shakespeare productions in addition to community performances and entertainment. Each March and April bring the Odessa Shakespeare Festival, with May including a Renaissance Festival.

The cottage, named after Shakespeare's wife, mirrors the original in Shottery, England with four antique-filled rooms and an open-fire stove.

Even more artistic design can be found at the **Ellen Noel Art Museum** (4909 E University, University of Texas of the Permian Basin campus, ☎ 915-368-7222), which boasts a permanent sculpture garden and rotating exhibits of historical and contemporary works.

Pictures of the **White-Pool House** (112 E Murphy, ☎ 915-333-4072) were used to lure settlers to the area. Charles White and his family built their house, designed to resemble their home back in Indiana, in 1887. Today it is Odessa's oldest structure. Different areas in the house are furnished with pieces from different decades, spanning the 1880s to the 1920s.

Not only was the area part of a monstrous sea so many centuries ago, there is lasting evidence of meteorite crashes between 20,000 and 30,000 years ago, with a **Meteor Crater** just west of town off US 20. Some 550 feet across and six feet deep, the crater is the second largest in the nation and the sixth largest in the world. Smaller craters surround the main one and iron from the estimated 1,000-ton meteor remains there today.

The **world's largest jackrabbit** (Texans have a thing about making sure they always earn that distinction), a sculpture at the corner of 8th St and Sam Houston, would shame the real pint-sized critter. Standing eight feet high, Mr. Jackrabbit is a popular photo stop.

Real live critters can be found at **Prairie Pete Park** (Sherwood Park), a prairie dog town open for curious onlookers. The park includes a playground and picnic tables to complete the afternoon hotspot.

Unique gifts can be found all around. The **Midessa Porcelain Doll Factory** (4209 South County Rd 1290, ☎ 915-563-5557) sprawls across more than 5,000 square feet, with dolls, furniture, kits and supplies.

The **Pecans International Grove** (☎ 915-367-6119) boasts a gourmet kitchen where the grove's products are glazed and packaged fresh.

If you're looking for an extended, rugged frontier-type vacation, call the **K-Bar Ranch Hunting Lodge** (south of town, ☎ 915-580-5880), where guides provide entertainment and grub for between one and four days. The owner says that, while there's not much water, there are "really good people and sky out the wazoo." A German visitor, overhearing the conversation, piped in that sunsets in Hawaii have nothing on the K-Bar.

Once guests that stay in a 12-bed bunkhouse know where the "icebox" is, they're on their own for the little things. Honeymooners are not allowed (right now) because privacy is too hard to come by at the homestead.

There is seasonal hunting for white-tail, quail, dove and ducks, and year-round hunting for exotics. The ranch always has between 15 and 20 exotic species on hand.

If you're just along for the ride and hunting's not your game, you can hunt for fossils, learn to shoot a gun and watch the ranch hands at work. There are bed and breakfast options, as well. Having only opened its doors to the public in the early 1990s, the K-Bar Ranch has already played host to a number of world travelers. They boast that 80% of their visitors become repeat customers.

West Texas

Information Sources

You can contact the **Odessa Chamber of Commerce** for more information (700 N Grant, 79760, ☎ 915-332-9111, www.odessachamber.com).

■ Where to Stay

K-Bar Ranch Hunting Lodge. Call for directions, ☎ 915-580-5880. $$-$$$$. An adventure on its own. See *Touring,* above, for more details.

Mellie Van Horn's Place, 903 North Sam Houston, 79761, ☎ 915-337-3000. $$. A former boarding house for school teachers, this inn offers 16 rooms and a dining area that can seat up to 55.

Rodeway Inn, 2505 E 2nd, 79761, ☎ 800-228-5160, 915-333-1528. $. Basic amenities, with children under 10 staying for free.

Radisson, 5200 E University, 79762, ☎ 800-333-3333, 915-368-5885. $$-$$$$. From middle-of-the road to luxury suites, the Radisson offers airport transportation, health club guest memberships and a heated outdoor pool and jacuzzi.

■ Where to Eat

 The Barn Door and Pecos Depot, 2140 N Grant, ☎ 915-337-4142. The modern Barn Door specializes in steak, with seafood and Tex-Mex items sprinkled throughout the menu. The Pecos Depot Lounge, attached to the restaurant, is Pecos' original Santa Fe Railroad depot, built in 1892.

Dos Amigos, 47th and Golder, ☎ 915-368-7556. Once a month this horse-barn-turned-Tex-Mex restaurant hosts bull rides. Its outdoor stage pulls in top name entertainers.

Mellie Van Horn's Place, 903 North Sam Houston, ☎ 915-337-3000. This inn doubles as a fantastic lunch time restaurant. In 1996 it was voted best new restaurant in Odessa.

Midland

■ History

There's beauty in Midland – in its remoteness, in its pockets of green, in its vast sunsets streaked with yellow and orange and red – but you have to be open to finding it. Because it's also flat, gray and dusty.

Located at the midway point between Fort Worth and El Paso – thus its first name "Midway," which was later changed to "Midland" – it was also a crossroads of famous trails: the Comanche War Trail, the Chihuahua Trail and the Emigrant Trail to California. It began as a farming community, settled by conservative, solid citizens from the Ohio River Valley and the Great Lakes region – much different from the rest of the West, which was more a haven for the wild, woolly and rambunctious.

By 1880, about 300 families called the community home and lived peacefully on area farms and ranches. Despite its quiet nature – which it retains today – Midland was the victim of the last Comanche raid into Texas before the tribe acquiesced to US rule.

The big change for Midland came in the 1920s when oil was discovered in the Permian Basin. While Midland didn't actually discover oil in its own county until 1945, the town became the administrative hub for the oil industry that moved into the area, housing over 150 oil companies. Between 1920 and 1960, the population of Midland doubled each decade, going through the booms and busts that characterized the volatile industry.

In booms, high-rises began dotting the downtown skyline. It is the tall city in the flat plains – austere and self-possessed. Midland shares an odd relationship with Odessa, its sister to the west, the blue collar worker of the pair. Both towns compete for bragging rights and one-up each other for social distinction. However, to the outsider, they are a pair.

One of Midland's claim to fame was a baby girl trapped in a well for days on end. Baby Jessica captured the hearts of America and gave Midland its 10 seconds in the world's spotlight. But don't mention Miss Jessica to the locals – most can't stomach any more about her and are apt to roll their eyes at you.

■ Touring

The **Museum of the Southwest** (1705 W Missouri, ☎ 915-683-2882 or 570-7770, www.museumsw.org), situated in a 1934 oil family's home that takes up an entire block, is dedicated to the preservation of Southwestern art and culture. In addition to traveling exhibits that change every six weeks on average, it is the permanent home for other pieces, including contemporary sculpture by Allan Houser and Doug Hyde. The complex also includes the **Marion West Blakemore Planetarium** and the **Fredda Turner Durham Children's Museum**, which provides a hands-on, interactive place for the kids.

The Midland Man

The Midland Man is now 22,000 years old and counting. Calling the **Midland County Museum** (301 W Missouri, ☎ 915-688-8947) home, a reproduction – the real one is kept safely locked up – of the Midland Man's skull (actually a woman's) was found on Scharbauer Ranch south of town. It provides evidence that woman (and man) inhabited the area at least 22,000 years ago.

The museum also showcases a hodgepodge of other regional artifacts that include the death masks of Butch Cassidy, Jesse James and Bob Ford, James' killer.

The **Confederate Air Force Flying Museum** (9600 Wright Drive, Midland International Airport, ☎ 915-563-1000, www.avdigest.com/aahm/aahm.html) should not be missed by war or aviation buffs. Displaying the most complete collection of flyable World War II aircraft, the museum's main goal is still to acquire and restore historic representatives of aviation history. **The Confederate Airforce** (CAF) maintains over 130 different planes from the US, Britain, Germany and Japan, showing about 20 of them at a time. They are rotated quarterly.

Flying demonstrations take place at the annual Airshow in October, re-enacting everything from Pearl Harbor to the final battles over the Pacific. Visitors have ringside seats for the display of aircraft and the pyrotechnics (☎ 800-CAF-SHOW for information). There's also a flight simulator if you'd like to experience the thrill of flying.

The Pliska Aircraft

This airplane hangs from the ceiling of the Midland Regional Airport. Thought to be the first aircraft constructed and flown in Texas, it was built by Midlanders John Pliska and Gary Coggins just two years after the Wright Brothers' adventure at Kitty Hawk. The entrepreneurs convinced cowboys to pay admission to see their contraption fly in Odessa, but they had to flee when the plane failed and the disappointed fans demanded their money back. The pair rescued the plane under the cloak of darkness, but supposedly never flew again.

Since oil is the body and soul of Midland, a trip to the **Permian Basin Petroleum Museum** (1500 I-20W, ☎ 915-683-4403), one of the largest museums in the world devoted to oil, would be worth your while. It features a great mix of interactive activities and historical artifacts. Among them: 3-D models of oil strata, the story of oil formation, displays about well-drilling techniques and photos of oil boom towns. You can travel through a tunnel that takes you back 230 million years and see what it looked like. You can experience a simulated oil blow out or try your luck at the "oil game."

Outside, in the "Oil Patch," the world's largest collection of drilling equipment is on display.

For the more research oriented, the **Nita Stewart Haley Memorial Library and J. Evetts Haley History Center** (1805 W Indiana, ☎ 915-682-5785) could occupy your attention for days. Emphasizing Texas and Southwestern history, this mainly research library includes some noteworthy exhibits of Western art and photographs among its 10,000 pieces. An original bell, cast in 1722, from the Alamo Mission, is one of its most famous pieces. They also have extensive information about horses on the Western range.

The **Brown-Dorsey Medallion Home** (213 N Weatherford, ☎ 915-682-2931) is open by appointment only. A tour through the 1899 home, Midland's oldest dwelling, will take you past Gothic arched windows, interior doors with airy transoms, and through the wine cellar.

The **Midland Angels** (☎ 915-683-4251 for information, www.midlandangels.org), a AA franchise of the California Angels, play from April to August. While adults breathe in the smell of baseball, children lay claim to the team's mascot, Juice the Moose.

Information Sources

Midland Convention and Visitors Bureau (109 N Main, ☎ 800-624-6435, 915-683-3381) or the **Midland Chamber of Commerce** (☎ 800-624-6435, PO Box 1898, 79702).

■ Where to Stay

Hilton, 117 W Wall, 79701, ☎ 800-722-6131, 915-683-6131. $$-$$$. Everything you could ask for, including one-day dry cleaning service and airport transportation.

Holiday Inn Country Villa, 4300 W Hwy 20, 79703, ☎ 800-465-4329 or 915-697-3181. $$. They even have miniature golf and a play area for the kids.

■ Where to Eat

Cattleman's Steakhouse, 3300 N Big Spring, ☎ 915-682-5668. Steak lovers' paradise enhanced with seafood offerings.

Wall Street Bar & Grill, 115 E Wall, ☎ 915-684-8686. Consistently great seafood and steaks have been bringing in the locals for decades.

Santa Fe Grill, 117 W Wall at the Hilton, ☎ 915-683-6131. Though its name is from New Mexico, its food is Tex-Mex.

Luigi's, 111 N Big Spring, ☎ 915-683-6363. A popular Italian trattoria with home-spun dishes served on red-checkered tablecloths for over 25 years.

Susie's South Forty Confections, ☎ 915-570-4040. They're open only during the week, but they serve up some of the state's tastiest pecan pralines and sweet concoctions.

Through the Davis Mountains

Fort Stockton

■ History

Like most of the places in West Texas, Fort Stockton was a stopping point for native Indians well before Texans settled here. They were attracted by a spring, now called Comanche Springs. In 1859, Texans, eager to protect travelers against violent Comanche attacks, established Fort Stockton at the crossroads of the great Comanche War Trail and the San Antonio-El Paso Trail.

The usefulness of the fort declined as more settlers moved West and the Indians lost their battle with American colonization. In 1886 the actual post was closed, though the community that had arisen on its edges remained.

■ Touring

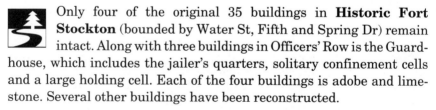 Only four of the original 35 buildings in **Historic Fort Stockton** (bounded by Water St, Fifth and Spring Dr) remain intact. Along with three buildings in Officers' Row is the Guardhouse, which includes the jailer's quarters, solitary confinement cells and a large holding cell. Each of the four buildings is adobe and limestone. Several other buildings have been reconstructed.

You might also enjoy the self-guided **Historical Sites Tour** that weaves through the heart of Fort Stockton. Maps are available from the Chamber of Commerce (100 Railroad Ave, ☎ 800-336-2166, 915-336-

2264) and there are signposts around town to guide you. Included in the stops are the **Grey Mule Saloon** (200 block of S Main).

Sheriff A.J. Royal

The Grey Mule was built and operated in the 1880s by Sheriff A.J. Royal, an infamous figure in Fort Stockton's history. Royal's reign as sheriff crossed the line into terrorism, his constituents believed, as six men were killed by his fast draw.

The townspeople took matters into their own hands. A black bean lottery was held among the area's prominent citizens, with the winner becoming the designated assassin. Royal met his demise in November 1894 and the murder was never solved.

The restored saloon is a nostalgic jump back into the Wild West.

Other historical sites you'll see around town include the **Old County Jail** (400 block of S Main), **St Joseph's Church**, the first church in Fort Stockton, and the **Zero Stone**, a rock that lies on the county courthouse lawn and served as the zero reference point for surveyors as they mapped most of West Texas.

The most famous figure – and most photographed – in contemporary Fort Stockton is **Paisano Pete** (Main St, just south of US 290), an 11-foot-tall and 20-foot-long roadrunner statue that serves as the town's welcome mat. Deemed the world's largest roadrunner (though the competition hasn't really shown up yet), Pete does little more than stand still for photo opportunities with travelers.

The **Annie Riggs Hotel Museum** (301 S Main, ☎ 915-336-2167) has taken a very active stance in preserving its history. A popular hotel on the stage route in the early 1900s, the building was restored and is maintained by a local historical society.

Ms. Riggs, the hotel's namesake, was a twice-divorced persevering local woman who ran things for more than a quarter-century. Her hotel, with its wraparound veranda and gingerbread trim, remains popular today.

The hotel's 14 rooms host a peculiar collection of early memorabilia. Among the items are a piano, one of the first brought west of the Pecos River, the desk at which A.J. Royal, the violent sheriff, was assassinated, a 22,000-year-old mammoth tusk found close by, and a safe with

West Texas

a hidden keyhole. There are also hundreds of artifacts, from kitchen gadgets to period clothing, that are representative of the early 1900s.

Comanche Springs

The lifeblood of the community early on, the springs were sucked dry in the 1950s after Fort Stockton tapped into the aquifer and went through a seven-year drought. An Olympic-size swimming pool now sits on the springs site, and serves as a social hub. Debate divides the city even today over governing and reviving the springs. They are still active but can't keep pace with consumption by irrigating farmers. Civic pride regularly butts heads with economic necessity.

If you're around during the third weekend in July, mosey by the **Water Carnival**, which has been celebrating the springs every year since 1936. Each year is different, featuring synchronized swimming, musical acts or dancing. But one thing remains the same: every event is either in the pool or around it.

On the southern edge of the springs lies **James Rooney County Park,** where you can enjoy swimming and picnicking on its lush grounds.

A more recent addition to the West Texas landscape, wine production is hitting its stride all around Fort Stockton. The Domaine Cordier Vineyard produces grapes used in **St Genevieve** wines (☎ 915-395-2417 or 395-2484), a line said to be on par with the Napa Valley wines. Although it was rough going in the early years for Texas wineries, stiff competition, aging vineyards and experience have made the wines hot commodities. Tastings and tours are held on Saturdays or by special appointment. There is a tour bus that starts and finishes at the Fort Stockton Chamber of Commerce.

Information Sources

For more information on Fort Stockton contact their **Chamber of Commerce** (☎ 915-336-2264, PO Box C, 79735).

■ Where to Stay

Best Western Sunday House, 3201 W Dickinson (US 290W), 79735, ☎ 800-528-1234, 915-336-8521. $$. All the normal amenities of a mid-range hotel with steambaths and jacuzzis available in some of the rooms.

Econo Lodge of Fort Stockton, 800 E Dickinson, 79735, ☎ 888-336-9711, 915-336-9711. $$. Two outdoor pools, a restaurant and a free breakfast buffet for guests.

■ Where to Eat

Sarah's, 106 S Nelson, ☎ 915-336-7700. Owned and operated by the same family for longer than any other Fort Stockton restaurant. Enjoy tasty tacos, enchiladas and chalupas.

Fort Davis

West Texas

■ History

Perhaps fulfilling its name's destiny, Fort Davis, a sleepy town where the human head count doesn't even hit a thousand, attracted the national spotlight in April 1997 with the stand-off between government officials and the Republic of Texas faction, a militia group dedicated to the secession of Texas. The small-potatoes outfit was lumped together with other separatists groups like the Branch Davidians and those at Ruby Ridge, although the outcome was much less destructive.

Ironically, Fort Davis took its name from Jefferson Davis, who, while acting as Secretary of War for the United States, established the fort as a safety valve for westward-moving travelers who were regularly attacked by Apaches and Comanches.

Jefferson Davis later went on to become president of the Confederate States.

■ Touring

The most tantalizing aspect of Fort Davis is its location. Nestled within the Davis Mountains at an altitude of 5,050 feet, Fort Davis is the highest town in the state. The Davis Mountains, with an average rainfall of more than 20 inches a year, is a virtual oasis in the middle of the Chihuahuan Desert of West Texas.

While most Texans battle heat waves during the summer, Fort Davis residents, because of the altitude, don't necessary pack their jackets away. Cool summer nights are the norm.

The **Fort Davis National Historic Site** (☎ 915-426-3225, TX 17 at the north edge of town) offers a grand display of the original fort. Established in 1854 to protect travelers on the San Antonio-El Paso road, the fort was abandoned by federal troops at the onset of the Civil War and later, in 1862, it was abandoned by the remaining Confederate soldiers.

The fort was reestablished in 1867 and was primarily protected by black infantry and cavalry members, respectfully nicknamed "buffalo soldiers" by the Indians, a tribute to the animal they considered sacred. The group, the Ninth Cavalry, was one of four black regiments organized to protect the government's policy.

Most historians agree that it is ironic, if not a little paradoxical, that the black soldiers played a key role in the post-Civil War suppression and ultimate vanquishing of the American Indians, especially amidst the mounting anti-black violence and hostility.

The 460-acre site includes some 25 original structures and the foundations and ruins of many more.

There are also **hiking trails** that lead visitors from the fort to the Davis Mountains State Park. Immediately after the trailhead you will have to pick either the right or left fork, which rejoin later. The right fork, though slightly longer, traverses more interesting terrain. The left fork affords a beautiful panoramic view of the fort.

The trail takes hikers to the fort's neighbor, the **Davis Mountains State Park** (Hwy 118 northwest about four miles, ☎ 915-426-3337, www.tpwd.state.tx.us). The diverse plants and wildlife within the park's boundaries represent the terrain of both the Davis Mountains and the Chihuahuan Desert. Two of the rare animals that call the desert home are the kangaroo rat, which never drinks water but manufactures it from seeds, and a group of all-female whiptail lizards, which are said to clone themselves naturally.

There are more hiking trails to follow, an amphitheater, picnic areas and a Southwestern pueblo-styled hotel, the **Indian Lodge** (☎ 915-426-3254). Some of the original rooms in the lodge were built by the Civilian Conservation Corps.

The **Chihuahuan Desert Research Institute** (☎ 915-837-8740, three miles south on TX 118) includes 507 acres, an arboretum and desert garden. The institute's headquarters are at Sul Ross University in Alpine. The actual desert begins in Northern Mexico, then wanders through Texas and up into parts of New Mexico and Arizona. The garden's collection includes more than 500 regional plant species and over 95% of the cacti that grow in the desert. The visitor's center is open from April through August. Mount Livermore lies to the north and Blue Mountain to the southwest, making for a scenic undertaking.

World renowned is the **McDonald Observatory** (☎ 915-426-3640, TX 118 north to Spur 78, www.as.utexas.edu/mcdonald), a University of Texas facility that perches atop 6,791-foot Mount Locke about 16 miles north of Fort Davis. The area's cloudless nights coupled with its distance from city lights and altitude above any desert dust, make it a perfect home for some of the world's largest telescopes.

Also just north of town is the **Prude Ranch** (☎ 915-426-3202, TX 118, five miles north, www.prude-ranch.com), a working ranch owned by the same family since the '30s. With both bunkhouse and motel-style lodging, it serves as a perfect retreat for any group. Its proximity to the observatory, the Marfa Lights (see page 361), the fort and the mountains, makes Prude Ranch a great central locale for a West Texas vacation. In addition to more civilized amenities, like tennis courts and a Jacuzzi, there is horseback riding and lots of ranch-style chow.

The **Neill Doll Museum** (☎ 915-426-3969, Court Ave and 7th St), which doubles as a bed and breakfast, has more than 350 dolls dating back to the mid-1800s. A trip to the **Overland Trail Museum**, named for a trail that once passed along the house's front steps, provides another retrospective look at the area with pioneer artifacts. The museum was home and office for Nick Mersfelter, an early settler who served as the justice of the peace, town barber and musician (it was rumored he could play most any instrument).

Possibly the best orientation to the diverse landscapes that surround Fort Davis can be seen by driving the **74-Mile Scenic Loop Road**, which both begins and ends in town. The path follows Texas Hwy 17 two miles south of town, west on TX 166 (which winds its way around to the north), southeast on TX 118, back to Hwy 17, which leads you back into town. The scenic tour includes nine roadside parks, the McDonald Observatory, the Davis Mountains State Park and Madera Canyon.

A trip by the **House of Shoes** (TX 118, north of TX 17) will open your eyes to the world of horse shoes. Proprietor Virgil Baldwin can make just about anything out of the shoes discarded by the four-legged creatures,

West Texas

from chairs to lamps to beds. Prices on each piece depend on the number of shoes needed.

Information Sources

Contact **Fort Davis Chamber of Commerce** (Box 378 Fort Davis, 79734, ☎ 800-524-3015, 915-426-3015, www.fortdavis.com).

■ Adventures on the Water

 The community of Balmorhea received its off-beat but attractive name from an odd source – a trio of Chicago investors with the last names Balcom, Morrow and Rhea. "Bal," "Mor" and "Rhea" purchased a $14,000 tract of West Texas plains to sell and enticed buyers with a free train ride to view their new town. The area's most enduring asset would prove to be **San Soloman Springs**. During the Depression, the Civilian Conservation Corp. (CCC) built the Balmorhea State Park out of Soloman Springs, which produced 26 million gallons of clear spring water a day.

Making the claim that it is the world's largest spring-fed swimming pool, **Balmorhea State Recreation Area** (☎ 915-375-2370, north on TX 17) boasts a swimming hole with a capacity of 3½ million gallons of spring water. At 30 feet deep and covering almost two acres, the pool could probably accommodate all of West Texas. In addition to a motel, there are campsites and RV hook-ups.

The gentle, waveless surface of Balmorhea's massive spring-fed pool belies a throng of fish species that lie just beneath the sparkling water's surface. The lake offers some of the best scuba diving in the state. Visibility can go up to 100 feet, with depths up to 25 feet. The pool's calmness is perfect for novices, as is the pleasant temperature, ranging between 72 and 78° all year.

Because of the relative warmness of Balmorhea's spring, it is used by divers year-round. Though it is not very deep, divers can earn their open water ceritification here.

Dive Operator

Although the park does not rent tanks, the **Desert Oasis** dive shop (☎ 915-375-2572), about 50 yards from its entrance, will rent tanks and provide general guidance.

If you're traveling through West Texas during the summer – especially with your family – you owe it to yourself to stop and at least take a swim. Top it off with an ice cream cone. There is no better way to beat the Texas heat.

■ Where to Stay

Butterfield Inn, Main St, ☎ 915-426-3252. $$. Four cottages. Jacuzzis and fireplaces in each cottage and apples in season.

The Hotel Limpia, Main St, PO Box 822, 79734, ☎ 800-662-5517, 915-426-3237, www.hotellimpia.com. $$-$$$$. Built in 1912, the hotel's 33 rooms have been restored to their original splendor, including Victorian parlors and fireplaces. There are also two gift shops on site.

Paradise Mountain Ranch, Hwy 166, west of town, ☎ 800-648-9162 or 915-426-3737. $$-$$$. A working ranch 15 miles west of Fort Davis on Hwy 166, the ranch provides furnished rooms sleeping 13. Includes complete country breakfast and horseback rides. The newest addition is a challenge course used for team-building exercises. A lodge will be their next project.

The Indian Lodge in Davis Mountains State Park, ☎ 915-426-3254. $$-$$$. A rustic full-service hotel with restaurant, gift shop and pool.

Boynton House, Dolores Mountain, 79734, ☎ 800-358-5929 or 915-426-3123. $$. Mexican Colonial hacienda atop Dolores Mountain. Private baths, TV, library, music/games/exercise rooms.

Neill Doll Museum, Court St, ☎ 915-426-3838 or 426-3969. $$. Unique Victorian historic landmark home furnished with antiques. Two rooms with double beds and private baths.

The Veranda Country Inn (B&B), 210 Court Ave, 79734, ☎ 888-383-2847 or 915-426-2233, www.TheVeranda.com. $$-$$$. One block west of Jeff Davis County Courthouse, the historic inn and guest house provides a getaway, spacious rooms/suites and generous breakfasts.

Wayside Inn, 400 W 4th St, 79734, ☎ 800-582-7510 or 915-426-3535. $$-$$$. At the base of Sleeping Lion Mountain. Country-style house with resident hosts.

The Webster House, Conrad & 2nd, ☎ 800-752-4145 or 915-426-3227. $$. Pinion pines shade the porch of this historic Victorian home, which has three bedrooms, two baths, fully equipped kitchen, butterfly garden and yard just three blocks from the courthouse.

Balmorhea Fishing Resort, PO Box 362, 79718, ☎ 915-375-2308. $. While it may not be what you expect in a resort, if you like fishing and camping, it might seem perfect. There are also RV hookups. Birdwatchers and rock collectors also like the grounds. Very inexpensive. Call for directions.

■ Where to Eat

The Drugstore, Main St, ☎ 915-426-3118. Things haven't changed much here, including the fountain soft drinks, floats, malts and good conversation.

Limpia Hotel Dining Room, Main St, ☎ 800-662-5517, 915-426-3237. Enjoy perusing their bookstore and gift shop before or after their fine home cooking.

Marfa

■ History

Marfa, population 2,400, is one of those towns where you'd better not blink for fear of missing the whole shebang. Despite its meager populace, the town has had more than its allotment of time in the national limelight. It served as the set for the 1956 Academy Award epic *Giant*, which provided a trampoline for co-stars Elizabeth Taylor and Rock Hudson and marked the last project young James Dean would ever work on.

On a grander scale, *Giant* provided an entire generation of movie-goers something palpable of the Texas spirit and landscape. What they saw in that movie (and what more recent generations saw in the TV series *Dallas*) was wide, sweeping and dusty, dotted with oil wells and a perpetual heatwave.

Parts of the leftover set have been used in filming several other movies, including the 1985 classic *Fandango*, which marked the beginning of Kevin Costner's propulsion to mega-star status.

■ Touring

The **El Paisano Hotel** (☎ 915-729-3145), built in 1927 and host to such dignitaries as Franklin D. Roosevelt, Harry Truman and John F. Kennedy, enchants even the most amateur of

Presidio County Courthouse, Marfa.

movie buffs with its memorabilia from the making of *Giant*. It acts as the area's museum.

The Marfa Lights

Despite all the Hollywood hype, the most extraordinary thing about the town is the Marfa Lights.

For over a century Texans have recorded sightings of a mysterious set of lights, most often seen about nine miles east of town at Mitchell Flats. No one has provided a definitive answer as to the lights' source but proposed explanations have ranged from mirages to St Elmo's fire to bats' wings carrying radioactive dust to piezo electricity, a phenomenon involving polarity and pressure.

There is a sign indicating the viewing area. Although many of the locals maintain that the mysterious lights are some type of hoax, scientists worldwide continue to study and hypothesize about their origin.

There's a Web site dedicated to the Marfa Lights (www.marfalights.com), which includes possible explanations and a calendar of area events that celebrate them.

Information Sources

To get more information on the Marfa Lights – or to view them for yourself – visit http://www.marfalights.com.

■ Where to Stay

 El Paisano Hotel, 207 North Highland St, 79843, ☎ 915-729-3145. $$-$$$. Vintage hotel frequented by FDR, Truman and Kennedy. It's a Texas treasure.

The Arcon Inn, 215 N Austin, ☎ 915-729-4826. $$-$$$$. Built in 1886, a historic Victorian gothic adobe, full of Colonial treasures collected from years of foreign residence. Dinner is also served on weekends to the public by reservation.

■ Where to Eat

 The Arcon Inn, 215 N Austin, 79843, ☎ 915-729-4826. The innkeeper's son is a professionally trained chef. He'll make a special dinner for you (by reservation only), or you can pick from the regular menu.

Carmen's Café, 317 San Antonio, ☎ 915-729-3429. A '50s-type establishment that pulls in the locals with consistently good Mexican food and steaks.

Alpine

■ History

The Murphys are probably not too happy with the town of Alpine. That's because in 1888 the townspeople outvoted the Murphys and changed the town's name from Murphyville to Alpine, drawing inspiration from the mountains that surrounded them. The minor revolt didn't change things thing too much, and the community still barely tops 5,500 residents.

Alpine is located in the most mountainous and largest county in Texas. Brewster County, at 5,935 square miles, is larger than Connecticut, Rhode Island and Delaware combined.

■ Touring

Rock hounds love the **Woodward Ranch** (TX 118 south to signs, ☎ 915-364-2271) about 16 miles south of town. You can hunt for over 70 varieties of gems, including red plume agate, pom-pom agate and opals. For a small fee, they will provide guide service on their over 3,000-acre spread. You can purchase the rough rocks by the pound or buy "pre-discovered" rocks from the ranch experts. They're very helpful in telling you where to look and what to look for. Enthusiasts can take advantage of RV hookups and camping facilities to make their stay last.

If Big Bend is your final destination, or you've already been there, a trip to the **Museum of the Big Bend** (Sul Ross University, US 90E, ☎ 915-837-8143) will quench your historical thirst. Exhibits showcase the region's history through its varied cultural influences, including the Indians, Spanish, Mexican and Anglo-Americans, who have all lived here. There's also a reconstructed general store and blacksmith shop.

Another stop to make before hitting Big Bend is the **Apache Trading Post** (2701 Hwy 90 W, ☎ 915-837-5506). The log cabin store maintains one of the largest collections of maps on Big Bend, along with information about all of the area's attractions. It also features a large display of Mexican and Indian jewelry and pottery.

West Texas

Information Sources

Alpine Chamber of Commerce (106 N 3rd, ☎ 915-837-2326) or **Sun Runner Tours** (☎ 915-364-2247), which offers both shuttle services and hiking, rafting and cycling tours for the Davis Mountains and Big Bend.

For more information on Alpine, visit their Web site at www.alpinetexas.com.

■ Where to Stay

Holland Hotel, 207 W Holland, 79830, ☎ 800-535-8040, 915-837-3844. $$-$$$$. They are renovating rooms in stages. There are also pricey penthouse digs with outdoor decks available. Free in-room breakfast and airport transportation, as well as other luxury services. Rooms are limited (12 and growing), so call well ahead.

Sunday House Inn, 1440 E Hwy 90, 79830, ☎ 915-837-3363. $$. 80 units, a restaurant, private club and outdoor pool.

The Corner House, 801 E Hwy 90, 79830, ☎ 915-837-7161. $$-$$$. A bed and breakfast with proprietors who came here for a visit and ended up staying for good.

■ Where to Eat

Alpine's Little Mexico, 204 W Muryphy, ☎ 915-837-2855. Authentic homemade Mexican and American food for over a decade.

Longhorn Cattle Company, 801 N 5th, ☎ 915-837-3217. Steaks, steaks, and more steaks, with barbecue and seafood if you're not in the mood.

McFarland's, 209 W Holland (Holland Hotel), ☎ 800-535-8040, 915-837-3844. If you've been roughing it and need some fine dining, scrub up and come on by. The fresh food menu changes twice daily. It's a private club, but they let outsiders in for a small fee. Reservations recommended.

To Big Bend Country

Marathon

■ History

Marathon is nothing more than a dot on the West Texas horizon. But it's the last substantial stop before Big Bend National Park and its 800 or so residents hold many of the secrets to Big Bend Country. The town, which got its name after a sea captain suggested the area looked much like Marathon, Greece, sits at the junction of US 90 and US 385, with Big Bend 80 miles due south.

■ Touring

Alfred Gage, the largest landowner in Texas at one time, had the **Gage Hotel** (102 W Hwy 90, ☎ 915-386-4205) built in the 1920s by Henry Trost, a renowned El Paso architect. Legend

The Gage Hotel.

has it that he sold and bought over a million head of cattle in the hotel's lobby.

All of the hotel's 19 rooms have been restored to their 1920s splendor and boast individual and eccentric names like Panther Junction and Dagger Mesa. If a bathroom is important to you, ask if your room has one. Not all of them do.

The hotel prides itself on mingling old with nouveau. You can enjoy your gourmet, chef-prepared enchilada dish on one of the porch's many rocking chairs. The hotel will also arrange rafting and hunting trips for you.

Marathon served as an auxiliary post – **Fort Peña Colorado** – beginning in 1881. Created to protect Texas pioneers from Indian attack, the fort is now a county park five miles south of town.

A little off the beaten path, 50 miles to be more exact, is an absolute must-see for anyone craving Texas folklore. **The Stillwell Store** (FM 2627, six miles off US 385, ☎ 915-376-2244) preserves not only the spirit of Texas, but the spirit of Hallie Stillwell, called the "matriarch of the Big Bend of Texas" by one biographer. The Stillwell Store serves as the Hallie Stillwell Hall of Fame, chronicling her life through articles of her past. Miss Hallie serves as an inspiration to the most stoic of Texans.

Hallie Stillwell

This West Texas pioneer died in 1997, just two months shy of her 100th birthday. The town of Marathon celebrated her birthday – her life – as planned on Oct. 20, 1997, with "Miss Hallie's" spirit only.

Miss Hallie (who has a Web site dedicated to her: www.misshallie.com) arrived in a covered wagon in 1910 with her husband, Roy Stillwell, whom she outlived. Their 22,000-acre ranch is mostly desert.

They say Hallie rode every trail in this part of the country, and still packed a gun until close to her death. She once shot a mountain lion between the eyes when it got too close for comfort. She also rode in a posse to oust Pancho Villa loyalists. Her accomplishments brought her to the city and to civilization, serving at Brewster County's justice of the peace in 1964 and writing an autobiography called *I'll Gather My Geese*.

She has received many accolades, having been included in the Cowgirl Hall of Fame and the Texas Women's Hall of Fame. *Texas Monthly*, the largest magazine in Texas, paid tribute by putting Hallie on its cover.

The Stillwell complex also includes an RV park and ranch. Hallie's daughter, Dadie, invites you to stay awhile. The store offers five-hour jeep rides down into **Maravillas Canyon**, where you can explore caves that sustained life thousands of years ago. Their habitation is still evidenced in pictographs and rock ceilings blackened by fire.

Terlingua/Lajitas

■ History

Terlingua is the most active ghost town around. When mercury was discovered in 1890 in area cinnabar, a boom town of close to 2,000 quickly developed. Millions were made on the quicksilver before the boom fizzled. It's just been recently that a new breed of Texan has come to Terlingua, which is a corruption of the Spanish "tres linguas" or "three languages."

No one is quite sure if the three languages were meant to refer to the three different native Indian groups that dwelt here or the odd juxtaposition of native American, Spanish and English. The name has stuck, even though the inhabitants haven't.

■ Touring

Terlingua's biggest claim to fame is chili. There are two chili cook-offs a year that attract chili connoisseurs from around the globe. Over 5,000 "chili-heads" pitch their tents and bed down in their RVs on the first weekend of November for the **Frank X. Tolbert/Wick Fowler Memorial Championship Chili Cookoff,** while hundreds concoct their special versions of the "bowls of red."

The chili is only half the story (maybe only a quarter). The party that surrounds it is legendary (you have to drink beer with chili). Musical legends are known to show up with only their guitar and campfire sing alongs are the norm. If you're looking for good people and a good time, a Terlingua chili cook-off will serve you well.

Terlingua is also a rendezvous point for adventurers wanting to tackle the Rio Grande and other area activities. Outfitters, who want to be as close to Big Bend as possible, have set up shop here. There's a list of out-fitters on page 379. Make sure that the outfitter you pick is licensed. Big Bend officials can provide you with an approved list.

Lajitas, or "flagstones," was originally established in 1915 to protect the border from Mexican bandits who liked to cross the Rio Grande nearby. Today Lajitas is a "resort" that has been rebuilt in early 1900s fashion, looking much like an old Texas border town.

The **Lajitas Trading Post** (☎ 915-424-3234) has been around since 1899 and is good for stocking up on supplies and on a little history. Hopefully, the dry goods aren't as old as the store.

Information Sources

If you have a hankering for good chili, contact the **Lajitas/Terlingua Chamber of Commerce** (☎ 915-371-2320, PO Box 336, Terlingua, 79852).

■ Where to Stay

Lajitas on the Rio Grande, Lajitas, ☎ 915-424-3471. $$-$$$. Just west of the park, the resort boasts over 80 rooms.

■ Where to Eat

Badlands, Lajitas, ☎ 915-424-3471. It have moved around town a few times, but the good Mexican food remains intact. Fill up on homemade bread and cookies at their adjacent bakery.

La Kiva Restaurant & Bar, Terlingua, ☎ 915-371-2250. The party's here, along with shower facilities and sumptuous barbecue. It is uniquely built into the side of Terlingua Creek in a makeshift cave. (A kiva is a ceremonial pit house dug into the ground where Indians socialized and worshipped.)

Starlight Dinner Theatre, Terlingua, ☎ 915-371-2326. The "theatre" in its name refers only to what used to happen in the historic building. A supper diner with standard fare.

The Eastern Edges

Sonora

Sonora is another Texas town where the locals don't really talk about street names and addresses. Things are just "up the road a piece." And they really are. With fewer than 3,000 full-time residents, the small town of Sonora sees more than its share of traffic, being at the crossroads of US 290 and IH-10, two major east-west highways. It's on the way to a lot of places and it's a good stopping point for a casual, homemade lunch.

Wool and mohair production have supplanted cattle as the town's primary trade, though cattle remain important. The town straddles a fine line between West Texas and Central Texas, not truly belonging to either. Its weather and topography are a cross between the two, not as arid and desert-like as the West, but also not hilly like much of Central Texas. It lies just west of the Edwards Plateau, the edge of the Hill Country.

■ Touring

Texans exaggerate a lot about how big and how bold things are. But not even Texans, a past president of the National Speleological Society said, can exaggerate the beauty of the

Caverns of Sonora (FM 1989, ☎ 915-387-3105). The town's masterpiece is a brilliant assortment of crystal formations, deemed by cavern experts as among the world's finest for their brilliance, beauty, color and delicacy. Don't be fooled by the beginning portion of the tour, which takes visitors through the dead portion of the caverns. They save the best for last.

The tours run around 1½ miles and aren't too strenuous, though there are a lot of steps in the stairway leading out of the caverns. There are also campgrounds for overnight guests.

Another high point for children at the caverns are peacocks that wander the grounds. Bring a picnic lunch (they have a snack bar, if you prefer) and enjoy the living zoo. If you're lucky, you'll find a peacock feather that's been shed to take home. The peacocks are somewhat tame, but they are still wild. It's not a petting zoo.

If you're in for a more extended stay, the **Covered Wagon Dinner Theater** performs close to the caverns in a natural amphitheater throughout the summer months. Call the area **Chamber of Commerce** (707 N Crockett, ☎ 915-387-2880) for more information about the performances that recall earlier eras and include a catered dinner.

While you're driving through town, you might want to take a quick stroll around the **Sutton County Courthouse** (Water Ave, ☎ 915-387-2711), which has been left pretty much as is since it was built in the 1890s. Its Second Empire design is unique to the area.

Information Sources

The **Sonora Chamber of Commerce** (☎ 915-387-2880, PO Box 1172, 76950) can provide visitors with additional information.

■ Adventures on the Water

 The **South Llano River**, near Junction, Texas, is indeed an oddity. Not only for Texas, but for the entire nation. Its clear and clean spring waters flow south to north, crossing over beds of solid Texas limestone and gravel. The scenery varies from lofty cliffs to a canopy of local pecan trees.

There are about 15 miles of river to enjoy before the Llano reaches Junction. It can be broken down into pieces, just ask area outfitters what will suit your needs best.

> ## ❋ Author's Tip
>
> If you put in at Goodman Cabins, make sure you know what you're getting into – it is 7.8 miles before you can get back out. That's fine for canoes and kayaks. But it's about nine hours for a tuber – beyond the fun threshold.

Most tubing is done within the **South Llano River State Park** (see listing below), which rents tubes and canoes. The rest of the river is usually best traveled by canoe or kayak. Junction is 60 miles east of Sonora off I-10, just a short jaunt by West Texas standards.

South Llano River Resources

South Llano River Canoes, one mile south of the state park on Park Road 73, ☎ 915-446-2220. Canoes and kayaks for rent, with shuttle service.

Goodman Cabins, Hwy 377, ☎ 915-446-3870. Cabins for rent, equipment rentals and shuttle service.

South Llano River State Park, Park Road 73, ☎ 915-446-3994. Primitive camp sites, RV hook-ups, walk-in sites and tube and canoe rentals.

■ Where to Stay

 Devil's River Motel, I-10 and Golf Course Rd, 1312 N Service Rd, 76950, ☎ 915-387-3516. $-$$. With almost 100 rooms, there's both a restaurant and an outdoor pool.

Twin Oaks Motel, 907 North Crockett, 76950, ☎ 915-387-2551. $. No frills motel lodging.

Zola's Motel, 1108 Crockett, 76950, ☎ 915-387-3000. $. If you're just passing through, it's an inexpensive place to rest your eyes.

■ Where to Eat

Los Jaritos, 104 E Glasscock, ☎ 915-387-2838. Mexican fare for the hungry.

Sutton County Steakhouse, Golf Course Rd at Devil's River Motel, ☎ 915-387-3833. That locals come to this motel restaurant is a testament to its place in Sonora. Big portions of Texas food like steaks and burgers.

Langtry

■ History

Langtry is the stuff of legend. Literally. The last official census placed Langtry's population somewhere below 50 and the small town – just a dot on Hwy 90 above the Rio Grande – exists only as a living tribute to its most famous resident, Judge Roy Bean.

Judge Roy Bean

Judge Bean, or Ol' Roy, exacted his own brand of justice. His saloon was often the courtroom and his patrons often the jury. Legend has it that he once fined a corpse $40 for concealing a weapon. (Someone should have the dead man's money.) It's also said that he once let off an Irish customer who had killed a Chinese railroad worker. He looked through his one law book and in true Bean form, said, "It don't say nothing in here about it being against the law to kill a Chinaman. Case dismissed."

Bean received national attention in 1896 when he defied Texas law, in addition to New Mexico law, Arizona law and Mexican law, and shuttled heavyweight contenders Bob Fitzsimmons and Peter Maher onto a sandbar in the Rio Grande where the law was murky. Each state had outlawed fighting, as had Chihuahua, and until Bean stepped up, it looked as if the heavyweight title match would have to be canceled. With only a few witnesses, Fitzsimmons won the match by knocking out Maher only two minutes into the first round.

And while his six-shooter, vigilante justice was not by the books – or even close – the self-proclaimed "Law West of the Pecos" was instrumental in quieting the raucous and violent railroad camp where Bean served as justice of the peace.

Bean's saloon, The Jersey Lilly, was a symbol of his devotion to Lillie Langtry, whose stage name was The Jersey Lily (with one "l"). Bean claimed the town was named for the raven-haired actress, as well, and he frequently wrote to the star asking her to perform in the town that he created as a tribute. However, other accounts say "Langtry" was named for the railroad foreman who chartered the area.

Lillie Langtry did finally come to town at Bean's request. Only she came in 1904, the year after Bean had died in his saloon of lung and heart complications.

West Texas

■ Touring

The Judge Roy Bean Visitor Center (Loop 25, one mile off US 90, ☎ 915-291-3340) serves several functions in addition to paying tribute to Bean with historical memorabilia and dioramas. It also acts as a way station for Texas visitors, supplying information and maps for the entire state. Out back is a cactus garden with more than 100 plant species native to the Southwest.

Seminole Canyon State Historical Park (20 miles east of Langtry, Park Rd 67 off US 90, west of Comstock, ☎ 800-792-1112, 915-292-4464) contains over 2,000 acres of park land. Scientists believe man first visited here 12,000 years ago, when bygone species of elephant, camel, bison and horse roamed the area and pine, juniper and oak woodlands were the norm for the canyons. Mammoth and bison fed the developing hunting culture.

By 7,000 years ago, the region underwent a climatic change that produced a landscape much like today's. This new landscape led to a gatherer society that also created many surviving pictographs.

Within the **Fate Bell Shelter** are some of the oldest pictographs in North America. Many experts believe the rock paintings – as much as 8,000 years old – are some of the most important finds in the New World. Fate Bell is also one of the oldest cave dwellings in North America.

More than 200 pictograph sites within the canyons are known to contain examples of early man's style of rock art, ranging from single paintings to caves containing panels of art hundreds of feet long.

Tours to see the pictographs involve a fairly tough hike to the bottom of the canyon and then up to the shelter. There are two tours daily, Wednesday through Sunday. You can also see Pressa Canyon by calling and making arrangements ahead of time.

There are campsites with showers available for overnight usage.

You can round out your visit to Seminole Canyon with traditional outdoor adventures including hiking, mountain biking and camping (showers are available).

Near Seminole Canyon is the **Pecos River Bridge Overlook** (east bank of Pecos River on US 90), the highest highway bridge in Texas at 273 feet above the Pecos. The panoramic view includes a Mexican mountain range and the Pecos as it empties into Amistad Reservoir.

High Bridge Adventures (PO Box 816, Comstock, ☎ 915-292-4495) will allow you to get a little bit closer to the rivers that ebb and flow through this corner of Texas by offering scenic boat rides of both the Pecos and the Rio Grande.

Information Sources

Contact the **Judge Roy Bean Visitor Center** for more information on Langtry (☎ 915-291-3340, PO Box 160, Langtry, 78871).

Special Attraction

■ Big Bend National Park

There's no stumbling across Big Bend National Park. With its 800,000+ acres tucked into a gentle crook of the Rio Grande River within the Chihuahuan Desert, the park is not on the way to anywhere. Its vastness and isolation have made it one of the most under-visited national parks in America.

But that doesn't mean it's under-appreciated. In fact, the people you meet here have been coming for a lifetime, having been brought by their parents for their first visit decades ago and perhaps introducing the next generation to the park's splendors. Many of the people that work here are tied inseparably to its earth, depending on its varied topography, endless vistas and quiet nights, interrupted only by the noises of nature, for their lifeblood.

Big Bend is about nature. Not about a busload of tourists lining the canyon walls snapping pictures before moving on to the gift shop. It's about unity with canyons, mesas, springs and desert. About being alone with coyotes and javelinas and watching thunderheads race along the desert plains. And it's about respecting nature in both its glory and its savageness.

Despite the park's location smack dab in the middle of a desert, Big Bend boasts climates and topography as varied as the state itself. The river basin – lined with natural hot springs that percolate through the mud – is blanketed by forest and rich vegetation. The mountain highlands are cool to the touch. Underground aquifers feed unexpected groves of cottonwoods and desert springs. The canyons – Santa Elena and Boquillas – are steep, severe and spectacular.

West Texas

Chisos Basin Campground.

And the basin – ohh, the basin – rises up from the desert floor like a mirage. You can feel the temperature dropping as you climb its dizzy, sheer walls and you must catch your breath while you teeter on its top edge before plunging into its lush garden. As the centerpiece of Big Bend National Park, the Chisos Basin is often the only respite on arid desert days.

The magic of Big Bend is found throughout its 112 miles of paved road and 157 miles of unpaved road. Its beauty is in the 1,200+ species of plants, 450 different types of birds, 75 mammal species, 56 reptile species and 40 different fish species. Not to mention the 65 hiking trails and 210 primitive trails.

There's no dropping by Big Bend. Stay a while and breathe deep. Wake to the smell of cowboy-brewed coffee and look across vistas where eagles soar and Mexico is in your back pocket. Big Bend is Texas: the Texas of legend. It is raw, yet remarkable.

And it is one of the few grand places left in the world unmolested by commercialism, though that won't last forever.

As the official map and guide to Big Bend so aptly says, "The truth is, Big Bend is more mood than place. Sometimes you must wait for it to capture you."

Big Bend Average Temperatures (°F)

Month	Average Maximum	Average Minimum
January	60.9	35.0
February	66.2	37.8
March	77.4	45.3
April	80.7	52.3
May	88.0	59.3
June	94.2	65.5
July	92.9	68.3
August	91.1	66.4
September	86.4	61.9
October	78.8	52.7
November	68.5	42.3
December	62.2	36.4

Note that temperatures in the mountains average 5-10° cooler, while those in the desert are 5-10° warmer.

West Texas

The Weather

Respect. That's what visitors must never forget about Big Bend National Park. If you don't respect its often cruel lands, it'll bite you in the backside and send you home.

The Terrain

Over 90% of the park is Chihuahuan Desert – a stunning, green and explosive desert, but desert all the same. The Chihuahuan Desert, which extends between El Paso and Pecos and down deep into Mexico, is one of four warm deserts in North America, the other three being the Great Basin, the Mojave and the Sonoran.

> ### ✳ *Take Care!*
>
> Desert means hot. Hot enough to make you sick and de-hydrated, perhaps leaving you with heat exhaustion or heat stroke. This is not meant to be a discouragement, only a reminder to be prepared. Generally, the park is very pleasant. But occasionally you may experience temperatures above 100°. Make sure you have water at all times and wear a hat during both cold and hot spells.

Traveling Tips

- If you're interested in the isolation and big, empty vistas that Big Bend normally provides, avoid Spring Break. College students flock to the camping sites during their week off in March. Other busy holidays include Easter, Thanksgiving and the week between Christmas and the New Year.

- As the chart shows, May and June are the hottest months in the park. August and September see the fewest visitors.

- Stock up with food and water and fill up with gas well before you get to the park – the Big Bend spread does have amenities, but they are few and far between. It's better to have everything ahead of time rather than depend on getting them in the park.

- There is no public transportation to or from the park. Amtrak serves Alpine (108 miles north) and bus services are available to both Alpine and Marathon from the park. The closest airports are El Paso (325 miles) and Midland (230 miles), which means you have to have a car.

- Be sure to bring a reliable car. The Chihuahuan Desert isn't where you want to break down. Also, there are several areas off the beaten path where park officials recommend a 4x4 all-terrain vehicle for access.

- There are four visitor centers that provide information and backcountry permits: **Persimmon Gap**, **Panther Junction**, **Chisos Basin** and **Rio Grande Village**. Reach them all through a central number, ☎ 915-477-2251.

Touring the Park

 If you're truly interested in the park, an extended visit with the park rangers at headquarters (Panther Junction) will serve you well. There are so many hikes and adventures to experience in this mega-park, that even an entire book couldn't address them all. Read up on the literature the rangers provide.

Beginning in the **Chisos Basin**, some of the highlights include a hike to the **Window**, a conspicuous gap in the cliffs that circle the lush Basin. A relatively short hike (5.2 miles round-trip), this trail is well-traveled and popular with families. It begins at the lodge and goes west along the Basin floor to the Window. Hikers are rewarded with a 200-foot waterfall, one of the highest in Texas. The return trip includes picturesque views of **Casa Grande**, one of the most distinctive formations in the area.

Perhaps the best-loved hike in Texas is Big Bend's **South Rim Trail**, a 14½-mile hike that affords hikers some of the most expansive and fulfilling views in the state. On clear days, you can see deep into Mexico. To really enjoy the strenuous hike, spend two days and plan an overnight campout along the trail in a designated area. Try to time it so you can take a break at **Boot Canyon**, a lush hideaway. The hike can be done in one day if you're in good shape.

Other popular trails include the **Lost Mine Trail**, **Emory Peak** (the highest peak in the Chisos Mountains – strenuous), and **Dog Canyon**. Again, check all the literature park officials have. It'll give you the most recent information as well as pertinent safety considerations involved with each trip.

West Texas

Entrance to Santa Elena Canyon.

North of Rio Grande Village Drive, in the Dead Horse Mountains, is the **Ernst Tinaja**. This tinaja, a Spanish word meaning "earthen jar" (in this case it means "water hole") was named for Max Ernst. He ran the post office and store here over a century ago before being murdered in 1908. The rocks and formations that have been enjoyed since Pancho Villa's time are tinged with all the colors of the rainbow, including mauves and blues.

Black Bears

The return of the black bear to the Big Bend has naturalists excited. Early this century bears were common, but by 1944, when the park was established, their numbers had dwindled to practically zero, the result of hunting and trapping and the changing environment. Bears were occasionally seen through the 1980s, but they were basically passing through from their permanent habitat in Northern Mexico.

In 1988 a visitor photographed a black bear mother with her three cubs; 27 sightings were reported that year. By 1996, sightings numbered 572. Researchers say that it is very rare for an animal eliminated from its natural environment to return without human intervention – the return of the black bear on its own is a remarkable event.

Big Bend biologists believe between 18 and 22 black bears live in Big Bend, primarily in the Chisos Mountains, where they thrive on juniper, pinon pine, madrone, oak and persimmon trees.

If you're camping in the Chisos backcountry, take special precautions to insure you won't be the recipient of an unwanted bear visit. When hiking, never leave packs or food unattended. Store all food and cooking gear in the bear-proof storage boxes provided at each camp site. Never take food inside your tent and prepare your food away from sleeping areas.

Big Bend Ranch State Park

Just west of Big Bend National Park, stretching between Presidio and Lajitas along the Rio Grande, lies **Big Bend Ranch State Park**. Encompassing over 277,000 acres of Chihuahuan Desert wilderness, the park is one of the newest additions to the area, having been purchased in 1988.

It is as richly varied as its larger counterpart, including two mountain ranges, extinct volcanoes, canyons and waterfalls. A Texas longhorn herd, reminiscent of the land's ranching days, is maintained at the ranch.

Not many people know about the park yet. You can find information about it on the Texas Parks and Wildlife Web site at www.tpwd.state.tx.us.

Rafting through the **Colorado Canyon** is a favorite Rio Grande trip. The same outfitters that service the national park provide service on this end of the river. There are also most of the same activities available, from hiking to biking to camping. Since the park is relatively new, it's still mostly primitive, but developing rapidly. There are two places to stay (for now) within the park. The **Big House**, the original Sauceda ranch house, can accommodate up to eight people, with kitchen privileges available. You'll feel at home here – because it is the home where the ranching family that ran this land lived from 1908. The **Sauceda Lodge** is more dormitory-style (a former hunting lodge) and can house up to 30 people.

West Texas

Information Sources

Call the **Big Bend Ranch Complex** (☎ 915-229-3416) for reservations or information on the park. **Texas Parks and Wildlife** (☎ 800-792-1112) can also provide information on the park.

Big Bend Outfitters

Big Bend Outback, West Hwy 90, Sanderson, ☎ 888-GO-OUTBACK, e-mail outback@bigbend.com. The Web site is www.bigbend-outback.com. A travel planning and booking agency that helps visitors with hotels, motels, outfitters and travel providers for the region.

Big Bend River Tours, Box 317, Lajitas, ☎ 800-545-4240, 915-424-3219. River rafting tours.

Big Bend Stables and Outfitters, Hwy 170, Terlingua, ☎ 800-887-4331, 915-371-2212. Day or overnight horseback adventures.

Desert Sports, ☎ 915-371-2727, Terlingua, www.Desertsportstx. com. One of the newest outfitters, they mix-and-match hiking, rafting and mountain biking adventures to suit your tastes and needs. Trips range from one day to 12.

Far Flung Adventures, Box 377, Terlingua, ☎ 800-359-4138, 915-371-2489. They organize Rio Grande rafting adventures.

Lajitas Stables, Star Route 70, Box 380, Terlingua, ☎ 915-424-3238. Guided trips on private land that borders Big Bend National Park.

Rio Grande Adventures, Hwy 170, Terlingua, ☎ 800-343-1640, 915-371-2567. Complete rental and guided rafting and canoe trips. Shuttle service also available.

Rio Grande River Outfitters, Lajitas, ☎ 915-371-2424. Based in the old Lajitas Trading Post, they offer rafts for rent.

Scott Shuttle Service, Hwy 90 West, Marathon, ☎ 800-613-5041, 915-386-4574, www.bigbend.com/river or e-mail scott.shuttle@bigbend.com. Provides guided raft and canoe trips on the Rio Grande and Pecos River, along with transportation service and accommodation arrangements.

Where to Stay in the Park

Chisos Mountains Lodge, Chisos Basin, ☎ 915-477-2291. $. It's the only game in town and not bad to boot. Reservations are recommended.

There are three developed campgrounds within the park: **Rio Grande Village** (100 sites), **Chisos Basin** (63 sites), and **Cottonwood** (31 sites). All have restrooms and water, but no hook-ups. Sites are on a first-come, first-served basis.

Where to Stay Outside the Park

Antelope Lodge, 2310 West Hwy 90, Alpine, ☎ 915-837-2451, e-mail antelope.lodge@juno.com. $. Rustic cottages with kitchenettes; the lodge isn't fancy, but it is convenient and offers special rates for extended stays.

Big Bend Motor Inn, TX 118, west in Study Butte, ☎ 800-848-BEND, 915-371-2218. $$.

Easter Egg Valley Motel, west of Study Butte on TX 170, ☎ 915-371-2254. $.

Heath Canyon Guest Ranch, on TX 2627 to the end of the pavement, ☎ 915-376-2235, e-mail heathcr@mcione.com. $-$$$. Right on the Rio Grande, there's a boat launch site, a café and a small airstrip. Accommodations range from bunkhouse to an entire house.

Lajitas on the Rio Grande, Lajitas, ☎ 915-424-3471. $-$$. Just west of the park, the resort boasts over 80 rooms.

Pope Ranch, PO Box 332, Marathon, ☎ 915-376-2200, www.bigbend.com/pope. Six miles from the entrance to the park, this is one of the largest working ranches in West Texas. They offer everything from backcountry camping to fully outfitted horseback trips to bunkhouse accommodations. They also organize star-gazing adventures (they have some of the darkest skies in West Texas), birdwatching and hunting parties (for javelina, trophy mountain lion and other seasonal attractions).

Terlingua Ranch, 18 miles north of Study Butte on TX 118, 18 miles east on marked gravel road, ☎ 915-371-2416. $. Off the beaten path, there's no TV and no room phones. Motel rooms, RV hook-ups and camp sites.

Where to Eat

Badlands, Lajitas, ☎ 915-424-3471. It may have moved around town a few times, but the good Mexican food remains intact. Fill up on homemade bread and cookies at their bakery.

Chisos Mountain Lodge Restaurant, Chisos Basin, ☎ 915-477-2291. You can't beat the view and they'll even rustle up box lunches to take out on the trail.

La Kiva Restaurant & Bar, Terlingua, ☎ 915-371-2250. The party's here along with shower facilities and sumptuous barbecue.

Starlight Dinner Theatre, Terlingua, ☎ 915-371-2326. The "theatre" in its name refers only to what used to happen in the historic building. A supper diner with standard fare.

Index

Index

Adventure Guides
from Hunter Publishing

ALASKA HIGHWAY

2nd Edition, Ed & Lynn Readicker-Henderson

"A comprehensive guide.... Plenty of background history and extensive bibliography." *Travel Reference Library on-line*

The fascinating highway that passes settlements of the Tlingit and the Haida Indians, with stops at Anchorage, Tok, Skagway, Valdez, Denali National Park and more. Sidetrips and attractions en route, plus details on all other approaches – the Alaska Marine Hwy, Klondike Hwy, Top-of-the-World Hwy. Color photos.

400 pp, $16.95, 1-55650-824-7

BAHAMAS

2nd Edition, Blair Howard

Fully updated reports for Grand Bahama, Freeport, Eleuthera, Bimini, Andros, the Exumas, Nassau, New Providence Island, plus new sections on San Salvador, Long Island, Cat Island, the Acklins, the Inaguas and the Berry Islands. Mailboat schedules, package vacations and snorkeling trips by John Michel Cousteau.

380 pp, $15.95, 1-55650-852-2

EXPLORE BELIZE

4th Edition, Harry S. Pariser

"Down-to-earth advice.... An excellent travel guide." *Library Journal*

Extensive coverage of the country's political, social and economic history, along with the plant and animal life. Encouraging you to mingle with the locals, Pariser entices you with descriptions of local dishes and festivals. Maps, color photos.

400 pp, $16.95, 1-55650-785-2

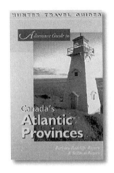

CANADA'S ATLANTIC PROVINCES
Barbara Radcliffe Rogers & Stillman Rogers
Pristine waters, rugged slopes, breathtaking sea-scapes, remote wilderness, sophisticated cities, and quaint, historic towns. Year-round adventures on the Fundy Coast, Acadian Peninsula, fjords of Gros Morne, Viking Trail & Vineland, Saint John River, Lord Baltimore's lost colony. Photos.
672 pp, $19.95, 1-55650-819-0

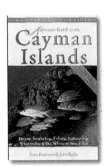

CAYMAN ISLANDS
Paris Permenter & John Bigley
The only comprehensive guidebook to Grand Cayman, Cayman Brac and Little Cayman. Encyclopedic listings of dive/snorkel operators, along with the best sites. Enjoy nighttime pony rides on a glorious beach, visit the turtle farms, prepare to get wet at staggering blowholes or just laze on a white sand beach. Color photos.
224 pp, $16.95, 1-55650-786-0

COASTAL ALASKA & THE INSIDE PASSAGE
3rd Edition, Lynn & Ed Readicker-Henderson
"A highly useful book." *Travel Books Review*
Using the Alaska Marine Highway to visit Ketchikan, Bellingham, the Aleutians, Kodiak, Seldovia, Valdez, Seward, Homer, Cordova, Prince of Wales Island, Juneau, Gustavas, Sitka, Haines, Skagway. Glacier Bay, Tenakee. US and Canadian gateway cities profiled.
400 pp, $16.95, 1-55650-859-X

COSTA RICA
3rd Edition, Harry S. Pariser
"... most comprehensive... Excellent sections on national parks, flora, fauna & history."
CompuServe
Incredible detail on culture, plants, animals, where to stay & eat, as well as practicalities of travel. E-mail and Website directory.
560 pp, $16.95, 1-55650-722-4

HAWAII

John Penisten

Maui, Molokai, Lanai, Hawaii, Kauai and Oahu are explored in detail, along with many of the smaller, less-visited islands. Full coverage of the best diving, trekking, cruising, kayaking, shopping and more from a Hawaii resident.

420 pp, $16.95, 1-55650-841-7

EXPLORE THE DOMINICAN REPUBLIC

3rd Edition, Harry S. Pariser

Virgin beaches, 16th-century Spanish ruins, the Caribbean's highest mountain, exotic wildlife, vast forests. Visit Santa Domingo, revel in Sosúa's European sophistication or explore the Samaná Peninsula's jungle. Color.

340 pp, $15.95, 1-55650-814-X

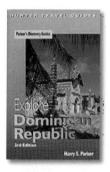

FLORIDA KEYS & EVERGLADES

2nd Edition, Joyce & Jon Huber

"... vastly informative, absolutely user-friendly, chock full of information..." Dr. Susan Cropper

"... practical & easy to use."
Wilderness Southeast

Canoe trails, airboat rides, nature hikes, Key West, diving, sailing, fishing. Color.

224 pp, $14.95, 1-55650-745-3

FLORIDA'S WEST COAST

Chelle Koster Walton

A guide to all the cities, towns, nature preserves, wilderness areas and sandy beaches that grace the Sunshine State's western shore. From Tampa Bay to Naples and Everglades National Park to Sanibel Island.

224 pp, $14.95, 1-55650-787-9

GEORGIA
Blair Howard
"Packed full of information on everything there is to see and do." *Chattanooga Free Press*
From Atlanta to Savannah to Cumberland Island, this book walks you through antique-filled stores, around a five-story science museum and leads you on tours of old Southern plantations.
296 pp, $15.95, 1-55650-782-8

GEORGIA & CAROLINA COASTS
Blair Howard
"Provides details often omitted... geared to exploring the wild dunes, the historic districts, the joys... " *Amazon.com Travel Expert*
Beaufort, Myrtle Beach, New Bern, Savannah, the Sea Islands, Hilton Head and Charleston.
288 pp, $15.95, 1-55650-747-X

GREAT SMOKY MOUNTAINS
Blair Howard
"The take-along guide." *Bookwatch*
Includes overlapping Tennessee, Georgia, Virginia and N. Carolina, the Cherokee and Pisgah National Forests, Chattanooga and Knoxville. Scenic fall drives on the Blue Ridge Parkway.
288 pp, $15.95, 1-55650-720-8

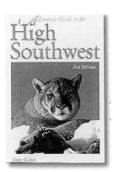

HIGH SOUTHWEST
2nd Edition, Steve Cohen
"Exhaustive detail... [A] hefty, extremely thorough & very informative book." *QuickTrips Newsletter*
"Plenty of maps/detail – an excellent guide." *Bookwatch*
Four Corners of NW New Mexico, SW Colorado, S Utah, N Arizona. Encyclopedic coverage.
376 pp, $15.95, 1-55650-723-2

IDAHO

Genevieve Rowles

Snake River Plain, the Owyhee Mountains, Sawtooth National Recreation Area, the Lost River Range and the Salmon River Mountains. Comprehensive coverage of ski areas, as well as gold-panning excursions and activities for kids, all written by an author with a passion for Idaho.

352 pp, $16.95, 1-55650-789-5

THE LEEWARD ISLANDS

Antigua, St. Martin, St. Barts, St. Kitts, Nevis, Antigua, Barbuda

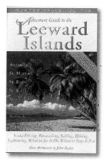

Paris Permenter & John Bigley

Far outdistances other guides. Day sails, island-hopping excursions, scuba dives, unique rain-forest treks on verdant mountain slopes, and rugged four-wheel-drive trails.

248 pp, $14.95, 1-55650-788-7

NEW HAMPSHIRE

Elizabeth L. Dugger

The Great North Woods, White Mountains, the Lakes Region, Dartmouth & Lake Sunapee, the Monadnock region, Merrimack Valley and New Hampshire's Seacoast. Beth Dugger finds the roads less traveled.

360 pp, $15.95, 1-55650-822-0

NORTHERN FLORIDA & THE PANHANDLE

Jim & Cynthia Tunstall

From the Georgia border south to Ocala National Forest and through the Panhandle. Swimming with dolphins and spelunking, plus Rails to Trails, a 47-mile hiking/biking path made of recycled rubber.

320 pp, $15.95, 1-55650-769-0

ORLANDO & CENTRAL FLORIDA
including Disney World, the Space Coast, Tampa & Daytona
Jim & Cynthia Tunstall
Takes you to parts of Central Florida you never knew existed. Tips about becoming an astronaut (the real way and the smart way) and the hazards of taking a nude vacation. Photos.
300 pp, $15.95, 1-55650-825-5

MICHIGAN
Kevin & Laurie Hillstrom
Year-round activities, all detailed here by resident authors. Port Huron-to-Mackinac Island Sailboat Race, Isle Royale National Park, Tour de Michigan cycling marathon. Also: canoeing, dogsledding and urban adventures.
360 pp, $16.95, 1-55650-820-4

NEVADA
Matt Purdue
Adventures throughout the state, from Winnemucca to Great Basin National Park, Ruby Mountain Wilderness to Angel Lake, from Cathedral Gorge State Park to the Las Vegas strip. Take your pick!
6 x 9 pbk, 256 pp, $15.95, 1-55650-842-5

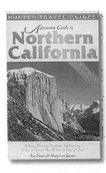

NORTHERN CALIFORNIA
Lee Foster & Mary Lou Janson
Waves lure surfers to Santa Cruz; heavy snowfall attracts skiers to Lake Tahoe; scuba divers relish Monterey Bay; horseback riders explore trails at Mammoth Lake. Travel the Big Sur and Monterey coasts, enjoy views of Yosemite and savor Wine Country. Resident authors.
360 pp, $15.95, 1-55650-821-2

PACIFIC NORTHWEST

Don & Marjorie Young

Oregon, Washington, Victoria and Vancouver in British Columbia, and California north of Eureka. This region offers unlimited opportunities for the adventure traveler. And this book tells you where to find the best of them.

360 pp, $16.95, 1-55650-844-1

PUERTO RICO

3rd Edition, Harry S. Pariser

"A quality book that covers all aspects... it's all here & well done." *The San Diego Tribune*

"... well researched. They include helpful facts... filled with insightful tips." *The Shoestring Traveler*

Crumbling watchtowers and fascinating folklore enchant visitors. Color photos.

344 pp, $15.95, 1-55650-749-6

SIERRA NEVADA

Wilbur H. Morrison & Matt Purdue

California's magnificent Sierra Nevada mountain range. The Pacific Crest Trail, Yosemite, Lake Tahoe, Mount Whitney, Mammoth Lakes, the John Muir Trail, King's Canyon and Sequoia – all are explored. Plus, excellent historical sections. An adventurer's playground awaits!

300 pp, $15.95, 1-55650-845-X

SOUTHEAST FLORIDA

Sharon Spence

Get soaked by crashing waves at twilight; canoe through mangroves; reel in a six-foot sailfish; or watch as a yellow-bellied turtle snuggles up to a gator. Interviews with the experts – scuba divers, sky divers, pilots, fishermen, bikers, balloonists, and park rangers. Color photos.

256 pp, $15.95, 1-55650-811-5

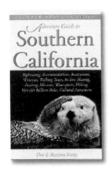

SOUTHERN CALIFORNIA

Don & Marge Young

Browse an art festival, peoplewatch at the beach, sportfish near offshore islands and see world-class performances by street entertainers. The Sierras offer a different adventure, with cable cars ready to whisk you to their peaks. A special section covers daytrips to Mexico.

400 pp, $16.95, 1-55650-791-7

VIRGIN ISLANDS

4th Edition, Harry S. Pariser

"Plenty of outdoor options.... All budgets are considered in a fine coverage that appeals to readers." *Reviewer's Bookwatch*

Every island in the Virgins. Valuable, candid opinions. St. Croix, St. John, St. Thomas, Tortola, Virgin Gorda, Anegada. Color.

368 pp, $16.95, 1-55650-746-1

VIRGINIA

Leonard Adkins

The Appalachian Trail winds over the state's eastern mountains. The Great Dismal Swamp offers biking, hiking and canoeing trails, and spectacular wildlife. Skyline Drive and the Blue Ridge Parkway – popular drives in spring and summer. Photos.

420 pp, $16.95, 1-55650-816-6

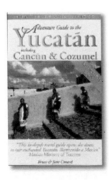

THE YUCATAN
including Cancún & Cozumel

Bruce & June Conord

"... Honest evaluations. This book is the one not to leave home without." *Time Off Magazine*

"... opens the doors to our enchanted Yucatán." Mexico Ministry of Tourism

Maya ruins, Spanish splendor. Deserted beaches, festivals, culinary delights.

376 pp, $15.95, 1-55650-792-5

Send for our complete catalog. All Hunter titles are available at bookstores nationwide or direct from the publisher.

ORDER FORM

Yes! Send the following *Adventure Guides*:

TITLE	ISBN #	PRICE	QUANTITY	TOTAL

SUBTOTAL	
SHIPPING & HANDLING (United States only) (1-2 books, $3; 3-5 books, $5; 6-10 books, $8)	
ENCLOSED IS MY CHECK FOR	

NAME:

ADDRESS:

CITY:STATE:ZIP:

PHONE:

Make checks payable to Hunter Publishing, Inc. and mail with order form to: Hunter Publishing, Inc., 239 South Beach Rd., Hobe Sound FL 33455; ☎ 561/546-7986; Fax 561/546-8040.